Communism in Indochina

Earlier versions of the twelve papers in this volume were presented at an ad hoc seminar on "Communist Movements and Regimes in Indochina" organized and chaired by Dr. Joseph Zasloff of the University of Pittsburgh for the Southeast Asia Development Advisory Group (SEADAG) of The Asia Society, New York. The seminar was held at the Asia House, New York, September 30-October 2, 1974.

The Asia Society, a nonprofit educational institution, was founded in 1956 to enhance American understanding of Asia and Asians and to stimulate meaningful intellectual exchange across the Pacific. Within this framework, SEADAG, which is funded by the United States Agency for International Development, seeks to promote and facilitate communication and collaboration among Asian and American scholars and policymakers concerned with development in Southeast Asia.

Communism in Indochina

New Perspectives

106229

Edited by
Joseph J. Zasloff
University of Pittsburgh
MacAlister Brown
Williams College

Lexington Books
D.C. Heath and Company
Lexington, Massachusetts
Toronto   London

Library of Congress Cataloging in Publication Data

Communism in Indochina.

  Papers originally presented at ad hoc seminar held Sept. 30-October 2, 1974 in New York and sponsored by the Southeast Asia Development Advisory Group of the Asia Society.
  Includes index.
  1. Communism—Indochina—Congresses. I. Zasloff, Joseph J. II. Brown, MacAlister. III. Southeast Asia Development Advisory Group.
HX398.5.C65   335.43'09597   75-18761
ISBN 0-669-00161-9

Published simultaneously in Canada.

Printed in the United States of America.

International Standard Book Number: 0-669-00161-9

Library of Congress Catalog Card Number: 75-18761

Contents

Introduction

Since the first preparation of these chapters on the Communist movements in Vietnam, Cambodia and Laos in mid-1974, events have moved rapidly in Indochina. Within a few months of the authors' final revisions, the demise of the non-Communist side in each of the Indochinese countries was accomplished. By the end of April 1975, the Communists had assumed full power in Cambodia and Vietnam, and in the succeeding weeks in Laos the coalition government agreed upon in 1973 eroded into effective Communist domination. A striking feature of the Communist victory was the sudden collapse of the non-Communist will to resist. Although there was Communist military pressure, particularly in Vietnam and Cambodia, it was not major new offensives which brought down the incumbent governments, but rather the serious demoralization of their military and political leadership. Following a series of local defeats, there began a rapid unraveling of the total fabric of resistance.

As several papers in this volume show, the war in Vietnam persisted despite the cease-fire agreement signed in Paris in February 1973. Both sides attempted to consolidate and expand their areas of control. Perhaps the final phase of Saigon's defeat began with the Communist offensive in the southwest province of Phuoc Long in mid-January 1975. As the province town and most of the province fell to Communist control, the shock to ARVN of military defeat was compounded by the clear indication to the Saigon elite that American military intervention was no longer available. Indeed, U.S. Congressional debate had made it evident that U.S. economic assistance would also continue to diminish. In the face of a March offensive in the Central Highlands, where the North Vietnamese had been assiduously improving their logistic capability, President Thieu and his generals decided, precipitously, to abandon the zone. A rout of ARVN ensued, beginning in the Central Highlands and followed by ARVN abandonment of Hue, the collapse of Danang, the spread of panic and the rapid crumbling of all significant resistance until the surrender of Saigon on April 30th.

The rapid military collapse of Phnom Penh came as less of a surprise, to Communists and non-Communists alike, than that of Saigon, since, as the papers in this volume indicate, the glaring political and military weaknesses of the Government were even more apparent. The Lon Nol side collapsed after the Khmer Communist forces had imposed a stranglehold around Phnom Penh in the final months of the war. U.S. bombing of Cambodia had been terminated by Congressional legislation in August 1973, and there were strong indications that continued U.S. military assistance would be drastically reduced or eliminated.

Right-wing elements in Laos were deeply disturbed by the sudden demise of their counterparts in Cambodia and Vietnam, and by the failure of the United States to react. A succession of political and military maneuvers within Laos crystallized their distress, and their will to continue the political struggle evaporated. On May 10th a number of Vientiane-side ministers resigned from the coalition government, and fled to Thailand, followed by several key right-wing army officers. Following these resignations, although the façade of coalition remained, the Communists were in effective control. The consolidation of Communist power then moved rapidly, although in non-violent Lao style. Pathet Lao troops moved into key towns of the South, under garlands of flowers offered by the FAR (Forces Armees Royales) commanders, and their numbers rose to 8,000 in Vientiane. The FAR military command was reshuffled under PL guidance, selected FAR officers were assigned to re-education courses, and a "purification" of the civil service, under the aegis of PL-led people's courts, was begun. At the same time, student and worker demonstrations against the U.S. mission in Laos, benignly managed by the PL leadership, brought a reduction in the number of official Americans in Laos to about 50 at the end of June 1975, and put future U.S. presence in Laos in doubt. Thus, with the assumption of power by the Pathet Lao, Communist victory in all of Indochina was complete.

The new perspectives on Communism in Indochina found in these pages deal with questions of both current and long-term interest during the interlude between the Paris Agreement and the Saigon capitulation. The questions puzzling scholars at that time remain of critical significance still. Among the recurring issues of interpretation, four stand out for their particular pertinence to future understanding of the region. First is the relative value which the Communist movements in Indochina have attached to their struggle for national independence as contrasted with their commitment to social revolution. Clearly these two goals are not mutually exclusive, but Duiker's and Thayer's chapters on the historical development of the Communist movement in Vietnam, illustrate the disagreement over the years about how much emphasis each goal should receive. In Laos and Cambodia the same ambiguous priorities have manifest themselves between the struggle against "imperialist forces" and the fight for a new social order. The Indochinese Communist movements may well remain, even in their moment of triumph, ambivalent about their two great objectives, not sure whether radical social restructuring and equalization or national independence and development should require top priority. Will the triumphant new regimes prefer to cast their societies wholly free from the intrusions of economic relations with capitalist states, and concentrate on eradicating feudal and bourgeois remnants at home? How will their commitment to socialist and national liberation doctrines affect their policies as leaders of independent states? The chapters on agricultural and military development in the North by Elliot and Turley describe a pragmatism within the DRV leadership, and the essay on Laos by Brown and Zasloff emphasizes the spirit of accommodation in Lao culture, tendencies which would project more moderation in the post-victory policies of Vietnam and Laos than that of Cambodia. There, the extraordinary violence perpetrated by the Khmer Rouge in 1974, as the chapters by Poole and Kirk indicate, and their abrupt emptying of the cities and towns following their seizure of power, suggest that the Khmer revolutionaries are more impatient than their Vietnamese and Lao colleagues for a radical transformation of society.

A subsidiary problem of assessing priorities in the struggle for national liberation or for social revolution has been the north-south split within the Vietnam Workers Party (VWP) resulting from the partition negotiated at Geneva in 1954. Several chapters in this volume contend that following both the Geneva Agreements of 1954 and the Paris Agreement of 1973, the DRV gave priority to socialist reconstruction in the northern zone over immediate liberation of the south, even though the goal of an independent, reunified Vietnam under Communist leadership remained unalterable. In view of the rapid, unexpected Communist acquisition of power by virtue of ARVN's collapse, the actual role of the southern Provisional Revolutionary Government (PRG) is now put into question. Although there is no doubt that the VWP, with its Politburo in the DRV, will provide the strategic direction throughout Vietnam, it is not clear whether it will move to rapid, formal reunification of the two Vietnams, or opt for a transition period in which there remains the framework of a Communist-led southern government. The DRV has been tactically sensitive to the political, social, and economic differences between the two zones of Vietnam, as our study shows, and they might deem it desirable to integrate the social groups of the south into the new system within the framework of a PRG. On the other hand, the external restraints which inhibited the DRV from giving priority to reunification in the past have now been removed, and the Party leaders may wish to move directly to their long-cherished objective.

A second persistent issue of interpretation raised in this study, with important implications for the future, is the relationship between Communist parties and states in Indochina. As the oldest and most developed Party of the largest and most powerful of the three Indochinese states, the VWP (and its predecessor, the Indochina Communist Party established in 1930) has played the dominant role within the Communist movement of Indochina but the degree of control over its partners in Cambodia and Laos remains obscure. The Lao Communist movement, from its origins in 1949, has received important guidance and support, as well as powerful direct military assistance from its Vietnamese senior partner. The dependence relationship of the Khmer Communists toward the DRV is not as long-standing nor as institutionalized as that of the PL, but the North Vietnamese have provided important training, logistical support, and direct military assistance at various stages of the Cambodian revolution. However, by 1972, as these pages show, major North Vietnamese involvement in the Khmer Rouge military operations, so important at the outset of the war in 1970, had substantially diminished, with the DRV then serving, in part, as "gatekeeper," funnelling aid which originated in the USSR and China to the Khmer Communists.

The extent of independence of the Khmer Communist movement from its DRV ally during the immediate post-victory period can be inferred from their different strategies. In contrast with the radical policies of the Khmer Rouge, mentioned earlier, the Vietnamese Communists moved more moderately, calling upon former GVN (Government of Vietnam) civil servants, for example, to resume their posts and render normal services. The Lao Communist movement also seemed more in tune with the North Vietnamese than the Khmer Communists did. Whether the Lao Communist leadership had moved on their own to keep in step with their neighboring revolutionaries, or whether they were reluctantly marching to the drum of the DRV leadership is not clear. Indeed, the DRV's own aims in Indochina remain an open question. Does the DRV wish a tightly assured hegemony over Laos and Cambodia, or even leadership in an Indochina Federation, for example, or is its aim more modest? In dealing with the neighboring Communist movements, does the VWP act with social revolutionary aims in the forefront, or rather with the conventional interests of a nation state?

A third issue raised by our study is the decision-making process within the parties. The chapter on cooperativization asserts that the DRV decision-making style in agricultural policy has included a deliberate, pragmatic sifting of evidence, and tolerance of competing views until the final decision is made. The chapter on the political role of the People's Army of Vietnam (PAVN) emphasizes that no disputes of lasting consequence have occurred, not only because of the external threat but also because of the strictures of Party discipline and ideology. Hence both low-key conflict resolution and openness to a variety of strategic ideas are considered typical of the PAVN. These observations, however, are not in themselves sufficient evidence of a decision-making style that can be projected onto the whole movement. Kattenburg's chapter on DRV external relations posits the rational actor model for purposes of analysis, while recognizing that bureaucratic politics models might equally well apply.

The mysteries of the inner councils of Communist decision making grow deeper as one moves from Hanoi to the Sam Neua headquarters of the Pathet Lao and to the unknown headquarters of the Khmer Rouge. The chapter on the Pathet Lao places the decision-making apparatus within the semisecret People's Party of Laos (PPL), whose top leaders remained in Sam Neua, following the formation of the coalition government. In the summer of 1975, it appeared that the harder-line policies of the Sam Neua group, assumed to be closer to Hanoi than their colleagues serving in the coalition government, were ascendant. A leave of indefinite duration for "rest" was imposed on several important PL ministers in Vientiane, following a party council meeting in Sam Neua. But the exact nature of deliberations, the manner and process of debate, the role of personality, of faction, and organizational interests, and the method and extent of DRV influence, remain in the realm of the unknown. We can assume, that bases for factions exist within the leadership (as Kattenburg has done, listing such factors as age, geographic background, training and education, political tendency, temperament, and organizational interests) but the actual expression of contrary viewpoints within the inner circle of the parties is scarcely visible, and may indeed be more limited than our own experience predisposes us to expect. The studies on the Khmer Rouge admit frankly that not only the decision-making process, but the identity of the key leadership is unknown to Western analysts, despite the Khmer Rouge victory in the spring of 1975.

A final uncertainty in Indochina raised in these pages is the issue of central control versus local autonomy within the Communist movements. As examples indicate in various chapters, the Nghe-Tinh uprisings of 1930-1931, the increase in the armed struggle in the South after 1957, and the "pressure from below" during the agricultural cooperativization campaign after 1959, all confronted the central leadership with the need to adapt to the initiatives and impatience of local cadres. The center managed to adjust, retaining its leadership, but its policies had been questioned and its control challenged. In the case of the raw terror inflicted by the Khmer Rouge in 1974, as described by Kirk, there remains doubt about the level of central control, and projections of disciplined authority in the post-victory phase in Cambodia are difficult to make.

Notwithstanding the total victory achieved by the three Communist movements in 1975, the potential exists for divergence between the aims of the central party leadership and local circumstances. Although the power of regional Communist organizations will undoubtedly be diminished by the achievement of full national liberation, there will remain strong ethnic, religious, occupational, provincial and other group identities. The extent of influence that these special interests will be able to generate within a unified national state is another of the interesting questions that has risen out of research in the revolutionary period.

The editors wish to express their gratitude to Tela C. Zasloff for her valuable editing of the entire manuscript and to Jerry Cawley for bibliographic and research assistance.

Part I:
Communism in Vietnam

A. Evolution of the Vietnamese
Communist Movement

1

Building the United Front: The Rise of Communism in Vietnam, 1925-1954

William J. Duiker

It has been nearly half a century since the birth of the Communist movement in Vietnam. The road has not been an easy one: two smarting defeats during the decade immediately preceding the Second World War; the long and bloody war of resistance against the French after the Pacific War; the frustrating peace at Geneva in 1954 capped off by the arrival of the Americans to replace the French. Then, two more inconclusive decades of struggle in an effort to seize the South. On the whole, however, the history of the Communist movement in Vietnam has been a saga of success, the rise of a small and elitist revolutionary organization in French-controlled Indochina to a highly effective political movement capable of controlling half of the population of Vietnam and contesting seriously for control over the entire nation.

Why has the Communist movement in Vietnam been so successful in recent decades, not only against its internal rivals, but also against the fighting forces of two powerful Western nations? At this point, scholarship on Vietnamese Communism is still at a relatively primitive level (compared, for example, with the amount of published research already available on the rise of Communism in China), but we are now at the point where we can begin to draw some tentative conclusions.

The present chapter is an attempt to trace the strategy which over forty-odd years has served to forge the Communist movement into a highly effective revolutionary organization, perhaps the most effective political weapon of its kind in contemporary Southeast Asia.[1] The Communist strategy which has been used to such great effect in recent years did not emerge full-blown with the birth of the first Marxist-Leninist party in Vietnam, but rather like its ideological counterpart in China, the Vietnamese Communist movement has developed as a result of years of trial and error.

Planting the Seed of Marxism

From a conceptual point of view, it might be said that Vietnamese Communism was born in 1920, when Lenin enunciated his "Theses on the National and Colonial Questions" at the Second Congress of the Communist International in Moscow. Lenin's famous theses were the first serious attempt by a European

3

Communist leader to adapt Marx's doctrine of class struggle to the predominantly agrarian, pre-capitalist societies in Asia. With Lenin's new formulation,
Marxism developed broad world implications, for Communist movements could
now be formed and cooperate with local bourgeois nationalist parties in Asian
societies even before the advent of capitalism. The new strategy has enormous
practical implications as well, for nationalism was the most powerful emotional
force in colonial and semi-colonial areas of Asia, and if Communism were to
form an alliance with indigenous nationalism against the common adversary of
Western imperialism, it would markedly improve the prospects for social
revolution in Asia.

In 1920, of course, Lenin's ideas were pure theory, and in practice would
present some difficult problems. What role should the Communist Party play in
an alliance with nationalist groups? Should it accept the leadership of bourgeois
elements? To what extent should it subordinate its own interests in the alliance?
With which elements in the nationalist movement should the Party cooperate?
Finally, and most important, at what stage should the Party cease to cooperate
with bourgeois elements and attempt to seize power for itself? In the brief years
before his death, Lenin provided some broad guidance, but many of these
questions evaded precise definition. "Local conditions" would be the determining factor.

Still, if Lenin's theses did not solve all the coming problems of Asian
revolutionaries, they were the decisive first step in the formation of a strategy
for Communist movements in Asia. Most importantly, Lenin's proposals unleashed a chain of events which resulted half a decade later in the creation of the
first truly Marxist political organization in Vietnam. It was as a result of reading
a French-language version of the theses in Paris that young Nguyen Ai Quoc,
later to be known to the world as Ho Chi Minh, decided to accept Marxism as a
tool for achieving the liberation of his Vietnamese countrymen, and thus in
1920 became a founding member of the French Communist Party. Five years
later, after spending a year receiving training as a Communist agent in Moscow,
Nguyen Ai Quoc returned to South China as a member of Borodin's Comintern
mission to the Kuomintang, with the assigned duty of forming the first
Communist movement in French Indochina.

Vietnam in 1925 was ripe for the new leadership that the young revolutionary hoped to provide. There had been active resistance to French control in
Vietnam for several decades, most recently in the anti-French scholar-gentry
movement led by the intrepid nationalist Phan Boi Chau.[2] By 1925, however,
Phan's movement had run its course due to French oppression, the death or
imprisonment of many of its leaders, the innate weakness of the movement and,
finally, the arrest of Phan himself by French police.

The dispersal of Phan's movement did not mark the end of resistance to
French rule in Vietnam. A new generation of Vietnamese—urban, middle class,
increasingly Westernized in schooling and outlook—was beginning to form in the

big cities. This new generation, many the sons and daughters of the traditional mandarin elite, sensed a continuing obligation to serve the proud heritage of Vietnam. In 1925, however, this inchoate sense of national identity lacked a concrete political focus. There were a few quasi-political parties like the moderate Saigon-based Constitutionalist Party under Bui Quang Chieu and its slightly more radical counterpart, the Youth Party; in the Center and the North, student groups and remnants of Phan's old organization made a few tentative efforts to organize.

Factionalism, regionalism, and vacillation over strategy and tactics kept the various groups from finding common ground, and they presented no serious challenge to French rule, although the colonial authorities kept an eye on their activities.[3]

The Revolutionary Youth League

The disorganized character of Vietnamese nationalism presented Nguyen Ai Quoc with an opportunity to build a Communist organization which would become the leading element in a vast anti-colonial movement dedicated to achieving national independence. The first priority, of course, was to form a nucleus dedicated to Marxist-Leninist principles. In early 1925 he began patiently to assemble his following—small groups of exiles in South China, remnants of Phan Boi Chau's old organization, restless students and intellectuals in the big cities—and in June he formed the first avowedly Marxist political organization in Vietnam, the Revolutionary Youth League (*Viet Nam Thanh Nien Cach Menh Dong Chi Hoi*). In recognition of the fact that most of the founding members had only a nodding acquaintance with Marxist-Leninist theory and practice, the new organization did not formally consider itself a Communist Party. Its goals were general, stressing patriotism and only the basics of Marxist theory. Its headquarters were located in South China, but it aimed at building up a dedicated membership from all progressive classes in all areas of Vietnam. Within two years it had become one of the largest and most cohesive secret political organizations in Vietnam.

Creating a Marxist revolutionary Party was only half the problem. The broader and perhaps more difficult task was to mould an effective anti-colonial force out of the disparate nationalist groups in the three regions of Vietnam. We need not discuss in detail the involved process of rivalry and negotiations that ensued. Suffice it to say that for the remainder of the decade the League attempted with varying degrees of sincerity to form an alliance with the more progressive nationalist groups in Vietnam—in particular with the Tan Viet Party, a quasi-Marxist organization based in Central Vietnam, and with the Viet Nam Quoc Dan Dang (The VNQDD), a Tonkinese Party composed of students and workers and ideologically similar to Sun Yat-sen's Kuomintang in China. The

Constitutionalist Party in the South was considered too pro-French for membership in an anti-imperialist alliance.

The League's efforts to forge a nationalist alliance had meager results. Mutual suspicion, regional loyalties, personal pique, and ideological distrust all combined to prevent a meaningful union of nationalist efforts. On the other hand, many of the more radical elements in other nationalist Parties were soon attracted to the League's program, and by the end of the decade it had become the most influential force within the nationalist movement in Vietnam.[4] There was a price to pay for this success. The composition of the Party was strongly middle class in background, and relatively few thought beyond the goal of national independence to the ultimate social revolution. Like its rivals, the League was fundamentally an elitist organization, and lacked a mass base. There was talk of broadening the proletarian base, of reaching out to the peasant masses, but in these early years such statements represented the ideal more than the reality.

In any event, by late 1928 the League's failure to form a Leninist-style alliance became less important, for the Sixth Congress of the Comintern had altered the policy of forming united fronts with nationalist groups in Asian socieites. Smarting under the failure of the Leninist strategy in China, where Chiang Kai-shek had struck at his Communist ally in April 1927, the Comintern issued a new world strategy for Communist Parties in colonial and semi-colonial societies which backed away from the policy of alliance with the anti-imperialist bourgeoisie. Communists were to strive for the "united front from below," to strengthen the mass base by winning the support from workers and peasants in preparation for a revolutionary "high wave" which Moscow felt was sure to come in the near future. The major duty of the League was no longer to search for alliances with its nationalist rivals, but to move into the factories and reduce the strongly bourgeois orienation of its own membership.

Split, Reunification, and Revolt

The year 1929 inaugurated a period of rapid change in the affairs of the Communist movement in Vietnam. Ideological and regional strains had been evident in the organization and erupted into full-scale conflict in 1929. For several months three rival organizations, each claiming to represent Marxist-Leninist orthodoxy, competed for the role of the leading revolutionary organization in Vietnam. The major cause for the split appears to have been ideological—some members resented the priority of national over social class concerns in the League's program—but regional and personal factors were at work also.[5] The Comintern was aghast at the sight of squabbling Marxist factions and angrily instructed the three groups to negotiate a settlement. When early attempts failed, the Comintern dispatched Nguyen Ai Quoc, who had been out of contact with Party affairs since mid-1927, to return to South China and obtain a settlement. In February of 1930, the now veteran revolutionary convened a secret meeting of representatives of the rival factions and achieved a rapid agreement on unification. For not the last time Nguyen Ai Quoc would play a key role in maintaining Party unity.

One result of the negotiations was the dissolution of the League and the formation of an official Indochinese Communist Party. The movement now entered the second stage of its brief existence. Having in the eyes of the Comintern reached the stage of ideological maturity, it could now concentrate on the main task of building up its strength and preparing for the ultimate seizure of power from the French. In the context of the world conditions at the time, it had entered its new existence at a propitious period in the history of the modern world. Since the Sixth Congress in 1928, the Communist movement had claimed it discerned a high wave of revolution in the capitalist world.

In the view of Moscow, this wave against world capitalism and imperialism, strengthened by the economic depression that struck the West in 1929, was fast approaching and would soon break in a number of countries around the world. The Comintern was not specific about whether or not Indochina was such an area, but all Communist Parties were expected to prepare for the possibility of local crisis conditions which would present an opportunity for a seizure of power.

As it turned out, the possibility was not long in coming in Vietnam, for 1930 marked a temporary high in the level of anti-French discontent there. The first indication was an abortive revolt by the VNQDD at military camps scattered around the fringe of the Red River Delta in February. Indications are that the VNQDD leadership saw little hope for success, but was driven to action by desperation. The ICP, scarcely formed, did not rise in response, apparently in the belief that the situation was not ripe.[6] Within weeks of the VNQDD uprising, indications of discontent arose elsewhere. Strikes at the Phu Rieng rubber plantation near Bien Hoa near Saigon were soon followed by work stoppages and riots at factories at Vinh in the Center and at Nam Dinh in the North. These incidents were economic in origin, and symbolized dissatisfaction with local working conditions more than the desire for a nationwide revolt, but there is no doubt that local Communist cadres, acting in accordance with Comintern instructions to raise the level of consciousness among all potentially revolutionary classes, were actively involved.

By mid-summer, discontent had extended to other areas throughout Vietnam and began to involve peasants—particularly in the Center where rural areas had been hard hit by high taxes, mandarin corruption, and flood conditions. In early September, full-scale revolt broke out in the central provinces of Nghe An and Ha Tinh and, under prodding by local Communist cadres, peasant rioters seized control at the district level and began to establish village "soviets," which drove the traditional leadership under cover, and confiscated the land of the wealthy for distribution to the poor.[7] The French reacted swiftly to the challenge with military countermeasures and severe repression against the local populace, and by early the next spring had begun to bring the situation under control. The soviet movement finally collapsed in early summer, and the area lapsed back into sullen silence.

The famous Nghe-Tinh uprising of 1930-1931 has been correctly viewed as a significant point in the history of the Communist movement in Vietnam. It was at once a glorious page in the history of the Party and a serious setback in its quest for power. In one sense it provided a model for the later development of the Vietnamese revolution and a number of lessons for future behavior. On the other it seriously weakened the movement and, at least temporarily, undermined its influence in Vietnam. For our purposes, the revolt had two major consequences: it destroyed the indigenous leadership of the Party and led to the temporary domination of the organization by elements trained in Moscow, and, secondly, it taught the Communists a few vivid lessons that the Comintern had only given in an abstract sense. First, it demonstrated the need for centralized control over the decisionmaking process. The uprising had not been deliberately instigated by the Party leadership but had been promoted by lower-level cadres reacting to local circumstances and to the highly generalized instructions of the Comintern. Secondly, it showed that local crisis conditions were not sufficient to justify a major insurrection unless the area could be adequately defended from attack. In 1930, large areas of Vietnam were quiet, and did not join the peasant riots in the Center, which soon collapsed before French power. Finally, it showed at least to some members of the Party, the potential of the peasantry, and its possible role as a basic force in the Vietnamese revolution.

Retrenchment

Whatever the long-term benefits of the events of 1930-1931 in Central Vietnam, there is no minimizing the immediate consequences to the Party. In the course of the uprisings and its aftermath, the French *sûreté* made strenuous attempts to destroy the ICP. Hundreds of Communists were arrested and a number were executed, including some of the top Party leaders. Communist figures estimate that nearly 90 percent of the active leadership of the Party was eliminated by French police activity, and the Party's organizational structure at all levels was badly decimated.

The early 1930s were thus necessarily a period of patient Party rebuilding. With the internal apparatus nearly totally destroyed, the ICP was forced to find new talent for the challenging days ahead. Fortunately, the Comintern had been making an effort to train potential young leaders at the famous University of the Toilers of the East (the Stalin School) in Moscow. Between 1925 and 1932, according to French sources, thirty-four Vietnamese Communists received training of from one to three years at the school. With the ICP badly in need of an infusion of new talent, the Comintern accelerated its training program in Moscow and began to send back graduates of the Stalin School to Vietnam in order to rebuild the Party apparatus. By 1932 two temporary headquarters abroad—one in South China and the other in Thailand—had been set up to supervise the revival of the Party from a safe distance beyond the border. A number of Stalin School graduates were seized by the French, but enough got through to provide a new leadership for the Party. Foremost among the new crop of leaders were Le Hong Phong, an ex-student at the Aviation School in Leningrad who was put in charge of the ICP's South China bureau, and Tran Van Giau, a Stalin School graduate who led the Party to a strong revival in Cochin China. Slowly but surely, the ICP began to revive.

The transfer of leadership, and the nature of the strategy followed by the Stalin School graduates, justify our entitling this period as the "Stalinist period" in the history of the movement. ICP programs closely followed the Comintern line—united front from below, concentration on working class areas, downgrading the visibility of the peasantry. The cornerstones of Nguyen Ai Quoc's program for the old League—a broad united front and nationalism—were abandoned and even criticized.[a] By all indications, the ICP dutifully followed Moscow's lead, and did not appear to question whether the Comintern strategy was appropriate to Vietnamese conditions.

For four years, the ICP presented a low profile in Vietnam. This apparent inactivity is somewhat misleading, however, for Communist efforts were beginning to pay dividends, particularly in the South, where Tran Van Giau led a revitalized regional apparatus, while in Saigon overt Party workers combined temporarily with Trotskyites in publishing the left-wing journal *La Lutte* and winning considerable support in Saigon municipal elections.[b] Efforts in Annam and Tonkin had less success. There the population was cowed, if resentful, and the Party was forced to locate its regional leadership in the North in the mountainous areas not far from the Sino-Vietnamese border.

Encouraged by the improving situation, the new Party leadership in South China began to plan for a national congress in 1934 to set forth a new political program for the ICP. Under the direction of Le Hong Phong, a preliminary meeting was held late in 1934, and a formal meeting took place the next March in the Portuguese colony of Macao.[c] With both Le Hong Phong and Nguyen Ai Quoc in Moscow attending the pivotal meeting of the Seventh Comintern

[a]To underline its attitude, the Comintern refused to admit any but proletarian candidates into the Stalin School during the early 1930s.

[b]The French intelligence services were aware of the revival of the Party, and persistently warned Paris of the effectiveness of the ICP's rebuilding efforts, and their own growing inability to deal with the situation.

[c]French sources are doubtful that a formal meeting was held at all, because of police harassment, and conjecture that the Macao leadership simply met the delegates individually as they arrived.

Congress, which was clearly about to enunciate a new world strategy for the Communist movement, the March congress had a provisional air about it. In the absence of clear directives from Moscow, the Macao congress drew up a program not substantially changed from that of the previous four years. Shortly after the close of the congress, however, Le Hong Phong returned from Moscow with the "popular front" strategy adopted by the Seventh Comintern Congress. Fearing isolation as a result of the rise of fascism in Germany and Japan, Stalin directed the Communist Parties in the world movement to broaden their alliances. Once again, "united fronts from above" were to be formed with moderate bourgeois Parties against the menace of fascism in Europe and Asia.

On seeing the disparity between the new Comintern policy and the Party program formulated at the ICP's Macao congress, Le Hong Phong called a plenary meeting of the central committee and a new program was drawn up in accordance with the new popular front strategy. The rapid shift in world strategy must have been confusing to the leadership as well as to the rank and file of ICP membership, but from all indications it appears that the Party accepted the new policy with relatively little grumbling. There are signs that some Party members were disgruntled at the prospects of initiating cooperation with bourgeois nationalist groups, and a few secret workers expressed their scorn of the "politicos" who worked openly among non-Communist groups. As Nguyen Ai Quoc was to write from abroad, the new strategy had broad implications for ICP policy:

At the present time the CPI should not make excessive demands (independence, parliament, etc.) so as not to fall into a snare prepared by the Japanese fascists. The party must limit itself to demanding democratic rights, freedom of organization, assembly and press, general amnesty for political prisoners—struggle for the right of legal activities. To realize these goals the party must successfully form a wide national-democratic front which would unite not only the local population of Indochina, but progressive French forces, not only of the working class, but also representatives of the national bourgeoisie.[8]

One suspects that he, at any rate, was pleased at the new direction world Communist strategy was taking.

The Period of the Popular Front

The change to a new strategy in 1936 coincided with similar changes taking place in France, where a popular front government, including socialists and with the support of the French Communist Party, took office in 1936 and, as part of its program, promised to convene a study commission on conditions in French colonies. The proposed commission quickly became the focus of ICP efforts to form a popular front in Indochina. In the summer of 1936, the radical journalist

Nguyen An Ninh, a sympathizer but not a formal member of the ICP, suggested in the pages of *La Lutte* that Vietnamese progressives should emulate the examples of nationalist groups in French Africa and form an Indochinese Congress (*Dong Duong Dai Hoi*) to gather the complaints of the Vietnamese people and pass them on to the proposed Colonial Commission when it made its trip to Indochina. Nguyen's suggestion was immediately supported by the ICP as a handy instrument to achieve broad nationalist cooperation against Japanese fascism as well as to raise the level of revolutionary consciousness among the mass of the population. Party journals called for the formation of hundreds of "action committees" (*uy ban hanh dong*) in villages and factories to gather local complaints which would then be submitted to a central committee comprised of all nationalist factions which was then taking shape in Saigon. This national committee, comprising—at least in the early stages—moderate Constitutionalists such as Le Quang Liem and Nguyen Phan Long as well as radicals and members of the ICP, began to cooperate in drawing up the plans for the proposed congress. For the first time, a true Leninist-style united front seemed to be in the making in Vietnam.

It was through the Indochinese Congress movement, then, that the ICP attempted to put its new and broader united front policy into effect. The immediate results were promising, but hardly reason for unbridled optimism. Outside the South, political Parties were illegal, and nationalist agitation in the late 1930s was of limited strength. with little scope for a broad front, the Party's activity was restricted to attempts at informal cooperation with other groups within the regional consultative assemblies. In Cochin China, where political activity was permitted and a number of moderate nationalist groups were already in existence, the potential for popular front activity was greater. There the open members of the ICP attempted to forge a cohesive alliance of moderates and radicals to propagandize the government for reforms and the formal convening of the proposed Indochinese Congress. The net cast by the Party was fairly wide—not only small radical Parties and individuals like Nguyen An Ninh were cultivated, but even "progressive" elements in the Constitution-alist Party and (on an informal basis) even the Trotskyites in Saigon. For the first time the Communist movement was beginning to conceive of the united front on a fairly broad scale.

Even in Cochin China, however, the Party's popular front activities looked better on paper than in reality. The moderate Constitutionalists—foremost representatives of the prosperous urban middle classes in Saigon—split over the issue of cooperating with the Communists, and by early fall the more cautious elements under Le Quang Liem withdrew from the Congress movement, leaving only a mildly left-wing "rump" of the Party under Nguyen Phan Long cooperating with the radicals. Even there, the degree of cooperation seems suspect: Nguyen Phan Long was led to cooperate more through his resentment of fellow-Constitutionalist Bui Quang Chieu than through sincere conviction, while the ICP grumbled that Nguyen Phan Long did not really have his heart in the Congress movement.

As for the Trotskyites, whatever possibilities had existed for cooperation with the ICP melted during the course of the popular front period. The Trotskyites, in the words of Party leader Ta Thu Thau, considered the front a "front populaire de trahision," a ruse used by capitalism to lure the proletariat away from revolution, and they refused to participate in the front with the Stalinist ICP. On its part, the ICP, possibly under the influence of the Stalinist purge trials in Moscow, retreated from any further contact with the Trotskyites. By mid-1937, hostility between the two groups reached a high level, and the potential for cooperation dissolved. All in all, the celebrated "popular front" in Indochina achieved little in the way of practical results. Not all the blame should accrue to the ICP. The nationalist movement in the South was by now almost chronically factional. On the other hand, the ICP (as later Communist historians admit) was excessively rigid in its attitude toward moderates. In addition, it had not begun to make a serious effort to build up the movement among the rural populace.[d] As for the proposed "Indochinese Congress" itself, the government in Paris, under pressure from French *colon* groups in Vietnam, soon retracted its original intention to send a commission to Indochina; it "studied the question" in Paris.

A fair assessment of the popular front period should not be entirely negative in tone, however. Although the ICP had only limited success in forming a broad united front, the period did serve the useful purpose of increasing the Party's visibility and prestige among the mass of the population. It is hard to avoid the conclusion that the ICP was the most—and indeed, the only—effective political force speaking for the nationalist cause in the late 1930s. Moreover, it is clear in retrospect that the popular front period did serve to move the ICP one tentative step toward a new strategy which would be appropriate to conditions in Vietnam. Once again, the Party was beginning to give a higher level of priority to the "national question" and to moderate its appeal for social revolution. For at least the early stages of the revolution, national independence would take priority over radical social change. The stage was being set for postwar success.

World War and the Formation of the Vietminh

The popular front in France died gradually in the years 1938 and 1939. The final blow which ended this early period in Communist cooperation with the liberal democracies was the signing of the Nazi-Soviet pact in August 1939. The signing of the treaty had immediate consequences in Indochina, where the

---

[d]This, of course, was in part a consequence of the excessive urban orientation enforced by Comintern directives during the early 1930s.

French authorities cracked down on the ICP's open activities and seized a number of its top leaders.

These events in late 1939 were to have momentous consequences for the history of the Communist movement. Under the stimulus of French oppression, the Party abandoned its urban base and its fundamentally urban strategy and retreated to the countryside where covert operations were easier to carry on. The movement to the villages marked the beginning of a new rural strategy for the Party. Heretofore it had only given lip service to the concept of a proletarian-peasant alliance and to the idea of the peasantry as the "basic force" of the Vietnamese revolution. True enough, peasants had been a central force in the Nghe-Tinh uprising of 1930-1931, and later in the decade the Party was relatively active in rural areas in the Mekong delta, in the narrow coastal central plain, and in the highlands of the Viet Bac. But, influenced by continued Comintern incentives to emphasize agitation among urban workers, by the essentially urban bias of the Party leadership and, in all probability, by the passivity of the Vietnamese peasantry, the ICP had not really devoted top attention to building a firm base in the countryside.[9]

During the French crackdown in late 1939, as in 1931, the Party leadership was stringently pursued and a number of leaders, including Le Hong Phong and new Party secretary-general Nguyen Van Cu, were seized and executed. Those that remained went into hiding, some fleeing across the border into South China to establish contacts with Communist elements abroad. By 1940, a series of events began to accelerate the move to a new policy: (1) the decline of the Comintern and the consequent absence of policy leadership from Moscow. As a result of the Stalin purges in the late 1930s, much of the Comintern leadership had been destroyed; as for the Soviet leadership, it was preoccupied with events in Europe and showed little interest in Southeast Asia. The ICP, which for so long had loyally followed the Moscow line, was now left substantially to its own devices; (2) the Bac Son uprising in the early fall of 1940. When Japanese forces crossed the border briefly in September to accentuate their demands for concessions from the French colonial government, local montagnard tribesmen, possibly spurred on by local Communist cadres, rose in revolt against the French administration in the area.[10] Although, technically speaking, the revolt did not succeed, the rebel forces, composed primarily of local minority Tay tribesmen among whom the ICP had been active for a decade, broke into guerrilla bands, managed to preserve the bulk of their forces in retreat and began to build stable base areas in the upland provinces around Bac Son and Cao Bang. The French made strenuous efforts to root them out, but they survived and grew. For the first time, the ICP now had a secure revolutionary base area from which to launch a people's liberation war at the close of the Pacific conflict; (3) the return of Nguyen Ai Quoc to South China. Absent from Vietnamese affairs since June 1931 when he had been arrested in Hong Kong, Nguyen Ai Quoc had spent nearly a decade abroad, first in the Soviet Union and then in North China, where he worked with Chinese Communist forces under the leadership of Mao Tse-tung. In the summer of 1940, conscious that an opportunity favorable for the liberation of Vietnam would come out of the approaching world war, Nguyen Ai Quoc returned to South China and got in touch with ICP elements in the border area. From within Vietnam, young Party leaders such as Vo Nguyen Giap and Pham Van Dong were sent north by the Central Committee to establish contact with the Communist leader.

It seems probable that Nguyen Ai Quoc was under the influence of Maoist guerrilla tactics in China, and was prepared to apply these tactics to Vietnamese conditions. Up until now, the Party had not given serious thought to elaborating a strategy for the seizure of power which would meet the unique requirements of the Vietnamese situation. The Soviet model of takeover—concentration of power in the cities, backed by the generalized support of the peasantry, with the ultimate seizure of power through an armed insurrection in the major population centers—was considered to be the natural process of takeover in Vietnam. Presumably the Party was aware of the societal differences between Vietnam and Tsarist Russia, and also familiar with the Maoist revolutionary variant in China. But, by all evidence, the ICP leaders gave little thought to the implications of such facts for the Vietnamese revolution. Now, driven by circumstances, the Party began to move cautiously toward the new strategy that it was to use with such success in the postwar period.

Considering the vital importance of the new trend in ICP thinking, it is curious that many of the details of the Party's decision to adopt the new line are missing. As a result, scholars of the period are forced to piece together the story from the scattered evidence at hand. Nguyen Ai Quoc evidently returned too late to have been involved in the decision to launch the Bac Son uprising, but he was in a position to take advantage of its immediate consequences. With his probable consent, the remnants of the guerrilla units involved in the fighting were instructed to form stable revolutionary base areas along the border. Here revolutionary guerrilla forces would be recruited and trained for the future general uprising. Meanwhile, in South China, the external leadership, now once again firmly in the hands of Nguyen Ai Quoc, would attempt to gather together the scattered nationalist elements—including VNQDDs, ex-followers of Phan Boi Chau and others—who had fled there as Japanese forces had gradually taken over control in Vietnam. Out of this potpourri the ICP would forge a national united front under its own leadership. Then, when the time was ripe, the Party would make its bid for power.[11]

As the ICP forces in the Viet Bac began to build up their strength, the broad outlines of a new political-military strategy were being ironed out. In late 1940, the ICP Central Committee within the country—isolated from contact with the exile leadership—had met in secret at a village near Hanoi and drew up a program calling for a broad anti-French and anti-Japanese alliance. By implication the plenum was moving in the same general direction as the leadership-in-exile under

Nguyen Ai Quoc. The new strategy was not inaugurated, however, until the famous Eight Plenum, held at Pac Bo in the mountainous center of the Viet Bac in May of 1941. The new strategy was based on two foundations, the one political and the other military. On the political side, the Party was to consider the cause of national liberation as the matter of highest priority in the current phase of the Vietnamese revolution. The goal of social revolution was by no means abandoned, but it was to be postponed until the cause of national independence had been achieved. As a tool to win independence, a broad anti-imperialist and anti-fascist front was to be created. This united front, called, after much thought, the League for the Independence of Vietnam (*Viet Nam Doc Lap Dong Minh Hoi* or, for short, Vietminh), would attempt to unite under its banner all progressive forces in Vietnam—not only the four classes of Leninist-style alliances, but even patriotic landlord elements and progressive anti-fascist Frenchmen. In the eyes of the Vietminh, anyone opposed to the Japanese was welcome in the new alliance. This front was to be under the firm control of the ICP, but the latter's role was to be muted in order to win the support of vacillating elements. Its social goals were to be kept general and sufficiently moderate to appeal to cautious urban elements, and the aim of national independence was to be given top priority.

The Vietminh front would hopefully provide the ICP with the broad base of support on a nationwide basis which had been so patently lacking from its revolt in Nghe-Tinh a decade earlier. In the eyes of Party leaders, however, Lenin's warnings that political struggle alone would not suffice to overthrow the class enemy were apropos, for the Japanese and French forces would never give up without a fight. Consequently, the final seizure of power would have to be achieved by means of an armed insurrection by revolutionary forces. And here the Party strategists were beginning to fashion an approach which would meet the unique requirements of the local situation. In conformity with the mixed character of Communist strength in Vietnam (i.e., in both rural and urban areas) the final uprising would involve a simultaneous insurrection both in the cities and in the countryside. Organized and paramilitary forces would be trained in the revolutionary base areas and gradually dispatched to other rural areas throughout the country to build up a nationwide guerrilla network at the village level. In the major urban centers, Party cadres would prepare the revolutionary elements in the population for city demonstrations and riots to be timed with the outbreak of struggle throughout the countryside. Where necessary, urban revolutionary elements would be bolstered by peasant militia brought in from surrounding districts.

Preparing for Insurrection

With the Eighth Plenum in 1941, the main lines of the ICP's war strategy had been laid out. For four years the Party prepared for the uprising to take place at the close of the war. From a military point of view, the build-up went on at two levels, a small people's liberation army serving as a backbone for the local militia units at the village level. The political task was more complex, and perhaps more difficult. As in previous years, it was easier to determine on a united front policy than to put it into effect. Several factors made the formation of such a broad nationalist alliance difficult: the severe repression of all political activities in Vietnam, which made any open Party activities there virtually impossible; the refusal of some nationalist and French groups (including anti-fascist Gaullists) to join hands with the Vietminh; and, finally, the excessive dogmatism and sectarianism of Party members which frequently hampered the prospects for sincere cooperation with other nationalist groups in Vietnam and in South China. With Nguyen Ai Quoc again in jail in 1943, the ICP groups in South China consistently alienated other nationalists with their high-handed attitudes, and no real cooperation was achieved until after Nguyen Ai Quoc (now under the name of Ho Chi Minh) was released in 1944.

Still, the political work went on. Front work was pursued, mass associations (*cuu quoc*) were set up among youth, women, peasants, and workers, and by 1944 the framework of an alliance of Communists with other nationalist groups began to emerge. One of Ho's major problems was to keep tight reign on enthusiasm in his own Party until the proper moment for a general uprising had arrived. Shortly after his release, he discovered that some overzealous elements in the Tonkin regional committee were planning to move before the end of the war. Only a last minute intervention on his part managed to prevent it. In any event, military preparations began to take priority over political work as the war neared its end, and Ho Chi Minh managed to enforce his view that the time for insurrection would arrive in the interval between surrender of the Japanese and the arrival of allied (or French) forces in the area.

The decisive moment came closer in March 1945, when Japanese authorities in Vietnam, sensing impending defeat and growing hostility from local French authorities, presented an ultimatum to the local French administration. When the latter procrastinated, the Japanese arbitrarily overturned French rule and granted paper independence to a Vietnamese government under Emperor Bao Dai. For Ho Chi Minh, the Japanese coup d'état simplified his own plans. Japanese occupation forces took control only in major population centers and made little attempt to take the reigns of authority in outlying areas, where the French administrative apparatus, now lacking central direction, still operated. The overthrow of the French central administration created a political vacuum in the rural areas that could be filled by local revolutionary forces in areas where the latter were sufficiently organized. Separate "liberated zones," areas where revolutionary power could be seized prior to a general uprising, could be established in advance of the war's end.

Immediately following the Japanese coup, then, the Party's Standing Committee met near Hanoi and issued a directive, "The Franco-Japanese conflict and our Actions." According to the directive, the period of greatest opportunity was fast approaching. The enemy had entered a period of crisis, with the war being lost, his ranks in confusion, a growing food problem leading to the threat of famine, unemployment in the cities, high taxes and confiscation of rice in the villages. All of this created a rising level of anti-Japanese sentiment in Vietnam, and an opportunity for Communist forces to take power in local areas, where conditions were appropriate. Where such open revolutionary control could be established up to the district or provincial levels, people's committees should be selected to replace the existing authority; elsewhere, secret militia units and a skeleton administrative structure should be set up and prepared for activation when the order for a general uprising was given. In general, the Party gave precedence to preparations in the rural areas, where the revolutionary strength tended to be stronger than in the cities. In practical terms, this implied that a Maoist-style rural strategy—with seizure of power first in rural areas—would be adopted, with village revolutionary forces moving thence to the cities to aid in the seizure of power there. By June of 1945, six provinces with a total population of one million—mostly in the Viet Bac—had come under the direct control of the Vietminh.

At the national level, also, preparations were underway to establish a provisional central republican government under Vietminh direction. On August 16, shortly after the Japanese surrender was announced abroad, the Vietminh called a national "People's Congress" at Tan Trao to establish a program and to select a National Liberation Committee which would serve as a provisional national government until elections could be held. The congress was strongly dominated by the Communists, since the ICP had selected the delegates and had held a Party congress at Tan Trao immediately prior to the convening of the People's Congress.[12] At this Party conference, it was decided that the period of maximum favorable opportunity (*thoi co*) had arrived. Japanese forces were on the verge of surrender, the French were in disarray, and allied forces from China and Great Britain had not yet arrived. This was the moment to launch the general uprising, and to be in possession of the country when the allied occupation forces arrived to accept the surrender of Japanese military forces in Indochina. The ICP decision was submitted to the People's Congress which ratified it unanimously.

According to plan, uprisings were to take place simultaneously in all rural areas where revolutionary power was considered sufficiently strong—in all provinces of Tonkin, and in selected areas in the South and the Center—with the aim of taking power at the provincial as well as at the local level. At the same time, armed propaganda detachments were to spark major demonstrations in the big cities which would be supplemented by militia forces brought in from neighboring rural districts. Takeover in the major cities of Saigon, Hanoi, Hué, and Haiphong was considered essential for success.[13] The uprisings began in the last two weeks of August, beginning in the urban areas with the revolt in Hanoi on the 19th. During the preceding four days, rural districts throughout the North had seized power, including three important communes near Hanoi. On the 19th, massive demonstrations combining urban workers and revolutionary bourgeoisie, peasants from the environs, and led by trained armed propaganda detachments, took place in the center of Hanoi, and they had soon neutralized Japanese forces and seized all strategic locations in the city. Because of the difficulty of communicating rapidly with other armed units, other major urban centers did not coordinate their actions with the uprising in Hanoi. Hué followed on the 23rd, and Saigon on the 25th. In each case, however, the uprisings were successful, and power fell to the revolutionaries.

Within less than two weeks, the Vietminh had seized power throughout most of Vietnam. Only a few areas—mostly in the rural areas in the South where sympathy with the Communists was lacking—remained outside of revolutionary control. Japanese troops remained generally neutral throughout the period of the uprising, and a few handed over their weapons to the revolutionaries. The puppet Bao Dai government in Hué resigned and Bao Dai himself somewhat reluctantly abdicated, turning over authority to a delegation sent by the provisional government now installed in Hanoi. The "August Revolution" had been a major success. In a relatively bloodless coup, the Vietminh had managed to seize de facto power in Vietnam. The degree of success is particularly striking in view of the weakened position of the ICP at the beginning of the war. The ingredients were ones which were becoming familiar to observers of the Communist movement in Vietnam—organization, discipline, dedication, and a striking amount of political astuteness. As the Vietminh leadership had foreseen, the end of the war had created a political vacuum in Vietnam, and they had known how to fill it.

The Period of Negotiations

As the ICP leadership was well aware, the Vietnamese revolution was not completed with the insurrection of August 1945. The Communists' main adversary—French colonialism—still had to be faced. The Vichy government, of course, had been discredited and the local French administration in Indochina had been deprived of power by the Japanese coup d'état of March 1945. But the Free French movement under General Charles De Gaulle had indicated in 1944 its own determination to preserve a French presence in Indochina. Once the Allied expeditionary forces had arrived, the Free French could be expected to make their move to return in force to Indochina.

Furthermore, Communist control in Vietnam was shaky at best. The Vietminh had taken power in the name of the nationalist-Vietminh alliance that had been formed in South China in 1944, but the National Liberation Committee appointed at Tan Trao on August 16 was strongly Vietminhoriented, and the takeover itself had been almost entirely engineered by the Communists. Non-Communist nationalists such as the VNQDD in the North, and the moderates in the South, were not likely to stand idly by while the Communists consolidated their power. Nor was the mass base of the new government in the rural and urban areas sufficiently firm to withstand a healthy degree of opposition. The Vietminh were generally welcomed by the populace as an indigenous political force symbolizing the desire of the Vietnamese people for social justice and political independence, but such generalized approval would not easily be translated into firm support in the event of a serious internal conflict among several indigenous forces.

The month of September thus inaugurated a period of intense political activity of almost unprecedented complexity. From the Vietminh point of view, the struggle had to be carried on at two levels—against the returning French and the Allied expeditionary forces and the Japanese troops on the one hand, and against their Vietnamese rivals within the nationalist camp on the other. From a theoretical sense, the problem was clear: the Vietminh could not hope to face both adversaries at the same time. Militarily they were too weak to be able to defeat the French and its external allies while at the same time competing actively against their internal nationalist competitors. They were thus required to mobilize a maximum amount of support against one enemy at a time, without at the same time diluting their own authority to the extent of losing control of the movement, and the support of the more radical elements within the nationalist camp. Under such circumstances, of course, the united front technique was the best approach, and their first move during the autumn of 1945 was to mobilize support from all potentially anti-imperialist elements in the population against French and other outside forces. The nucleus of Vietminh strength would have to come from workers and peasants, but significant help was expected from the highly nationalist urban petty bourgeoisie, and even from the more patriotic elements among the wealthier classes. Some elements—Bui Quang Chieu in Saigon, Pham Quynh in Hué, Ta Thu Thau, the Trotskyite leader in Cochin China—were considered too far gone to save and (whether on central or local orders is not yet clear) were assassinated.

The simple statement of the problem above hardly indicates its delicacy. Social and economic conditions were harsh as the war ended, with famine rising in the rural areas and unemployment and economic crisis in the cities, and far-reaching governmental measures were called for to alleviate the suffering of the people. Yet the behavior of the provisional government in Hanoi would have to be sufficiently moderate to avoid unnecessarily alienating the moderate elements within the nationalist alliance, for if the latter were driven to support the French, or even to abstain from the coming conflict, the Vietminh's chances for victory would be severely compromised.

The measures taken by the government indicate the care with which the Vietminh attempted to construct their anti-imperialist front. Social and political measures were announced to win mass support: the personal tax was abolished as well as the French-run monopolies, rent on land was limited to 25 percent of the harvest; worker legislation limited the work day to eight hours, and democratic rights were guaranteed, including equality for all regardless of age, sex, religion, or ethnic background. Finally, beginning steps were taken to establish democratically elected people's councils at all levels of government, and national elections were promised for the creation of a formal central government. In an attempt to solve the problem of hunger, rice stocks confiscated by the Japanese were distributed to the needy, and farmers were urged to grow other quick-producing crops to supplement the coming rice harvest. The government was careful to avoid the impression of moving toward radical measures, and no nationalization of property or land took place.

In retrospect, such measures can be seen as a respectable effort to win the zealous support of revolutionaries and at least the tolerance of moderate anti-imperialist elements in the population. In practice, the innate suspicion of many moderates for the Communists and the long-standing hostility between the ICP and such non-Communist revolutionary elements as the VNQDD made any true reconciliation and cooperation extremely difficult, if not impossible. Non-Communist Parties and factions led by such figures as Vu Hong Khank, Nguyen Tuong Tam, and Nguyen Hai Than had reluctantly joined with the Vietminh in South China in 1944, but their suspicions of the Communists ran deep, and such distrust was only exacerbated by the dominant role of the Vietminh in the waning days of the war. Their own trump card lay with the Chinese expeditionary forces who were to occupy all of Indochina north of the 16th parallel as the war came to a close. As Chinese troops entered North Vietnam in the fall of 1945, VNQDD and Dong Minh Hoi leaders returned to Tonkin, began to seize control of areas taken by the Vietminh, and, certain of the backing of the Chinese, took a hard line in negotiations with the Communists.

The ICP attempted to play a cautious game with its rivals: its broad policy was to isolate the leaders of rival groups and to win over their followers, but in delicate periods when negotiations with the French were taking place, the Vietminh leadership attempted to placate its rivals with such minor concessions as offering them high positions in the government. Periodically they were forced to give ground to the nationalists—in late fall when Chinese troops were still present in force in the North, in March of the succeeding year when Ho Chi Minh signed the preliminary and very moderate Ho-Sainteny agreement which conceded a long-term French presence in Vietnam, and later in 1946 when a Vietnamese delegation went to France in an attempt to negotiate at Fontainebleau a peaceful compromise on the issue of independence and French control. At the same time the Vietminh made rigorous efforts to keep the nationalists from a share in power and, when possible, took a hard line toward their rivals. By the fall of 1946, when occupation forces had been withdrawn and war with

France appeared inevitable, the Communists made little effort to disguise their unwillingness to share power. VNQDD elements were purged from the government, removed from the National Assembly, and occasionally assassinated. Eventually nationalist leaders like Vu Hong Khanh and Nguyen Hai Than fled to China and the Vietminh managed to help in the formation of a puppet VNQDD which joined the Communist-dominated united front.

Generally, the Vietminh attempt to build a broad united front in the North was successful. Potentially hostile elements such as the Catholic hierarchy either supported the Vietminh or took a neutral stance. Even the Chinese occupation forces, who did not hide their basic sympathy with the nationalist Parties, were led to tolerate Vietminh control over the government. Eventually the Vietminh's essentially Communist coloration became evident, however, and a new and wider front, the Lien Viet Front, was added in the hopes of gaining additional support from cautious moderates in the country. In addition, the ICP dissolved itself (maintaining, of course, its secret organization) in a gesture to reduce the suspicions of moderates that the resistance movement was entirely Communist-controlled.

In the South, the situation was equally complicated and even more difficult. In the first place, the British expeditionary force under General Douglas Gracey was more openly sympathetic to the French and immediately released imprisoned French troops to cooperate in the effort to destroy Vietminh strength in Cochin China. In the second place, Communist strength in Cochin China was measurably weaker than in Tonkin. French security measures in the months immediately following the disastrous 1940 uprising had decimated Communist forces in the South, and although the Party had recovered sufficiently by 1945 to play a major role in the August Revolution, it was not in a strong enough position—particularly in rural areas—to establish liberated zones. Finally, moderate nationalist groups, such as the Constitutionalist Party and pro-Japanese elements, religious minorities such as the Cao Dai and the Hoa Hao, and the anti-Stalinist Trotskyites, were relatively well organized in the South, and were serious rivals to the Communists for control over the Vietnamese nationalist movement.

Under the circumstances, it is perhaps surprising that the Communists did as well as they did in the South in the weeks immediately following the end of the war. Communist strength during the takeover of the city of Saigon on August 25 had been based primarily on workers, peasants from the countryside, and the one-million-strong Vanguard Youth movement under covert ICP member Pham Ngoc Thach. In the difficult negotiations with the non-Communist nationalist groups in the Committee of the South, the Vietminh did relatively well, and briefly, because of rival confusion, had a controlling voice in that nationalist front body. Ultimately, however, the ICP found itself overmatched. French troops, aided by British expeditionary forces and the remnants of Japanese occupation troops in Cochin China, drove the Vietminh out of Saigon and attempted to eliminate their strength even in the rural areas. As the French regained control, they began to organize non-Communist and relatively pro-French elements to form an anti-Communist front. In the complex political situation, various groups competed for control. Driven to near desperation, by French harassment and slippage in their own ranks, the Southern leadership under Tran Van Giau and, later, Nguyen Binh, turned to terrorism and scorched-earth tactics, assassinating a number of the leaders of rival groups. Troops were sent by the ICP from the North, but it was already too late, and although throughout most of 1946 the Communists controlled much of the Cochin Chinese countryside, the French were able to consolidate their own authority in Saigon and the major delta cities.

The long struggle of the Communists to defend the gains of the August Revolution by political maneuvering came to an end in December 1946. While many of the details of Communist policy are unknown to us, it seems evident that they postponed military confrontation as long as possible, in order to build up revolutionary strength. From mid-summer, however, it became apparent that French policy was hardening and that Paris was not seriously interested in a negotiated settlement. In control of much of the South, with token occupation forces in the Red River Delta in the North, the French apparently decided to force a military solution. At bay, the Communists finally concluded that armed struggle was inevitable.

The War of Resistance, 1946-1954

The Vietminh was forced into a military confrontation with the French at a time when Communist military strength was not yet up to an open struggle with the colonial regime. It seems clear enough that Ho had attempted to put off conflict as long as possible for this reason. Now that such a conflict was inevitable, the Communists gave the military build-up the highest priority. As for the strategy to be followed, some aspects are still subject to controversy, but the broad outlines of Communist policy during the War of Resistance are clear enough. They intended to utilize the basic elements of the strategy originally worked out in South China during the war: (1) in the military strategy, use of the guerrilla war approach, relying on rural base areas to build up strength, division of revolutionary armed forces into main force, guerrilla, and village militia. In accordance with the Maoist "three-stage" concept, Communist activity would move from a predominantly defensive approach through a period of equilibrium and ultimately, when enemy strength and morale was sufficiently worn down, to a final stage of military confrontation in a general offensive in both rural and urban areas; (2) in the political sphere, adoption of a united front approach to win maximum nationalist support in the war effort. Such a policy would require, of course, that the "national" issue should take precedence over social revolution, and that Marxist slogans should be subordinated to the appeal to patriotism. In recognition of the role of the peasantry as the "basic force" of the revolution, the Party would recruit primarily in the rural areas. On the other hand, workers and the patriotic middle classes in the cities could be useful in undermining stability in enemy-controlled areas, and, ultimately, would assist Communist main forces in seizing the cities at the culmination of the war.

Time does not permit us to make a detailed analysis of Communist policies during the eight-year War of Resistance. Nor, for lack of documentation, is it easy to determine the degree of Communist success in building up the united front in the years leading up to Geneva. Certainly, support from the population was sufficient to sustain the movement during its difficult stage of retrenchment and build-up. And, throughout the entire period of the war, relatively few Vietnamese gave a firm commitment to the anti-Communist forces. On the other hand, it appears that the Communists were only partially successful in building support for their cause. In key areas, support for the Vietminh was marginal. Among the urban population, the Communists had some success in winning over intellectuals, students, and some merchants. Relatively few, however, seem to have given active aid or left French-controlled areas to join the war effort. Even among the working population in Saigon, there was some decline in active support, particularly after 1950. Then, too, the Communists had difficulties with the various ethnic and religious minorities—the Catholics, the overseas Chinese, the Hoa Hao and the Cao Dai—and achieved minimum support from these groups during the bulk of the war.

Such spotty indications of weakness should not be interpreted as a sign that the united front was not working. Vast numbers of non-Communist Vietnamese throughout the country remained uncommitted during the war, and under the circumstances, this can be considered as a tribute to the astuteness of Communist political strategy. The Communist stronghold in the villages served them well, and provided them with the troop strength that permitted them to hold their own, and more, against the French. But the period shows the limited degree to which the Communists could expect to win active support from moderate elements in society. The Communists appear to have conceded this point in 1950-1951 when the composition of the government was narrowed and moved perceptibly to the Left. The Party itself was revived with the new name of the Vietnam Workers' Party, and the government initiated several moves in the direction of more radical land policies to win peasant support.

For a variety of reasons, then, it is difficult to analyze with precision the success of Communist united front policies during the War of Resistance. The united front succeeded in undermining support for the enemy, but Vietminh strength was based more in rural than in urban areas and the final, partial victory in 1954 seems to be a tribute as much to military astuteness as to political success. Such, at any rate, is the tentative conclusion here. A final assessment of this period must await further analysis.

Conclusions

The rise to power of the Communist movement in postwar Vietnam was due to many factors: (1) to the flexibility of the movement as a whole, which enabled it to reduce its early weaknesses; (2) to the personal leadership of Ho Chi Minh, who at key points prevented regional and ideological conflict from breaking down the party; (3) to the assistance of the Comintern, which provided guidance at an important point in the history of the Party, and finally, (4) to the inveterate factionalism of its rivals in the nationalist movement, who displayed a persistent inability to unify in the cause of national independence.

Perhaps the salient feature in the rise to power of Communism in Vietnam was its ability to don the mantle of nationalism. The formation of the Vietminh front in 1941 was the culmination of a long, sometimes interrupted process whereby the Party was able to become the most effective political organization opposed to French rule in Vietnam. The highly patriotic character of Vietnamese Communism has suggested to some the possibility that national concerns continue to have priority over Marxist ones in the Communist movement. This is by no means impossible, and it is certainly true that "nationalism" continues to be a major emotional factor in North Vietnam today. Similarly, there is a pragmatic character to the movement which suggests that ideological, social revolutionary concerns are perhaps somewhat less important than in China. Yet a brief look at the history of the Party shows a consistent dedication to Marxism, and a willingness to stay within the ideological tracks of more powerful Socialist powers, such as the Soviet Union and the People's Republic of China. There is little evidence that the Vietnamese Communists, any more than their Chinese cousins, were ever simple "agrarian reformers." If unification becomes a reality, the Party will in all likelihood turn its energies to building a Marxist utopia in Vietnam.

Another striking aspect of the history of the Party has been its success in avoiding regional factionalism, a problem which has been such a major factor in preventing cohesion among non-Communist groups. There were slight indications of regional suspicion during the prewar years, but as a whole the Party took care to obtain a satisfactory regional mix. Since World War II, the Party strength has tended to concentrate in the North and parts of the Center, a reality which was recognized at Geneva in 1954. There are a variety of reasons for this, which we need not go into here. The last two decades of struggle have seemingly intensified an ideological North-South clash within Vietnam which the Party had avoided in the past and must now deal with. In any event, it is clear that by 1954 the Communists had "Vietnamized" Marxism, and had built a strong and indigenous movement solidly based on support among the population. By then the Communist leadership had taken the optimistic view, and prepared to turn on its new adversaries—the Saigon government of Ngo Dinh Diem and its new ally, the United States.

Notes

1. In writing this article, I have relied in part on material recently released by the government of France at the Archives Nationales de France, Section Outre-Mer, Rue Oudinot in Paris. This material, which contains information on the rise of nationalism in Indochina between the two world wars, is of invaluable benefit to the student of modern Vietnamese history. Of particular interest are French *sûreté* files and reports labeled SLOTFOM (Service de Liaison avec les originaires de territoires de la France d'Outre-Mer) held at Rue Oudinot. I am greatly indebted to Professor Milton Osborne for pointing out the existence of these files to me. Hereafter this source will be cited as SLOTFOM.

2. The rise of the nationalist movement in the early twentieth century has been competently treated by David Marr, in *Vietnamese Anticolonialism, 1885-1925* (Berkeley: University of California Press, 1971).

3. Papers by Milton Osborne, William Frederick, and Hoang Ngoc Thanh in Walter F. Vella (ed.), *Aspects of Vietnamese History* (Honolulu: University Press of Hawaii, 1973), deal with this period. SLOTFOM, Series III, has a number of documents and reports dealing with nationalist activities during the mid-twenties. The general impression of factionalism and impotence is borne out by the material held in these files.

4. Such, at any rate, was the conclusion of the French *sûreté*. For French intelligence reports on the League, see SLOTFOM, Series III, carton 48.

5. For a discussion, see William J. Duiker, "The Revolutionary Youth League: Cradle of Communism in Vietnam," in *China Quarterly* (July-September 1972): 475-499.

6. Some local branches of the Party allegedly wanted to strike, but the newly-formed Party leadership forbade any action. SLOTFOM, Series III, Carton 48, Dossier entitled "Les Associations Anti-Francaise en Indochine et la propagande communiste," monthly report of February-March 1930.

7. Two recent English-language studies of the period are Milton Osborne, "Continuity and Motivation in the Vietnamese Revolution: New Light from the 1930s," in *Pacific Affairs* (Spring 1974), and William J. Duiker, "The Red Soviets of Nghe-tinh: An Early Communist Rebellion in Vietnam," in *Journal of Southeast Asian Studies* (September 1973).

8. SLOTFOM, Series III, Carton 48, Dossier 44, monthly report of September 1936 has a detailed exposé of united front tactics.

9. This issue has excited some controversy in recent years. Jean Chesneaux, in his *Tradition et Revolution au Vietnam* (Paris: Anthropos, 1971), p. 220, contends that the shift to a rural strategy occurred only in the late 1930s. Tran Van Giau disagrees, and in an article in *Nghien Cuu Lich Su*, No. 142 (January-February 1972), p. 26, asserts that the Party had been devoting considerable attention to the peasantry throughout the 1930s. Without further evidence to the contrary, I am inclined to agree with Chesneaux on this point.

10. This period is discussed in John T. McAlister, *Vietnam: The Origins of Revolution* (New York: Doubleday, 1971).

11. The most detailed discussion of this period is found in King Chen's *Vietnam and China, 1938-1954* (Princeton: Princeton University Press, 1969).

12. Material on this conference is relatively scarce. For an informal, almost "folksy" recollection, see Tran Huy Lieu, "Di du Quoc Dan Dai Hoi o Tan Tro" (Attending the National Conference at Tan Trao), in *Nghien Cuu Lich Su*, No. 17 (August 1960).

13. A Communist model of the process is located in Ho Hai, "Mot vai y kien ve moi quan he giua nong thon va thanh thi nuoc ta trong thoi ky 1939-1945" (A few opinions on the relationship between the rural villages and the cities during the period 1939-1945), *Nghien Cuu Lich Su*, No. 52 (July 1963), pp. 15-18. See Truong Chinh, *Primer for Revolt* (New York: Praeger, 1963), p. 42.

2 Southern Vietnamese Revolutionary Organizations and the Vietnam Workers' Party: Continuity and Change, 1954-1974

Carlyle A. Thayer

Introduction

Vietnam's physical geography as well as the pattern of colonial history have created problems of regionalism with which the Vietnam Workers' Party (VWP) has had to contend. From the earliest days Party leaders sought to form a national Central Committee composed of members from all three regions: South, Center and North. Party policy, based on resolutions approved by the Central Committee, were carried out by regional committees (*xu uy*) which, although subordinate to the Central Committee, were also given enough autonomy to enable them to adjust Party policy by taking into account the special characteristics of their region.

As a result of changes ushered in by the Second World War, and resulting from an abortive uprising in Nam-Ky in 1945, the Party's center of gravity shifted from the South to the North. This led to a situation of uneven development in the Party's southern organization which soon lagged behind the other regions. In 1951, partly in response to this development, the VWP created a special Central Committee Directorate for Southern Vietnam (*trung uong cuc mien nam*) to which senior Party officials were assigned.

In 1954 as a result of a variety of pressures, the VWP agreed to reach a negotiated settlement to the eight-year-old war it had waged against France. Part of the settlement called for the temporary partition of Vietnam pending unification elections. In accepting this solution Party leaders also concluded that henceforth they would have to pursue two different strategic tasks in each zone: socialist construction in the liberated North and a national democratic revolution in the occupied South.

Accordingly the Party withdrew its military units from the southern zone and concentrated on building socialism in the North. It was expected that disunity in the South coupled with external support from France and Russia in favor of implementing the political provisions of the Geneva Agreements, would eventually lead to Vietnam's unification. In this new situation the Party conducted a

The author would like to express his appreciation to David Elliott, William Gausmann, and Robert J. O'Neill for their helpful comments and criticisms of various drafts of this chapter. In addition he would· also like to thank the Southeast Asia Development Advisory Group of The Asia Society for travel funds which enabled him to attend the conference on Communist Movements and Regimes in Indochina: The Politics of Transition.

27

major reorganization by which the special southern Directorate was downgraded into two regional committees, one for the extreme South (*Xu Uy Nam Bo*) and one for the southern portion of central Vietnam (*Xu Uy Trung Bo*).

The VWP's political-administrative organization remained in place; indeed there was no requirement to do otherwise. The Party's organization at lower echelons was reorganized to prepare for an expected two-year-long period of political struggle culminating in reunification elections. However, with its military forces withdrawn and faced with the obdurate policies of the American-backed Diem regime, the Party's plans proved disastrous. By 1956 the VWP's organization in southern Vietnam was forced on the defensive as the Diem government mounted a series of repressive anti-Communist campaigns. Instead of immediately resuming all-out military conflict, the Party chose instead a long-range strategy to rebuild the southern movement. This policy stressed southern self-reliance and restrictions on the use of armed force (armed self-defense was permitted) as conditions prevailing in the North precluded any alteration of existing priorities. By 1958 it was clear that this policy was similarly unsuccessful as the Party's strength and fortunes in the South fell to their lowest state since Geneva.

Throughout 1959-1960 the Party thrashed out a new strategy for the South, one which would mean a greater involvement by leaders in the North and greater use of the resources at their command. It should be pointed out that the VWP never accepted, even in principle, the partition of Vietnam into two different states. They did accept the realities of the existing situation which at that time dictated a cautious involvement in the South. The new strategy of waging a war of national liberation was fully elaborated at the Third National Congress of the Vietnam Workers' Party in September 1960. Over the course of the next year a second Central Committee Directorate was reestablished in the South and charged with overseeing the creation of a new front, the National Front for the Liberation of South Vietnam (NFL). Party cadres, veterans of the Resistance War (1945-54), and a variety of non-Communist opponents of the Diem regime were enlisted as members of this Front. Vietnamese who had regrouped to the North in 1954 returned home to play their part.

The structural relationship between the VWP and the NFL which emerged at this time has not been altered. The VWP remains a nationwide organization which operates under the direction of its Central Committee and Political Bureau. The Directorate for Southern Vietnam is directly responsible to the Central Committee in the conduct of its duties in implementing VWP policy in that region. It is staffed by Party members and is headed by those who hold positions on the VWP Central Committee.

In southern Vietnam the VWP has redesignated itself as the People's Revolutionary Party (PRP). The PRP as such was instrumental in forming the NFL and can properly be termed its vanguard. Party members occupy positions at all levels within the NFL structure and in one sense can be said to "control" the Front because they represent the best organized and disciplined group.

In 1969 a Provisional Revolutionary Government of the Republic of South Vietnam (PRG) was formed. Its most prominent members were drawn from the NFL's Central Committee and from the Alliance of National Democratic Peace Forces. The PRG is an organization which Party leaders deem appropriate for the present stage of the national democratic revolution. In other words, with the start of peace negotiations in Paris in 1968, the "objective realities" of the situation called for the establishment of a governmental structure equal in status to that of the Republic of Vietnam (RVN, i.e., the Saigon government). In the Party's view, the PRG is the current instrument by which the national democratic revolution is being carried out. Until it is completed the Party's policy will be to share power at the "national" level in the South with various non-Communist personalities not aligned with the American-supported Thieu regime.

The Historical Precedents (1930-1951)

The Influence of Regionalism

From its formation in 1930 the Party has continuously experienced problems of coordination between the Central Committee and subordinate echelons. Prior to the sixth plenum in 1940 the Party experienced periods of uneven, spotty, and uncertain growth. In part this was due to the colonial division of Vietnam into three parts which allowed, for a time, overt Party political activity in Cochin China (Nam Ky, now Nam Bo). The Party attempted to adjust to these regional differences by guaranteeing membership on the Central Committee to regional representatives.

During 1931-32 the Party suffered from severe French repression following in the wake of a mutiny at Yen Bay (led by its rival the Vietnam Quoc Dan Dang) and the failure of its attempts to establish revolutionary "soviets" in the provinces of Nghe An and Ha Tinh. Recovery occurred first in the South and from 1935-39 the Party's center of gravity was located there. This was a very important period of development as certain cadres gained experience in both electoral politics and in conducting a united front with elements of the then thriving Trotskyite movement. The Central Committee, which in 1930 had originally moved to Saigon from Haiphong, and had moved overseas during 1932-35, was once again ensconced in Saigon.

The signing of the Hitler-Stalin pact, the outbreak of the Second World War and the Japanese occupation of Indochina, albeit with the cooperation of the French Vichy government, suddenly and radically changed the Party's fortunes. It was outlawed and driven underground by the French, and in the South was severely repressed for the second time following an abortive uprising there in November 1945. This incident, the Nam Ky uprising, marks a decisive turning point for those in the South, because from this time the Party's center of gravity shifted to the North where it has remained. This meant a continuation of difficulties in communications between the Central Committee and its subordinate regional committee in Nam Bo. The situation was exacerbated by the uneven development which followed, for over the next few years, 1942-43, the Party grew in size and organizational complexity much more rapidly in the North than in the South. Development in Nam Bo was further retarded in the face of competition from several rural based politico-religious sects and an urban-based Trotskyite movement.

Subsequent postwar history was to reinforce this estrangement between North and South. For example, during the course of the August Revolution in 1945 when the Party directed the seizure of power from the Japanese, developments in the South were complicated by two factors. In the first instance, Party weakness meant that it had to share power with forces not under its control. In the second, as a result of British action, the French colonialists were permitted to return and to regain power by force of arms. Thus an unprepared southern Party leadership was thrown into the countryside where for a brief time, it faced attack from both the French and its former Saigon coalition partners.

The "Vietminh" Complex (1941-1951)

In May 1941 at the Party's eighth plenum, the decision was taken to form an anti-Japanese and anti-French united front. This was named the League for the Independence of Vietnam—or Vietminh—(formed from shortening the original Vietnamese *Viet-Nam Doc Lap Dong Minh Hoi*). This was the embryo of what by 1945 and after was to emerge as the premier organization leading the struggle for Vietnam's independence. It was both Party-inspired and -directed, but it is important to note that many non-Communists joined it and some even served on the national leadership committee.

In 1946 another front was formed, the *Hoi Lien Hiep Quoc Dan Viet Nam*, or Lien Viet, for short. In both cases the efforts to create a front was designed to rally into one organization a variety of individuals and organizations who agreed on some minimal program. The Party has always shown itself flexible in these matters, rarely permitting ideological dogma to get in the way of the national liberation struggle.

In 1944 the Vietnam People's Army (VPA), known then as the Armed Propaganda Brigade for the Liberation of Vietnam, was formed. It proved instrumental in seizing power during the August Revolution. In September 1945 a Party-led provisional government declared Vietnam's independence and thus created another structure, the "government" of the Democratic Republic of Vietnam (DRVN). It should be noted that it was under this provisional government that Party members in Saigon claimed their authority.

By the outbreak of hostilities there were three structures of importance controlled by the Party: the Vietminh Front, the DRVN government, and the VPA. During the Resistance War this entire complex was popularly known as the Vietminh despite the incorporation of the Vietminh Front into the Lien Viet Front in 1951. This confusion has served to obscure the Party's real role. However, in the period before 1951, this confusion may very well have been real as the Party was not officially in existence. Ho Chi Minh, for example, writing in 1947, in fact used the word "organization" as a semantic dodge for "Party."[1] But the Party did exist. In Nam Bo a regional committee was created in embryo as early as December 1945 when Hoang Quoc Viet, a member of the Central Committee, was sent south for this purpose. Other Party personnel filled key positions in the structure that was being set up. The following year Ho Chi Minh dispatched a non-Party man, Nguyen Binh, to Nam Bo with the task of creating order out of the prevailing confusion. This he did, but not very successfully. At that time, it would appear, Nguyen Binh and Le Hien Mai (alias Duong Quoc Chinh) took charge of military operations. Le Duan and his deputy Le Duc Tho assumed direction of political affairs and Pham Ngoc Thuan directed political cadres serving in the military. Insofar as there is information, Le Duan, Le Duc Tho, and Le Hien Mai were all members of the Party, Duan and Tho being members of the Central Committee. Nguyen Binh was reported to have joined sometime during 1947-48.

The Vietnam Workers' Party Emerges (1951-1954)

The success of the Chinese Communist revolution in 1949 had direct repercussions in Vietnam. The Party was no longer forced to conduct its struggle for independence in isolation from the rest of the world. The arrival of Communist troops on the northern-most border opened up access to a sanctuary which was quickly exploited. No doubt because of this change in Party fortunes, which included victory in a series of military engagements in the Viet Bac region (and Chinese and Russian diplomatic recognition of the insurgent DRVN government) it was decided to have the Party become public. This it did in early 1951 under the name Dang Lao Dong Vietnam (Vietnam Workers' Party).

The problem of regional coordination was dealt with by upgrading the Nam Bo Regional Committee into a directorate under the control of the Central Committee, and by assigning members of the Central Committee to staff it. This meant an upgrading of Nam Bo from one of six interregions (*lien khu*), the basic organizational structure existing from 1948, into a special area of attention. Formerly each interregion was headed by a committee which directed both political and military affairs. The committee was headed by a senior military officer who reported directly to the Central Committee. The new Directorate for Southern Vietnam was literally the Party's command post for that region. It was

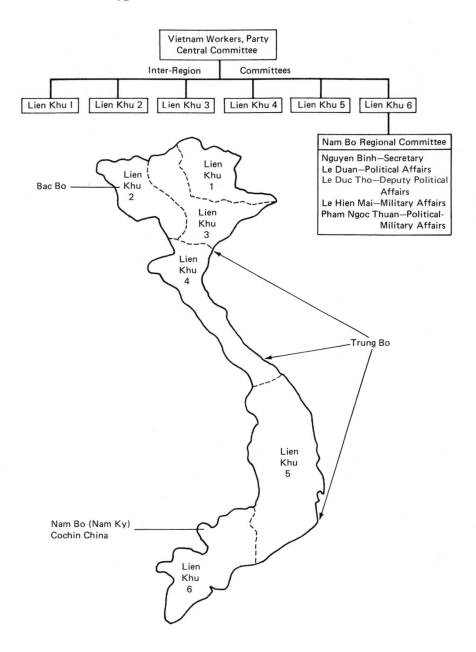

Figure 2-1. The Vietnam Workers' Party and the Nam Bo Regional Committee, 1948-1951

headed by a committee of six members of the Central Committee who, although subordinate to the Central Committee, were given increased authority for operations in their region. According to French intelligence sources the new Directorate was initially staffed by six men: Le Duan (secretary), Le Duc Tho (deputy secretary), Ha Huy Giap, Pham Hung, Nguyen Van Kinh (who operated then under the alias of Thuong Vu), and Ung Van Khiem. If Bernard Fall is correct in stating that by March 1953 the VWP Central Committee contained only nineteen full and ten alternate members,[2] the importance of this Directorate can be gauged by the fact that five of its members were of the former status and the sixth of the latter.

It is interesting to note that before the 1954 conference held in Geneva, partition at the 17th parallel may very well have represented the actual balance of forces on the ground at that time.

The National Democratic Revolution in the South (1954-1960)

Two Strategic Tasks

In 1954 the VWP leadership made the momentous decision to seek a negotiated end to the war. From the time this switch in policy was first broached until shortly before it was accepted as the new line, the Party was engulfed in heated controversy. There were those, particularly in the military and among certain cadres assigned to the South, who wanted to continue the war. However once negotiations began, the intra-Party arguments turned quickly to the specific details of any future settlement. There is some evidence that the Central Committee considered two basic possibilities: (1) the so-called leopard spot solution with regroupment of forces into enclaves and (2) partition brought about by regroupment of forces on either side of a parallel. The latter possibility was accepted.

The reasons why the Party accepted the terms contained in the Geneva Agreements is not our main concern here. What is important was that for the first time in the Party's history, different strategic lines were drawn up to guide the revolution in the North and in the South. In other words, accompanying the decision to accept partition came another decision, equally significant, which was to carry out socialist construction in the northern regroupment zone (henceforth the DRVN) and to carry out a national democratic revolution in the southern regroupment zone. Priority was accorded to the former task, and success in building socialism there, it was argued, would have an irresistible impact on developments in the South.

Cadres stationed in the South were not all happy with this turn of events. In fact it seemed to them as if history were repeating itself, with the 1954 Geneva

Agreements taking the place of the Franco-Vietnamese agreement of 1946 (at that time Ho Chi Minh left the future of Cochin China to a referendum which never took place). According to Tran Van Bo, a deputy secretary on the western Nam Bo interprovince committee, who went under the nom de guerre "Le Van Chan":

When the Geneva Agreements were signed, there was already much ill will against the Central Committee and Ho Chi Minh, because people felt that the South was always to be treated as a sacrificial animal when it came to reunification. Now the Southerners were called upon to sit by and tolerate more sacrifices. They felt that the Party and Ho Chi Minh had turned out to be more stupid than the French, the Americans, or even Diem himself.[3]

Reorientation in Nam Bo

The signing of the Geneva Agreements set in motion a rapid change from war to peace in which the military shield which had protected the Party's administrative apparatus was to be withdrawn and replaced by the enemy's forces (the French Expeditionary Corps and the State of Vietnam's so-called Vietnam National Army). This change required a total restructuring of the Party's organizational complex in the South. During the period of phased regroupment (which was to last for 300 days) the Party ordered the dissolution of all national salvation associations (*hoi cuu quoc*) connected to the Lien Viet Front. Specific policies were drawn up for areas which the Party controlled in varying degrees. In the contested areas this meant disbanding the Party-controlled village councils. In the urban areas, on the other hand, where it was felt that the waging of political struggle would prove decisive, the Party assigned certain selected cadres for underground operations.

The Party organization, thought to number between 50-60,000 in 1954, was trimmed for the anticipated period of underground existence. All members were forced to participate in a "reduction of cadres" movement which succeeded in lowering the number of effectives to 15,000 by 1957.[4] Meanwhile the Party shifted its exposed facilities deep into the resistance base areas, particularly in the Plain of Reeds (*Dong Thap Muoi*). An estimated 10,000 men with military experience, of whom no more than 5,000 were considered well armed, were divided up into a variety of stay-behind groups. Some of these men remained in small units and were stationed in inaccessible regions. Others were assigned to Party provincial committees to fill in gaps left by departing cadres or to form the skeletal framework for armed self-defense units should the need arise.

Most importantly, the Central Committee Directorate which had overseen these disruptive changes was itself reorganized. Along with many other key cadres, members of the Directorate also joined the exodus to the North. By early February 1955 it was confirmed that at least four of the six Directorate members were in Hanoi (Ha Huy Giap, Pham Hung, Le Duc Tho, and Ung Van Khiem). On the occasion of May Day 1955 the Party newspaper *Nhan Dan* published the names of several secondary-level cadres of the "Trung Uong Cuc Mien Nam" who were in the North and who had received the Resistance Medal (Third Class) for their services. It seems that at this time the Directorate was almost certainly downgraded into the previously existing regional committees for Trung Bo and Nam Bo. Le Duan remained as secretary in Nam Bo. He was assisted by Pham Hung who, although he had regrouped, was to return to Saigon first as the DRVN representative on the ceasefire committee for the South, and then on the VPA High Command's Liaison Mission to the International Commission for Supervision and Control (ICSC).

The partition of Vietnam at the 17th parallel sheared off two provinces which had been under the jurisdiction of the Lien Khu V Committee. The remaining provinces were reorganized under the command of the Trung Bo Regional Committee. Nguyen Van Vinh served as its secretary and Nguyen Dang took charge of supervising the skeletal regional forces.

The Failure of Political Struggle (1954-1956)

In September 1954 the VWP Political Bureau met and set forth a resolution and directives for the next two years which were carefully synchronized with the various provisions of the Geneva Agreements. It was expected that the terms of the Agreements would be honored by the French and that unification would take place as planned, or that reunification would come about as the result of endemic political instability in the South. Several scenarios have been suggested, most of which posited some form of coalition between the Party and other social forces in the South which would eventuate in negotiations with the DRVN, leading to the peaceful reunification of Vietnam. Yet another scenario considered the possibility of a Party-led coup d'état.

The Nam Bo Regional Committee was given a great deal of discretion within the framework of the Political Bureau's resolution. During 1954-55 it conducted a political struggle movement demanding consultations between the two zones and which directed its attention to alleged violations of the Geneva Agreements. With the outbreak of armed conflict between the Binh Xuyen and Hoa Hao armed forces on the one hand and the Diem government on the other, the Party quickly negotiated alliances with elements of the former. During 1956-57, as was later admitted, these units served as "the prop of the people's struggles" alongside reactivated Party units.[5]

After the deadline set for consultations had passed, the Party directed its efforts at coordinating the political struggle movement in Nam Bo with DRVN diplomatic maneuvers on the international level. Both efforts failed. In Nam Bo, beginning in mid-1955 and picking up considerably in 1956, the Republic of

Vietnam inaugurated an "Anti-Communist Denunciation Campaign" aimed specifically at rounding up "former members of the Resistance." This campaign was accompanied by military operations aimed at destroying the armed forces of the insurgent coalition which, at this time, had styled themselves variously, the Peace Alliance (*Lien Minh Hoa Binh*), the Vietnam Liberation National Front (*Mat Tran Quoc Gia Giai Phong Viet Nam*), and the Vietnam People's Liberation Movement (*Phong Trao Giai Phong Nhan Dan Viet Nam*).

The initiative passed to the Diem government and the Party organization in Nam Bo was forced on the defensive. As its fortunes fell, disillusionment set in, especially after the July 1956 deadline set for elections had come and gone. Many cadres had firmly believed that these elections would be held and when the deadline passed they saw little prospect for rapid reunification. Thus Party morale declined at the same time as Diemist repression increased and Party membership accordingly declined to lower levels.

The interaction between the Nam Bo Regional Committee and the Party's Central Committee over this situation has been detailed elsewhere.[6] For our purposes it is worth noting that after 1954 the Party's Central Committee began to convene regularly, about twice a year, and it received reports from the South to which it responded by issuing directives. During 1954-56 the Nam Bo Committee was quick to point out the disastrous nature of the Party's southern strategy. But the Central Committee was unable to respond appropriately as it was deeply involved in problems of socialist construction and land reform in the North.

In August 1955, for example, the decision was taken at the VWP's eighth plenum to form the Fatherland Front. This move clearly indicated that Party leaders were thinking beyond the outlines of the Geneva Agreements in their quest for reunification. An executive committee of the Fatherland Front was formed in the South later that year. Although its platform provided membership for former enemies, and was used to attract certain non-Party personalities, the Front itself never became a mass organization. At this time the Party still felt that consultations might be held, although belatedly, and instructed its cadres in the South to push the political struggle against "My-Diem" (the American-backed Diem) as a means of weakening the hand of the DRVN's prospective conference partner.[7] The plenum also sanctioned Party support for the sects who at that time were engaged in combat with troops of the Army of the Republic of Vietnam (ARVN).

In line with the implementation of both policies, over the course of September-November 1955, the return of selected cadres regrouped in the North began.[8] In September a number of delegations concerned with political, propaganda, cultural, and military affairs made their way to Nam Bo. In October a group of at least fifty highly trained cadres arrived in the Mekong Delta where they leavened the interprovincial committees (*lien tinh uy*) in eastern, central and western Nam Bo. Undoubtedly this infusion, miniscule by later standards, greatly facilitated the Party's just burgeoning relationship with the sect remnants and contributed to the formation of a skeletal Fatherland Front organization.

The dividends expected from this change in policy were not received. In late 1955 and in early 1956 there were renewed signs of disenchantment within the Nam Bo Regional Committee. In particular Le Duan was quoted as urging the overthrow, as soon as possible and by military means, of the Diem government if Vietnam was to achieve reunification.[9] In March/April 1956 at a conference convened by the Nam Bo Regional Committee in the Plain of Reeds to review its policy of political struggle combined with reliance on the sects' armed forces (implemented from September 1955 onwards), Le Duan once again expressed his strong feelings in favor of immediate military action. These views were incorporated into a fourteen-point plan of action which included, among other things, suggestions for establishing bases in Cambodia, for the formation of at least twenty battalions in addition to self-defense forces and the building up of stockpiles of military equipment.[10]

It would seem a reasonable assumption that the views of this conference were transmitted to the Central Committee for consideration at its ninth plenum, held from April 19-24, 1956. At this plenum Khrushchev's new policy of peaceful coexistence and his denunciation of Stalin's cult of the individual as well as Soviet reluctance to support DRVN initiatives to reconvene the Geneva Conference (or to hold elections) were revealed to the entire Central Commitee for the first time. Truong Chinh, the VWP Secretary-General, left no doubt as to the policy which would be followed despite disclaimers from certain quarters. In his report to the ninth plenum he stated:

there are some people who do not yet believe in the correctness of this political program (of the Fatherland Front) and in the policy of peaceful reunification of the country, holding that these are illusory and reformist. The view of the Twentieth Congress of the Communist Party of the Soviet Union on the forms of transition to socialism in different countries, and on the possibility of preventing war in the present era, has provided us with new reasons to be confident in the correctness of the policy of the Viet-Nam Workers' party and the Fatherland Front in the struggle for national reunification.[11]

By June 1956 directives based on the resolutions of the ninth plenum reached Nam Bo where they were discussed at a meeting of the Regional Committee. Although the Committee's plan of action did not receive complete endorsement, the Nam Bo Committee did receive instructions to consolidate existing base areas and to maintain and revitalize those armed units which had been developed. Similar instructions were received concerning the Party's organization. First priority was assigned to improving conditions and rebuilding the apparatus. Renewed emphasis was to be placed on the political struggle with special stress on the program of the Fatherland Front.

The Path of the Southern Revolution
(1956-1958)

Disagreement within the Party over the correct line on reunification continued throughout 1956. A *Nhan Dan* editorial of July 22, 1956 pointed out at least four distinct viewpoints current at that time:

1. There are a number of compatriots who have always been simple in their thoughts. They did not figure out all the schemes of the enemy and were, therefore, sure in their minds that when the two years' time was over, elections would certainly be held.

2. There are a number of compatriots who lack confidence in the future of the struggle for national unification because they see that the enemy is daily consolidating his forces and going all-out to terrorize and massacre our compatriots in the south.

3. There are a number of compatriots who believe in victory but do not believe in peaceful methods.

4. Then there are a number of compatriots who believe in final victory but who are reluctant to carry on a long and hard struggle, and who are anxious to find a more effective method of achieving national unification more quickly.

While it is not entirely clear which persons held what viewpoint, nor even whether the "compatriots" referred to were members of the VWP Central Committee, the views of the Nam Bo Regional Committee are known as they were set forth in a remarkable document entitled *On the Revolution in South Viet-Nam.* A recent Hanoi publication has confirmed this document's existence and has ascribed its authorship to "the leaders in Nam Bo."[12] Other evidence points to Le Duan as the principal author with the possible assistance of Pham Hung. Fortunately a rendition of this important document, obtained by RVN security officials in March 1957, is available for our use.[13]

It has been argued elsewhere that this document, while it might have been discussed in draft form at the tenth plenum in September 1956, was probably presented at the eleventh plenum in December 1956.[14] In either case the exact date is not crucial, insofar as insistence from cadres in the South for a change in unification policy coincided with a change in Party leadership precipitated by failures in the conduct of the agrarian reform campaign in the North. Truong Chinh was forced to give up his post as VWP Secretary-General, Hoang Quoc Viet and Le Van Luong were dropped from the Political Bureau (but retained their membership on the Central Committee), and Ho Viet Thang was expelled from the Central Committee. There is evidence that the question of southern policy was also involved in causing this shake-up, but it could only have played a very minor part.[15]

The policies derived from *On the Revolution in South Viet-Nam* were to serve as the basic guidelines until major changes were agreed upon in 1959. In summary, a long-term strategy was devised which continued to place primary emphasis on political struggle, while at the same time permitting preparations for armed struggle. In other words, the new policy accepted the view that revolutionary violence would be necessary at some future time but in the meantime only preparations for its use were approved. In fact the authority of the 20th Congress of the Soviet Communist Party was invoked to clinch the argument that a revolutionary movement could develop according to a peaceful line. The document outlined four specific tasks:

1. The revolution must be led by a revolutionary party based on a class viewpoint, representing the workers and laboring classes according to the doctrine of Marxism-Leninism.

2. A broad and firm worker-peasant alliance must be developed.

3. The national front must be developed, consolidated and expanded.

4. The enemy's internal contradictions must be exploited so as to weaken and isolate him; our own forces must be introduced directly into his ranks.

According to a subsequent Party history of this period, the policies outlined in *On the Revolution in South Viet-Nam* in fact settled an ideological crisis which has arisen in the South, for it

outlined a new strategic orientation for the South Vietnam revolution, a strategic mission in which everyone could have some confidence. It is necessary to continue the national democratic revolution in South Vietnam and it is necessary to use force to overthrow the feudalist imperialist regime (of Ngo Dinh Diem).[16]

An analysis of the eleventh plenum's decisions, which appeared in the Party's theoretical journal *Hoc Tap*, confirmed that the struggle for national unification had been discussed. Shortcomings were ascribed to the fact that "the long and difficult nature of the struggle had not been fully understood" but that this would be corrected as the Party had "set forth immediate tasks" to remedy this situation. These tasks unfortunately were not enumerated in the analysis but the *Hoc Tap* account clearly revealed that a dispute over priorities was continuing. According to the journal:

We must always remember that our country is still divided into two regimes, therefore while consolidating the north we must plan to win over the south. The consolidation of the north is the key task in realizing national unification. Therefore we must not allow the winning over of the south to detract from the requirements of consolidating the north.[17]

This intra-Party dispute continued throughout the next two years. An official history commenting on the fourteenth plenum held in November 1958, for example, revealed that

The Party also struggled to overcome inappropriate understanding of the close inter-relations of the task of socialist revolution in the North and that of liberating the South, characterized by the fear that the advance of the North toward socialism would hinder the struggle for Viet Nam's reunification. The Party pointed out that (it) was just in order to create favorable conditions for the struggle to liberate the South and achieve the reunification of the country that the North must advance rapidly, vigorously and steadily toward socialism.[18]

National Liberation (1959-1960)

Sometime in early 1957 the secretary of the Nam Bo Regional Committee, Le Duan, was summoned north to assume new duties. In fact he became the VWP's de facto Secretary-General, although not formally appointed to the post until 1960 (other sources report that he was secretly appointed to the post in April 1959). In October 1957 Le Duan was identified as a member of the VWP Political Bureau and the following month he accompanied Ho Chi Minh and Pham Hung to the fortieth anniversary celebrations of the Russian October Revolution in Moscow. Le Duan's public appearances came after a three-year period in which his activities went unreported in the DRVN press and radio. His importance at this juncture was further underscored when on his return from Moscow he addressed an extraordinary Party conference (the thirteenth plenum held in December 1957) on the significance of the 1957 Moscow Declaration, while Ho Chi Minh, the nominal Party Secretary-General, remained in Russia.

The rise of Le Duan to this important Party post brought into the VWP councils a powerful advocate for greater involvement in the South. As has been indicated, the Party was divided on the issue of the interrelationship between the building of socialism in the North and the carrying out of the national democratic revolution in the South. After Le Duan's appointment, however, VWP policy tilted more and more in the direction of greater commitment in the South.

There were other personnel shifts of note. Also in 1957 Nguyen Van Vinh was recalled from his post on the Trung Bo Regional Committee to head the newly created Reunification Department. This department was directly responsible to the Central Committee and was charged with overseeing all matters connected with southern regroupees. According to one source these "matters" concerned the organizing and equipping of various Party and administrative cadres infiltrating and exfiltrating southern Vietnam.[19]

During 1957-58, it is now clear, cadres in the South intensified their expressions of impatience with the restrictions placed on the use of armed force. Apparently a secret directive accompanied the final version of *On the Revolution in South Viet-Nam* permitting "the extermination of traitors" (*tru gian*).[20] It was also at that time that non-Communist observers noted a rise in the number of political assassinations, especially of Saigon government officials. This has now been admitted by semi-official sources:

By 1958, the punishment of local tyrants and the destruction of the grassroots administration of the Diem regime had become a widely-extending mass movement. Some of the tyrannical agents at the top of the administration at district and even provincial level were executed one after another.[21]

Developments followed different paths in the various areas under the command of the Nam Bo and Trung Bo regional committees. During 1957 and in early 1958 ARVN renewed its anti-Communist suppression in the Mekong Delta area. For the first time these Saigon units penetrated Communist base areas such as the U Minh forest, the Dong Thap Muoi and War Zone D. According to a later account:

The revolutionary movement suffered heavy losses. Hundreds of thousands of cadres and people were arrested or massacred. The self-defense organizations in the countryside were broken up. The armed forces in the resistance bases had to be reduced. In particular, the resistance army of the religious sects dwindled into a mere token force.[22]

These reverses prompted Party cadres to review their current tactics. They reached the conclusion that "they could no longer limit themselves to purely defensive methods. The most urgent thing was to punish the cruel agents and tyrants." Throughout the remainder of 1958 self-defense organizations were restored. Eastern Nam Bo became the center of this activity where regular armed forces " of the people" and sect military units combined to step up their activities. At the end of 1958 a "Command of the People's Armed Forces" was established which coordinated action with the revitalized sect forces, this time operating under the acronym Cao Thien Hoa Binh Alliance (formed from the Vietnamese: Cao Dai-Thien Chua Giao [Catholics]-Hoa Hao-Binh Xuyen). The total force in eastern Nam Bo probably totaled three battalions; six companies survived in the U Minh area of western Nam Bo.

In central Vietnam the Party faced similar problems and they too "discussed methods of struggle which would be more effective than just political struggle alone." In late 1957 the Trung Bo Regional Committee received "materials" from the Nam Bo leadership "containing the view-points of the leaders of the struggle in South Viet Nam as a whole." According to one account these documents concluded that "there was no other way out than to use people's revolutionary violence" but that it was necessary "to prepare for an armed uprising to wrest back power for the people."

Accordingly Tran Nam Trung, a pseudonym used by "the top leader of South Central Viet Nam," on his own initiative, made the decision to start preparations for an armed uprising pending "the decision about a new line." These preparations were undertaken gradually and were restricted to two testing grounds: portions of Quang Ngai and Ninh Thuan provinces. In July 1958 a congress of representatives of various ethnic minority groups met to discuss plans for an uprising in Tra Bong district, Quang Ngai province.

Later in that year it was clear that not only was pressure building up on the Central Committee to change its policies on the use of force, but that certain cadres were in fact taking this initiative themselves. Despite these pressures, however, as late as August 1958 the Nam Bo Regional Committee at its third conference opposed an increase in the use of revolutionary violence as a violation of the Party line.[23] Shortly thereafter Le Duan made an inspection tour of the South. No doubt these complaints against the current line of political struggle fell on sympathetic ears. According to one directive dated December 1958, issued to an unnamed subordinate organization in the Highlands, the VWP Central Committee had decided to open "a new stage of the struggle." Coincidently American intelligence sources began picking up indications that "guerrilla-secure (base) areas" were being prepared in the Highlands, the Plain of Reeds, and in War Zones C and D.

Undoubtedly Le Duan's inspection tour was designed to gather material and impressions for the full-scale review of the southern situation which followed on his return. It should be recalled that in late 1958 the VWP's southern organization had entered its "darkest period" and that by mid-1959 its ranks were virtually decimated. The political struggle movement had already ground to a halt under the impact of Diem's anti-Communist campaigns. According to a later history of this period, *Tinh Hinh Nam Bo*, the Party's situation was grim indeed:

By mid-1959 the Party had only 5,000 members left in Nam Bo. Many Party organizations (*dang bo*) were almost completely wiped out, for example, the Gia Dinh Party organization. Even after it received many replacements, the Gia Dinh Party organization was completely destroyed. The secretary of the province committee committed suicide. The Go Vap and Tan Binh district party organizations after the restoration of peace had more than 1,000 comrades, in 1957 after the consolidation of party chapters (*chi bo*) there were only 385 comrades, but by mid-1959, however, there was only one comrade left in Go Vap and there were only five comrades left in Tan Binh. All the remaining district committee members were either arrested or killed. The Kien Tuong province Party organization located in the center of the Plain of Reeds, in mid-1959 had just one chapter of three Party members for 21 villages.

Other areas such as Go Cong, Cho Gao and My Tho town were "white areas."

We do not yet have a complete report, but the number of cadres at the district, province and regional committee levels that were killed between 1954 and 1959 were in the hundreds, and the numbers of Party members at the chapter levels killed was in the thousands.

The Fifteenth Plenum (January 1959)

It was in these circumstances that the Party Central Committee convened its fifteenth plenum. According to an official history of this meeting:

In January 1959 in an important conference South Viet Nam's revolutionary leaders pointed out that South Vietnamese society was a neo-colonial and semi-feudal one. The Ngo Dinh Diem administration was a reactionary, cruel, war-like one which had betrayed the national interests. It was obviously a U.S. tool for aggression and enslavement. The direction and task of the South Vietnamese revolution could not diverge from the general revolutionary law of using revolutionary violence to oppose counter-revolutionary violence, rising up to seize power for the people. It was time to resort to armed struggle, combined with political struggle to push the movement forward.

In the light of this conference, the people of South Viet Nam passed from various forms of political struggle to insurrections.[24]

At that time the Central Committee adopted a resolution permitting the use of "all appropriate means" to push forward the liberation of the South. British observers, presumably attached to their Consulate in Hanoi, reported to the Americans that they took this to mean armed force.[25] The VWP Central Committee also decided to accelerate developments in the political sphere. The fifteenth plenum set up a "war steering organization" for the South which "was (to be) realized no sooner than after May 1959."[26] This was in embryonic form what was to emerge as the second Central Committee Directorate for Southern Vietnam in October 1961. Its duties were to oversee the formation of a new united front in the South.

Flowing from other decisions made at the fifteenth plenum, preparations were undertaken to increase the numbers of regrouped cadres returning to the South. Two groups, Doan 559 and Doan 603, were created to oversee infiltration by land and by sea, respectively. Special border crossing teams were set up and DRVN personnel began securing communication routes to the South through Laos. The Pathet Lao "offensive" of mid-1959 was later connected to this activity.

It was not until May 1959 that the VWP Political Bureau met to translate the fifteenth plenum's resolutions into operational directives. Once these were

drawn up they were transmitted south for study and discussion before implementation. Then, according to one account,

In the summer of that year (1959), a historic resolution reached them [Party
cadres in the South], giving them the green light for switching from political
struggle alone to political struggle combined with armed self-defense and support
activities. A new page had been turned in the history of the South Vietnamese
revolution.[27]

In March and April 1959 the first provincial armed units to be formed in the
Highlands since 1954 were activated in Quang Ngai and Ninh Thuan provinces.
After receipt of "the resolution on the orientation of the movement" Party
leaders in Trung Bo approved long-standing plans for an uprising of the Kor
minority peoples in Tra Bong district of Quang Ngai. These were carried out in
August.[28]

Similar developments occurred in Nam Bo. The new VWP policy of combining political struggle with armed struggle was discussed at all levels from
mid-1959 on. In September two companies of ARVN's 23rd Infantry Division
were ambushed, inaugurating what Australian correspondent Denis Warner has
dubbed as the start of the second Indochinese war. An official Party history
dates the historical turning point in Nam Bo to the month of October. From
that time Party cadres in the South took to the offensive and military action
with battalion-size units, as distinct from the previous armed propaganda and
self-defense unit forays, increased. During Tet 1960 the Party flexed its military
muscle and in a well-coordinated attack, overran the headquarters of the ARVN
23rd Regiment in Trang Sup, Tay Ninh province. Weapons captured at Trang
Sup were distributed elsewhere, contributing to the success of what Party
historians term the period of "concerted or simultaneous uprisings," marked by
the general uprising in Ben Tre province in January 1960.

The Third National Congress of the VWP
(September 1960)

In September 1960 the VWP held its Third National Congress, planning for
which had been announced after the tenth plenum in September 1956. The
four-year delay in holding the Congress was undoubtedly due to a variety of
factors, including disagreement over what the strategic line for the South should
be. The Congress itself, the most authoritative body the Vietnam Workers' Party
can convene, not unexpectedly ratified the changes in policy and personnel that
had been developing for some time. New Party statutes were also approved.

Le Duan's political report, the most important document to be tabled at the
Congress, called for the creation of a broad National United Front in the South.

It was approved and formed the basis of the resolution of the Congress which announced two strategic tasks for the Vietnamese Revolution at that stage:

Firstly, to carry out the socialist revolution in the North.

Secondly, to liberate the South from the rule of the American imperialists and their henchmen, achieve national reunification and complete independence and freedom throughout the country.

These two strategic tasks are closely related to each other and impel each other forward.

The resolution clearly gave priority to socialist construction in the North for it explicitly stated that "to carry out the socialist revolution in the North is *the most decisive task* for the development of the whole Vietnamese revolution, for the cause of national reunification ... our compatriots in the South have the task of directly overthrowing the rule of the American imperialists and their agents in order to liberate south Viet Nam."

Whereas the VWP had previously drawn distinctions between the strategic tasks in the two zones, and had expected the southern cadres to exercise self-reliance in carrying out the national democratic revolution by peaceful means, the Party now committed itself to a greater involvement in southern affairs. However southern cadres were still expected to carry the main burden in employing armed struggle.[29] Probably the main reason for this was that the VPA was in no state for sustained combat at that time. General Vo Nguyen Giap made this clear in a speech to the Third National Congress: "hundreds of thousands of volunteer-fighters have been demobilized. Our army is almost entirely made up of new recruits (who) ... have not yet been tempered (in combat) and whose political standards are rather low." Therefore, concluded General Giap, "(t)he modernization of the army is a most necessary work, amounting to a whole technical revolution requiring great efforts."

The new leadership lists made clear the VWP's commitment to modernization of the army as at least six military officers were appointed to the Central Committee. The Party's commitment to national liberation under southern leadership was also made evident. Among the new thirteen-member Political Bureau were included four individuals who had post-Geneva experience below the 17th parallel. This list included Le Duan, who was now ranked second after Ho Chi Minh. Le Duan had also been named VWP First Secretary (the title Secretary-General having been dropped). The Secretariat, charged with overseeing the daily concerns of the Central Committee, included among its seven members four cadres with lengthy experience in the South, all of whom had in fact been born below the 17th parallel: Le Duan, Pham Hung, Le Duc Tho, and Nguyen Chi Thanh.

Southern representation was also increased on the Central Committee as a whole, as possibly twelve cadres were secretly appointed. These included second-echelon members on the Nam Bo Regional Committee who assumed top positions in the 1957-59 period when more important cadres like Le Duan were ordered north. Their names appeared on RVN "Viet Cong Order of Battle" rosters in 1956 and 1959, and were inadvertently revealed by a DRVN official in 1962 (Nguyen Van Cuc, Le Toan Thu, Pham Van Dang, and Pham Thai Buong).[30]

As was noted above the Party adopted new statutes at this time. Of particular interest is article 24:

The Central Executive Committee may also design a number of its members to set up a central directorate in charge of leading Party activities in especially important Party chapters. The central directorate is placed under the leadership of the Central Executive Committee.

In effect this article gave sanction for the creation of a second Central Committee Directorate for Southern Vietnam similar to the one which had existed in Nam Bo from 1951-55. Southern Vietnam had indeed become an "especially important Party chapter."

The Second Indochinese War (1961-1973)

Nam Bo After the Fifteenth Plenum: The Second Central Committee Directorate

Following decisions made at the fifteenth plenum and the Third National VWP Congress, steps were taken to upgrade the Nam Bo Regional Committee into the second Central Committee Directorate for Southern Vietnam. Personnel for this Directorate were gathered from among the newly appointed members of the VWP Central Committee, who were either confirmed in their positions in Nam Bo or were dispatched from the North.

By September 1961 preparations had advanced sufficiently for a conference to be held at the site of the Nam Bo Regional Committee. Tran Luong, a newly appointed member of the Party's Central Committee, and Tran Van Quang, a member of the VWP's Central Military Committee, were present. At that time it was decided to merge the Nam Bo and Trung Bo regional committees into a "TWC" (*trung uong cuc*). In October the Directorate held its first plenary session where it was decided, according to the draft resolution of the meeting, that:

The best way to develop the *S*(outh)*V*(iet)*N*(amese) Revolution consists of concurrently developing the armed and political struggles, because they constitute the basic conditions for our Revolution to advance forward and attain its final goal, that is, the General Uprising. We must have the proper leadership from the Party.[31]

The draft resolution discussed in some detail Party cadre shortcomings which had emerged over the previous difficult years. In particular, it was pointed out that "Party agents were not widely developed because of a lack of cadre and Party members. The number of casualties during the recent years were serious while the immediate and forthcoming requirements of the movement increased." One of the proposed solutions was to "strengthen unity in the Party, between lower and higher echelons, agencies and the Party Committee, former and new cadre or Party members, and local and *newly arrived personnel*" (emphasis added).

The creation of the new Directorate was part of a major reorganizational drive, linked, as we shall see, to the formation of the National Front for the Liberation of South Vietnam. During 1959 and 1960 it has now been estimated, around 4,500 regroupees returned to the South. Given the state of the Party organization this influx must have dramatically raised the movement's capabilities.

The Party also strengthened its southern organization by recruiting former Resistance cadres into an Association of Former Resistance Members. Organizational work, begun in early 1960, continued throughout the next year under the direction of Tran Nam Trung. In late December 1961 the Association called a meeting at which it was decided to announce the formation of the People's Revolutionary Party (*Dang Nhan Dan Cach Mang*, PRP) on January 1, 1962.[32]

The creation of the PRP did not mark the emergence of a new Marxist-Leninist Party independent of the VWP. Indeed, the international Communist movement has accorded no recognition to it.[33] The southern branch of the VWP was merely revitalized and renamed the PRP in recognition of the fact that Vietnam was "divided into two regions having different social regimes" and, according to an announcement made when the PRP was formed, "(t)he Viet-Nam People's Revolutionary Party is the party of the working class and the laboring people in South Viet-Nam. It is also the party of all patriots in South Viet-Nam."[34]

The PRP was fashioned as a "vanguard group" to lead the struggle against U.S. imperialism and the Diem regime (My-Diem) in the South while in the North the VWP continued with its task of socialist construction. The connection between these two organizations was maintained by the newly created Central Committee Directorate, provision for which had been made in the new Party statutes.

The precise organizational relationship between the Directorate and the PRP is unclear. It seems likely from the scanty evidence available that the Directorate operates as a kind of standing committee for the PRP's Central Committee. The Directorate as an organization is responsible to the VWP's Central Committee while at the same time being responsible for PRP affairs in the South.

The importance of the Directorate can be gauged from the calibre of personnel assigned to its top posts, as well as from the fact that it has been retained as an organizational device linking the VWP and PRP continuously from

1961 to the present (March 1975). Nguyen Van Linh (alias Nguyen Van Cuc) served from 1962-1964 as the Directorate's first secretary. At that time Linh had just been made a covert member of the VWP's Central Committee. No doubt he was chosen because of his long experience in the South. Linh was replaced in 1964 by Nguyen Chi Thanh, a VPA General equal in rank to Vo Nguyen Giap and a member of the VWP Political Bureau. General Thanh brought with him experience as head of the VPA Political Department; he also carried with him instructions to oversee for the first time the use of native northerners—organized in their own military units—for combat in the South. In mid-1967 General Thanh died (or was killed) and Nguyen Van Linh once again assumed the Party's top post in the South. Linh was probably elevated to membership in the VWP Political Bureau at that time. Later in the year Pham Hung, a native of Vinh Long province and likewise a member of the Political Bureau, came south to assume the post of secretary of the Directorate, a post which he holds at present.

Several other members of the VWP Central Committee have long been active in the Directorate's affairs. The roster includes: Tran Van Tra, Tran Luong, Tran Do, Nguyen Don (recalled in 1967), and Hoang Van Thai (recalled in 1974). All of these individuals are also senior officers in the VPA.

The National Front for Liberation

It was at the VWP's fifteenth plenum that plans for forming a new united front were set in train. Throughout 1959 a limited amount of organizational activity was undertaken but it was not until late December 1960 that it was possible for a small organizing committee to convene and declare the formation of the NFL. Copies of the new Front's program were distributed to press and diplomatic circles in both Saigon and Phnom Perih before being broadcast by Radio Hanoi. At the December meeting a provisional Central Committee was formed charged with organizing the NFL's first Congress.

Very little is known about this first organizing conference. According to Douglas Pike about sixty persons were involved, ten of whom represented specific organizations.[35] The VWP played an intimate role at this time, as later evidence indicated that Tran Nam Trung, Nguyen Van Linh, Vo Chi Cong, Phung Van Cung, and Tran Bach Dang were all present. Members of the Democratic Party likewise played prominent roles including Huynh Tan Phat and Tran Buu Kiem. It is likely that representatives from elements of the Binh Xuyen, Cao Dai, and Hoa Hao were present, as, most likely, were representatives from the Party's administrative committees and military forces in central, eastern and western Nam Bo as well as from Trung Bo.

By the time the NFL held its first Congress the VWP had reorganized and retitled itself, various armed forces had been unified under one command (under Tran Nam Trung) and a host of liberation associations had been both created and assembled under the Front's banner.[a] At the first Congress a thirty-five-member Central Committee was formed. The numbers were increased to sixty-four at the time of the second Congress held in January 1964.

The relationship between the NFL's Central Committee and the Directorate for Southern Vietnam is one characterized by the interchangeability of personnel. Several prominent members of the VWP/PRP occupy top posts in the Front's Presidium: Vo Chi Cong, Tran Nam Trung, Tran Bach Dang, Pham Xuan Thai, and Nguyen Huu The. It also seems probable that several prominent members of the Democratic Party as well as other individuals are in fact covert Party members. Tran Buu Kiem and Phung Van Cung are most often mentioned in this regard by American intelligence sources.

Toward the Provisional Revolutionary Government

VWP policy towards the South has undergone several changes since the formation of the NFL. In the years 1960-63 the emphasis was on building up a largely southern self-sufficient movement directed against the American-supported Diem regime. It was in this period that the Front structure rapidly expanded in size, membership and influence while at the same time drawing on the pool of cadres regrouped in the North since 1954. The basic organizational structure and indeed key leadership personalities have changed only slightly in the meantime.[b]

In late 1963 the VWP Central Committee made the decision to escalate the war because of increased American presence in the South and because of the fact that the Diem regime had been toppled in a coup and Party leaders rightly foresaw a period of political instability emerging there. By late 1964 native northern troops (as distinct from regroupees) were making their way south. Shortly thereafter American and VPA main force units were slugging it out on various battlefields in South Vietnam. The massive commitment of VPA regular divisions to southern Vietnam had the effect of increasing the responsibility of the VWP Central Committee in the conduct of the war as well as reinforcing the crucial role of its Directorate for Southern Vietnam. The advent of "big unit warfare" during 1965-67 served to retard a concentration on political issues

[a]During 1961 the following organizations were formed: Peasants' Liberation Association, Women's Liberation Association (March 8th), Workers' Liberation Association (May 1), Youth Liberation Association (December 25th), Students' Liberation Association (January 9) and Cultural Liberation Association (sometime early in the year).

[b]Huynh Van Tam, the PRP's first Secretary-General was replaced by Tran Nam Trung in 1963 when Tam undertook overseas assignments for the NFL. Nguyen Van Hieu served as Secretary-General of the NFL from March 1962 until he too took up overseas duties in late 1963. He was temporarily replaced by Tran Buu Kiem who served until the second NFL Congress in 1964 when Huynh Tan Phat was appointed to that post which he holds at present.

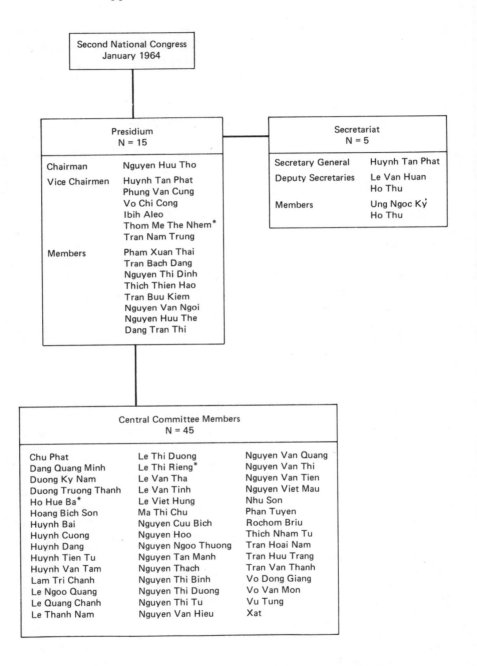

Figure 2-2. National Front for the Liberation of South Vietnam—Leadership

which had developed prior to then. In fact the second NFL Congress was the last; no third Congress has yet been convened.

The appointment of General Nguyen Chi Thanh as secretary of the Central Committee Directorate in 1964 in many respects symbolized the nature of these changes. General Thanh, a native of Thua Thien province in central Vietnam, was a member of the VWP Political Bureau with long experience in Party-Army affairs. Under his secretaryship a three-tiered decision-making structure emerged in which the VWP Political Bureau and Central Committee decided in general terms on major issues (peace negotiations, bloc relations, diplomatic/international policies, general military strategy and important Party and Front policies). In the final quarter of every year the VWP Central Committee would meet in plenary session and draw up a resolution providing general policy guidance for the South. Directorate officials would contribute to this process and the views of Nguyen Chi Thanh and his deputy, Nguyen Van Linh, would be considered before the resolution was transmitted to the South. The Directorate would then convene a special conference to discuss and endorse the new policy guidelines and sometime during the first quarter of the new year would produce its own detailed annual resolution related to specific events in the region (and no doubt timed to coincide with the advent of the dry season). The Directorate appears to take a more tactical approach than the Central Committee although it may possess the option of a veto in certain matters.

At the third tier the NFL Presidium (and in special circumstances the entire Central Committee) would receive and discuss the Directorate's views. The NFL leaders would then draw up guidelines for lower echelons and for constituent organizations to implement by way of political mobilization. Eventually watered-down versions of the highest directives would be discussed at all levels.

In 1967 in response to the failure of the Buddhist Struggle Movement of the previous year, the NFL changed its political program. The new NFL program was specifically drawn up to appeal to adherents of the so-called "third force," that is Vietnamese personalities who were neither pro-Communist nor pro-Saigon government. As such, the 1967 political program represents an adjustment on the part of Party leaders to the fact that there was a possible break in the political alignment of various forces which had been frozen since 1963. It should be recalled that the Saigon government ended the dissidence in central Vietnam and thereafter moved into a period of increased political stability perhaps best symbolized by the presidential elections held in 1967. The NFL's 1967 political program in effect argued that there was no third way for non-Communists who opposed these developments.

During Tet 1968 VPA and NFL military forces launched a dramatic nationwide assault which enveloped almost all provincial capitals as well as the major cities of Saigon and Hue. Although the "success" of this offensive will long be debated, its results are clear. The 1968 Tet Offensive was a sharp blow to America's solar plexus. It effectively knocked out American determination to keep fighting and thereafter the U.S. government moved rapidly to seek an end to the war and a disengagement of its forces. The much vaunted rural pacification program was set back. On the other side of this ledger one must note the appallingly high number of casualties suffered by the attacking forces and their signal failure to bring about an urban "General Uprising." But the offensive did have one side effect, little noticed at that time: it effectively toppled a number of prominent non-Communist fence-sitters into the NFL's camp. In the course of the Tet Offensive various revolutionary committees formed in Hue, Da Nang, Saigon, Cholon, Can Tho, and elsewhere. These groups made contact with the NFL in the liberated areas and in April 1969 were amalgamated into an Alliance of National Democratic Peace Forces (ANDPF). The personalities who comprised the Alliance leadership were urban intellectuals, long active in non-Communist opposition to various Saigon governments. In June 1969 members of the ANDPF were given prominent positions in the newly formed Provisional Revolutionary Government of the Republic of South Vietnam which drew its other members from among the ranks of the NFL.

It is curious to note that the formation of a provisional government by the NFL had been predicted by Western intelligence observers evey year since 1962. When the predictions failed to materialize these very observers took this to mean that difficulties obtained in the NFL's camp.[c] The formation of the PRG in 1969 must be related to the Paris Peace talks and the desire of Party leaders to form a government capable of claiming legitimacy alongside the RVN.

The composition of the PRG's Council of Ministers and Advisory Council is an illustration of two things: (1) the Party's inclination to play a background role and to share state power, at the national level at least, with non-Communists and (2) the Party's powerful role, nevertheless, within the PRG. The posts of Minister and Vice Minister of Defense are held by public Party officials while the posts of Minister of the Interior, Minister and Vice Minister to the President's Office are held by covert Party members.

Conclusion

This chapter has detailed some of the structural and organizational forms fashioned by the Vietnam Workers' Party over the years to meet changes in the political environment brought about by massive foreign intervention on behalf of an anti-Communist regime in the southern region of Vietnam. Throughout the period 1954-74 the VWP's leadership of various southern Vietnamese revolutionary organizations has been constant. At no time has a serious threat to this leadership emerged. What has varied over time has been the VWP's will and

---

[c]Interestingly there is some evidence to suggest that the Soviet Union opposed the creation of a "revolutionary government" during the 1960s because they did not want to back such an organization until it had demonstrated that it could survive and succeed.

capacity to successfully conclude the national democratic stage of the revolution in the South.

The 1973 Agreement on Ending the War and Restoring the Peace in Vietnam provided international endorsement for the PRG's role in the political future of Vietnam. Taking this into account VWP leaders view national reunification as a long-range prospect. The Party has accepted the idea that intermediate forms of organization will have to evolve over time before the North and South can mesh their political structures. In these circumstances the Party has postponed in the South its program of Socialist revolution in favor of national liberation leading to the independence of Vietnam (i.e., the removal of all foreign influence incompatible with Vietnamese self-determination). The failure of the Thieu regime in the past two years to enter into a political settlement, coupled with the obvious reluctance of the American Congress to give President Ford more funds to support his Saigon ally, meant that the tempo of war once again picked up. Now since the Theiu regime has been defeated, the Party will probably have little trouble implementing its control through its already existing structure, a structure which has served the Party so well in the past.

Notes

1. *An Outline History of the Viet Nam Workers' Party* (Hanoi: Foreign Languages Publishing House, 1970), p. 58, footnote 1.

2. Bernard B. Fall, *The Viet-Minh Regime: Government and Administration in the Democratic Republic of Viet-Nam* (New York: Institute of Pacific Relations, 1956), pp. 42-44. My knowledge of this early period also owes much to an interview I had with Ha Huy Giap, VWP Central Committee member in Canberra, June 18, 1974.

3. Jeffrey Race, *War Comes to Long An: Revolutionary Conflict in a Vietnamese Province* (Berkeley: University of California Press, 1972), p. 74.

4. *Tinh Hinh Nam Bo Tu Sau Hoa Binh Lap Lai Den Hien Nay* (The Situation in Nam Bo from the Restoration of Peace to the Present), p. 25; this document appears to be a high-level policy review possibly written by the Nam Bo Regional Committee in 1961. A copy of the Vietnamese original is in the author's possession. Cited hereafter as *Tinh Hinh Nam Bo.*

5. Ta Xuan Linh, "How Armed Struggle Began in South Viet Nam," *Vietnam Courier* [Hanoi] No. 22 (March 1974), p. 21.

6. Carlyle A. Thayer, "Origin of the National Liberation Front: Debate on Unification Within the Vietnam Workers' Party," *Vietnam Report* (Saigon: Vietnam Council on Foreign Relations) Part I (July 15, 1974) and Part II (August 1, 1974).

7. United States Central Intelligence Agency, *Central Intelligence Weekly Review* (October 27, 1955).

8. "Hanoi and the Insurgency in South Vietnam," p. 34; Dispatch by Dennis Bloodworth from Saigon in *The Observer* (London) of January 15, 1956; and Voice of the Dai Viet National Liberation Troops in Vietnamese to Vietnam, November 1, 1955, 0500 GMT.

9. U.S. Central Intelligence Agency, Report No. CS-82270 from Singapore of January 16, 1956 and Report No. FVS-107 from Singapore of September 21, 1956.

10. United States Department of State, *Working Paper on North Viet-Nam's Role in the War in South Viet-Nam* (Washington, D.C., 1968), Appendices, Item 19, "Translation of a document found on the person of a political officer with Communist forces in Zone 9 of the Western Interzone on Nov. 27, 1956." Cited hereafter as *Working Paper.*

11. *Nhan Dan* [Hanoi] , No. 786, April 28, 1956, p. 3.

12. Ta, "How Armed Struggle Began in South Viet Nam," p. 22.

13. *Duong Loi Cach Mang Mien Nam*, document number 1002 in the Jeffrey Race collection of *Vietnamese Materials* on deposit at the Center for Research Libraries in Chicago, Illinois.

14. Thayer, "Origin of the NLF," Part II, p. 12.

15. See for example *Nhan Dan*, No. 900, October 30, 1956, p. 2.

16. *Experiences of the South Vietnam Revolutionary Movement During the Past Several Years*, Item 301 in Appendices to the U.S. Department of State's 1968 *Working Paper.*

17. *Hoc Tap* (November-December 1956) reprinted in *Nhan Dan*, No. 1030, December 30, 1956, p. 2.

18. *An Outline History of the Vietnam Workers' Party*, p. 87-88.

19. "Interrogation of a Signal Platoon Leader in the Viet Cong's 5th Military Region," *Working Paper*, Appendices Item 84.

20. Race, *War Comes to Long An*, p. 82-84.

21. Ta, "How Armed Struggle Began in South Viet Nam," p. 22.

22. Ibid. Unattributed quotations in the following paragraphs are taken from this source.

23. *Tinh Hinh Nam Bo*, p. 32.

24. *An Outline History of the Viet Nam Workers' Party*, pp. 108-109.

25. Telegram from the American Embassy in Saigon to the Department of State, Washington, D.C., dated March 7, 1960 in *United States-Vietnam Relations, 1945-1967*, Book 10, pp. 1255 and 1263.

26. Republic of Vietnam, Ministry of National Defense, Joint General Staff J2, *Study of the Activation and Activities of R, 1960-1964*, p. 25.

27. Ta Xuan Linh, "Armed Uprisings by Ethnic Minorities Along the Truong Son," *Vietnam Courier*, No. 29 (October 1974), p. 18.

28. The Hanoi periodical *Nghien Cuu Lich Su* (Historical Research) has provided several intimate accounts of this period, in particular see issues No. 138 (1971), No. 146 (1972) and No. 148 (1973).

29. See the remarks by Truong Chinh in the April 1961 issue of *Hoc Tap* designed to counter a belief among regroupees that the Party's recent change in policy meant that they would shortly be returning to the South.

30. "Agents from the North Lead Viet Cong," *The Sunday Telegraph* [London] of July 29, 1962, p. 24.

31. *A Draft of the Resolution Adopted by R in Its Open Conference in Oct 61*, translated in the U.S. Department of Defense's *Intelligence Information Report* (March 17, 1970), p. 12.

32. Wilfred Burchett, *Vietnam Will Win* (New York: Monthly Review Press, 1970), p. 151. This section on the PRP also relies on an interview with Nguyen Van Tien member of the NFL Central Committee in Canberra, May 5, 1973.

33. Carlyle Thayer, "Vietnam: Republic of Vietnam (Vietnam Cong San Dang)," in Richard F. Staar (ed.), *Yearbook on International Communist Affairs* (Stanford: Hoover Institution Press, 1974), p. 559; in the late 1960s the Socialist Unity Party of East Germany in discussing various Communist Parties founded since 1960 failed to mention the PRP although it did include the Cambodian People's Revolutionary Party and the Laotian People's Party, see: *Neues Deutschland*, No. 82, May 22, 1968, p. 5.

34. Liberation News Agency dispatch of January 13, 1962 carried by Radio Hanoi in Vietnamese to South Vietnam, January 18, 1962, 0422 GMT.

35. Douglas Pike, *The Viet Cong: The Organization and Techniques of the National Liberation Front of South Vietnam* (Cambridge: The M.I.T. Press, 1966), p. 83.

3

The Paris Agreement and Revolutionary Strategy in South Vietnam

Gareth Porter

The Lao Dong Party and "National Democratic" Revolution

An analysis of the strategy of the Lao Dong Party since the Paris Agreement must begin with the objectives and overall strategy of the Party in the present stage of the revolution in the South. For while this stage of the revolution is "Communist" in its leadership and inspiration, its objective is not Communism nor the imposition of a government wholly controlled by the Party.

While a reunified socialist Vietnam remains the ulitimate goal of the revolution, the present phase is still part of what is called the "bourgeois democratic" or "national democratic" revolution, which is conceived primarily as a struggle against foreign imperialism and for national independence. Although this phase has not excluded class struggle against "feudal landlords" and the land tenure system existing under colonialism, this anti-feudal theme has remained distinctly secondary to the main theme of national liberation struggle by a national united front, made up of four classes: workers, peasants, the petit bourgeoisie, and the national bourgeoisie.[1]

Although the Lao Dong Party calls the anti-imperialist phase of its revolution the "bourgeois democratic" revolution it asserts that it has been led from the beginning by the Vietnamese working class, through the Lao Dong Party itself. But those whose class interests and background may incline them against a Communist system are still considered to be an integral part of the revolution for independence.[2] And the Party has not insisted that all those who want to participate in the anti-imperialist struggle submit to the Party's direction. On the contrary, it has been willing to work along parallel lines with groups and individuals in South Vietnam unwilling to join either the Party or a political front under its leadership.[3]

The corollary to the national united front during the struggle is the concept of the "government of national and democratic union" which is the immediate political objective of the national democratic phase of the revolution in the South. Such a government, as called for in the National Liberation Front's 1960 program, would represent "all social classes" as well as different parties and religions.[4] Ministerial positions would be shared among Party members, personalities who have collaborated closely with them in the past, and other independent figures who have stood for peace and reconciliation. While symbolizing the national united front and the absence of a political monopoly by the Communists, a coalition government in which non-Communist tendencies are represented, would not fundamentally alter the Party's overall political preeminence. For at every stage of the struggle in South Vietnam, as in the earlier war against the French, the Party remained the only nationwide, disciplined and cohesive political organization in the country. When the repression of that organization by armed force is no longer a factor in the political equation, the Party would constitute the dominant political force in the country, with effective direction of the government.

Assured of dominant political power, the Party would nevertheless refrain from pushing for a socialist South Vietnam for a considerable period of time after the establishment of a national union government. It would concentrate instead on the restoration of a minimum degree of national unity and the elimination of the worst social, economic, and cultural effects of colonialism, foreign intervention, and continuous war. "We are in no hurry to establish socialism there," said Central Committee spokesman Hoang Tung in 1973.[5] During this period of normalization, which could take many years, reunification with the North would be out of the question.[6] However, trade, cultural and other ties between the two zones would be rapidly developed.

The political structure and policies of the Party after the conclusion of the present war would be significantly different from those in the North following the war against the French. In 1954, the North Vietnamese government had already been a Lao Dong Party government openly for four years. It moved rapidly to complete the process of eliminating the system of feudal land tenure and then immediately began the collectivization of agriculture within four short years. However, in the South, there are several reasons why the strategic line of the Party calls for a more gradualist postwar policy. In the first place, the legal and political position of the Democratic Republic of Vietnam during the first war was quite different from that of the NLF and the Provisional Revolutionary Government (PRG) since 1960. The DRV, under the Lao Dong party's leadership, had uncontested legitimacy as a resistance government in North Vietnam for many years. After Geneva, most of those bourgeois intellectuals and others who opposed the Party's leadership or who were openly anti-Communist moved to South Vietnam rather than remain in the North. But in the South, since 1960, most of the southern intellectuals have refused to recognize the National Liberation Front and more recently, the Provisional Revolutionary Government, as a resistance government. The urban population has had virtually no contact with the revolutionaries.

Moreover, there are not only more than a million Catholics in South Vietnam who are tightly organized and anti-Communist, but also the Hoa Hao and Cao Dai sects, which are by no means united in their anti-Communist political attitude but which have been used by the United States and the Saigon regime against the revolutionaries. Hundreds of thousands of young men have known nothing but fear of the Communists, having spent their entire adult lives in the Saigon army. The cumulative effects of foreign intervention and prolonged war has been the creation of far more suspicion and fear of the Communists than existed in the North in 1954. A delegation of French Communist Party leaders who visited Hanoi in 1965 reported that North Vietnamese leaders "recognized frankly the reservations which a large fraction of South Vietnamese people have with regard to Communism and their rejection of Hanoi's leadership."[7] Before the Party could begin to carry out a socialist program in the South, therefore, it would have to successfully heal these political wounds left by the war and achieve a degree of social and political consensus which has been absent during three long decades of war.

Finally, there are fundamental differences in social structure which make any effort to force a rapid collectivization on the southern economy a highly risky course. The rural population in the South is now dominated not by the poor and landless peasantry, as in the North in 1954, but by the self-sufficient small farmers of the Mekong Delta who have sufficient land to support their families due primarily to land distribution programs initiated by the National Liberation Front itself. It will be much harder to persuade these peasants that collective ownership of the land is in their interest than it was in the North, where individual parcels were so tiny even after land distribution by the DRV that a high proportion of the poor peasants could still be wiped out by a bad harvest. The Party is likely to be hesitant about imposing collectivization as a national policy in the South.

In general, then, the national democratic revolution in the South has posed problems for the Lao Dong Party which were not present in the North. The Party must concern itself with the problem of restoring a stable social and political order and must postpone demands for radical socialist transformation of society.

Because the Party's political objectives in the South are substantially different from those of the Vietminh in the first war, the role of the Provisional Revolutionary Government in the Party's strategy has been widely misunderstood. The formation of the PRG was aimed at establishing a bargaining position from which to force the United States to give up Saigon's claim to exclusive sovereignty. The central issue in the Paris talks in 1969 was that of the sovereignty of the U.S.-sponsored Saigon regime. The Americans made it clear that the Republic of Vietnam's constitutional structure was not negotiable, and that any "national reconciliation" had to take place within that structure. In keeping with this position, the United States and Thieu offered to permit the NLF to participate in elections under the RVN constitution. The DRV and NLF refused to recognize the RVN constitution, which they saw as merely a reflection of the U.S. military occupation of South Vietnam. They demanded instead that it be superseded by a coalition government.

By transforming the Front into a government in June 1969, the revolutionary side was in a better position to demand that both sides agree not to impose their political regimes on the country during an interim between peace and the choosing of a new government by free elections. Again, the PRG did not need to impose itself as the government of South Vietnam in order to achieve the aims of the national democratic revolution; it needed only to deny to the U.S. client regime its claim of sovereignty over all of South Vietnam.[8]

The Party not only defined the objective of a bourgeois democratic revolution in South Vietnam in terms of foreign intervention in Vietnam but has also had to adapt its strategy and tactics to that intervention. Throughout the war, the military, political, and diplomatic actions of the DRV and the NLF have been determined in large measure by actions taken by the United States to maintain its client regime. Given the disparity in resources between the United States and the Vietnamese, moreover, the Party could not hope to complete the national democratic revolution except by a series of phases, in which the United States would be progressively weakened and finally defeated. The Party's ideological training journal warned in mid-1972 that the struggle in the South "will have to pass through many transitional phases in order to achieve victory step by step."[9]

The process of defeating an enemy with such an enormous power behind it called for the most sober appraisal of the "balance of forces" at each stage. As the training journal said, the Vietnamese knew how to "defeat them in a way most compatible with the balance between our forces and the enemy's in each historic phase." It also required a patient willingness to sustain temporary reversals in some areas while building up the revolutionary forces and waiting for circumstances to change in a way which would be more favorable to the revolution.

Finally, the revolutionary struggle in the South has from the start utilized a strategy which closely coordinated military action with political struggle by the civilian population and agitation within the enemy's own army. And while armed struggle was indispensable to defeating American and Saigon military and pacification plans, it was political struggle which served both as the basis for the armed struggle and which would provide the final push which would overthrow the enemy's regime. Political struggle involved primarily what the Party called "political violence": mass demonstrations; strikes in factories, schools, and other institutions; and occupation of urban centers by civilians from the surrounding countryside. And in the final stage of the struggle to overthrow the client regime in Saigon, direct political action would again hold the "preponderant position" in revolutionary strategy.[10]

These three elements—the limited aims of the "national democratic" revolution in the South, the necessity to "achieve victory step by step" in order to ward off direct American military reintervention, and the central role of political struggle—provide the keys to the Lao Dong Party's strategy, both before and after the signing of the Paris Agreement.

The Paris Agreement and the
Revolution's "New Phase"

Nearly two decades after accepting a compromise settlement which ultimately denied them reunification, and after more than a dozen years of armed struggle, the acceptance of another agreement which fell short of the removal of the U.S. client regime in Saigon must have been a disappointment to Vietnamese revolutionaries, North and South. But the Vietnamese leaders are pragmatic revolutionaries who recognize that in certain circumstances, temporary compromise with their enemy may be advantageous, provided that such an agreement does not compromise the fundamental principles for which the movement has struggled for so long. They knew that the balance of forces within Vietnam and, more important, in the world outside, was not yet favorable enough to make possible the establishment of a government of national union in South Vietnam.[11]

The Paris Agreement represented a compromise between the original PRG demand for a coalition government to replace the Saigon regime and the original U.S. demand that the sovereignty of the Republic of Vietnam be preserved in the settlement. While the RVN managed to avoid signing an agreement which recognized the PRG by name, the agreement signed by the United States named the PRG as one of the parties to the agreement. More important, both the two-party and four-party texts of the agreement accepted the legally coequal status of the PRG and the RVN by allocating a zone of control to the PRG and giving it an equal role in the determination of the modalities of the final agreement on internal political matters.

The absence of any reference in the agreement to northern troops in the South implied that the revolutionaries in the South were justified in calling on northerners for help in their struggle. The Saigon regime remained intact under the agreement, but was obliged to loosen its grip over the political process before an election: the agreement called on Saigon to permit both Communist and non-Communist opposition activists to operate legally within its zone of control; to release the tens of thousands of political detainees in Saigon's jails; and to recognize an independent and politically equal "third segment" as part of the formation of the National Council of National Reconciliation and Concord.

Since there was no enforcement mechanism for the political provisions of the agreement, the Thieu regime could be expected to resist the implementation of these provisions. But this very resistance would be used by opponents of the Thieu regime to chip away at its control and hasten the process of its disintegration.

The Party's strategy in the South after the Paris Agreement reflected its judgment that the Agreement was a major turning point in the "national democratic" revolution. The Paris Agreement marked the end of the revolution in which armed struggle was the main form of the struggle and the beginning of a "new phase" in which the political struggle was the dominant form, while armed struggle played a supporting role. The new strategic guideline for the South was to "closely combine political struggle with armed struggle and legal struggle, using political struggle as the base, and armed struggle as support, while bringing into full play the legal effects of the Agreement."[12]

Because the Paris Agreement had both raised the status of the PRG and the anti-Thieu "third force" and provided a mechanism for eroding Theiu's authority and control, the "legal" political struggle constituted a major new front, which would interact with the Party's other forms of political struggle. A January 1973 Central Office South Vietnam (COSVN) directive on the Paris Agreement said, "We must closely coordinate the masses' struggle in the three strategic areas [mountains, rural areas and urban areas] with the struggle of the overt organizations which are provided for in the agreement. . . ."[13]

Both DRV and PRG leaders used the terms, "protracted," "difficult," and "complex" in describing the struggle for implementation of the Agreement, indicating that Party leaders did not foresee the early demise of the Saigon government or an early end to the struggle.[14] No spectacular leaps forward were forecast by the Party leadership in 1973. Instead the emphasis was placed on gradually changing the balance of forces in favor of the revolution, defeating the enemy "bit by bit."[15]

Party leaders were under no illusions that the United States would carry out the agreement and thus play into their hands. A directive from COSVN predicted that the United States would try to "maintain by all means and under new forms their military involvement in the south while increasing their economic and cultural infiltration as well as political intervention" and that it would use its "lackeys" to "sabotage the implementation of the Agreement, unceasingly instigate limited conflicts which include the possibility of a resumption of [war] . . . ."[16]

Despite its assumption that Saigon would probably violate the ceasefire, People's Liberation Armed Forces (PLAF) units were ordered to stop the pre-ceasefire military offensive when the ceasefire deadline arrived, as documents captured or later reconstructed by U.S. intelligence showed, and to respect the in-place ceasefire provisions of the agreement.[17] These orders did not forbid fighting in the defense of the zone occupied at the time of the ceasefire by the PRG, but did rule out attacks outside that territory.

The willingness of the PRG to hold to a defensive posture even if Saigon did not do likewise was predicated on a fundamental decision by the Lao Dong Party leadership that its primary interest lay in avoiding any action which would provoke U.S. military reintervention. The DRV needed a period of peace in order to reorganize and rebuild its war-shattered economy, just as it had after the first resistance war.[18] A high level of fighting in the South could bring a high risk of a resumption of bombing in the North by an unpredictable Richard Nixon. As one high Party official wrote in April 1973, "We must be extremely vigilant against extreme war-mongering forces."[19] A dampening of the military conflict, on the other hand, would bring a reduction of American interest in Vietnam, and increase the prospects that Nixon's options would be circumscribed and bombing in Indochina ruled out.[20] In order to deprive Nixon of the occasion for intervening with airpower once more, the Party leadership determined that any incursions by Saigon would have to be dealt with in piecemeal fashion, and that no effort would be made to keep Saigon's forces off balance by continuing to pose the threat of a counteroffensive.

Having made its decision to maintain a defensive military posture, the DRV and PRG had an obvious interest in stabilizing the ceasefire lines. The implementation of the in-place ceasefire would not only take the pressure off the PRG zone and permit the Communists to consolidate the economic and military strength of the zone, but would represent a political victory as well. For it would confirm the "reality of two governments, two armies and two areas of control," which the Thieu regime still wished to deny.

The hope was that Saigon's offensive operations could be fended off by a defensive military action combined with popular pressures on Thieu to implement the agreement and successful proselyting within the Saigon army to disobey orders violating it. As a COSVN directive issued in March 1973 said, if the revolutionaries could "prevent the enemy from striking into our territory, bring the political and military-proselyting movements of the masses up to requirements, and coordinate the military victories which have forced the enemy to cease his advances" they could "repel the enemy's plot to impede the Ceasefire Agreement. . . ." Although it was conceded that "it is not possible to avoid having scattered, small military engagements," the revolutionary forces had to "try hard to hold the enemy back" and "force him to implement the Agreement."[21]

By this time, Saigon's military had recaptured villages and other territory lost in the days just prior to the ceasefire deadline and was threatening other vulnerable areas of PRG control. The Party's restrictive military policy was creating some confusion within the PLAF. COSVN directive 03 said that "in many areas" people were "still confused about the application of the struggle principles and methods in the new situation, while the enemy is infringing on us . . . and is secretly causing us a number of difficulties. . . ." It had to warn against the desire to "contend with the enemy's incursions by expanding the scope of military attacks on all the battlefields, as the only way quickly to recover lost territory." At the same time it noted the danger of "passivity, feeling that even use of the military cannot restore the previous position."[22] A leading Party spokesman wrote at this time that there was a "possibility" of "actively repulsing" Saigon's offensive operations against the PRG zone. But he implied that Saigon might succeed in pushing the PRG out of its "leopard spots" in the populated areas, threatening the whole balance of forces in the South.[23]

These admonitions, which recalled COSVN's concern about similar "rightist" and "leftist" deviations during the difficult period of political struggle from

1956 to 1959,[24] were necessary because the Party was defining a military policy which put the PLAF at a strategic disadvantage. It permitted Saigon to mass its forces against a particular objective without fear of a Communist counteroffensive. The result was that the PLAF response lagged considerably behind the ARVN offensive thrust.

"Political Violence," Political Struggle and Military Proselyting

As discussed above, in the new phase of the revolution, the Party's strategy relied primarily on political struggle in order to weaken the hold of the Saigon regime on the countryside as well as the cities and force the ultimate implementation of the Agreement's political provisions. While emphasizing that the Agreement by itself would not be a "complete weapon" which would "replace other types of struggle,"[25] the Party made it clear that the political struggle would revolve around the Paris Agreement.

The form of the struggle between us and the enemy is: The enemy distorts the Ceasefire Agreement, impedes the implementation of the Agreement, creates suspicion and divisors and hatred among the people, and maintains the tense situation. We disseminate the Agreement broadly, bring out the significance of the Agreement as a great victory, open up the movement of struggle to demand that the enemy implement the Agreement, and follow the trend in demanding peace and national concord among all classes of people—even within the puppet army and puppet government—and this forms our new struggle position in the new situation.[26]

The political struggle strategy rested on the belief that Thieu's obdurate refusal to permit democratic freedoms and to move toward reconciliation and peace would contribute to his political isolation and at the same time strengthen the revolutionary movement. The main thrust of the political struggle was to be concentrated on specific popular demands relating to the Paris Agreement, such as for freedom of movement and other democratic liberties which the Paris Agreement was supposed to guarantee, or for an end to the drafting of young men and the upgrading of local militiamen to the status of regular ARVN troops.[27]

The ultimate objective of the political struggle was not simply to raise people's consciousness but to get them to act in defiance of the Saigon government's orders. These actions represented the "higher level" of the political struggle, which the Party called the "political violence of the masses."[28] "Political violence" in this context referred not to the use of armed force, but to the revolutionary character of actions which would mark an open break between the population and the Saigon regime.

In contested areas or areas controlled by Saigon, people would be urged to "apply by themselves the rights to freedom, democracy, freedom of movement, freedom to earn a living, and disregard the enemy's reactionary policies and regulations."[29] One of the most important tasks was to organize people to return to their former ricefields or orchards despite Saigon government orders to stay away. "Where the enemy tries to stop them," one document says, "they must break out in violent struggles to return to their land."[30] Families were also to be urged to demonstrate at outposts to demand that sons and husbands lay down their arms and return home.[31]

To deal with the possibility that Saigon would try to suppress such "illegal" direct actions by civilians, the Party urged that they be coordinated with "military proselyting offensives" with the local Saigon government self-defense organizations. The military proselyting operations would attempt to persuade the soldiers not to use force against their compatriots. Where necessary, the strategy called for the use of armed units to support political struggles by "killing cruel tyrants and destroying enemy units playing the key role in oppressing the people." But again, the preferred method of using force against Saigon's self-defense forces was to "rely on fifth columnists who foment revolts to kill cruel tyrants, destroy enemy posts and motivate enemy personnel to defect."[32]

Proselyting in enemy units is another form of "political violence" which has always been distinguished from other kinds of political struggle in order to give it greater emphasis. When Saigon increased its armed forces to over 1.1 million men, the importance of military proselyting increased accordingly.[33] PRG Minister Nguyen Van Hieu pointed out in 1973 that approximately one out of three South Vietnamese families has at least one member in the ranks of the Saigon army.[34]

The Paris Agreement brought fruitful opportunities for political struggle with ARVN soldiers. With the Americans gone and the PLAF still militarily strong, many ARVN soldiers were eager to make accommodations with the Communists. As a COSVN directive described the situation only two months after the ceasefire, Saigon officers and men, "although closely controlled by the enemy and forced to go on operations of infringement and to build outposts, want to make peace with us in order to feel secure themselves and want to bring about circumstances favorable to their returning home to make their living in the new situation. . . ." In some provinces, the document asserted, "a full hundred outposts have contacted us and want to make peace with us."[35]

Most of the military proselyting was still done by civilians. COSVN called on its branches to "use the force of the masses as the main force for attacking outposts to force the enemy to make peace" rather than using armed forces "extensively to make such peace contacts." The PLAF would remain in the background to support such actions with armed force if necessary.[36]

But another important tactic in military proselyting was to invite individuals or groups of ARVN soldiers to discuss the Paris Agreement with PLAF cadres and soldiers. According to one Communist account, "hundreds of policemen, thousands of security and self-defense forces, and tens of thousands of civil defense forces have met, exchanged opinions and discussed matters with units of the Liberation Armed Forces in their localities." At these meetings, Saigon soldiers were urged to refuse orders to carry out "land-grabbing operations" and pacification operations. Many soldiers pledged that they would do so in the future, and whether or not they kept their promise, the Saigon soldiers who attended such meetings undoubtedly acquired a greater understanding and sympathy for the Communist side.[37] North Vietnamese *People's Army Magazine* called the tactic "a new stage of development" of the military proselyting campaign of the revolution.[38]

Even when the PLAF was attacking Saigon units, military proselyting was given high priority. COSVN instructed its branches that, "in every military action, before, during, and after fighting the enemy, it is possible and necessary to use the reasoning leading into various articles of the Agreement to [appeal to], inhibit, warn, or accuse the enemy...."[39]

Strengthening the Revolutionary Forces

According to the Party's strategic doctrine, only by gradually changing the overall balance of forces to the advantage of the revolution can the client regime finally be overthrown. While consolidating the PRG zone economically and militarily, therefore, its post-Agreement strategy called for increasing the revolution's political and military forces.

One of the most important advantages of the Paris Agreement to the PRG was the elimination of the threat of American bombing. Even if the Saigon government continued to violate the ceasefire, this reprieve from U.S. bombardment would permit the PRG to strengthen its zone by normalizing its economic life and carrying out major improvements in the lines of the communications within the zone. While the PRG zone was large in total land area, it was relatively underpopulated and lacked the roads, logistics bases, and air defenses which would make it more readily defensible. A major effort was made in 1973 to correct these deficiencies. During the first year, the PRG claimed "more than 1 million hectares" of ricefields left fallow due to bombing and shelling had been put back into cultivation.[40] The PLAF still required a significant percentage of the total rice supply in the zone, necessitating both contributions from the population within the zone and purchases from the Saigon zone. But PRG authorities were able to pay premium prices to farmers in the Saigon zone of control for their rice, both for military needs and for resale to civilians in the PRG zone at low cost.[41] (In addition, the PRG zone reportedly had a surplus of manioc, traditionally used by Vietnamese to supplement their diet in times of economic difficulty.[42]) Saigon's National Assembly deputy from Quang Ngai province reported in the spring of 1974, "People who have gone back to their zone have attested that there is no famine there as there is in the nationalist zone."[43]

The objective of the PRG's efforts to raise the standard of living in its zone was not only to meet the needs of its existing population, but also to attract people from the Saigon-controlled zone. A *Liberation Army* editorial exhorting PLAF soldiers to increase production said, "Our compatriots in areas still under temporary enemy occupation, motivated by the improved living conditions in the liberated areas, will enthusiastically go to the liberated areas to earn their livelihood. . . ."[44] Special programs were designed to induce the return of former residents of the NLF-PRG zone as well as others living under Saigon's control. Early in 1974, the PRG began to organize tractor teams especially for the purpose of helping returnees from the Saigon zone begin cultivating lands which had lain fallow. Special credit terms were extended to returnees to buy buffaloes and repay in kind. Cash grants awaited each family coming over to the PRG zone amounting in some areas to as much as $40 to $50 per person.[45]

Although there are no statistics on the population flow from the Saigon zone to the PRG zone, in 1973 and 1974 it appears to have been considerable, particularly in Central Vietnamese provinces like Quang Ngai, where refugees and other unemployed families were going hungry due to high rice prices and the lack of help from the Saigon government. According to RVN National Assembly Deputy Mai Ngoc Duoc, an estimated 10 percent of the people living in the Saigon-controlled area of Quang Ngai moved to the PRG zone to escape starvation.[46] Population movement back to the PRG zone by refugees living under Saigon's control has also been reported in the Mekong Delta. In My Tho province, where the NLF-PRG zone had been seriously depopulated during the years of heavy bombing and shelling, nearly 1,000 families were reported by Liberation Radio to have moved from the Saigon zone to their "native places" in October and November 1973.[47]

A second aspect of the consolidation of the PRG zone has been the building of a major new road network which knits together the long eastern part of the zone along the Laotian and Cambodian borders stretching from the demilitarized zone all the way down to the town of Loc Ninh and links it with the PRG-held areas of the central coastal plains from Quang Tri down to Binh Dinh. These roads, built with North Vietnamese bulldozers, made it possible to distribute goods and services throughout the zone in a fraction of the time required before the Agreement. They also dramatically increased the mobility of the PLAF. The PRG has constructed, repaired or extended a dozen airports in Quang Tri, Kontum, Binh Long, and Tay Ninh provinces, most of them captured from the Americans before the Agreement.

At Khe Sanh the PLAF also constructed a major logistics base for the entire PRG zone, with a truck park and storage area, all guarded by surface-to-air missiles—the first such base to be built by Communist forces within South Vietnam. In combination with the airfields and the road network, this sophisticated logistics complex increased the PLAF's military potential considerably.

While improving the infrastructure of the PRG zone, Communist strategy after the agreement emphasized the importance of increasing the forces under the PLAF command. For, as Directive 03 warned in March 1973, "opposition to the enemy will not win victory unless there is a change in the ratio of military forces between us and the enemy." Only under those circumstances, it said, "can the situation be made to change quickly, can every enemy plot for obstruction and instigating contention and conflict be smothered, can the enemy be stopped or dealt with in timely fashion should he adventurously reinstigate the civil war, and can we force the enemy to implement the Ceasefire Agreement and defeat him."[48]

Published estimates of North Vietnamese combat strength in the South indicated that the number of northern troops remained stable from the time of the ceasefire until late 1974.[49] It seems likely that an ambitious military recruitment campaign in the South accounted for the alleged buildup of "North Vietnamese" troops in 1973 and 1974. U.S. intelligence specialists pointed out in April 1975 that the Southern component of the Communist army in the South had increased from less than 40,000 at the time of agreement to 100,000 main force troops.[50]

Vietnamese military doctrine emphasizes the importance of maintaining the three types of military forces (main force, guerrillas, and local militia) in "proper balance," and the main weakness of the PLAF in the past few years has been in its guerrilla and militia forces. A study document issued early in 1974 frankly admitted the primary military weaknesses of the revolutionary side: "the guerrilla warfare movement is not yet strong."[51] Guerrilla forces were the key to the political struggle which the Party hoped would weaken and disintegrate Theiu's power at the base. In contested areas where the influence of the revolution is high, said the January 1973 COSVN directive, "We must build guerrilla forces, armed security forces" and "make proper use of these forces to support the people's struggle movement."[52] "The building of armed forces," the same directive stated, "must be closely associated with the building of political forces," which it called the "principal task." The Party called for increasing its own membership as well as that of mass associations, with particular attention in the building of Party chapters to be focused on contested and Saigon-controlled areas.[53]

1974-1975: Military Pressure and the Paris Agreement

As discussed above, at the time of the Paris Agreement, the Party adopted a restrictive military policy and placed primary reliance on political struggle to weaken Thieu, in spite of its knowledge that Thieu would continue to maintain the offensive militarily. There were two primary reasons for this strategy: first, Party leaders feared the resumption of U.S. bombing if its military reaction was too strong. And second, it was hoped that Saigon's offensive thrust could be blunted by a combination of defensive military action, political protest, and military proselyting. Saigon was able to take advantage of the restraints placed on the PLAF, however, to increase its own territorial control throughout 1973.

Hanoi apparently came to the conclusion sometime in the latter half of 1973 that Saigon's military and pacification operations could tilt the balance of forces dangerously in Saigon's favor if it were permitted to continue. Hoang Tung, the Central Committee's most authoritative spokesman, declared in a 1975 interview, "If in the last two years, Thieu had succeeded in wiping us out in the Delta area, eliminating our infrastructure in areas that don't dispose of armed forces ... to complete Saigon's control of the Delta, he could have consolidated his administration and army, developed the economy and liquidated the third force."[54]

In October 1973, the PRG announced a shift in military policy which permitted the PLAF to attack ARVN not only where a violation of the ceasefire had occurred, but at any point where Saigon might be vulnerable.[55] For the first time, therefore, the Communists were threatening to go on the counteroffensive at places of their own choosing, hoping to keep Saigon's forces off-balance and to deter truce violations. Such a policy could ultimately be extended to include a major offensive campaign by the PLAF against the Saigon zone, but North Vietnamese leaders were not yet ready to risk the possible consequences of such a major shift in policy. "If we use our forces to smash the Saigon army," said Hoang Tung to an American journalist early in 1974, "It would open the possibility of a renewed war with the United States. ... That is why our efforts are to try to keep the war on a small scale and to force the other side to implement the Paris Agreement and have real peace."[56]

With PLAF military moves still limited essentially to the mountainous area already dominated by the Communists, Saigon continued its efforts to expand its area of control in the populated plains in late 1973 and early 1974. In January 1974, Thieu called openly for the first time for attacks on Communist base areas.[57] By the end of February 1974, Saigon had gained control of as much as 15 percent of the territory held by the PRG at the time of the ceasefire.[58]

But as the Nixon administration's political crisis deepened, the PLAF did step up its counteroffensive, moving into the lowlands with its main force units for the first time. From May to August 1974, the PLAF seized a series of district towns and other ARVN strongpoints. Moreover, the drive failed to generate the same threats of reintervention which had been issued from time to time in 1973. In August the Nixon presidency was coming to an end under a cloud of scandal, and Congress voted to appropriate only $700 million of the $1 billion in military aid authorized for the Saigon government for fiscal year 1975.

With the virtual disappearance of the threat of resumed U.S. bombing, the second reason for military restraint was removed. In a directive written some time after the military and political developments of the summer, the Party's Central Office in the South analyzed the significance of these developments: "When we stepped up the people's warfare in the lowlands and the border area, raiding their bases or destroying their sub-sectors, district seats, infantry battalions and battle groups the puppet army met with lots of difficulties and the U.S. did not dare intervene openly," it observed. The economic situation in the South was in rapid decline, it said, and U.S. aid would be "further reduced." The result would be to increase the "bitter and irreconcilable antagonisms between every social class and the Saigon government," which would "certainly lead sooner or later to a new, widespread and strong movement of all social strata."[59]

All of this added up to a new and highly favorable balance of forces, which would make it possible to speed up the "step by step" process of defeating the enemy. The COSVN directive indicated that the party expected a "turning point of a decisive character" as a result of future military action.[60] Further victories in the lowlands were expected to encourage the urban political struggle movement against Thieu, increasing the prospects for his replacement by a more moderate Saigon regime. "Our operations in the lowlands as well as those of the main forces are geared to the backing of the urban movement so that it can move forward," said the document.[61]

After the opposition movement in the cities did step up its activities against Thieu in August, September, and October, the DRV and PRG began to focus the military and political struggle on the objective of replacing Thieu with a regime publicly committed to the political accommodations embodied in the agreement. On October 8, the PRG called for Thieu's ouster and "the establishment in Saigon of an administration willing to implement the Paris Agreement."[62]

Thus began a major shift in revolutionary strategy, in which an offensive military posture, combined with stepped-up political struggle, would be aimed at forcing Saigon into a general crisis, from which there would be no exit except by a change of government. The Party had no illusions that such a political change would come until the situation had become desperate for Saigon. A Binh Dinh Party Conference resolution in September 1974 warned, "Only when we have thwarted 'pacification' and encroachment by the enemy and have caused the Saigon regime to be faced with a danger of collapse and are ourselves in a better position and stronger will there be the possibility of a ceasefire.... Only when the ... puppet clique is overthrown and replaced by another force which is willing to implement the Paris Agreement is there a possibility that peace can be restored."[63]

In the new situation, there were "two possibilities" regarding the policy of the United States and Saigon, according to the Central Office: "If in the coming period the balance of forces between the enemy and us tilts to our side, and the enemy meets with increased difficulties, they [may be] compelled to cling to the Agreement and implement small parts of it to impede our advancement, save their deteriorating situation and [then] sabotage the Accord." On the other hand, if Saigon authorities "do not want to carry out the Accord and the present war gradually widens into a large scale one, we again have to wage a decisive revolutionary war to defeat the enemy to win total victory."[64]

The Party would "take advantage" of the first possibility, it said, and at the same time "ready ourselves" for the possibility of an expanded war. The Central Office was thus suggesting that a return to the implementation of the Paris Agreement was possible after a change in Saigon's leadership and in a situation in which collapse of the whole administration was threatened. In spite of the Party's willingness to press the attack until final victory, if necessary, it was still ready to return to the political track if the opportunity presented itself and "take advantage" of it by bringing into play its considerable resources for political struggle.

The 1975 campaign, aimed at forcing a political solution either by threatening to cause the disintegration of Saigon's forces or actually causing it, began with an attack on Phuoc Long province late in December and early in January, culminating in the fall of the province capital on January 6. This was only an indication that the PLAF would aim at important political targets, in order to administer a major blow to Saigon government morale and bring maximum political pressure to bear on the United States to force a change in government. In March, the PLAF carried out a carefully planned attack on Banmethuot, with the collaboration of the Montagnard autonomy organization, FULRO, which had formally pledged its allegiance to the Saigon government in January 1969.[65] The success of the Banmethuot attack and the prospect of other such attacks elsewhere in Military Regions I and II, triggered an effort by Thieu to execute an orderly retreat from the Central Highlands and from Hue. The result, however, was a collapse of morale and discipline within ARVN, as the retreat turned once more into anarchy and chaos. The plan to make a stand at Danang fell apart with the disintegration of Saigon's administration and without a significant battle.[66]

With the collapse and retreat of ARVN all along the Vietnamese coast, the revolutionaries were suddenly in a position of overwhelming superiority in military power, from which they could capture Saigon with relative ease. ARVN had lost nearly half of its main divisions in the Central highlands and coast. Its main force troops had been reduced from 250,000 at the time of the agreement to only about 100,000.[67] By the beginning of April, North Vietnamese and Southern PLAF troops were moving into positions in the Saigon area from which they could cut off access routes and close down the airport.

Even with Saigon clearly indefensible, there were signs that the U.S. Embassy and the Ford Administration were not yet ready to act decisively to end the war. Reports in the U.S. press referred to the "air of unreality" pervading the U.S. Embassy on the possibility of holding Saigon.[68] Party leaders were determined not to allow the war to be prolonged. They would give the United States one last chance to make a political change in Saigon which would eliminate the violently anti-Communist political tendency from the Saigon government; but if that change did not come quickly, they would take the city without negotiations.

The general order to prepare for an attack on the city was given by the Communist general staff, according to a PRG spokesman, on April 4.[69] In the two weeks that followed, Communist forces gradually tightened their noose around Saigon, increasing the political pressure for a rapid and decisive political change. Then, on April 19, PRG spokesman Vo Dong Giang announced that his government would enter Saigon and take over if there was no move by Saigon to settle the war by negotiations.[70] That same weekend, PRG officials passed on an ultimatum to U.S. officials through diplomatic channels demanding that Thieu resign by midnight, Tuesday, April 22, and offering to negotiate a tripartite coalition with a Saigon regime which was clearly differentiated in its policy and personnel from the Thieu regime. The ultimatum apparently gave the United States only a few days to come up with an acceptable Saigon government.[71] In the context of Colonel Giang's announcement, the PRG was clearly giving the United States and Saigon a deadline by which there had to be a political solution to avoid a military takeover of Saigon.

The U.S. Embassy did act with decisive speed to force Thieu's resignation on Monday night, April 21, thus appearing to open the way for a political settlement.[72] But instead of bringing in a figure clearly committed to accommodation with the PRG in the past, such as former General Duong Van Minh (Big Minh), the United States agreed to Thieu's replacement by Vice-President Tran Van Huong, who had collaborated closely with the United States ever since 1964 and had been Thieu's running mate in the farcical 1971 Presidential election. For the next seven days, Huong and the National Assembly played out a meaningless gesture to the RVN Constitution, instead of moving with dispatch to summon a peace cabinet from outside the circle of pro-American leaders. It was not until Sunday night, April 27, that the Assembly finally voted to transfer power to Big Minh.

By that time, it was already too late. For nearly a week, following Thieu's resignation, the Communist forces, which had been in a position to take Saigon at any time they wished, had maintained a relative military lull, apparently in order to give the United States a chance to produce a peace government.[73] But at 5 p.m. on Saturday, April 26, that lull had ended, signalling that the deadline for a political solution had passed.[74] Saigon was rocketed for the first time since the Paris Agreement was signed, and the airport came under heavy attack. A PRG spokesman in Paris made it clear that Minh had to agree to abolish the Saigon administration and dismantle his war machine in order to avoid an attack on the city, which meant surrendering to the Communist forces.[75] By Monday night, all roads leading out of the capital were cut.

On Tuesday, Minh assumed the position of President of the RVN and immediately sent his Vice-President and Premier to the PRG's headquarters at Tansonnhut Airport to accept the PRG's new terms for a negotiated ceasefire.[76] But he no longer represented an army or administration which he could offer to dismantle, for as he assumed his new position, the entire military and civilian leadership of the RVN was leaving the country, rushing to the airbase to be evacuated by the Americans.[77]

The PRG officials at Tansonnhut told Minh's emissaries that there was nothing to negotiate.[78] On Wednesday, Minh announced the surrender of his government and army, and most of the city's defenders quietly laid down their arms, pulling out of their positions and moving into the center of Saigon.[79] Shortly afterward, PLAF troops smashed into the palace grounds in tanks without significant resistance. The thirty-year struggle for Vietnam was over.

Conclusion

The Paris Agreement was always seen by the leadership of the Lao Dong Party at two levels: on one level, the political terms of the agreement represented a defeat for the United States and the Thieu regime in that, carried out strictly, they meant an end to Thieu's tight police controls and monopoly over the political process. At another level, Thieu's refusal to carry out those terms would provide a new legitimate basis for carrying on a political struggle and, at an appropriate time, an armed struggle, in order to overthrow that regime and replace it with one consistent with the objective of the national democratic revolution.

When it signed the Paris Agreement, the Lao Dong Party recognized that the problem of war and peace was still to be decided in Washington and not in Saigon. They knew that, despite having signed the document, the United States would not end its intervention in Vietnam. They assumed, therefore, that there would remain for some time a balance of forces which ruled out any simple or short path to final victory. Based on a realistic analysis of the strengths and weaknesses of the two sides, they established a strategy which would gradually redress their own weaknesses, while seeking to deprive the Saigon regime of its main advantage, which was the abundant material support of the United States and the threat of reintervention by U.S. airpower.

It is clear, in retrospect, that the Party achieved the early success of the revolution in the South with the least cost to its people by avoiding a military confrontation in spite of Thieu's provocations, at a time when American policy was still bellicose and military aid to Thieu was still at its peak. By its willingness to accept temporary setbacks for the PRG in territory and population control, the Party leadership gained valuable time in which to consolidate the PRG's military strength, weaken the morale of Saigon's forces, and allow to develop the long-term trend in the United States toward disengagement from Vietnam. The

Nixon administration's political crisis and the steadily worsening economic situation in the United States only accelerated the trend which the Party leaders had already noted early in 1973. The fact that the revolutionary forces were able to take Saigon in 1975 following a campaign of only six weeks in which only one significant battle (the diversionary fight over Xuan Loc in early April) was fought, and without any opposition from Saigon's defenders, is a tribute not only to the tactical military skill of the Communist generals, but more important, to the strategic wisdom of its political leadership.

Notes

1. For a discussion of the "national democratic" revolution, see part 1 of Truong Chinh, "The Strategic Line of Our Party," *Hoc Tap*, January 1960; Le Duan, *The Vietnamese Revolution: Fundamental Problems, Essential Tasks* (Hanoi: Foreign Languages Publishing House, 1973), pp. 21-40.

2. A key COSVN document in 1970 pointed to the urban movement against the Thieu regime and the United States as a development of major importance to the success of the revolution in the South. See Study of COSVN Resolution 10, COSVN Directive 01/CT71, Viet-Nam Documents and Research Notes, Document No. 99, October 1971, p. 4.

3. See the interview with NLF official Nguyen Van Hieu by Prof. George McT. Kahin, in *The New Republic*, October 14, 1967, p. 17.

4. "Program of the National Liberation Front of South Viet-Nam," in *The Viet-Nam Reader* (New York: Random House, 1965), pp. 216-217.

5. "A Vietnamese Vision: An Interview with Hoang Tung," *Indochina Focal Point*, July 1973, p. 2. This document consists of quotations from Hoang Tung in three separate interviews given to visiting American delegations in March, May, and June 1973.

6. "Only when the forces in South Vietnam are truly united can there be eventual reunification of Vietnam," said Hoang Tung in 1973. "You may see Vietnam unified, but not me— because I am a bit old." "A Vietnamese Vision," p. 2.

7. George Chaffard, *Les Deux Guerres du Vietnam* (Paris: La Table Ronde de Combat, 1969), p. 363.

8. For a full discussion of this point, see Gareth Porter, *No Peace for Vietnam* (Bloomington, Indiana: Indiana University Press, forthcoming).

9. Hong Nam, "A Number of Matters Concerning Strategic Line," *Tuyen Huan* (Training), no. 7-8, July-August 1972.

10. See LeDuan, *The Vietnamese Revolution*, pp. 62-76; Vu Can, "The NFL and the Second Resistance in South Viet Nam," *Vietnamese Studies*, no. 23, (1970) *South Viet Nam: From the NFL to the Provisional Revolutionary Government*, pp. 26-45.

11. See Nguyen Khanh Toan, "President Ho and International Solidarity," *Hoc Tap*, no. 11, November 1972.

12. COSVN's Directive 02/73 "On Policies Related to the Political Settlement and Cease-Fire," *Viet-Nam Documents and Research Notes*, Document No. 113, June 1973, p. 7.

13. Ibid., p. 8.

14. See, for example, the speech by Maj. Gen. Le Quang Dao, in *Quan Doi Nhan Dan*, May 15, 1973; "Revolutionary Struggle, the Real Strength of the Revolution and the Revolutionary Armed Forces," *Tap Chi Quan Doi Nhan Dan* (People's Army Magazine), no. 4, April 1973. For similar language in discussing the peaceful political struggle following the Geneva Agreement, see "Appeal of the Lao Dong Party," Vietnam News Agency, August 5, 1954; speech by General Vo Nguyen Giap, Vietnam News Agency, July 11, 1956, *Nhan Dan*, July 12, 1956.

15. COSVN Directive 02/73, p. 6.

16. Ibid., p. 4.

17. *New York Times*, January 24, 1973. Similar orders had been reported to be in effect when the Party expected a ceasefire in late October 1972. See *New York Times*, November 23, 1972.

18. In an authoritative article on the revolutionary tasks of the two zones after the Paris Agreement, Hoang Tung wrote that the "central task of the new period" for North Vietnam was "the task of carrying out economic and cultural development, strengthening the nation's defense forces, and transforming the country into a prosperous and strong one." Hoang Tung, "Our Very Great Victory and Our New Task," *Hoc Tap*, no. 4, April 1973.

19. Ibid.

20. Hoang Tung referred to the appearance of a "neo-isolationist" trend in the U.S., which would oppose renewed military intervention in Vietnam. Ibid.

21. COSVN Directive 03, *Viet-Nam Documents and Research Notes*, Document no. 115, September 1973, pp. 8-9.

22. Ibid., pp. 12-13.

23. Hoang Tung, "Our Very Great Victory and Our New Task."

24. See Tinh Hinh va Nhiem Vu 59 (Situation and Tasks for 1959), a captured Party document, no. 1025 in the Jeffrey Race collection, available from the Center for Research Libraries, Chicago.

25. COSVN Directive 03, p. 11.

26. Ibid., p. 5.

27. COSVN's Directive 02/73, p. 12.

28. Ibid., p. 7.

29. Ibid., p. 13.

30. "Plan of General Uprising When a Political Solution is Reached," captured Party document, dated October 4, 1972, captured by ARVN on October 9, 1972, translated by USIS, Saigon (xerox copy).

31. COSVN's Directive 02/73, p. 13.

32. Ibid., pp. 13-14.

33. In a ten-point declaration on January 25, 1972, the PRG said that families whose members had been "forcibly enlisted by the United States and Thieu" were considered "unfortunate victims of the American policy of aggression," and pledged that there would be "no discrimination" toward them. Quoted in Nguyen Van Hieu, "Stability and Peace Can be Achieved in Vietnam," *Le Monde Diplomatique*, June 1973.

34. Ibid.

35. COSVN Directive 03, p. 17.

36. Ibid., p. 18.

37. Local accommodations between ARVN troops and the PLAF were admitted by the ARVN 22nd Division commander to be "chronic" around Kontum city and cause for serious concern. See Evans and Novak, "Conquest by Accommodation," *Syracuse Post-Standard*, May 18, 1973.

38. Nguyen Ngoc Giao, "The New Stage of Development of the Military Proselyting Activities of the Liberation Army of South Vietnam, *Tap Chi Quan Doi Nhan Dan*, (Liberation Army Journal), no. 10, October 1973.

39. COSVN Directive 03, p. 14.

40. Hanoi Radio, December 20, 1973.

41. A *Liberation Army* editorial called on PLAF soldiers to increase production in order to "partially" meet the PLAF's needs for food. At the same time "reducing the people's contribution. . . ." But on the other hand, an American volunteer worker in Quang Tri province observed in the autumn of 1973 that the first RVN 1000-dong notes to appear in the province "came out of the mountains" and were used by the PRG to purchase rice and other foodstuffs in the market.

42. Mai Ngoc Duoc, "Nhan Dinh ve Van De Phan Phoi Gao va Nan Doi tai Tinh Quang Ngai," (Observations on the Problem of Distribution of Rice and Hunger in Quang Ngai Province), April 1, 1974 (mimeographed). Deputy Duoc was once Province Chief of Long An Province under Diem.

43. Ibid.

44. Quan Giai Phong editorial, Liberation Radio, October 25, 1973.

45. Hanoi Radio, November 30, 1973; Liberation Press Agency, February 3, 1974; Diane Jones, "Eyewitness: Liberated Zones," *Indochina Focal Point*, March 1-15, 1974, p. 2.

46. Mai Ngoc Duoc, "Obserations."

47. Liberation Radio, December 9, 1973.

48. COSVN Directive 03, p. 13.

49. Maynard Parker, chief of *Newsweek*'s Hong Kong bureau wrote in the autumn of 1973, "Although the North has sent approximately 145,000 men to the South since the ceasefire, they have also exfiltrated nearly 115,000 men back to North Vietnam. The resulting net increase of 30,000 men basically

accounts for casualties and other routine replacements and indicates no new massive buildup of men in the South. . . ." "Vietnam: The War That Won't End," *Foreign Affairs*, January 1975, p. 368.

50. Robert Shaplen, "Letter from Saigon," *The New Yorker*, April 21, 1975, p. 132.

51. "Communist Guidance on 'New Phase' of the 'Revolution' in South Vietnam," *Viet-Nam Documents and Research Notes*, Document no. 117, April 1974, p. 8.

52. COSVN's Directive 02/73, p. 14.

53. Ibid., p. 15.

54. Quoted in Gareth Porter, "Pressing Ford to Drop Thieu," *The New Republic*, February 8, 1975, p. 20.

55. The New Orders to the PLAF were broadcast on Liberation Radio, October 15, 1973.

56. Quoted in "North Vietnam: Reconstruction and Vigilance," *International Bulletin*, no. 6, March 25-April 17, 1974.

57. Thieu publicly called on his troops to carry out operation "in the areas where their army is now stationed," *Washington Post*, January 5, 1974. In February 1974, ARVN began major offensive operations in all four military regions. Report by Father Levi Oriel Broqueto to the Vatican, translated from French into Vietnamese by the Dinh Huong Committee, p. 23.

58. *Thailand, Laos, Cambodia and Vietnam: April 1973.* U.S. Senate, Committee on Foreign Relations, Subcommittee on U.S. Security Commitments abroad, Staff Report, 92nd Congress, 2nd Session, May 8, 1973, p. 33.

59. Directive NR. 08/CT74, "COSVN's Directive 08: North Vietnam's military Plans for 1975," translated by U.S. Embassy, Saigon, (mimeographed), pp. 11 and 13.

60. Ibid., p. 12.

61. Ibid., p. 17.

62. Liberation Radio, October 8, 1974.

63. Resolution of the Third Province Party Conference of the Fifth Term (September 18-30, 1974), "Binh Dinh Province Resolution: Communist Plans for 1975," translated by U.S. Embassy, Saigon, (mimeographed), p. 15.

64. Directive NR 08/CT74, p. 15.

65. See *Le Monde*, March 14, 1975; *Le Figaro*, March 19, 1975.

66. Don Oberdorfer, "Near the End of an Era," *Washington Post*, March 30, 1975.

67. *Time*, April 28, 1975, p. 13.

68. A secret Senate Foreign Relations Committee staff report referred to this "air of unreality," as reported in *Washington Post*, April 17, 1975.

69. *Washington Post*, April 20, 1975.

70. Ibid.

71. *Washington Post*, April 26 and 27, 1975; May 5, 1975.

72. *Time*, May 5, 1975, p. 12.

73. *Washington Post*, April 24, 1975.

74. Vietnam News Agency, Hanoi Radio, April 30, 1975; *Washington Post*, April 28, 1975.

75. *Washington Post*, April 28, 1975.

76. *Washington Post*, April 30, 1975.

77. *Washington Star*, April 29, 1975; *Chicago Tribune*, April 29, 1975.

78. *Washington Post*, April 30, 1975.

79. Ibid.

Part I:
Communism in Vietnam

*B. External Relations Strategy
of the DRV*

4

Fighting While Negotiating:
The View from Hanoi

Allan E. Goodman

[Author's Note] This chapter draws heavily on statements made by North Vietnam to its own people and on instructions to Party and army officers that have all been monitored or captured and then translated by agencies of the U.S. government. Some of this material Hanoi wanted Washington to read; some it did not. I have seen none of the material in the original and could not in any case vouch for the accuracy of the translation; but what I have read and what I shall quote reflect what U.S. negotiators relied on in developing a profile of Hanoi's intentions. To the twelve principal U.S. negotiators I have interviewed, the relevant data about Hanoi's attitudes toward negotiations are represented by the extracts reproduced here.

I apologize in advance for those extracts that seem awkward, jargonistic, or that appear to unnecessarily belabor a single point. But I have rarely found that a conclusion can be lifted from the setting of the argumentation and rhetoric supporting it. That such argumentation is often lengthy reflects the nature of the medium as often as it does the complexity of the message. Since most of what is quoted here came from speeches or interviews, the extracts tend to be somewhat longer than if they had been drawn from a polished book. For some helpful hints in interpreting ideological jargon, see R.N. Carew Hunt, A Guide to Communist Jargon *(New York: Macmillan, 1957).*

North Vietnam came to the Paris talks with a fighting-while-negotiating[1] strategy not to end the war but to win it. It agreed to secret and, later, semi-public talks believing it had achieved a position of strength; it was prepared, consequently, to step-up the fighting in the South as the surest route to a military victory. For Hanoi, negotiated settlement was a contradiction in terms; negotiations[a] are undertaken only to facilitate military victory and a settlement could only be based on what had been achieved on the battlefield, not at the conference table. This chapter reviews Hanoi's use of negotiation as a tactic of protracted struggle and examines North Vietnamese perspectives on the relationship between negotiations and a settlement of the war.

[a]Hanoi chooses its words carefully. "Preliminary talks" refers, with one exception, to the 1964-1968 contacts between DRV and U.S. representatives where conditions for the 1968 Paris Meetings—called official conversations—were specified. What took place during these talks and conversations was characterized by DRV representatives as "discussion." The word negotiation was rarely used by Hanoi though the U.S. and third party representatives used it frequently.

As the Vietnam experience shows, negotiation is neither limited to formal interaction between and counter proposals among adversaries,[2] nor to a process by which a bargain or compromise between two positions is struck.[3] Following a strategy of fighting-while-negotiating, adversaries may actually believe a negotiated settlement is not possible and use negotiations to assure (or prevent) a military victory. For both sides, negotiation was an extension of warfare and not a means of conflict resolution. For Hanoi, fighting-while-negotiating required avoiding a premature cease-fire and seeking an agreement that provided for a continuing capability to conduct military operations in the South. Washington also needed time. Both the Nixon and the Johnson administrations wanted to train and test the South Vietnamese army and to see filled the vacuum created by political instability in Saigon and the government's administrative incompetence in the countryside. The political future of the South, consequently, could not be left ambiguous until Washington thought Saigon ready to face the Communists in the political and military arenas.

Hanoi made no secret of its use of negotiations to whipsaw Washington into peace terms by weakening the U.S. will to continue the war. What is striking is the extent to which Hanoi succeeded in achieving what it had set out to do. The twelve U.S. negotiators I have interviewed, for example, all indicated that at some point they were taken in by Hanoi's strategy. As one put it, "I can't begin to count the number of cables I saw reporting that Hanoi was about to make some concession, which ended by commenting: 'at last real negotiations have begun'. Two months later, of course, the so-called serious negotiations would have collapsed and the movement toward a concession was revealed to be a feint." While some U.S. negotiators are convinced that an agreement on such issues as troop withdrawals and prisoner-of-war exchanges could have been reached in 1968, they attribute the prolonged negotiations to Washington's desire to assure that the Saigon government would last at least eighteen months after an agreement was concluded and to President Nixon's search for a more lasting peace, built upon the foundation of the GVN's military and administrative capabilities, on the one hand, and Hanoi's acceptance of that reality on the other hand.

As the present situation in South Vietnam indicates, beyond certain limited obligations now substantially fulfilled, the Paris Agreement on Ending the War and Restoring Peace in Vietnam is moribund. But then there was nothing in the behavior of any party to that Agreement indicating that the basic, conflicting goals of each had undergone modification or, in fact, were negotiable. What is striking, in fact, about the decade of Vietnam negotiations is the consistency with which both sides followed fighting-while-negotiating strategies, each believing in the efficacy of force, not diplomacy. As Hanoi has maintained ever since it first sought direct talks with Washington, negotiations could not be expected to settle a conflict so fundamentally linked to the course of a revolution.

Causes and Consequences of Hanoi's
Fighting-While-Negotiating Strategy

Each agreement accepted by Hanoi embodied less than Hanoi originally sought (see Table 4-1). Every agreement has soured, every peace conference has been followed by warfare. Because of this experience, Hanoi has repeatedly warned its people that negotiations do not foreshadow the end of their struggle.

But negotiation has bought Hanoi time and preserved its military advantage. In 1945-46, under the principle of *hoa de tien* (conciliation for future advance), the Vietminh sought to delay the outbreak of war while a national united front was organized. In 1947, a French overture was rejected because it required giving up the foreign advisors so crucial to the training of the PAVN. Negotiations were sought with France in 1954, in part, to preserve what was left of the PAVN after years of warfare and the siege of Dien Bien Phu. And when the United States launched its air war with North Vietnam, overtures were made to use the promise of negotiations to have the bombing stopped. Despite the lack of an agreement on direct talks until 1968, the United States responded to such North Vietnamese overtures by authorizing 452 days of bombing pauses of various types out of the 809 days of the air war.

Experience has taught the North Vietnamese to be distrustful of their adversaries' diplomacy[4]—e.g., to focus on the 377 days when there was no bombing halt—and uncompromising in the struggle for a united Vietnam. As one Asian diplomat who negotiated twice with North Vietnam observed: "It was always clear that their basic goal was unification.[5] Any agreement had to represent a step toward that goal." Because basic goals do not vary, there is a characteristic[6] rigidity in North Vietnamese diplomats. Thus, agreements with them are nearly always reached at the eleventh hour and not through give-and-take over the sessions of a conference. This has occurred, for example, when Ho accepted an agreement in 1946 that his delegation had just refused, when Pham Van Dong proposed partition in 1954, when Mai Van Bo met secretly with a U.S. representative in Paris during August 1965 and proposed a Geneva-type conference on Vietnam and mutual troop withdrawals while soft-pedalling insistence on a total bombing halt, and when Le Duc Tho presented Henry Kissinger with a draft of an "agreement to end war and restore peace" in October 1972. This eleventh-hour diplomacy once led Henry Kissinger to describe the North Vietnamese as "the most difficult people to negotiate with that I have ever encountered when they do not want to settle. They are also the most effective that I have dealt with when they finally decide to settle."

Whatever the specifics of the debate of negotiations within the Politburo,[7] what Hanoi sought and when was determined by the necessity of accommodating three principles derived from its experience of negotiating. The first is the "tradition of determination to fight and win,"[8] growing out of the Dien Bien Phu experience. In the pre-talks period this meant that Hanoi would agree to

Table 4-1
North Vietnam's Record at Negotiating While Fighting

Conference (or Appeal) & Participants	DRV Goals or Proposal	Final Accord	Explanation (if DRV goal not achieved)
Secret talks, Ho & Jean Saint-eny, September 1945-March 1946	National independence; unity; terms of future association with France; neutralization of non-Communist Nationalist opposition	March 6, 1946 Vietnam to be "free state ... belonging to ... French Union"; referendum on unification; cease-fire; presence of French troops permitted during 5-year "Vietnamization" and withdrawal program	International situation unfavorable for independence struggle--resistance would bring devastation, not victory; complete independence could be achieved within terms of agreement and peacefully. Giap: "We have negotiated primarily to protect and strengthen our political, military, and economic position."
Official conversations, Ho & Adm. d'Argenlieu, March 24, 1946	Major negotiations should take place in Paris	Two conferences would be held: preparatory conference in Dalat and official negotiations in Paris	
Dalat conference, VNQDD leader Nguyen Tuong Tam, Giap, & French High Commissioner's Office, April 17-May 11, 1946	Membership in French Union referred to in March 6 agreement impaired sovereignty; French financial and technical assistance in exchange for special French commercial and diplomatic status	NONE	Tam: there was "general agreement that the conference failed to reach agreement on anything."
Fontainebleau conference, Pham Van Dong & Max André, July 6-September 13, 1946	Economic and political autonomy within the French Union and dates for referenda	NONE	France recognized Cochin China as an autonomous republic on May 30 and held a second conference on August 1 to which the Vietminh were not invited.

Event	Proposal	Response	Comments
Secret talks, Ho & the French Prime Minister and Minister of Colonial Affairs, September 14-15, 1946	Same as above	*Modus vivendi:* French cultural and economic activities could resume; joint cooperation on a cease-fire. No formal recognition of Vietnamese independence or date set for referenda.	Ho, desiring to restrain Vietminh from launching premature armed struggle and to provide time to neutralize political opponents, accepted terms the official delegation had refused.
Radio broadcast appeals, Ho to Léon Blum, December 29, 1946; January 1, 7, and 10, February 18, March 5, 1947	Cease-fire	No French response	
April 20, 1947, appeal of DRV Foreign Minister to French people	Cease-fire and negotiations for "reaching a peaceful settlement to the conflict"	NONE	Ho-Paul Mus meeting revealed unacceptable French demands. Ho characterized the situation: "a coward is what I should be if I accepted these conditions."
Ho interview published in *Expressen*, November 28, 1953	An armistice and negotiations "to solve the Vietnam problem by peaceful means"	NONE	Bidault vetoed establishing contact with Ho arguing that "The Vietminh is at the end of the tether."
Geneva conference, May 7-July 21, 1954	Independence and unity	Temporary partition	"In the new combination of circumstances, the former watchword 'resistance to the end' must be replaced by 'peace, national unity, independence, democracy . . .' When people embark on negotiations, they have to make reasonable mutual concessions." Ho Chi Minh, 15 July 1954, secret speech to the Central Committee.
Ho to Diem, summer 1963	Negotiations to settle the conflict without outside interference	NONE	No response from Diem.

Table 4-1 (cont.)

Conference (or Appeal) & Participants	DRV Goals or Proposal	Final Accord	Explanation (if DRV goal not achieved)
May 18, 1965, Mai Van Bo to the French government; approach repeated in June and four meetings held August-September	The NLF, April 1965, proposed four points as working principles for negotiations, not preconditions for a Geneva-type conference; both sides right of self-defense should not be impaired by cease-fire; mutual troop withdrawal; South Vietnamese negotiations to solve political problems after U.S. troops withdrawn; peaceful reunification.	NONE	No U.S. response initially, then private contact established. Substantial agreement reached on basic principles of a settlement before contact terminated without explanation by Hanoi.
Pham Van Dong to Canadian diplomat Chester Ronning, March 11, 1966	DRV willing to enter talks—"unconditionally of the four points"—if U.S. unconditionally, stops bombing and all other acts of war.	NONE	U.S. disapproved of Ronning mission and saw no new initiative stemming from it. Pham Van Dong said that U.S. counterproposal presented on Ronning's second trip constituted a rejection of DRV's offer.
Foreign Minister Nguyen Duy Trinh's speech, December 30, 1967	DRV willing to enter talks if U.S. unconditionally stops bombing and all other acts of war against DRV	NONE	U.S. studied initiative until the 1968 Tet Offensive.
Le Duc Tho and Nguyen Thi Binh, June-July 1971, at Secret Paris meetings and in interviews with U.S. journalists.	U.S. prisoners could be returned if Washington fixed a date and withdrew forces and its support to the Thieu government. Cease-fire in the South would occur with the establishment of a coalition.	NONE	Hanoi publicly offered to separate the military from the political aspects of the proposal in order to permit the return of U.S. POW's, but refused this in the secret talks.

Le Duc Tho presents a draft peace document to Henry Kissinger, October 8, 1972.	U.S. recognition of unity of Vietnam; end of all U.S. hostile acts against territory of DRV, U.S. troop withdrawal, POW exchange and civilian detainees to be released, creation of an administrative structure to govern South Vietnam prior to general elections.	"Agreement on Ending the War and Restoring Peace in Vietnam" signed January 27, 1973.	Final accord augments truce supervision forces and their capability to initiate investigations, leaves the fate of civilian Vietnamese prisoners up to future negotiations between Saigon and the PRG, and deletes the phrase "administrative structure" from Article 12. Long-standing goals of the ouster of the Thieu government and insistence that political and military issues had to be settled simultaneously were unilaterally dropped.

Sources: Table is based on accounts of negotiations appearing in: Dennis J. Duncanson, "Two Vietnam's or One," *World Today* 25 (1969): 404-414. Nguyen Khac Huyen, *Vision Accomplished? The Enigma of Ho Chi Minh* (New York: Macmillan, 1971). Jean Lacouture, *Ho Chi Minh* (New York: Vintage, 1968). Jean Lacouture and Philippe Devillers, *End of a War* (New York: Praeger, 1969). Donald Lancaster, *The Emancipation of French Indochina* (London: Oxford University Press, 1961). Robert Randle, *Geneva 1954* (Princeton, N.J.: Princeton University Press, 1969). David Kraslow and Stewart Loory, *The Secret Search for Peace in Vietnam* (New York: Random House, 1968). Tad Szulc, "How Kissinger Did It: Behind the Vietnam Cease-Fire Agreement," *Foreign Policy* #15 (Summer 1974): 21-69. Other private papers available to this writer.

negotiate only on the attack, not under attack. Hanoi would not even respond to U.S. offers made during bombing pauses until the bombing had been resumed to avoid indicating that bombing would affect North Vietnamese behavior. Communist overtures for talks or elaborations of peace proposals tended to come *after* "periods in which they had inflicted relatively heavy casualties on the South Vietnamese . . ."[9] Once engaged in talks, the Dien Bien Phu tradition required the coordination of the military with the diplomatic struggle, making negotiation an extension of warfare. As General Vinh observed:

Fighting while negotiating is aimed at opening another front with a view to making the puppet army more disintegrated, stimulating and developing the enemy's internal contradictions and thereby making him more isolated in order to deprive him of the propaganda weapons, isolate him further, and make a number of people who misunderstood the Americans clearly see their nature.[10]

As the negotiations became protracted, Hanoi counted on impatience to produce concessions. The Dien Bien Phu tradition required that massive military offensives occur when victory appeared near or when they were likely to produce a shock in their adversary's political system such that the latter's terms would soften.

Hanoi's second principle of fighting while negotiating centered on the commitment to a *protracted* struggle. As Truong Chinh observed:

Time works for us. Time will be our best strategist. . . . To protract the war is the key to victory . . . if we prolong the war . . . our forces will grow stronger, the enemy forces will be weakened. . . . Those who want "lightening resistance war and rapid victory," who want to bring the whole of our forces to the battlefront to win speedy victory and rapidly to decide the outcome of the war, do not profit from the invaluable experiences of history. . . . All they would achieve would be the premature sacrifice of the bulk of forces in a few adventurous battles; they would commit heroic but useless suicide.[11]

In practice, however, throughout the fighting-while-negotiating stage, support within the Politburo for continuing a protracted struggle had to be continually mobilized. In a widely cited speech to the Lao Dong Central Committee in July 1954, Ho cautioned that despite the overwhelming victory at Dien Bien Phu:

The following errors might occur: leftist deviationism—people intoxicated by our continual victories will want to fight at any price, fight to the end. Like men who cannot see the woods for the trees, they are mindful of the enemy's withdrawal yet pay no heed to his maneuverings; they see the French [defeated] but not the Americans [who may still intervene]; they are full of enthusiasms for military action and underestimate diplomatic action. They do not understand that side by side with armed battle we are carrying on our campaign at the international conferences, with the same objective in view. . . . They put forward excessive conditions, unacceptable to the other side. They want to rush everything and do not realize that the struggle for peace is hard and complex . . .

Rightist deviationism takes the form of negative pessimism and unprincipled concessions. Having no faith in the strength of the people, the rightists weaken its will to fight. They have gotten out of the habit of enduring hardship and no longer aspire to anything but a quiet and easy life.[12]

The need to counteract such tendencies was no less apparent a decade later. In a February 1966 article in *Nhan Dan*, Le Duc Tho observed that the problem was "rightist deviationism":

A small number of comrades have developed erroneous thoughts and views . . . they have made an incorrect assessment of the balance of power between the enemy and us and of the enemy ruses. . . . Now they see only difficulties and do not see opportunities; display pessimism, perplexity and a reluctance to protracted resistance. . . . They fail to see clearly the enemy's deceptive plot of peace negotiations for what it is, and they rely on outside aid [i.e., are too responsive to apparent Soviet pressure for talks].[13]

By 1971, Le Duc Tho was probably arguing against the "leftist deviationism" manifest in the plans of Giap and Truong Chinh to launch an all-out offensive in 1972. In any case, the principle of protracted struggle contributed to prolonging the negotiations and the war in the hope of wearing down Washington's will and, thereby, softening its terms.

The third principle upon which Hanoi based its fighting-while-negotiating strategy involved the need for insulation against pressure from allies. Despite the fact that Hanoi has been dependent on Moscow and Peking for economic, technical, and military assistance since 1954, references to allied pressures at prior international conferences are rare. Indeed, analysts of public statements and radio broadcasts from Hanoi point out that only in 1972 did commentators openly take up the subject of selfish and deceived "foreign influences" pressuring for an agreement. Throughout that summer, Hanoi radio and newspapers focused on the fact that détente was actually a ploy of the Nixon doctrine to "break the national liberation movement" by appealing to the "narrow, immediate interests of a country" and by encouraging complacent Communist powers to forget that "communists must persist in revolution, and should not compromise." Prior to Soviet President Podgorny's June 1972 visit to Hanoi to convey the rather substantial concessions Kissinger had made in Moscow, the *Nhan Dan* commentator—the nom de plume for an angry Polit-buro—characterized détente in these terms:

Nixon [has] even raved about a switch from an era of confrontation to an era of negotiation, but the Nixon doctrine points out that the United States will unceasingly intensify its strength for the negotiations . . . to intimidate and commit crimes against other peoples to force them to accept the arrogant US conditions . . .[14]

·After Podgorny's visit the tone of commentator articles did not change and by August, Hanoi was reminding its allies that "... if out of the narrow interests of one's nation one tries to help the most reactionary forces avert the dangerous blows [it is] just like throwing a life-buoy to a drowning pirate ..."[15] These critical remarks recalled in veiled terms the dangers of repeating the Geneva Conference, about which Douglas Pike observes:

The traumatic effect of this loss on the DRV leaders is particularly evident with respect to two negotiational fears: fear of negotiations at premature levels, and fear of negotiations that do not take place at meetings firmly under their control with respect to agenda, participants, and certain other matters.[16]

Such fears no doubt came into play when Moscow was an intermediary between Washington and Hanoi in 1968, when Mao urged the PRG to take a leaf from the Chungking negotiations[17] and appear to compromise by dropping insistence on Theiu's ouster in return for complete U.S. withdrawal and a considerable reduction in U.S. military assistance, and, possibly, when both the USSR and China were used in May 1972 to convey a secret U.S. proposal that, despite closely coinciding with Hanoi's basic demands, "produced no real results."[18]

Throughout the decade of the Vietnam negotiations, it appears, Hanoi sought to avoid both being pressured into an agreement or discouraged from seeking one by its allies. None of the foregoing, of course, was unknown to Washington, suggesting that *however* Washington responded to Hanoi's overtures, an agreement would come only when Hanoi was ready and largely on Hanoi's terms. As one participant in the secret talks in 1972 observed in an interview: "Le Duc Tho told us that the Politburo decided on the issues of war and peace by a majority vote. This meant, Tho said, that no decision was likely to be precipitous, easily reversed, or deviate dramatically from their strategy."[19] If the pursuit of a fighting-while-negotiating strategy limits the nature of the agreement that can be sought, the need to accommodate the three principles (and their proponents) described above further prolongs the process by which even such a limited agreement can be reached.

The Paris Talks, the Paris Agreement, and Beyond

No U.S. agency that responded to the twenty-nine questions posed by Henry Kissinger in National Security Study Memorandum No. 1 (see Appendix A), a cornerstone of the Nixon administration's negotiating strategy, believed that Hanoi had come to Paris out of weakness:

All consider it unlikely that Hanoi came to Paris either to accept a face-saving formula for defeat or to give the U.S. a face-saving way to withdraw. There is an agreement that Hanoi has been subject to heavy military pressure[20] and that a desire to end the losses and costs of war was an element in Hanoi's decision. . . . The respondents agree that the DRV is in Paris to negotiate the withdrawal of U.S. forces, to undermine GVN [Government of Vietnam] and USG [United States Government] relations and to provide a better chance for VC victory in the South. . . . Hanoi's ultimate goal of a unified Vietnam under its control has not changed.

To Hanoi, starting direct talks in 1968 would buy time, devalue the U.S.' bombing bargaining chip, and heighten dissension within U.S.-GVN ranks.

Direct talks did not, in Hanoi's view, require that the military actions it was conducting in what was characterized as self-defense be stopped. "To ask for 'reciprocity' as a condition, or 'restraint' as a price, is nothing but a trick to blur the distinction between the aggressor and the victim of aggression."[21] By Hanoi's logic, the only negotiable issues were the terms of and timing for the end of U.S. aggression and this Hanoi made clear in Minister Xuan Thuy's first statement at the Talks on May 13, 1968:

. . . these official conversations . . . are aimed at determining with the American side the unconditional cessation of the U.S. bombing raids and other acts of war against the Democratic Republic of Vietnam and, thereafter, at discussing on other problems which interest both sides.

At the second meeting, Xuan Thuy presented the DRV's bill of particulars on the "military acts that violate the sovereignty and territory of the Democratic Republic of Viet-nam" that must be stopped; over the next 174 sessions of the conversations and the perhaps fifty secret meetings, Hanoi did not waver from this basic stand.[22]

U.S. troop withdrawal, of course, did not come because of what happened at the conference table. North Vietnamese agreement to talk achieved only the halt of the U.S. bombing of the North but even this was gradual and not complete. U.S. withdrawal came, according to Hanoi, as Washington's "will of aggression" was defeated by the DRV's demonstration that its forces could always outlast those of the United States. As one high-level DRV official observed: "The US may be powerful, but you are not more powerful than we are on our own soil."[23] While war-weariness was important to generate, what had to be clearly defeated was U.S. strategy.[24] "The U.S. will accept a withdrawal of all their troops only after they have been struck hard by us and when they realize that if they carry on the war, they will suffer heavier defeat."[25]

This defeat was, in Hanoi's view, the 1972 Easter Offensive. In December 1971, Truong Chinh declared:

The 19th Plenum of the VWP Central Committee pointed out [presumably over the objection of Le Duan[26]] that it is necessary to muster the utmost efforts of the entire Party, armed forces and people in both parts of our country . . . to persist in and step up the resistance war, to heighten the determination to fight and win and to advance toward complete victory in order to liberate the South . . .[27]

U.S. intelligence analysts think this was the signal in Hanoi's jargon that a 1972 offensive "was coming and would be all-out." And, indeed, the Easter Offensive became the "largest and most comprehensive strategic offensive ever opened on the battlefield."[28] Having demonstrated a capability to pose a substantial military threat in the South, Hanoi could then consider the overtures Henry Kissinger had made in Moscow that May.

Hanoi responded to Kissinger's May offer by narrowing the scope of the agreement sought through expressing a willingness—vaguely hinted at before—to separate military from political issues, and not press for either Thieu's ouster or the imposition of a coalition before a cease-fire. This tactic would permit an agreement without a need for Hanoi to compromise on political issues. It would leave the political future of South Vietnam ambiguous.[29] All it required for success was time and intransigence. As the State Department and the U.S. Embassy in Saigon correctly predicted in their response to National Security Study Memorandum No. 1 in 1969: "Hanoi is negotiating . . . because it believes that we will have to look for compromise formulas in the talks, and that its own intransigence, coupled with continued military initiative, will add to public pressures on the Administration to make such compromises."[30]!The fact that Hanoi was putting on pressure by announcing on October 25, 1972 that an agreement was near—the first time it had leaked news of the secret talks with the United States since they began in 1964—meant, moreover, that Hanoi guessed the United States would refuse to sign the agreement outlined in the English-language document Le Duc Tho gave Henry Kissinger in Paris on October 8, 1972,[31] once the significance of the Vietnamese version was explained by Thieu to Kissinger.

Since an agreement was not signed by either party as scheduled, it is likely that, although Le Duc Tho had anticipated the intransigence of South Vietnamese President Thieu, he could not move his intransigent Politburo colleagues who were unconvinced that the United States was acting in good faith. Throughout the negotiations and especially from May 1972 onward, for example, Hanoi had repeatedly asked for assurances that the United States was authorized to negotiate for the GVN. U.S. negotiators also think that the North Vietnamese did not fully believe that Kissinger could prevail over advocates of war within the U.S. military and so kept civilians evacuated from Hanoi long after the threat of retaliation for the Easter Offensive had passed.[32] When the agreements were not signed as scheduled, Hanoi made plans for the analogue to the U.S.' operation Enhance-plus, the effort to augment war material in the

South before the cease-fire and before further resupply would be restricted to the terms of the agreement then developing. Such resupply efforts were heavily dependent on navigational coordination and transport resources located in Hanoi and thus a tempting target to a U.S. president known for his belief that intensifying the war would bring Hanoi to terms. Thus, U.S. negotiators and analysts argue, Hanoi expected there would be some kind of force used when it ceased in early December to negotiate seriously and had been repeatedly warned by Kissinger that unless progress was made in the talks, the bombing would be resumed. Hanoi's continued intransigence despite Kissinger's warning thus greatly disturbed the president, who wanted "a Vietnam agreement signed before the inauguration," and who saw the bombing as the only way to re-start the talks.

Militarily, the Christmas bombing was the most successful U.S. operation of the war. B-52 evasion tactics had decisively defeated the SAM defense system and when the bombing ended, less than a two-day supply of missiles remained in the inventory. If an agreement had not been so close, the laser-guided bomb and the sheer amount of tonnage dropped[33] might have foreshadowed a new phase of the war. So effective were these raids, in fact, that consensus was growing within the highest circles in the Pentagon that a military victory, not peace, might be at hand in Vietnam.

Despite the bombing, however, the North Vietnamese could rationalize a return to Paris because, as Washington promised, if talks were again begun, there was nothing Le Duc Tho would have to accept that he hadn't already agreed to accept in October. Of course, North Vietnamese accounts of the final days leading to the Paris Agreement stress that it was Washington, not Hanoi, that had to return the October draft agreement. The key session appears to be that held on the eighth of January.

Comrade Le Duc Tho reiterated his condemnation during a memorable private meeting on 8 January 1973, in a tone of severity and intensity that was unprecedented in the almost 5 years of negotiations. At times, the U.S. representatives had to suggest that the comrade speak in a lower tone, lest newsmen waiting outside overhear.

Embarking on this new meeting phase after the B-52 incident, on the conference table between us and the United States there remained a number of problems arising from the U.S. demand to change what had been agreed upon earlier; at this time, no protocols had been compiled. The United States advanced the proposal for civilian movement through the DMZ, which was actually a scheme to perpetuate the partition of our country and consolidate the puppet Saigon administration. It did not want to return civilian prisoners and sought to prolong the timetable for a return. It wished to downplay the role of the national council of national reconciliation and concord. It also proposed various methods of signing the agreement in an attempt to negate the role of the PRGRSV.

We exposed the U.S. schemes in these proposals and resolutely rejected them. After the heavy U.S. defeat in the massive campaign of raiding Hanoi and other localities by B-52s, and faced with the sharp arguments and the persistent and resolute struggle attitude of our delegation, in 4 days of discussions the U.S. representatives gradually withdrew their proposals and had to accept the content of the agreement already agreed upon in October 1972—which the bombs dropped by B-52s had failed to budge.

One extremely heated topic of discussion dominated the conference table for 5 consecutive years and lingered on almost until the conclusion of the conference. This was the persistent U.S. demand for the withdrawal of northern forces from the South. Comrade Le Duc Tho pointed out that the United States could not place an aggressor on the same footing with those subjected to aggression, and that the Vietnamese people were authorized to fight their aggressor enemy anywhere in their country. The United States finally had to withdraw and give up this demand, and officially recognized that, from a political, spiritual, and legal standpoint it could no longer demand a withdrawal of northern forces.

There was still another extremely difficult issue—that is, the United States tried to exclude its war compensation to us from the agreement. It used this issue as a bargaining card. We declared frankly that the dollar could not be used to buy or exchange, that the responsibility of the United States was to pay its debt owed to our people, and that we were determined to persistently collect this debt at all costs. The United States had to agree to acknowledge in the agreement a U.S. contribution to healing the wounds of war in our country. This contribution really means reparation for the victims of aggression.[34]

Four days later, at Gif-sur-Yvette, the drafting of the agreement was completed.

Negotiations may be entered to protract a conflict or to permit the reallocation of scarce resources. Agreements can be signed to win recognition of basic principles that will ultimately triumph. Thus, just as entering negotiations protracted the struggle, the Kissinger-Tho agreement is now regarded as

... the basis upon which our people can continue their struggle in the new stage to consolidate the peace, step up socialist construction in North Vietnam, complete the national, democratic revolution in South Vietnam, and advance to the peaceful reunification of the country. This is consistent with our analysis and policy; Vietnam must advance on the path of revolution, the revolution must win victory gradually. . . .[35]

In words highly reminiscent of those used by Ho Chi Minh to characterize the victory at Dien Bien Phu, Le Duc Tho observed that the Kissinger-Tho agreements mark "only an initial victory. Our people in both zones, north and south, still have to struggle before we can reach our goal of building a peaceful, unified, independent, democratic and prosperous Viet Nam."[36]

While Hanoi has thus prepared itself for a prolonged political and military struggle until Saigon collapses, it has not allowed for the possibility of the survival of an independent, non-Communist regime in the South.

With the conclusion of the 1954 Geneva Agreements, one-half of Viet Nam was liberated. With the signing of the 1973 Paris Agreement, another half of this remaining half has officially escaped the imperialist yoke. The Paris Agreement recognizes the existence in South Viet Nam of two administrations, two armed forces and two zones of control. Does this entail the threat of a new and permanent partition of Viet Nam, now split into three parts? Drawing lessons from their* experiences of 1954, the Vietnamese negotiators dismissed all US-Saigon proposals for regrouping belligerent forces into a number of well-defined areas: such an operation would facilitate the execution of Nguyen Van Thieu's plan to liquidate "Viet Cong pockets" at a given moment with the support of the USA or, if need be, to perpetuate the division of South Viet Nam. On insistence of the DRVN and PRG, the USA had finally to agree that the cease-fire be carried out on the spot, which makes the map of South Viet Nam look like a "leopard skin."

But this very "leopard skin" must disappear within the shortest time. The existence of two zones, the recognition of which is imperative in the present phase in order to achieve a solution to South Viet Nam's internal problems, is not intended to last indefinitely.

Certainly it is not a *complete* victory and this is also a question of the relation of forces reflecting itself in the Agreement concluded: the PRG . . . will have to coexist for a certain time with the puppet regime. . . . As shown by the events since January 1973, the situation "half-war, half-peace" will be the backcloth for a multi-sided struggle on the ground in South Viet Nam with its political, economic and also its military aspects.[37]

If the Saigon government does not collapse from that struggle, the epitaph of the Paris Agreement may have been inadvertently written when Hanoi warned its allies in August 1972 about separating military and political issues: "Such a cease-fire cannot eliminate the cause of the war. Instead such a cease-fire will permanently maintain the factors for waging war again at any time."[38]

Communist sources indicate that sometime in 1975—after reconstruction and development programs are firmly launched—the Politburo will chart the future course of the revolution in the South by determining the mix of political and military resources required for the struggle.[39] As important as domestic priorities will then be, the variables that dictated strategy during the war will determine it in the period ahead. Hanoi will have to weigh the importance of détente to its allies as external military assistance is sought for future offensives and to estimate the staying power of the Saigon government at a reduced level of American assistance. Consequently, the key to future developments from Hanoi's perspective may lie as much in Washington as in Saigon. Both détente and support to the Thieu government depend on Washington's initiative and a desire to influence both may lie behind the DRV's repeated calls for the normalization of US-DRV relations.

These began with the publication in January 1974 of a White Book that, after thirty pages of discussion of how the United States had violated the Paris Agreements, abruptly concludes by outlining the basis for "normalization" of relations, the first time that process was specifically identified:

The United States must put a complete end to its military involvement and intervention in the internal affairs of South Viet Nam, seriously carry out its obligation regarding the healing of the wounds of war in the Democratic Republic of Viet Nam, and strictly respect the fundamental national rights of the people of Laos and Cambodia. Such a course would show that the United States has drawn practical lessons from an out-of-date policy and it would bring about favorable conditions to progress to the normalization of the relations between the Democratic Republic of Viet Nam and the United States on the basis of respect for each other's independence and sovereignty, and non-interference in each other's internal affairs.[40]

This proposal came less than a month after the United States and DRV reached a secret understanding that made U.S. reconstruction assistance to the DRV contingent on the level of DRV-initiated military activity in the South, suggesting that as late as December 1973 Washington expected that Hanoi would ultimately accept a cease-fire. By mid-year, however, neither side had taken steps to implement that understanding and Moscow rather than Washington was the major source of Hanoi's "post-war" reconstruction assistance. At this writing, the situation remains much as Henry Kissinger characterized in a letter to Senator Edward Kennedy: ". . . North Vietnam remains the aggressor. . . . We would welcome policy shifts in Hanoi which would ease the tension and thus permit us to review policy in light of a new situation."[41] But just as is the case when negotiating, Hanoi does not propose normalization of relations as a signal that it is prepared to compromise on basic goals. Both the normalization of US-DRV relations and a permanent end to the Vietnam War depend on where the southern boundary of the DRV is located. Unfortunately, drawing such a dividing line across Vietnam has been both a consequence of negotiations to end warfare for one generation and a cause of war for another.[42]

Notes

1. The phrase first appears in strategy discussions in a speech by General Nguyen Van Vinh (Chairman of the Lao Dong Party Reunification Department and Chief of Staff, People's Army of Vietnam) to the 4th Congress of the Central Office for South Vietnam (COSVN), April 1966, and summarized in Joint U.S. Public Affairs Office, "The Position of North Viet-Nam on Negotiations," *Viet-Nam Documents and Research Notes*, No. 8, (Oct. 1967), p. 4. This authoritative speech was regarded by the U.S. Mission, those engaged in secret negotiation initiatives, and the delegation to the Official Conversations in Paris as a major adumbration of the DRV approach. See, for example, the prominence given it by the U.S. delegation to the Paris Talks in its "Working Paper on the North Vietnamese Role in the War in South Viet-Nam," State Department Press Release, May 1968. Of the dozen or so comparable references

to the tactic of negotiation in North Vietnamese statements, moreover, the talk of General Vinh is widely cited. Indication of the extent to which this line was disseminated can be found in the 24 RAND Corporation interviews on "Viet Cong Knowledge of Paris Negotiations," Reel AD 741314 of the Defense Documentation Center for Scientific and Technical Information, as well as in the following extract from the Joint U.S. Public Affairs Office, "NFL Thoughts on Peace Negotiations, World Policies; A Cadre's Notes on a High Level 1967 Reorientation Course," *Viet-Nam Documents and Research Notes*, No. 14 (January 1968): "Negotiations, if we are to have negotiations, will serve mainly to provide us the groundwork from which to launch our general offensive. Another reason is to expose the enemy's political attack upon us and to show that ours is the just cause and his the unjust. This means that the war will be settled only on the battlefield, not in the conference room. To have such negotiations, we must fight more fiercely. Only in such a situation can we authorize negotiations to take place. Thus, when hearing that negotiations are about to take place, we must attack the enemy more strongly all over the country" (p. 9).

2. I.e., ". . . a process in which explicit proposals are put forward ostensibly for the purpose of reaching agreement on an exchange or on the realization of common interest where conflicting interests are present." Fred C. Ikle, *How Nations Negotiate* (New York: Praeger, 1967), pp. 3-4.

3. I.e., ". . . mutual recognition of a conscious difference between what is initially demanded at the conference table and what the party expects as the final solution." Wilfred A. Bacchus, "The Relationship Between Combat and Peace Negotiations: Fighting While Talking in Korea, 1951-1953," *ORBIS*, 17 (Summer 1973): 547.

4. For a demonstration that both sides' behavior was inconsistent with their peace rhetoric, see Jeffrey S. Milstein, *Dynamics of the Vietnam War: A Quantitative Analysis and Predictive Computer Simulation* (Columbus, Ohio: Ohio State University Press, 1974), pp. 67-76.

5. Washington's most experienced analyst of North Vietnamese affairs put it this way: "Over the years the DRV leaders have evaluated each proposal for a political settlement—whether it came from U Thant, Pope Paul, or the U.S. State Department—in terms of their fundamental objective, namely unification. Ho Chi Minh has asked himself of each proposal or offer: *Will it move us, even in a small way, toward unification?* If the answer was yes, then he was interested." Douglas Pike, *War, Peace, and Viet Cong*, (Cambridge, Mass., M.I.T. Press, 1969), p. 150. (Emphasis in original.)

6. The best operational definition of Communist rigidity I have yet seen is by Lester Pearson: "The manners and methods of the Communist diplomat . . . have reflected the proletarian nature of the revolution in his country. They are characterized by toughness, a brutal use of words, an obstinate refusal to admit to two sides of any argument, and an attitude of suspicious restraint. . ."

Diplomacy in the Nuclear Age (Cambridge: Harvard University Press, 1959), p. 4. See also C. Turner Joy, *How Communists Negotiate* (Santa Monica, Calif.: Fidelis Publishers, 1970); Arthur Lall, *How Communist China Negotiates* (New York: Columbia University Press, 1968); Kenneth T. Young, *Negotiating with the Chinese Communists: The United States Experience, 1953-1967* (New York: McGraw Hill, 1968); and Raymond Dennet and Joseph E. Johnson (eds.), *Negotiating with the Russians* (Boston: World Peace Foundation, 1951).

7. In 1969, Douglas Pike characterized the partisans as follows: ". . . Regular Force [quick victory, alternating small scale and guerrilla war techniques with sudden massive offensives] and Neorevolutionary Guerrilla War strategy [protracted conflict with victory through modernized guerrilla war tactics] advocates [i.e., Ho, Giap, Le Duan versus Truong Chinh, Le Thanh Nghi, Le Duc Tho] rule out neither tactical negotiations nor nonmilitary efforts in general. . . . The quarrel comes over the relative degree of emphasis each is to get, the allocation of resources, or the correct decision to be made in those specific instances . . . where the interests of one must be served ahead of the interests of the other. . . . But in the final analysis they would agree . . . that victory must be decided in the field, not at the bargaining table or in the political arena in the South." Pike, *War, Peace, and the Viet Cong*, p. 149.

8. Vo Nguyen Giap, speech reported in *Nhan Dan* (December 22, 1968), pp. 1, 4 and translated in Joint Publications Research Service (JPRS), Translations on North Vietnam #505 (February 14, 1969), p. 12. See also his "Vietnamese Military Traditions," Vietnam Courier No. 1 (new series) (June 1972).

9. Jeffrey S. Milstein, *Dynamics of the Vietnam War*, p. 70.

10. Vinh, Speech to COSVN, p. 4.

11. Truong Chinh, *Primer for Revolt* (New York: Praeger, 1963), pp. 112-113. One dissent to the view that time is on the side of the Communists remains relevant today: Communist taxation practices "in combination with the failure of the Vietcong to fulfill promises, seem to be causing an ever-widening number of South Vietnamese to become disillusioned and disgruntled with the Vietcong. In retrospect, this makes . . . the GVN look better than it once did: there was some aid (with few strings attached); taxes were at least three times lower or negligible compared to the VC's taxes; work on strategic hamlets was less demanding than for the Vietcong's combat hamlets; and freedom of movement, marketing and communication were not nearly so restricted." Victoria Pohle and Constantine Menges, "Time and Limited Success as Enemies of the Vietcong," RAND Corporation Papers, P-3491 (October 1971), p. 4.

12. The Selected Works of *Ho Chi Minh* (Hanoi: Foreign Languages Publishing House, 1962), pp. 458-462.

13. Reported in *Deadline Data on World Affairs* (February 3, 1966).

14. "Negotiations Under the Nixon Doctrine," *Nhan Dan* (May 18, 1972) and translated in Foreign Broadcast Information Service (FBIS) *Daily Report: Asia and Pacific* (May 22, 1972), p. K15. See also Commentator, "The Revolutionary

World Peoples Oppose the Nixon Clique," *Nhan Dan* (May 21, 1972) and translated in FBIS (May 22, 1972), pp. K1-2.

15. Editorial, "Victory of the Revolutionary Trend," *Nhan Dan* (August 17, 1972), p. K8.

16. *War, Peace, and the Viet Cong*, pp. 154-155.

17. Mao Tse-tung, *On the Chungking Negotiations*, (Peking: Foreign Languages Press, 1961).

18. Szulc, "How Kissinger Did It," p. 45.

19. This characterization is strikingly verified in a most creative study of how Le Duan, Truong Chinh, Pham van Dong, and Vo Nguyen Giap evaluated the risks involved in five turning points of the war. See Robert F. Rogers, *Risk Taking in Hanoi's War Policy: An Analysis of Military Versus Manipulation in a Communist Party-State's Behavior in a Conflict Environment*, Ph.D. dissertation, Georgetown University, April 1974.

20. By the start of the Paris Talks, the DRV had, among other things, lost over 80 percent of its POL storage facilities, two-thirds of its electrical generation capacity, all of its steel and cement factories, and an estimated half a billion dollars since the bombing began. No one today holds that the 1965-1968 bombing brought Hanoi to Paris or that the threat of resuming it produced substantial concessions on Hanoi's part. It did provide the United States with an important bargaining chip in getting Hanoi *to* a conference table in the sense that a halt could be offered to the North Vietnamese in return for talks conducted not solely on the basis of the four-points. For Washington in 1968, halting the bombing was far easier to do than withdrawing—i.e., the only other reason Hanoi had to hold discussions with the United States. But, if this assessment is correct, using the bombing to get Hanoi to the table made it that much more difficult to imagine the Communists making any real concessions at the table. The bombing stiffened their spirit and until the 1972 Christmas bombing, did not create serious difficulties to their war effort in the South. (See, for example, Oleg Hoeffding, *Bombing North Vietnam: An Appraisal of Economic and Political Effects*, RAND Corporation Memorandum RM-5213-1-ISA (December 1966) and *Harrison E. Salisbury's Trip to North Vietnam*, Hearings before the Committee on Foreign Relations, U.S. Senate, 90th Congress, 1st Session, (February 2, 1967). By attempting to use the resumption of bombing as a threat to induce Hanoi to give in on any basic issues, the United States was, in effect, assuming that a country that had refused to give in to save 90 or 95 percent of its industrial capacity would do so to save the little that was left. See, for example, "To Gain a Better Understanding About Our People's Complete Defeat of the U.S. Imperialist's War of Destruction, *Tuyen Huan* #12 (December 1968), and translated in JPRS #501 (February 5, 1969), pp. 14-15.

21. DRV Foreign Minister Nguyen Duy Trinh, in an interview with CBS News reporter Charles Collingwood in Hanoi, and reported in *Vietnam Courier*, No. 160 (April 15, 1968), p. 2.

22. Even during the secret talks in October 1972, Hanoi considered the withdrawal of U.S. troops "the first basic problem." "Our position is that because the United States invaded our country with U.S. and satellite troops, all these troops must be unconditionally withdrawn; the Americans must withdraw in a clear-cut period of time. . . ." Huong Nam, "Clearly Recognizing Our Just Stand and Exposing the Enemy's Deception Peace Agreement," *Thoi Su Pho Ton* #10 (October 1972), p. 33 and translated in JPRS #1295 (December 13, 1972), p. 16.

23. DRV Foreign Ministry spokesman Ngo Dien to Robert S. Byrd, Chief of the Washington Bureau of the Knight Papers during an interview in Hanoi and reported in *Congressional Record* (June 10, 1970), p. E5414.

24. See, for example, Chien Binh (the military commentator for *Nhan Dan*) "US Strength Obviously on the Downgrade," *Viet Nam Courier* No. 168, (June 10, 1968), p. 4; General Van Tien Dung, "Resolutely March Forward and Completely Defeat the American War of Destruction," Ibid., No. 1973 (July 15, 1968), supplement; "Abrams Won't Be Able to Stave Off U.S. Total Failure in Viet Nam," Ibid., No. 178 (August 19, 1968) p. 5; "Total Failure of U.S. 'Clear-and-Hold' New Strategy Inevitable," Ibid., No. 189 (November 4, 1968); and "Landmarks Since 1960 in the PLAF March Towards Complete Victory," Ibid., Nos. 195 (December 16, 1968), p. 4, and 196 (December 23, 1968), p. 4.

25. From a circular issued by the Current Affairs Committee of COSVN, February 12, 1969, and translated as " 'Decisive Victory': Step by Step, Bit by Bit," *VietNam Documents and Research Notes,* #61-62 (June 1969), p. 5.

26. For a well-informed presentation of this view, see Henry S. Haywood, "Hanoi Builds Unity Front for Kissinger Visit," *The Christian Science Monitor* (February 7, 1973), p. 1.

27. Address to the Third Congress of the Viet-Nam Fatherland Front, Hanoi, December 17, 1971, and translated in "Bases of Power in the DRV," *Viet-Nam Documents and Research Notes*, No. 107 (October 1972), p. 59.

28. *Tuyen Huan* (November-December 1972). For a review of the achievements of the offensive and its contribution to the political and diplomatic struggle, see Trung Dung, "The Unparalleled Expansion of the Revolutionary War in the South," *Tap Chi Quan Doi Nhan Dan* #10 (October 1972), pp. 1-6 and translated in JPRS #1308 (January 3, 1973), pp. 27-34, and "V.B.," "The April Offensive," *Vietnam Courier*, No. 1 (new series), (June 1972), pp. 3-6.

29. For an analysis of what this then meant to both Hanoi and Saigon, see my "Leaving the Future Up for Grabs: The Political Consequences of the Vietnam Cease-Fire," *Asia Quarterly* (1973/2): 93-109.

30. For an assessment of how this happened during the negotiations over Korea and the significance of that experience to the Vietnam negotiations, see the interview with General Mark W. Clark, "Do Truce Talks Mean Peace?" *U.S. News and World Report* (March 20, 1967), pp. 42-44.

31. For a summary of the main features of this document, see "Statement of

the DRVN Government on the Present State of the Negotiations Relating to the Viet Nam Problem," *Vietnam Courier* No. 1 (new series), (November 1972), pp. 4-5.

32. See "Hanoi Municipal Installations Strengthen Combat Forces and Promote People's Air Defense," *Hanoi Moi* (December 14, 1972), p. 1 and translated in JPRS #1320 (January 19, 1973), pp. 1-2.

33. These were the heaviest raids of the entire war. See the description and assessment of the attacks summarized in Robert Hotz, "B-52s Over Hanoi," *Aviation Week and Space Technology* (February 12, 1973): 7.

34. Hong Ha, "Paris: A Year Ago Today, and the Final Days Leading to the Paris Agreement on Vietnam," Hanoi Radio broadcast, January, 1974, and translated in JPRS #1514 (February 20, 1974), p. 17. For Hanoi's annotation of the agreement's significance to the success of the revolution, see Nguyen Van Lieu "The Paris Agreement on Viet-Nam and the Great Politico-Juridical Problems of our Time," *Vietnam Courier*, No. 12 (new series), (May 1973), pp. 26-30.

35. Speech by Xuan Thuy at the formal meeting held to commemorate the 1st anniversary of the signing of the Paris Agreement on Vietnam," *Nhan Dan*, (January 30, 1974), p. 3 and translated in JPRS #1528, (March 27, 1972), p. 4.

36. Speech of Le Duc Tho, Peking, February 2, 1973, as reported in *Welcome The Signing of the Paris Agreement on Viet Nam* (Peking: Foreign Languages Press, 1973), p. 29.

37. Hoang Nguyen, "The Paris Agreement on Viet Nam: Glimpses of the Past and the Future," *Vietnam Courier*, No. 16 (new series), (September 1973), pp. 9, 10.

38. Hanoi Radio broadcast, "Why is it necessary to solve the South Viet-Nam problem on the basis of linking the military aspect with the political aspect?" August 13, 1972, and translated in FBIS (August 15, 1972), pp. K-23-24. Current DRV analyses of the Paris Agreement, of course, stress that such a separation of issues did not take place by pointing out that Articles 2, 3, and 10 make clear that "The cease-fire is . . . the primary, sine qua non, condition for a settlement of the political problems." Ha Van Lau, "Some Military Problems," in Institute of Juridical Sciences, Committee of Social Sciences of the DRV, *The Paris Agreement on Vietnam: Fundamental Juridical Problems* (Hanoi, 1973), p. 88.

39. See, for example, Le Thanh Nghi, "Report on the Tasks and Guidelines for Economic Restoration and Development in the DRV in 1974 and 1975," delivered at the opening of the fourth session of the National Assembly, Hanoi, February 4, 1974; address of Truong Chinh at Conference of Delegates, Ho Chi Minh Working Youth Union, February 20-21, 1974; and, the editorial "Understanding the Revolution Passed by the 22nd Party Plenum: Continuing to Build the Material and Technical Base of Socialism and Strengthen the Potential of North Vietnam," *Hoc Tap* #3 (March 1974), pp. 1-10.

40. Ministry of Foreign Affairs, Democratic Republic of Vietnam, *One Year of Implementation of the Paris Agreement on Viet Nam*, (Hanoi, January 1974), p. 30. A similar formula is suggested by Le Duc Tho in a January 27, 1974, interview with a Hungarian correspondent in Hanoi. Reported in JPRS #1513, (February 15, 1974), p. 10.

41. Quoted in Stephen Wermiel, "Kissinger Denies S. Viet Has Political Prisoners," *The Boston Globe*, May 27, 1974, p. 27.

42. See, Tran Van Dinh, "Reunification: Key to Peace in Vietnam," *War/ Peace Report* (December 1968), pp. 3-4.

**Appendix 4A
Why Hanoi Is Negotiating
While Fighting: The View
in National Security Study
Memorandum No. 1, 1969**

104

| | Answers: | |
Study Questions & NSC Suggested Hypotheses	State Department & Embassy Saigon	Joint Chiefs of Staff & Field Commanders
1. Why is the DRV in Paris?		
a. Out of weakness, to accept a face-saving formula for defeat	No	No
b. To negotiate mutual troop withdrawal and/or a political settlement promoting communist victory in the South	Hanoi "came more and more to realize that it could not win the conflict by continued military and international political pressure, and that it would have to negotiate in order to make the American forces leave. It also sensed that the constitutional structure in South Viet-Nam, supported by the South Vietnamese Army, was developing in a manner which might preclude NLF participation unless the NLF could be negotiated into the picture."	"...all echelons generally agree that the preponderance of evidence indicates that North Vietnam is in Paris because of a decision that it would be less costly to get the bombing stopped and to negotiate the U.S. out of South Vietnam (SVN) than to continue fighting for another five to ten years, and that they are pursuing objectives *b* and *d*."
c. To give U.S. a face-saving way to withdraw	No. "Hanoi's desire for an end to the war is not yet combined with any readiness to yield on certain basic issues. . . ."	This may have been an early goal but has not been mentioned since 1967.
d. To undermine the GVN and U.S./GVN relations, and to relieve U.S. military pressures in both North and South Vietnam	Yes. Hanoi "hopes that the very fact of negotiations and NLF participation will lead to unraveling of the South Vietnamese political and administrative structure and to a strong if not necessarily widespread South Vietnamese movement for political accommodation with the NLF."	See above.
e. To end losses and costs of war on best terms available	Yes. "North Viet-Nam was beginning to feel greater pressure toward the middle and latter part of 1967, as the bombing became heavier. The Communist leadership also became worried that it was losing members of the important Southern cadre element in its Southern structure at a rate which, if	

continued over a long time, would leave the Viet Cong unable to compete effectively in the South. It wanted to open possibilities for greater emphasis on political warfare, and also to reduce the chance that the U.S. might escalate further."

f. Other comments

"We should not be under any illusions that the conclusion of some negotiated accord with the Communists will necessarily mean peace and quiet in Vietnam. Instead, it seems very likely that even if they withdraw their forces and turn to the reconstruction of North Viet-Nam, the Communists will want to use the post-war period to continue their political struggle against the GNV and to continue their drive to take over the South completely. One of their key purposes in negotiations will be to work out conditions which will optimize their chances for success in continued political warfare, in the long if not necessarily in the short term."

2. Will Hanoi compromise?a

Yes. "Some of the same pressure which drove them to negotiate *will* also drive them to modify their own terms and conditions over time. The Communists will want to pick the best possible moment for compromise, when we have yielded on the things which they consider vital but before they themselves have had to give up anything of critical importance. This will require delicate and sensitive timing. It is thus not correct to say that the Communists are not negotiating "seriously." They are negotiating seriously, in the sense that negotiations are an important element in their strategy, and that they would like to see the war end by a negotiated settlement favorable to themselves. But the required evolution in their position will come slowly.

"In describing the new policy [a highly reliable agent just four days prior to the bombing halt] said that in the near future the VC may approve negotiations with the GVN and the Americans in order to bring about a cease fire and a coalition government. But it must be emphasized from the beginning that a coalition government is only temporary. The parallel was drawn with someone on a long journey. One must stop and rest before continuing. The ultimate goal is still a Communist South Vietnam. There might be a cease fire, but after a period of time there would be another general uprising. U.S. withdrawal is an equally important objective and receives equal attention."

"CINCPAC (Commander in Chief, Pacific) ... notes that Hanoi has not acknowledged the presence of the North Vietnamese Army (NVA) forces in South Vietnam. The Communist position has not changed. This was reaffirmed by Ha Van Lau on 19 January 1969 when he asked the press to stress that the basis for the Paris talks remained the four points of the National Liberation Front (NLF) of South Vietnam. Having secured major concessions in 1968, i.e., total halt of aerial, naval and artillery bombardment in North Vietnam, and representation in Paris without being required to reciprocate, his next objectives would most likely be the withdrawal of U.S. troops and continued exacerbation of US/GVN relations."

Answers:

Study Questions & NSC Suggested Hypotheses	State Department & Embassy Saigon	Joint Chiefs of Staff & Field Commanders
		DICTA suggests that the GVN's political situation is so precarious that Hanoi has no incentive for compromise.
	"Hanoi's expectations from the negotiations appear to have changed considerably over the past months. There is fairly good evidence—in the way Hanoi responded to the March 31 speech, its statements about it at the time and afterward, and its conduct at the negotiations—that the leadership first thought they were going to get an American surrender, papered over with a few face-saving devices. As the weeks wore on, and it became apparent that this was not in the cards, and as the situation on the ground continued to deteriorate, Hanoi decided it would have to make concessions to achieve its immediate strategic goal—cessation of the bombing. And Hanoi did make concessions." (Embassy Saigon did not specify.)	
	The Embassy also thought that "the prospects are bleak enough for them so that they will, in the end, make significant concessions (in terms of their own withdrawal) to get us out. They may even relinquish their effort to obtain a favorable political settlement in the negotiations, provided they feel the play of forces in South Viet-Nam in the wake of the agreements reached holds out good promise for their military or political take-over of South Viet-Nam in the next few years."	
3. Is Hanoi under active pressure at the Paris Talks from Moscow (for) and Peking (against)?	"Sino-Soviet rivalry has left Hanoi relatively free from such pressures" and both powers appear to have limited leverage on decision-making in Hanoi.	"There does not appear to be significant pressure." "Hanoi over the years has been extremely adroit at balancing between the two by avoiding involvement in the Sino-Soviet ideological split and leav-

4. How sound is our knowledge of the existence and significance of stable "Moscow" and "Peking" factions within the Hanoi leadership, as distinct from shifting factions, all of whom recognize the need to balance off both allies?

Our knowledge is "imprecise," "speculative and amorphous" and, Embassy Saigon observed, "such characterizations are probably an impediment to . . . understanding . . . the political dynamics of the North Vietnamese leadership." "It is not accurate to state that these differences of opinion reflect the existence of "Moscow" or "Peking" factions. The Hanoi leadership is sufficiently xenophobic that its members must be considered "Vietnamese" first, with any other loyalties running a distant second. However, over the years patterns of attitudes have developed which suggest that some members of the *Lao Dong* Politburo are more attuned to the Chinese view of the world, and want to emulate policies which had been used by the Chinese, at least prior to the Cultural Revolution, for which we can see little sympathy in any quarter. Others tend more toward Russian ideas. It is generally believed that Truong Chinh, third-ranking man in the Politburo, is among those most sympathetic to China, whereas Pham Van Dong, and Vo Nguyen Giap (numbers four and six respectively) are more pro-Soviet. Party First Secretary Le Duan, second-ranking in the Politburo, is reputed to be neutral. At most, however, these leaders simply lean on some issues in one way or the other—and perhaps feel Vietnamese long-range interests are better served by closer cooperation with one or the other large ally. But they are not committed to full acceptance of either view."

Politburo disputes "concern methods, timing, and priorities—not ultimate objectives."

ing the subtle impression that attempted intimidation by one might force it into the arms of the other."

"We see through a glass darkly if at all." "Our knowledge of DRV politics and key personalities remains fragmentary and largely second hand."

"There is reason to believe a heated review of strategy for the 'fight-talk' phase of the war took place late last summer (1968)," but, over the years, in the DIA/JCS view, the groupings in the Politburo have been as follows:

a. *Militant.* Favoring an extreme and aggressive approach to both foreign and domestic policy:
(1) Le Duan.
(2) Le Duc Tho.
b. *Moderate.* Inclined to greater caution in domestic and foreign policy:
(1) Pham Van Dong.
(2) Pham Hung.
(3) Vo Nguyen Giap.
(4) Le Tanh Nghi.
(5) Van Tien Dung (alternate member).
c. *Neutral.* Open to persuasion:
(1) Truong Chinh.
(2) Nguyen Duy Trinh.

But whatever the internal alignments in the Politburo may be, the most important consideration favoring unity and discouraging open identification by a person or group with either China or the Soviet Union has been the widely shared fear of alienating either. This need to delicately balance and offset relations with the two Communist giants explains Hanoi's dispute and the muting of internal preferences by Politburo members."

---

aThis question was not originally in the outline of NSSM-1 but is suggested by the dicta of each agency's reply.

5 DRV External Relations in the New Revolutionary Phase

Paul M. Kattenburg

Introduction

The Democratic Republic of Vietnam (DRV) must be viewed in long historical perspective. Its first great hero and leader, President Ho Chi Minh, as well as his present-day successors, regarded it to be the principal *state* embodiment of the Indochinese people's struggle for independence and socialism. This struggle, begun by the Indochinese Communist Party in 1930 in the crucible of French colonialism, was continued in the anti-Japanese resistance of 1940-45, and renewed in the ensuing "heroic war of independence" of 1946-54 and in the consolidation period of 1954-59. It has had as its most recent phase the fourteen years (1959-72) of revolutionary war in South Vietnam, Laos, and Cambodia, presumably concluded with the signing of the Paris Agreements on January 27, 1973.

With the Paris Agreements, the revolutionary struggle has entered a new phase, under changed international and regional circumstances. The DRV objectives remain those of "independence" and "socialism," for all the peoples of Indochina. On these fundamentals, the DRV leaders have no differences. Thus, while the *state* embodiment of the revolution in the current phase confines the DRV geographically to North Vietnam, and the Provisional Revolutionary Government of the Republic of South Vietnam (PRG) to its zones of control in the South, the DRV explicitly maintains its *presumptive* right to speak for the entire Vietnamese people.[1] It maintains a similar right with respect to Laos and Cambodia, but within the framework of strict respect for the "fundamental national rights," i.e., the "independence, sovereignty, unity, and territorial integrity" of these two countries.[2]

This chapter deals only with the current phase of the revolutionary struggle. Present DRV insistence on the realities of "two parties, two administrations, two zones of control, two armies and three political forces" in South Vietnam does not even attempt to conceal the ultimate aim of Vietnamese reunification under that one leadership which, through correct guidance of the struggle in all its

I am indebted to the Institute of International Studies, University of South Carolina, for sponsoring travel and research which contributed to this chapter, and for holding the October 1973 workshop on North Vietnam at which I gleaned many ideas from the participants. I am also indebted to Donald I. Berlin for diligent research, and to all those in Southeast Asia who helped make my trip in mid-1974 so beneficial.

phases, has earned the right to lead. In the meantime, the DRV conducts its foreign policy in the present, with the belief that some day there must, and therefore there will be, *one* Vietnam linked in close bonds of friendship with one Cambodia and one Laos.

The DRV and the Paris Agreements

Hopes for Their Implementation

At enormous cost in lives and its own internal development, the DRV in the Paris Agreements secured international confirmation of "two parties, two armies, two administrations, and two zones" in South Vietnam; and tacit international, including U.S., acceptance of continued presence of DRV forces in South Vietnam. It also obtained the possibility of maintaining forces in Laos and Cambodia—areas of vital DRV interest—and reconfirmation of the basic framework of neutrality for the states of Indochina devised in the Geneva Agreements of 1954. Moreover, the Agreements greatly reduced the threat of American or U.S.-allied ("SEATO") attacks upon North Vietnam, although the DRV continued to reckon with what it would regard as possible irrational moves by the United States, the Thais, or others.

These were not insubstantial gains. As a result, the DRV is no longer the pariah of international and regional Southeast Asian politics that it was in the high containment phase of the cold war. To the extent that it feels secure, and feels it can subordinate its aims for victory in the South to the needs of reconstruction in the North, it is no longer forced to accept the degree of dependence upon Moscow and Peking which its own philosophy of self-reliance seriously countermands. This is especially important when Moscow and Peking find it difficult to unite upon any common action. However, South Vietnam has not receded in importance to the DRV. The priority of South Vietnam in current DRV considerations is a question more of method than substance. The Paris Agreements indicate that the *means* of struggle in the current revolutionary phase have undergone substantial change.

Sometime in 1972, or possibly earlier, the DRV top leadership decided that the revolution should enter another phase once the U.S. invaders were "defeated" (by this term the DRV meant "compelled to withdraw from Vietnam"). A decision was made to stage one more major offensive in South Vietnam even after U.S. words and action had already demonstrated U.S. intention to withdraw. This was the highly successful Spring Offensive of 1972. Important territory was seized which later became the basis for PRG zones of control, heavy casualties were inflicted upon GVN armed forces, and a severe psychological blow was dealt to the Thieu regime. At the same time, the 1972 offensive was extremely costly in terms of the number of DRV casualties and especially

PRG forces and cadres killed, rounded-up, decimated or otherwise lost to the DRV/PRG cause. Shortly after the offensive the DRV made the concessions—specifically, return of U.S. prisoners, separation of military and political provisions, and tacit agreement to let Thieu remain in office—necessary to bring about the Paris Agreements.

The DRV has steadfastly maintained in its public pronouncements that it would fully implement the Agreements and that it held GVN and the United States wholly responsible for their full implementation. Had there been full implementation, two specific DRV objectives (in addition to American withdrawal) would have been achieved: (1) PRG zones of control in South Vietnam would have been clearly demarcated by the Joint Military Commission (GVN/PRG) (even in the absence of specific guidance in the Agreements[3]); and (2) the "National Council of National Reconciliation and Concord" would have been created, giving the DRV, through the PRG, some legitimate voice in decisionmaking in a Saigon government for the first time since the beginning of the Indochinese revolution.

Therefore, implementation in spirit if not to the very letter of the Paris Agreements would have served DRV purposes. In the immediate post-Paris phase, these purposes would have been the construction in Saigon of a three-segment government presiding over elections, in which the Communist voice—muted or otherwise—would have been heard, as well as the existence within South Vietnam of secure, recognized and self-reliant zones of Communist control. Such a situation might have continued for an indefinite period (say three to five years), or—depending on local opportunities and on the international context—might have been superseded rather more quickly by an outright Communist attempt to seize power.

Such an attempt to seize power in Saigon would have required utilization of revitalized PRG city capabilities, and of PRG rural forces and cadres augmented by direct DRV manpower and logistics support. In addition, implementation of Article 13 on the military forces of the two parties would most probably have led, had a coalition regime been established in Saigon, to the gradual demobilization, or perhaps the rapid collapse of the Republic of Vietnam Armed Forces. Communist forces might also have been reduced, although they might easily have hidden weapons and melted into the countryside without losing their remobilization capacities. Moreover, sizable DRV forces, however dispersed, would have remained in South Vietnam.

Effects of Non-Implementation

Non-implementation of the Agreements has presented many serious difficulties for Hanoi. First, Hanoi has had to continue to rely on Moscow and Peking for arms and supplies necessary for an eventual resumption of full warfare. Second,

Hanoi has had to contend with the vagaries of Washington politics and the possibility of U.S. reintervention. Third, Hanoi has had to contend with the likelihood of further weakening of PRG and of its own forces.

On the other hand, the DRV must have also seen numerous opportunities in non-implementation. First, the DRV has room to maneuver in Laos and Cambodia, a factor discussed below. Second, there has been a progressive weakening of the Thieu regime as the economic situation has deteriorated in South Vietnam with dwindling U.S. aid and a growing swelling of the cities with refugees. The DRV no doubt calculates that the growing squeeze of the poor in South Vietnam will further demoralize the GVN armed forces and augment PRG ranks. Third, the DRV probably sees rising international revulsion at GVN and U.S. failure to honor the Agreements, particularly their political provisions. Fourth, the DRV probably counts on continued internal dissension within the United States over sustaining costly military and economic aid for South Vietnam. Finally, and perhaps most important, the DRV rests secure in its own certainty that the South cannot restore but can only aggravate the balance in favor of eventual Communist takeover, while the North gains a much-needed respite. There is a fatalism about Vietnamese Communist calculations, permitting slow-paced groundwork for late, more vigorous pursuit of the struggle. The DRV leaders may well have concluded that a final, crushing military assault can be conducted later with relative international impunity and with great chances of success. Then, a long, painful transition period through a coalition regime in the South would not be necessary. The PRG could take power in Saigon through collapse of ARVN in combat and of the GVN through war-weariness, terror assaults, and political subversion. Thus, instead of a mixed regime eventuating in Saigon through precarious and difficult negotiations, the installation of the PRG would confirm—but only for a time—the transitional nature of two Vietnams as set forth in the Paris Agreements.

It is therefore prudent to surmise that the DRV planned policies in 1972 to cover both implementation and non-implementation of its agreement with the United States. Events in 1973-74 leave little doubt as to what happened: Saigon has not implemented principal provisions of the Agreement and the DRV, while carefully maintaining a public posture of outrage, has violated select provisions in response; the United States has, within limits, followed Saigon's lead—probably due as much to U.S. military and bureaucratic momentum as to conscious planning in Washington; and there is recrudescence of fighting in the South. It is logical to expect Communist forces to be preparing to launch a culminating assault.

The DRV's Indochina Policies in the Proximate Future

Politics and Leadership in the North

Despite a certain ambiguity the DRV press in 1973 and especially 1974 has stressed "peace and socialist construction in the north" and a "peaceful" reunification of the fatherland. The speech by Vice Premier and State Planning Minister Le Thanh Nghi on February 4, 1974 is especially revealing of DRV priorities, listing goals for 1974 and 1975 in order of importance: (1) promptly heal the wounds of war; (2) strive to restore and develop the economy and culture; (3) continue to build the socialist material-technical base; (4) consolidate social- ist relations of production; (5) consolidate the socialist regime; (6) stabilize the people's livelihood; (only next to last) (7) consolidate national defense; (and last) (8) strive to fulfill the duty to the heroic South.[4] The relegation of "na- tional defense" and "the heroic South" to last in the DRV priorities is very significant. In a subsequent statement, Le Thanh Nghi argued further that DRV industrialization must proceed in an environment of peace.

Other pronouncements in 1974 also indicated the DRV Politbureau's empha- sis on the internal problems of North Vietnam and a decreasing concern with the South. Articles in *Hoc Tap* and *Nhan Dan* stressed that while the struggle of "our people" in the South has been fully reflected in the DRV's commitments, now was the time to enhance the building of socialism in the North. The lead editorial in the March, 1974, issue of *Hoc Tap*, for example, was revealingly entitled: "Let us continue to build the material-technical bases of socialism and increase the potential of the northern part of our country."[5] Whether such statements indicate a possible factional struggle in the DRV, with a "pro-North- ern" (or "socialist construction") wing opposing a "pro-Southern" (or "militant revolution") element remains highly speculative. Decision mechanisms of the DRV government and of the Communist Lao Dong Party which controls it, and even the men most significantly involved, are little known to Western analysts. North Vietnam is a relatively small and underindustrialized country, marked by thorough hierarchical Party control of the entire polity, and a relatively low level of institutionalization. There is no open press or other significant forum of free expression. Most of our information comes from official pronouncements and commentaries on events, plus an occasional foreign observer's report.

However, not much more may be needed to understand the formation of DRV policies if the following assumptions can be made: that the number of key decisionmakers is small; that security and secrecy pertain; that decisions are reached collectively by a process in which personality, political, affiliational, and other individual traits of decisionmakers blur in favor of a common outlook; that this outlook conforms to what the elite consensually determines to be the "mass" or "national" interest on the basis of a prudent cost-benefit calculation; and that the official pronouncements and commentaries are designed to com- municate the elite's consensual view.

The key men of Hanoi are indeed a small, close-knit group. Average age sixty-two, they have with few exceptions known and worked with each other uninterruptedly since the 1930s; they share the same generational experience and to a large degree the same life-styles; they have known great hardships and few moments of relief and tend to be conspiratorial; they have been sustained by what they regard as high aspirations and great ideals; they probably share a feeling that they have been in the vanguard of the "world's people."

These qualities were epitomized in Ho Chi Minh, their leader for so many years, who lived an extremely spare and sober existence. "Uncle Ho" had no palaces and enjoyed few personal perquisites. Carefully, he cultivated modesty and the appearance of the sober life-style: spartan quarters and clothes, the sandals of the people. Accordingly, his acolytes developed few tastes for high living and material privilege. In fact, the trappings of power were a disincentive for the leaders of the DRV—it was better to be modest and anonymous, perhaps dangerous to stand out. (The fact that he stood out somewhat may have been a problem for General Vo Nguyen Giap after the death of Ho.) As for decision-making processes, conditions are conducive to collegiality and consensus, and to the relatively easy acceptance of the views of peers like Le Duan and Pham Van Dong with long and successful service.

Nevertheless, there may be considerable differences among points of view in the Hanoi Politbureau. For example, there may be a wing led by Le Thanh Nghi that gives priority to reconstruction in the North, and another led by Vo Nguyen Giap that favors priority to the struggle in the South. Perhaps these different viewpoints are forcefully expressed. But once those most respected in the collegial power group give a signal, the group as a whole probably falls quickly into line. Democratic centralism may function at its best in the Hanoi Politbureau.

There is no mystery as to who the leading men are, even if we still know relatively little about them. Party First Secretary Le Duan sets the general philosophy and overall policy of the DRV Government, and Prime Minister Pham Van Dong is the principal operator and executor of its actions. Just behind them is Truong Chinh, Chairman of the Standing Committee of the National Assembly. Despite his reported illness and diminished prominence since mid-1973,[a] we must add Defense Minister Vo Nguyen Giap to the top quadrumvirate of leaders because of his past record of leadership and heroism. Perhaps alone among them, Giap is genuinely popular among the masses, millions of whom have served in the armed forces under his inspiration and command.

The next echelon of Lao Dong Politbureau members includes men whose roles in foreign policymaking are important. Nguyen Duy Trinh, as Vice Prime Minister (one of several) and Minister of Foreign Affairs, heads the growing bureaucracy charged with external relations. Le Duc Tho, although charged primarily with assisting Le Duan in Party organization (and therefore very close to the latter), was chosen as chief negotiator for the Paris talks with Henry Kissinger. Ton Duc Thang, who holds the formal title of President of the DRV, receives key foreign visitors—and so does the old and eminent Hoang Quoc Viet, President of the Vietnam General Federation of Trade Unions and chairman of

---

[a]Indications are that Vo Nguyen Giap underwent medical treatment in the Soviet Union in early 1974. After having dropped out of public view for about six months previously, Giap reappeared in Hanoi on May 7, 1974, where he delivered his annual speech commemorating the fall of Dien Bien Phu. Observers commented that he had lost much weight, and speculation arose that he was suffering from cancer.

several friendship associations with friendly foreign powers. General Van Tien Dung currently appears to be directing DRV military affairs.

In addition to this handful of leaders, all cut in very much the same mold, the following should be mentioned: Le Thanh Nghi, Minister of State Planning; Hoang Van Hoan, Vice Chairman of the Standing Committee of the National Assembly; and Tran Quoc Hoan, Minister of Internal Security whose star has been recently rising. Politbureau member Pham Hung participates in almost all key DRV decisions; and the Politbureau maintains its own foreign affairs expert, Xuan Thuy, much experienced in the diplomacy of the cold war. Propaganda experts and publicists (like Nguyen Khac Vien of *Vietnam Courier* and Tran Trang Quat of the Vietnam-American Solidarity Committee), as well as diplomats and bureaucrats, also play important roles. Still, the top group is small enough and sufficiently homogeneous that we may speak of a rational, consensual process. Accordingly, DRV policy output is less uncertain, erratic, and subject to rapid change due to power struggle than that of most democracies and even that of many, including large, socialist states.

It is, however, undeniable—and unprovable—that there may be opposing factions within the DRV leadership. Factors that may shape factions are: geographic background (southerners, centralists or northerners); age (middle versus old); training and education (whether only in Hanoi, or in Moscow or Peking, or elsewhere in the socialist world, or in France); political tendency and temperament (in the sense of radical-militant-impulsive versus moderate-reflective-delaying); and organizational interest. One would expect a North Vietnamese general to be just as devoted to the welfare of the armed forces as a general anywhere, and a construction engineer to place maximum emphasis on the industrial sector. Yet the rewards for collegial outlook are high and deprivations for "personalism" can be serious. Accordingly, although factions probably exist, they tend to be impermanent and to shift with issues—and therefore not as relevant to foreign policy as the element of consensual rationality.

Just before Giap's return in May 1974 Van Tien Dung was promoted to full four-star rank. It now appears that Dung, regarded as a protegé of Le Duan (who may well fear Giap's great popular standing), has been directing military affairs in the DRV since at least November of 1973. Commentators who identify Giap as a "proponent of a massive offensive strategy," seem to forget that his reputation rests almost entirely upon a clever combination of armed struggle and political struggle, which he characterized under the general heading of "People's War." On the contrary, it was Van Tien Dung and some of the other younger commanders who stood for the rapid development of a "modern, conventional Army" with the complex technological wherewithall required for sophisticated warfare, to be conducted by an ill-trained and poorly-suited population. It is therefore difficult to draw any automatic conclusions from the apparent transfer of power from Giap to Dung. Certainly, any conclusion that Dung's rise to power signifies that "moderation" now pervades the northern leadership would seem unwarranted.

Another rivalry frequently mentioned is that alleged to exist between Le Duan and Truong Chinh, with the latter identified with those elements in the *Lao Dong* who give greater stress to ideological purity and the traditions of resistance and mass mobilization.[6] Le Duan is assumed to be more moderate and—although not himself a northerner—more devoted to concentration upon socialist construction in the North. Once Truong Chinh began to fall from favor with Ho Chi Minh after the errors he committed in the implementation of land reform in the late fifties in North Vietnam, Le Duan increasingly replaced him in Ho's immediate entourage (the others being Dong and Giap). Accordingly, Le Duan—who has risen steadily to his present position of "primus inter pares"— may have incurred the enmity of Truong Chinh. But this says little about their respective positions on potentially divisive issues.

Finally, we should take note of the increasingly prominent role played in DRV decisionmaking by Politbureau member Le Thanh Nghi, a technocrat with considerable economic expertise, who has long coordinated all foreign aid coming into the DRV. Nghi is now Vice Prime Minister, Chairman of the State Planning Commission and head of the Party Central Committee's "Patriotic Emulation Movement," which strives to stimulate high productivity, high quality, frugality, and an emphasis on science, technology, and management. Perhaps the most striking evidence of Nghi's increased influence was his important economic policy speech, mentioned earlier, delivered to the fourth session of the DRV National Assembly on February 4, 1974. In this, Nghi painted a very bleak picture of the DRV's economic situation as a direct consequence of the years of U.S. bombing and of the sustained war effort in the South. He maintained that in the current phase, North Vietnam would have to heal the scars of the "protracted, violent war that has caused such grave consequences"[7] by concentrating first and foremost on the 1976-80 orthodox five-year plan.

Le Duan's views appear largely to parallel those of his protegé, Le Thanh Nghi. Both are strong advocates of technical know-how, the use of work incentives and the rapid development of heavy industry. From all available evidence, both favor concentration upon the North now—with the struggle in the South taking second place. Whether or not this is opposed by others, it does seem at the moment to be the DRV basic policy.

Strengths and Weaknesses in the North

It is clear that the DRV's own assets and capabilities will play the major role in determining the outcome of an assault in the South. A brief review of these assets suggests several areas of major strength, as well as some serious weaknesses. On the positive side, the DRV's magnificent leadership continues intact and, so far as can be determined, united. Agricultural problems in the DRV appear well under control with the better crops of the last few years, maximum energy now being devoted to raising foodstuffs, and apparent Chinese willingness to supply the DRV with rice to the extent necessary to make up deficiencies. (PRG/DRV forces in South Vietnam appear also to have adequate rice supplies.)

Furthermore, the DRV can count on economic support from both socialist and non-socialist sources, in addition to the CPR and USSR. Eastern Europe has been forthcoming in some areas; so have Sweden, Australia and Japan, and negotiations are in progress with a number of other Western countries.[8] Industrial recovery is progressing, as indicated by the return to full production of the Thai Nguyen steel and industrial complex—but the expansion of the industrial base remains slow. The DRV manpower situation has improved with the diminution of the war drain; potential soldiery is now arising from among those born in the relatively high birthrate years of the recovery period, 1954-59.

The DRV armed forces merit special consideration. There are some 200,000 combat and 50,000 administrative troops in the People's Army of Vietnam (PAVN), of which from all available sources the very great majority (up to about 185,000) are deployed within South Vietnam where they supplement the roughly 30,000 People's Liberation Armed Forces (PLAF)—or PRG—regulars and some 30,000 PLAF guerrillas.[9] (There are no doubt additional militia and home guards disposed within the home base of North Vietnam.) But the striking thing about the PAVN is that it has now for the most part become a very strong conventional armed force, including considerable aviation capability, and organized for heavy conventional combat. Since 1968, large volumes of sophisticated and extremely powerful weapons have been added (through Soviet and Chinese supply) to this army's arsenal.[b]

In the most recent phase (1972-74), advanced weapons have been or were expected to be furnished, such as Soviet medium and heavy tanks equipped with 122 mm guns; Soviet rocket launchers with ranges varying from 10 to 30 km; Soviet SAM anti-aircraft missiles of very advanced design; and Soviet SS missiles with ranges up to 60 km.[c] It is not inconceivable that PAVN, which has long been training pilots in the socialist world and whose MIG's on the whole fought very well against U.S. air attacks over North Vietnam, will in the future dispose of significant bombing capabilities against South Vietnamese targets.

---

[b]Based on interviews with reliable U.S. official sources in Saigon. These weapons include the latest available versions of: flamethrowers; recoilless guns; dual AA guns; regular and advanced field artillery; highly advanced middle- and long-range rocket launchers; advanced model trucks; amphibious tanks; medium and heavy tanks; advanced mortars and grenade launchers; highly advanced small weapons including pistols. submachine guns, and assault rifles; medium and heavy tracked artillery tractors; tank recovery vehicles, dual gun-mounted; antitank guided missiles; AA heat-seeking missiles; armored personnel carriers. (Several of these new weapons are of East European, as well as of Soviet and Chinese origin.)

[c]Ibid.

But the DRV faces substantial problems as well. First among these is the uncertainty of its relations with Moscow and Peking, a topic which is addressed further below. There are continued long-range effects on humans, vegetation, and industry resulting from the intense U.S. bombing to which the DRV was subjected; and there remain substantial fears that bombing might sometime be resumed. The DRV still faces an extraordinarily complex job in dredging and demining even small rivers—for at the end of the war the United States had been able to deny use of almost the entire inland navigation complex in addition to closing the port of Haiphong.[10] Major difficulties are involved in restoring and improving the transportation and communications network. There is an almost total absence of civil air communications, and of equipped airports capable of receiving large-size transports. Infrastructure in most domains remains weak to mediocre.

Moreover, the army is still in the re-gearing phase from "insurgency" to fully conventional character. While the weapons may be there, the men trained to use them frequently are not. The commanders charged with tactics must be further trained and, in many instances, their mentalities readjusted to the sophisticated managerial and other tasks involved in fully conventional warfare. Environmental and computer technologies required for effective use of sophisticated weapons, particularly in air and counter-air warfare, are still lacking. The same lack of advanced technological skills also plagues industrial recovery and the extension of the internal communications network.

DRV Policy for the South

Meanwhile, the groundwork is being laid in South Vietnam for the eventual activation of all assets. In this respect, several factors of importance must be considered. First, there has been a continuing shift of population within South Vietnam from rural areas to urban centers over the past several years, which raises questions of changing strategies on the part of both sides in the conflict. On the Communist side, this requires the perfecting of urban guerrilla warfare tactics and the devising of a general political/economic/military urban strategy which seems thus far to have eluded Communist planners. Second, the PRG's present areas of control are inhospitable, remote, generally poor in resources, and relatively underpopulated. This requires the gradual expansion of the PRG into zones which are more capable of providing the manpower and resources that will be needed later. The area along the coast south of Danang is an excellent example. Here past NLF/DRV influence permits the PRG to spread out rather easily; consequently, it is not surprising that much of the 1974 fighting was concentrated in that area. Similarly, the area northwest of Saigon adjoining secure North Vietnamese rear bases along the frontier in Cambodia offers opportunities exploited in mid- and late 1974. A northward expansion from secure rear bases in the southern Mekong Delta also took place in late 1974.

Next, a "Third Political Force" must be activated with the help of the PRG and DRV to provide a maximum of harassment for GVN during the final phases of the struggle. It was generally apparent throughout 1973 and early 1974 that a "third force" existed in the minds and wishes of many South Vietnamese and the actions of a few; but until late 1974 it did not emerge as a significant factor and GVN had an easy time repressing its every manifestation. The problem for Communist leadership here is at least twofold: on the one hand, the Buddhist hierarchy and bonzes who would be expected to provide the backbone for the third force must be brought into an activist, militant stage, resisting efforts of GVN authorities to buy them off. As of late 1974, the process of activating the pagodas and linking them to other sectors of the third force seemed to have started in earnest. This process was by no means, however, controlled solely or even fully by the Communists. The latter have to contend with a very strong-minded though frequently disunited Buddhist leadership.

The second problem for the Communists relates to means by which government repression can be eluded or mitigated whenever the third force manifests support for causes which the Saigon regime links to Communist propaganda—such as "peace," "neutrality" or even simple calls for the replacement of the Thieu regime. The growing frequency of Catholic-led demonstrations against Thieu since mid-1974, and increasing denunciations by leading Catholic prelates of government repression and economic policies, has undoubtedly eased the task of the Communists in this respect, since Catholic-led movements are more difficult for the Saigon regime to repress. Communist influence in bringing the third force into existence or in currently manipulating its activities should not be exaggerated. The "force" has a momentum and life of its own and is more a useful adjunct to Communist purposes than it is a Communist tool.

The PRG itself suffers from several serious deficiencies in addition to those already stated. Is the PRG a mere appendage of the DRV which will be discarded when it is time to assert DRV control directly? As mentioned at the beginning of this chapter, the DRV has not abjured the right to speak for all the people of Vietnam, nor has it in any way given up the objective of ultimate reunification. At the same time, both international and Vietnamese circumstances in the late sixties and early seventies seem to have persuaded the DRV to favor the establishment of a separate transitory regime led by Communists in the South. The PRG will prove to be an extremely useful instrument to the DRV when and if the Saigon regime collapses. At such a time, the PRG will be available to take over in Saigon as effective proxy for the DRV for at least several years.[11]

Laos and Cambodia

Laos and Cambodia remain vital areas in the DRV's strategy to reunify Vietnam. During the long armed struggle phase concluded in 1972, the North Vietnamese were primarily concerned with securing the eastern regions of these countries—the so-called "Ho Chi Minh trails" corridor in Laos and the Cambodian provinces immediately adjoining western South Vietnam—as staging, supply, and sanctuary areas for the war in South Vietnam.

Currently, North Vietnamese forces in Cambodia and Laos are concentrated in the Vietnam border regions and, in fewer numbers, in the northwest provinces near Thailand. The DRV may be increasingly concerned that security threats to its position in both Laos and Cambodia may in the future arise from Thailand. But for the present, North Vietnamese forces in both Laos and Cambodia play an essentially passive role. Neither in Laos, where the Pathet Lao have now become the dominant political-military force in the country, nor in Cambodia, where the Khmer Rouge are in military and political ascent, does the PAVN need perform more than the admittedly important role of logistical provider. Its direct engagement is neither required in Laos, nor advisable in Cambodia.

Close friendships and proprietary interests have been developed by the DRV leadership with the Pathet Lao leaders as well as more recently with the leadership of the Cambodian Front of National Union (FUNK), the real directing element of the Royal Government of Khmer National Union (GRUNK), whose figurehead leaders are Prince Sihanouk and Prime Minister Penn Nouth in Peking. The true leaders of the GRUNK, Khieu Samphan and Ieng Sary of the FUNK, conduct their side of the Cambodian civil war from the very large portions of the country which their armed forces, supplied by North Vietnam, have liberated in the past four years. The DRV has great influence upon the Pathet Lao and considerable influence upon the FUNK—many of whose leaders were trained in Hanoi. However, both Moscow and Peking possess influence upon these leaders as well. As a result, since they are not solely dependent on the DRV for the achievement of their objectives, the Pathet Lao and FUNK leaders may have a degree of leverage in Hanoi.

In Cambodia, Khieu Samphan and Ieng Sary's lieutenants include some 4,000 Khmer political cadres trained over the past twenty years in Hanoi, and a few hundred who received training over the same period in Moscow and Peking. When Khieu Samphan and Ieng Sary last visited Hanoi, on their return from a world tour in May 1974, the greetings and exchanges were cordial but not more so than they had been in Peking. Should the GRUNK regime gain the additional votes it lacked in 1974 and be admitted to the United Nations as the representative of Cambodia, it would become the first of the Communist-influenced Indochinese regimes to have been so legitimized by the world community. This, along with the close relations maintained between Peking and the GRUNK, and possible DRV fears of Thai reactions to GRUNK, may raise some problems for the DRV. Accordingly, it is possible that the latter, as principal supplier of FUNK forces, is placing some restraints on the FUNK's proceeding to final victory in Cambodia. At the same time, the DRV may also be discouraging FUNK from negotiating a settlement with Lon Nol and the Americans, because a settlement in Cambodia might reduce Hanoi's leverage with Washington and Saigon regarding an eventual accommodation in South Vietnam.

Summary

In conclusion, with respect to the proximate future of DRV policies toward the Indochinese countries, the following points stand out: (1) The DRV is continuing to emphasize reconstruction, resupply and extension of the northern base during the current phase, while at the same time reviving assets in the South. (2) Plans are being made for a final assault, which will take place when the moment is fully ripe. (3) If, meanwhile, circumstances should change (for example, a severe diminution of U.S. aid to South Vietnam) and lead to either a rapid major offensive or serious implementation of the Paris Agreements, including clear demarcation of zones of control and the formation of joint political organs, DRV policies might adapt to new possibilities in the South. (4) The timing of the final assault will depend largely on the state of ARVN and GVN, the readiness of DRV armed forces, and on the capabilities of PRG forces in the South, particularly in the southern urban areas and most especially in Saigon. (5) In the interim, Laos and Cambodia offer the DRV considerable opportunities for political, diplomatic, and strategic maneuver.

Recent Trends in the Hanoi-Peking-Moscow Relationship

Some observers believe that since January 1973 there has been a slow but steady deterioration in Hanoi's relations with both Moscow and Peking. Most of the evidence suggests that North Vietnam is a bit closer to the USSR than to China.

In December 1973, a delegation of the USSR Supreme Soviet headed by S. Niyazbekov, deputy chairman of the Presidium and member of the CPSU Central Committee, visited North Vietnam. The speeches and communiques from this visit suggest that Moscow is considerably less enthusiastic about the "liberation struggle" in Vietnam than is Hanoi. While Niyazbekov spoke of the Vietnamese as only "ultimately" achieving the "peaceful unification of Vietnam," DRV responses assigned liberation of the South more urgency.[12] The visit to the Soviet Union of "Republic of South Vietnam" (PRG) President Nguyen Huu Tho in late December 1973 may have represented an attempt to rectify deteriorating relations between Moscow and the PRG. Previously, a December 1, 1973 Liberation Radio summary of the previous ten months of "diplomatic success" for the PRG had thanked Peking profusely for its help, but noticeably made no mention of any diplomatic USSR assistance. The article was long and the failure to mention Moscow was probably intentional. Nguyen Huu Tho's subsequent visit to Moscow was apparently an attempt to fill this void and thus to "conclude a year of big successes in the diplomatic field of the RSV Provisional Revolutionary Government."[13] Rather hopefully, Hanoi's leading organ *Nhan Dan* editorialized that "the Soviet Union will continue its strong support to the (PRG) in the struggle to attain their revolutionary objectives in the new stage."

Conflicting evidence is available on the status of DRV-Soviet relations in early 1974. Robert S. Elegant of the *Los Angeles Times* has maintained that North Vietnam and the Soviet Union entered upon a period of embittered relations at this juncture. The DRV, according to Elegant, accused the USSR of being "faint-hearted" as regards the liberation struggle in the South and reneging on promised economic and military aid.[14] As against Elegant's view, it could be pointed out that the USSR did send a number of official delegations to North Vietnam in the early months of 1974 and was represented at both the Third Congress of the Vietnam General Federation of Trade Unions and the Fourth Vietnam Women's Congress. The Chinese, by contrast, were most noticeably unrepresented at either of these events. Furthermore, Soviet leaders warmly received DRV Premier Pham Van Dong in a March-April 1974 visit to the USSR.[15]

North Vietnam's relations with China seem to be somewhat more troubled than those with the USSR. Apparent Chinese opposition to any step-up in military activity in South Vietnam, and the CPR's involvement in the Paracel Islands dispute, seem to have embittered these relations. A high level delegation from the PRG, led by President Nguyen Huu Tho and including Foreign Minister Nguyen Thi Binh, visited China on what was described as an "official friendly visit" between November 18 and 23, 1973. The delegation was received by Chairman Mao and its activities were prominently featured in the press. In banquet speeches, however, there was a marked difference between what was said by guests and hosts in references to the behavior of the United States (whose Secretary of State, Dr. Kissinger, had visited Peking a week previously). Nguyen Huu Tho consistently linked the "United States and the Saigon administration" when apportioning blame for the breaking of the cease-fire and warned that, if this continued, "the South Vietnamese people would empower themselves to strike back." Chou En-lai, however, speaking on the same occasion, referred to the United States only as having been defeated in the war, and did not link the United States with Saigon as responsible for breaking the cease-fire. In a similarly cautious manner, he made no reference to the possible need to strike back. The implication seemed to be that the Chinese were likely to urge caution and restraint on the PRG and on North Vietnam.[16]

In the joint communique which followed the visit, a compromise formula seems to have been devised in which both sides condemned the "acts in contravention and violation of the Paris agreement committed by the Saigon administration with the support and connivance of the United States." But even in the final communique, the difference of emphasis between the two sides remained obvious.

In December 1973, the North Vietnamese party newspaper *Nhan Dan* made an oblique reference to the Sino-Soviet dispute and implicitly criticized both of the "big brother" allies:

The Nixon administration views as a main achievement the improvement of its relations with a number of socialist countries. But Nixon himself stated that this would not have occurred if there were no serious discrepancies within the socialist camp. This means that the Nixon-Kissinger clique has applied the strategy of reconciling with this or that socialist state to deeply aggravate the contradictions among socialist countries and to create a feud.[17]

While the foregoing remarks were ostensibly directed at the United States, Peking and Moscow were almost certainly the real targets of Hanoi's jibes.

On January 9, 1974, a delegation of the China-Vietnam Friendship Association arrived in the liberated zone of Quang Tri Province led by Chinese Central Committee member An Ping-sheng. National Liberation Front spokesmen denounced "the Saigon administration with the support of the U.S. imperialists." The remarks of the leader of the Chinese delegation were noteworthy in that he saw the anti-United States struggle as having terminated a year previously (disagreeing with the Liberation Front) and a year of "reconstruction" just concluded. Violations of the Paris accords were Saigon's alone—the United States deliberately, it appears, not mentioned by the Chinese visitor.[18]

Official DRV spokesmen were generally evasive on the Paracel Islands issue. A Japanese correspondent, however, indicated that an authoritative diplomatic source in Hanoi had said:

Based on the spirit of equality, mutual respect, and good neighborly friendship, the countries concerned should fully study it and settle it by negotiations. The question of territorial sovereignty is an extremely sacred issue to any nation. Since a border or territorial dispute between mutually adjoining nations has its historical background, it needs extremely complex and fully careful studies whenever a dispute occurs between them.[19]

These comments might be regarded as a mild diplomatic rebuke at the Chinese who were very quick to apply force in the Paracels dispute. Should Peking's claims in the South China Sea be fully legitimized, the DRV will be left with little or no maritime terrain. China's promulgation of very strict rules of passage in the Hainan Strait several years ago[20] could also be a point of future dispute between the DRV and Peking in that this Strait constitutes the principal maritime route into Haiphong for vessels coming from Hong Kong or Yokohama.

Peking's representation by only a letter at the Vietnam General Federation of Trade Unions Third Congress was one of the most serious indications of a DRV-Peking rift in early 1974. The letter maintained that "the Chinese people pledge to lend their unchanged, firm support to the Vietnamese people and to resolutely support the Vietnamese people's struggle until complete success."[21]

But the Chinese language was on the list of languages available for simultaneous translation at the meeting, and the Chinese decision not to attend was probably sudden and intentionally dramatic.

Another area of brewing controversy concerns economic policy. North Vietnamese Party leader Le Duan has been increasingly stressing that his country would give priority to the development of heavy industry. This differs from the Chinese model, which stresses agriculture as the foundation of the economy. Le Duan told the DRV National Assembly delegates that "it is wrong to rely solely on agriculture to advance to large scale production" and that to do so was a "negation of the historical role of the working class"[d]—a statement that may well have been a deliberate slap at China for insufficient assistance of the type desired. During March 1974, DRV-Chinese relations deteriorated further with the closing down without explanation of the single Chinese-language newspaper in Hanoi. Almost simultaneously, the Sino-Vietnamese Friendship Association suspended its activities there.

These recent viewpoints expressed by the DRV toward Moscow and Peking confirm a general feeling by observers that the DRV is not having an easy time in its triangular relations with these capitals. During the armed revolutionary phase of 1965-73 (after massive U.S. intervention), the DRV had used its desperate need for logistical support as a means of pressuring both Moscow and Peking. The fact that the present stage is more subdued, makes it more difficult for Hanoi to pressure its senior partners, particularly when both of the latter are engaged in detente policies with the United States.

One suspects that, in the current phase, contentions between Hanoi and Moscow and Peking might develop in the following five main areas.

1. The extent of continued military-logistical and economic assistance to the DRV from both parties. Moscow is continuing to supply sophisticated weapons, but in a restrained manner and possibly in diminishing volume, and is remaining within the limits prescribed by Art. 7 of the Agreements—periodic replacement of damaged or destroyed war equipment "on the basis of piece-for-piece, of the same characteristics and properties." However, this limitation—while it does apply to the United States and South Vietnam, and to the DRV and PRG forces in the South does not apply to Soviet materiel sent into the DRV proper. Similarly, Peking is continuing to provide some military assistance. Both parties are providing economic assistance, with Peking possibly providing more with its recent inputs of rice. However, both Moscow and Peking are finding such continued assistance to the DRV onerous, and the tendency is clearly toward a phase-down, as with the United States vis-à-vis South Vietnam.

2. The extent of continued support of all types, including diplomatic, to the PRG in South Vietnam. From all available indications, the Soviet Union has not

---

[d]Although this is a theme frequently stressed by Le Duan it is rare for the DRV leader to address the issue so pointedly.

been enthusiastic in pressing the PRG's case in world forums or in its various bilateral relations. To the degree a PRG regime would establish relations with, or be supported by, Peking, support for it would wane in Moscow. Indeed, the PRG may be closer to Peking than to Moscow. If so, Peking-PRG ties would be a significant factor accounting for the palpable cooling of relations in recent months between Peking and Hanoi. A degree of CPR influence upon the PRG might parallel its reported influence upon the FUNK leadership in Cambodia. The CPR might wish to see states arise in both Cambodia and South Vietnam which would be more independent of Hanoi than the latter could tolerate. Hanoi might even find this dangerous in terms of potential effects upon the ultimate goal of reunification.

3. Preservation of its influence in Laos is a cardinal objective for the DRV. The DRV would no doubt prefer independence from Moscow's or Peking's wishes with respect to Laos—wishes which might well respond to such international demands as detente with the United States.

4. Similarly, the extent of DRV influence in Cambodia, where, as already mentioned, Peking has a close relationship with the FUNK (and with its parent, GRUNK). A close FUNK relationship with Peking—Soviet support for both Sihanouk and the FUNK has clearly been no more than perfunctory—might lead to unwelcome Soviet pressures on Hanoi to remove or restrain its support to FUNK.

5. Finally, the extent of U.S. influence in the area. The current Soviet-Indian alignment may have opened new opportunities for Soviet encroachment on the Asian mainland, as well as new fears in Peking. Moreover, Moscow's relations with the Pathet Lao and Indonesia, and potentially with Thailand, have probably long been watched with suspicion in Peking. Moscow is probably correspondingly suspicious of CPR influence in Southeast Asia. Accordingly, both Moscow and Peking are probably united in their desire to see a more gradual disengagement of the United States from the Southeast Asian mainland than the DRV could tolerate, due to the fact that Moscow and Peking probably both regard U.S. presence in Southeast Asia as containment of the other.

As a result of these trends in the region, as well as the overriding importance to the DRV of the Sino-Soviet conflict, it is clear that the DRV faces both major problems and major strategic constraints in its foreign policy. Hanoi may have hoped that in constructing a peace with the United States and removing U.S. presence, the DRV itself would be essentially dominant in the area, with a tolerable coalition government in South Vietnam, as well as neutralized and sympathetic coalition regimes in Laos and Cambodia. At the same time, through U.S. assistance under Article 21 of the Paris Agreements, the DRV might have laid the bases for a closer relationship with the United States itself. The failure of the Agreements in South Vietnam has thus far negated such possibilities.

The DRV, the United States and the
Southeast Asian Region

The United States clearly lost interest in 1974 in concluding an accord with the DRV under Article 21 of the Paris Agreements for economic aid in the reconstruction of North Vietnam, and the DRV also seems to be lowering the priority of seeking a rapprochement with the United States. If the Agreements had been implemented in South Vietnam to a point minimally acceptable to the DRV, it might have been disposed to accept some continuing U.S. role in Indochina, particularly in the light of its increasingly complex relationships with Moscow and Peking. The DRV might have also felt that the United States would have wanted to build a new structure of peace in the region, which it had begun to elaborate in the negotiations with the DRV leading to the Paris Agreements, by seeking to influence a regime (the DRV) which would most probably play a dominant role in the future of Southeast Asia.

Although none of this has yet come to pass, the basic factors just alluded to have not disappeared. Moreover, a basic compatibility seems to have been established between Secretary Kissinger and the North Vietnamese leaders, particularly Le Duc Tho, who is very close to Le Duan. This compatibility may survive the vicissitudes of the present. In this regard, President Ford has not established any particular rapport with the South Vietnamese leadership, but has on the contrary established personal rapport with leaders in Peking. Moreover, the DRV leaders seem to have greeted with relief both President Nixon's departure and the continuation of Secretary Kissinger in office.[22]

It has been argued that North Vietnam has consistently misinterpreted U.S. public opinion, the role of the U.S. Congress, and the importance of leading American figures. On the contrary, the DRV has made few mistakes in its analyses of the American scene and of the long-range directions of American policy. For example, the DRV has correctly sensed that in this phase of revolutionary struggle in South Vietnam, U.S. financial and material support of the Thieu regime will gradually dwindle and eventually cease altogether. Moreover, the DRV conceivably believes that in a "peaceful" phase, the pressures of leading American sectors, particularly the oil multinationals, will eventually lead the U.S. government to seek some form of relationship with North Vietnam.

Current issues dividing the two countries include: (a) continued U.S. support for the Thieu regime and its general castigation of the DRV as most responsible for the non-implementation of the Agreements; (b) the question of U.S. personnel still missing in action; and (c) economic aid and relations. With respect to the first issue, the DRV counters by placing full responsibility on the United States and Thieu, a case supported by many countries aligned with the United States as well as by non-aligned and socialist countries. In any event, the GVN has at least as much responsibility to bear as DRV/PRG for the breakdown of the cease-fire, and the GVN was far more responsible for the collapse of the political negotiations and for not perfecting the restitution of political prisoners under Article 8c of the Agreements. This point is likely to continue damaging U.S. efforts to obtain a final accounting of MIA's from the DRV or the Pathet Lao. The United States in any case has little leverage in the MIA issue. Although it is unclear whether the DRV knows the burial places of many (if any) legitimate MIA's, a gesture to satisfy U.S. public opinion might be made by the DRV and the Pathet Lao as part of a settlement of larger issues.

But if DRV efforts on the political-diplomatic front fail to change the South Vietnamese situation, the DRV will count on the renewal of protracted warfare and finally on a culminating military assault. If this occurs, and Thieu is overthrown in favor of a Communist-dominated regime, the DRV probably expects the United States to bow to the situation. The only U.S. alternative, to return to war, would appear most unlikely, even with the use of airpower alone. Accordingly, the DRV is probably confident that events are going its way. If so, the DRV may well foresee profitable future relations with the United States, initially on the economic front. Reconstruction assistance, to both South and North Vietnam, would then be more than ever required, and possibly less controversial. For, while current economic and military assistance to GVN is clearly controversial in the United States, and while the notion of assistance to the DRV could not be seriously entertained as long as there is some interest in keeping the issue of the MIA or Paris Agreements alive, these factors could rapidly change in the event of a "clean-cut" DRV/PRG military victory in South Vietnam. In such a case, assistance to "all Vietnam" might well become sufficiently acceptable publicly to be sustained by the U.S. Congress.

The possibility that U.S. investors and traders would be attracted to the DRV should not be overlooked, even in the present indecisive phase. North Vietnam may have, in the Tonkin Gulf and adjoining coastal seas, energy resources that would look increasingly attractive to U.S. firms as the Japanese begin seriously to explore and exploit them. Conversely, the North Vietnamese market must sooner or later open to sophisticated suppliers in such products as civil air transport, communications and telecommunications equipment and industrial and construction technology. U.S. investors are likely to be on the lookout for the slightest signal of diminution of U.S. government support of Thieu, owing to changes in the U.S. administration, congressional sentiment, or other factors. In the longer range, assuming the disappearance of Thieu and installation in the South of a regime compatible with ultimate DRV goals, it is conceivable that United States-DRV relations may develop fairly steadily in the direction of closer association. This would assume that Hanoi would continue to operate independently from Moscow and Peking, and as a national Communist state.

If this were to be the case—and we are speaking now, say, of the time frame 1976-80—the DRV would emerge as a significant power on the Southeast Asian mainland. The creation of a zone of DRV hegemony in Indochina, assuming the continued survival through the decade of four separate but generally compatible regimes, each with major Communist participation, would make Indonesia the DRV's only potential rival for influence within the whole Southeast Asian region. The relations between these two countries, now marred by mutual ignorance and a number of mutual suspicions, would then become important to watch.

Currently, the state of DRV relations with most of the other Southeast Asian countries seems arrested—pending the resolution of the problems in Vietnam and Indochina as a whole. Again, had the Paris Agreements been implemented in South Vietnam, a more promising pattern of intraregional relations might have developed, easing the possibilities of a total U.S. disengagement from at least the mainland of Southeast Asia. With respect to Thailand, the U.S. tendency has been too pronounced to consider the DRV as a serious threat to Thailand while ignoring the threat which Thailand has posed to the DRV. Direct Thai participation with Meo irregulars in the Laos war will not soon be forgotten by the PL/DRV. Similarly, Laotian right-wing extremists on Thai soil, U.S. bombing bases in Thailand directed at the DRV and the rest of Indochina, and Thai regulars fighting in Vietnam at the height of the war have not inspired DRV trust of Thailand. At the same time, certain DRV activities during the entire armed struggle phase raised fears in Bangkok. Some of these activities, particularly those involving Thai insurgents in the North and Northeast, may still be continuing under PL/DRV aegis, but Thailand has shown less public concern over them since the Paris Agreements were signed.

In fact, Thailand seems now to be seriously interested in placing one foot in "the other camp"—the Pathet Lao, North Vietnam, China beyond—while retaining its other foot, though less solidly than before, in such regional associations as ASEAN and in bilateral relations eyed suspiciously (as is ASEAN) by the Communist powers. In mid-1974, Thailand eased her twenty-five year stand against the granting of Thai citizenship to Vietnamese refugees long in that country, a gesture no doubt calculated to gain goodwill in Hanoi. Since then, unofficial Thai visitors have gone to Hanoi and official exchanges are in the planning stage. Nonetheless, the remaining U.S. bases in Thailand present an obstacle to Thai-DRV rapprochement, even if they appear to have been no bar to Thai efforts at closer relations with Peking. It is likely that the DRV will await the evolution of events in Laos and Cambodia before committing itself to closer relations with Bangkok. Part of the problem will be the sort of relations Thailand would maintain with a coalition in Laos which had moved closer to Hanoi, and the Thai reaction to a possible revolutionary regime in Cambodia (if no negotiated solution is found) which might be independent of Hanoi and close to Peking. The Thai military might possibly move to clear out what it regards as highly hostile forces on the western borders of Cambodia—or, for that matter, the Thai borders of Laos. Probably, however, the DRV fears Thai political capabilities in Laos and Cambodia more than it does a military assault. A prudent DRV policy—and there is nothing to indicate that DRV strategy in Laos and Cambodia is anything other than prudent—will take full account of Thai concerns for these countries, as it takes account of those of Moscow and Peking.

Peripheral to the Southeast Asian region, the DRV's current diplomacy is one of prompting the recognition of the PRG by as many countries as possible— particularly the more important ones, which seek opportunities in the DRV just as the latter seeks assistance from them. Such a country is Japan, to which the DRV is apparently not disposed to grant more concessions until it has demonstrated some greater support for the PRG. In this case, DRV reconstruction requirements seem to take second place to the needs of aggressive diplomacy in the current struggle phase. France is a similar case, where—despite the possibilities of substantial assistance to the DRV—the DRV is showing little interest until the French move more concretely to upgrade the PRG's prestige. In the case of Australia, on the other hand, the DRV seems to have been better disposed, conceivably because of Australia's potential influence on U.S. policy in Southeast Asia. Britain, like France or Japan, has received no preferential treatment.

The DRV's policy of seeking PRG recognition by these powers is somewhat puzzling in that, after all, the formal acceptance of a South Vietnamese government, even of Communist hue, would seem to be flying against the ultimate goal of reunification. However, the DRV is clearly confident that the formation of a friendly regime in South Vietnam—either a coalition, for a period, or the PRG itself—is the surest path to reunification.

Notes

1. See Chapter V of the Agreement on Ending the War and Restoring Peace in Vietnam, signed in Paris, January 27, 1973.

2. Article 20(a) of the Paris Agreements.

3. See Chapter 6 of the Agreement and Protocols. Although the Agreements leave this specific question ambiguous, the writer has reason to believe that the North Vietnamese were given the impression that Saigon would be pressed further toward clear demarcation of zones of territorial control between GVN and PRG. On details of the negotiations leading to the Paris Agreements and their immediate aftermath, see Tad Szulc, "How Kissinger Did It," *Foreign Policy* (Summer 1974).

4. "Le Thanh Nghi Delivers Economic Report at National Assembly Session," Hanoi in Vietnamese to Vietnam 0435 GMT February 6, 1974 as reported in *FBIS Asia and Pacific*, February 22, 1974, p. 6.

5. "HOC TAP Editorial on the Development of Northern Potential," Hanoi HOC TAP in Vietnamese, March 1974, pp. 1-10 as reported in *FBIS Asia and Pacific*, April 8, 1974, K9.

6. See Truong Chinh, *The Resistance Will Win*, 3rd ed. (Hanoi: Foreign Languages Publishing House, 1966).

7. "Le Thanh Nghi Delivers," *FBIS Asia and Pacific*, February 22, 1974, p. 9.

8. See Report by Richard Moose and Charles Meisner, *Vietnam, May 1974* (A Staff Report prepared for the use of the Committee on Foreign Relations, U.S. Senate, 93rd Congress, 2nd sess., August 5, 1974).

9. Estimates of PAVN strength vary widely and Western commentators frequently confuse total PAVN strength with the numbers of its forces deployed in South Vietnam, augmented by PLAF forces. Estimates cited here are based on *Strategic Survey*, Institute of Strategic Studies, London, 1974, as modified by field interviews.

10. Based on a statement by a U.S. official who was a member of the U.S. demining operations team in North Vietnam.

11. See Chapter 2 in this book by Carlyle A. Thayer, "Southern Vietnamese Revolutionary Organizations and the Viet-Nam Workers' Party, 1954-1974."

12. "Niyazbekov Banquet Speech," Hanoi Vietnam News Agency in English GMT December 21, 1973 as reported in *FBIS Asia and Pacific*, December 21, 1973, K5.

13. "LPA Commentary Hails the Visits to Fraternal Countries," Liberation Radio in Vietnamese to South Vietnam 1000 GMT January 1, 1974 as reported in *FBIS Asia and Pacific*, January 3, 1974, L1.

14. This Robert S. Elegant news story was originally printed in the *Los Angeles Times* and appeared in *The State* (Columbia, S.C.) on April 4, 1974.

15. See the Indochina section of the March 21, 1974 *FBIS Soviet Union Daily Report*.

16. See "Quarterly Documentation," in *China Quarterly* (January-March 1974).

17. "Part 2 of Hoang Xuan article: 'The Nixon Administration and International Detente'," Hanoi *Nhan Dan* in Vietnamese November 24, 1973, p. 3, as reported in *FBIS*, December 6, 1973, K13.

18. "PRC Friendship Group Visits PRG Liberated Area," Hanoi Vietnam News Agency in English 1556 GMT January 16, 1974 as reported in *FBIS* January 15, 1974, K3 and reportage of other days in this time period.

19. "Authoritative Source Said to Comment on Paracels Issue," Tokyo AKAHATA in Japanese January 26, 1974, p. 4 as reported in *FBIS Asia and Pacific*, January 28, 1974, K9.

20. Donald L. Berlin, *Ocean Politics in Southeast Asia*, M.A. Thesis, University of South Carolina, 1974, pp. 113 and 154. See also: Cheng Tao, "Communist China and the Law of the Sea," *American Journal of International Law* (January 1969): 61.

21. "Further Coverage on Activities at 3rd Trade Union Congress," Hanoi in Vietnamese to Vietnam 0415 GMT February 12, 1974 as reported in *FBIS Asia and Pacific*, February 13, 1974, K2.

22. Premier Pham Van Dong commented September 2, 1974 that "the recent collapse of the Nixon administration reflects the deterioration of U.S. imperialism in various spheres and also shows the grave crisis of the U.S. society, a crisis which has been caused mainly by the failure of present and past U.S. aggressive wars in Vietnam and elsewhere in Indochina." "Premier Interviews on Vietnamese Situation, U.S. Role," Tokyo AKAHATA in Japanese September 2, 1974, p. 1 as reported in *FBIS Asia and Pacific*, September 6, 1974, K3.

Part I:
Communism in Vietnam

C. Development in North Vietnam:
The Army and Agriculture

The Political Role and Development of the People's Army of Vietnam

William S. Turley

The Lao Dong (Workers') Party has nurtured the People's Army of Vietnam (PAVN)[1] on the principle that it should draw its main strength from the social and political factors underpinning the Vietnamese Revolution. Such links between the military and society qualify the PAVN as a revolutionary army and are among the principal reasons for the Democratic Republic of Vietnam's (DRV) ability to achieve objectives and withstand pressures that many observers have believed would overtax its resources. Moreover, since its official founding on December 22, 1944, the PAVN has encountered an uncommonly broad range of social, political and combat situations and coped with challenges of foreign powers which other "people's armies" have not had to confront in equal intensity. The PAVN therefore is the institution that has reflected the unique characteristics of the revolution most accurately and that, after the Party, has contributed most to defining Vietnamese Communism.

The PAVN has passed through fairly distinct stages of development determined by the political, strategic, and technological conditions which have prevailed in different periods of the revolution. This development can be traced in the consolidation of a political work system in the army, in the changing social composition and political requirements of military leadership, in the impact of military modernization and regularization, and in the search for new strategy and tactics, especially during the war in the South. Since space has been limited to these topics, a thorough analysis of the PAVN's relationship to Vietnamese society and its role in specific policymaking processes must be left to a much larger work.

Political Work and Leadership in a Revolutionary Army

The first military formations under the Lao Dong Party during World War II were very small guerrilla units. The "Viet-Nam Propaganda Unit" formed under Vo Nguyen Giap in 1944 and considered to be the direct precursor of the PAVN, had only thirty-four men. Such units, of necessity, were concerned more with "political struggle" and their own survival than with the subtleties of political organization within armed forces. But in the spring of 1945, when it became opportune to plan for a general uprising and the number of men under arms had increased to 1,000, the problem of political supervision came to the fore.[2] A "Revolutionary Military Conference" held in April took steps to centralize control over the armed forces and install political representatives at high levels of command under a Revolutionary Military Committee;[3] and at a Vietminh Conference in June, instructions were issued to appoint political officers in the army and intensify the political training of new soldiers.[4] This was the origin of the Party's political apparatus in the new army.

Faced with Japan's imminent defeat and the almost certain return of France, the Party was compelled to organize at a hectic pace, and it had to do so among people who were unfamiliar with its goals and working methods. In consequence, political work in the army was devoted mainly to selection of recruits, political indoctrination, strengthening of discipline, and fighting "against the tendencies to pillage and regionalism."[5] So long as the overriding goal was national liberation and social reforms were moderate, political work concentrated on enhancing military effectiveness and mass mobilization with little concern for the class interests of officers and men. This is not to say that the tasks of political officers in the earliest stages of the Resistance were simple; on the contrary, they required great energy, eloquence, and political acumen because of the delicacy of the national united front and the onrush of unanticipated events.

In establishing a system of political officers in the army, the Party was able to draw from the experience of the Soviet Red Army and the People's Liberation Army of China. Yet it is important to recall that the justifications for and duties of political officers were different in the Red Army and PLA because of the particular circumstances of their origins and the nature of the conflicts which shaped their development. In the Soviet Union, the duties of political officers were largely internal to the army, particularly since many were placed alongside military commanders who were former Tsarist officers of questionable loyalty. In China, after a decade of civil war, the loyalty of military commanders, most of whom were long-time Party stalwarts, was not so much in need of supervision as were the attitudes and behavior of the troops and the relations between units and surrounding populations. Political officers in the PLA therefore became more deeply involved than their Soviet counterparts in education, propaganda, and general political work in both the army and civilian society. The early Vietnamese experience was most like that of China, inasmuch as the original top military commanders—Vo Nguyen Giap, Phung Chi Kien, Le Van Chi, Chu Van Tan—were established revolutionaries whose loyalty was not suspect and the main problem was to create a sympathetic environment and an army capable of retaining popular support.

There were certain aspects of the Vietnamese situation, however, that diverged from the experience of both China and the Soviet Union. These differences were evident in the political work system and the "lessons" drawn from foreign countries as summarized in a booklet entitled *Political Officers in the Army*. Written before August 1944,[6] this booklet made clear the Party's intention of placing its military arm on the proper political footing and under close supervision even while fighting behind a national united front.

Because of the extreme fluidity of the situation and the need to build military organizations very rapidly and to use military units in combination with mass movements, an extraordinarily large proportion of the first generation political officers' duties were devoted to mobilizing the masses, a task which was complicated by widespread feelings of political and military inefficacy, traditional distaste for the military profession, and stubborn village communalism. As described in this booklet, political officers were expected to work alongside the people during harvests to spread the message that "to become revolutionary soldiers is the duty of the People" and to tell them of the glory and advantages that would follow liberation. Social reform, discussed in general terms, was a minor element in this message. Inside the army, the officers' primary duties were to improve troops's understanding of national liberation, help raise military and technical abilities, and instill a sense of discipline; with respect to enemy forces, they were to encourage defections, especially among Vietnamese. In keeping with the principles of the national united front, political officers at regiment level and above were considered to be "representatives of the people's government, that is, representatives of the Vietminh organization in the army,"[7] which held out the theoretical possibility of appointing political officers who were not members of the Party though presumably cadres of the Vietminh front. Thus the duties and formal command structure of the political officers reflected the overriding concern with the nationalist character of the movement and the need for the broadest possible base of popular support.

The political apparatus initially created in the army foreshadowed all future Party organization in the army. All military affairs were placed under the authority of a Military Committee, the precursor of today's Central Military Party Committee (the functional equivalent of China's Military Affairs Committee), and the military command structure was paralleled by a system of political organs and political officers administered by a separate Political Directorate (later subordinated to the CMPC, a half-civilian half-military committee directly under the Central Committee). At brigade and division levels, political organs consisted of a secretary and assistant secretaries and bureau for administration; organization, investigation, mobilization and morale; propaganda and education; civilian proselytization; and enemy troop proselytization. Political officers were installed down to the companies, which ideally were to have about two hundred men and were the basic political and tactical unit in an essentially guerrilla army. Within the company, much of the actual political assignments and face-to-face contacts with troops were carried out by individuals in each platoon designated by the company political officer; these individuals also were called political officers but in effect were assistants to the company officer.[8] Subsequently, full-time political officers often were assigned to platoons. Such an intensive political work system was devised to cope with the social and political conditions that made the Vietnamese situation similar to that of China.

Although the Vietnamese did not have as serious a problem as the Soviets in using non-Communist military officers, this general concern was reflected in the assignment of clearly superior authority to the political officers. Collective decisionmaking was the ideal, but the decisions of military commanders with respect to strictly military affairs were subject to approval of political officers, while the latter did not require a military countersignature to their orders on political affairs. The reason for this arrangement in the particular, temporary conditions of the Resistance were stated clearly:

Do political officers have the power to supervise the command staff? When the revolution has just begun, a large part of the officers in the revolutionary army will come from the ranks of the imperialist army (i.e., the *Garde Indochinoise* and other Vietnamese auxiliaries to the French colonial army) and they will have weak political consciousness, and therefore the political officers definitely will have the power to supervise the command staff.

Later, in accordance with new circumstances, there will be a revision.[9]

Actually, the army grew so fast after the August Revolution, and the number of officers that could be obtained from the ranks of Vietnamese in the "imperialist army" was so small even if all of them had joined the Vietminh, that the proportion of officers from this particular source in the total number was low. At the same time, however, the PAVN did not enjoy such a long gestation period as China's PLA but rather had to cope with extremely rapid, large-scale recruitment of political and military neophytes. These circumstances demanded giving decisive superiority to political officers, but such a doctrine could not always be fastidiously applied. How, then, did this system of political organization in the army, prescribed before the Party had built large military forces, work in practice?

Because of unstable and strenuous conditions in the early phases of the Resistance and the shortage of qualified personnel for both military and political positions, political officers were not placed from the very first in all units or linked into a mature organizational hierarchy. A certain degree of informality, both necessary and permissible in military formations most of which still were little better than guerrilla bands, persisted until 1948. Formalization of the political apparatus in the army took place in that year in conjunction with creation of a formal system of military command in preparation for creation of regular main force units.[10] Although political officers were assigned to some units in 1945, the system evidently was implemented sporadically and the officers did not begin to exercise the broad supervisory role theoretically intended for them until about 1949. The reasons for the relatively subdued role of political officers until this time were that a sufficient number of qualified cadres was not available, extremely demanding extra-military duties diverted their energies, the national united front required restraint in Party leadership, and many political officers were themselves not "hard core" elements hence not considered fully reliable. The reason was not, as has been alleged, that a political work system for the army was opposed by high-ranking military leaders.[11] The highest-ranking military leaders had begun their revolutionary careers, after all, as political organizers and now were members of the Central Committee and Political Bureau.

Of course there were conflicts between "political" and "military" points of view, but mainly at tactical echelons, and between tactical echelons and operations planning sections. The potential for such conflicts grew in proportion to the extent that particular operations had strategic political goals independent of the military outcome or depended on local political factors for success. "Purely military cadres" insisted on launching attacks that were extraneous to larger political objectives or after combat refused to engage in political tasks among the people—such as helping harvest crops, rebuild houses, and provide security—that were essential to winning and maintaining popular support.[12] It was in the setting of such conflicts that "politics took command," political officers made their most direct contributions to military decisionmaking, and politicization of the revolutionary army in accordance with Party precepts occurred.

As indicated earlier, the general character of the army and its relation to Party goals was conditioned by the social composition of both its military and political cadre. If the number of officers that could be recruited from the colonial forces was small relative to needs, the number of educated, "bourgeois" individuals that joined the Vietminh and were rapidly promoted to positions of command immediately after the August Revolution probably exceeded expectations. The reminiscences of one "petit bourgeois intellectual" about his recruitment and qualifications for promotion vividly illustrate this situation:

The uprising occurred in Hue the 19th of August, and toward the end of August when the Viet Minh began recruiting youths to become soldiers I joined up. At that time, Mr. _____ who now works here [in Saigon] at the Ministry of Foreign Affairs also joined the Viet Minh army, then called the national salvation army or the liberation army, and I remember he was made a battalion commander because he had a university degree. A large number of us at that time had passed university or high school degree examinations because at first in Hue it was the intellectuals, university and high school students who participated. Therefore anyone who had one of these degrees could become a unit commander, and without a diploma one became a plain soldier. As for me, I had not yet graduated from high school, but not fifteen days later I was made an assistant squad leader, when I was still a secondary school student . . . Towards the end of 1945 . . . [after having proved myself in operations in the South] I returned to Hue because as a student I had some cultural level and was allowed to finish my studies, whereupon I was made a platoon leader, and that was my first command.[13]

After additional study of one month, in late 1946 at the age of twenty-two this man was made a company commander; in 1948 he became a battalion commander and in 1950 an assistant regimental political officer. Underscoring the social gap between officers and men, he compared his small physique to that of the sturdy peasants he commanded and commented on their simple-mindedness and rusticity.

Another officer, of "worker" origin, confirmed the absence of class criteria and the requirement of education in recruiting policies, linking them to the social and political goals of the movement at that particular stage of its development:

From the beginning, in choosing cadres to develop the Party, people were chosen without distinction as to class, as the class struggle prior to 1955 was not clear. Persons who had culture and could speak with cunning or who had resources to support them in their activities or families who had contributed to the revolution were promoted in the Party. In fact, it was mainly such persons who were inducted first into the Party.

. . . (B)efore 1954 the position of political officer can be said to have gone to anyone and to any class, so long as he had culture and could speak relatively coherently, that is, cleverly. . . . Even though units were said to be forces of the workers and peasants, landlords too could become political officers and exercise the powers of leadership.[14]

At high echelons, few such individuals, especially if non-Party, were given important decisionmaking authority or made privy to the inner workings of the Party,[15] but there was an obvious concern in this early period to obtain the services of as large a number of persons of talent as possible and to remain consistent in practice with the principle of the national united front. When the Party, after a period of self-proclaimed disbandment, reappeared in 1951 and clarified its leadership role in the Front, political officers became more prominent and class-based criteria for selection and appointment began to be applied, though with due regard for previous service to the Revolution. It was thought prudent to tighten political controls and establish more orthodox recruitment procedures by recruiting a larger proportion of individuals who because of social origins and position in the class struggle would be absolutely reliable.

Once the war was over, doctrinal consistency during accelerated land reform of 1955-56 demanded that establishment of the dictatorship of the proletariat through class struggle be accompanied by parallel policies in other institutions. It must be emphasized that this program did not aim merely to strengthen the Party's role through its political officers in the army, but to correct what was considered laxness in the earlier recruitment of both political officers and military commanders. As one DRV commentator has observed, "There were a number of deviations in expanding the Party which we had to correct later."[16]

Therefore, while the basic tasks of political work in the army remained the same, if somewhat less involved in popular political mobilization and more in military administration and training, more effort was made to recruit "hard core" elements at some cost to educational level and "cleverness" of speech.[17] The expansion of the political apparatus in conjunction with consolidation of Party control over the revolution ended any remaining informality or low profile in political work.

The legacy of the Resistance was a quasi-modern army deeply marked by the special political requirements of the war against France. Because of the need throughout the war for broad national support and for knowledge and training that were virtually monopolized by persons the Party defined as "bourgeois," an inordinately large proportion of military and political leadership cadres were drawn from social classes above the "basic level." When the class struggle was heightened with land reform, many of these persons experienced a freeze on their upward advancement or were shunted off into construction projects; but they were not systematically or abruptly excised from the ranks, and those who had attained division rank before 1954 generally were exempted from such restrictions.[18] Significantly, military service was considered equal to Party service as a criterion of worthiness for exemption from the full effects of class struggle. The same DRV commentator who noted deviations in Resistance recruitment policies also pointed out that persons who served in the military had "lived and fought under the banner of democratic proletarianism, not under that of bourgeois democracy, and therefore were not outside the ranks of the working class ... [A]side from the Party ..., the people's army was more deeply imbued with democratic proletarianism than any other element in the worker-peasant system of dictatorship."[19] In this respect, the Lao Dong Party may have been more lenient toward persons of high social status in the army at war's end than the Soviet or Chinese Communist Parties, at least so long as leniency was expedient in the interests of retaining national unity and educated leadership, as it was in 1954 and to some extent long afterward. The PAVN, along with the Party and state administration, thus reflected the great importance of nationalism in the Vietnamese Revolution and reliance on the modern education and skills concentrated in a small, formerly privileged class.

Military Doctrine

In addition to the distinctive social characteristics it shared with the Party and state, the army inherited a large body of military doctrine, or distillations of experience, and emerged as the foremost embodiment of what may be called the Resistance ethos. These doctrines, experiences and traditions were summarized as Vietnam's "unique military art." The essence of this military art was the maximization of the popular character of people's war to overcome a better armed and more numerous enemy, and on this principle the doctrine claimed continuity with Vietnam's history of heroic wars of resistance against China.[20] The Resistance against France was said to be a "creative application of Marxism-Leninism to the unique Vietnamese situation" which had existed throughout the nation's history, namely, Vietnam's extreme weakness in size and power relative to its adversaries. This situation required development of tactics, strategies and organizational forms to enable "the few to defeat many, quality to defeat quantity, and weakness to defeat strength."[21] The PAVN necessarily was preoccupied with compensating for its limited material resources by perfecting the "human factors" of high morale and political consciousness ("redness"), and with drawing upon the active assistance of the masses produced by political mobilization. Thus the army was expected to be highly visible in political roles, either in the socialization of its men to revolutionary values and extraordinarily high standards of self-sacrifice or as the beneficiary and agent of political work in society at large. As the PAVN's chief-of-staff, Van Tien Dung, observed:

Throughout the war, our arms and equipment were weaker than the enemy's. Thus we could only develop political and moral superiority, and only then have the courage to attack the enemy, only then dare to fight the enemy resolutely; only then could we stand solidly before all difficult trials created by the superior firepower that the enemy had brought into the war.[22]

Because of the PAVN's stunning victories over French forces and the military hubris which followed Dien Bien Phu, the "human factors" assumed mythic proportions and created in some circles an exaggerated faith in the effectiveness of motivation, political indoctrination, and mass mobilization against forces using vastly superior weapons. In general, however, the Resistance did not give rise to such a profound mystique of "men over weapons" as sometimes expressed by Mao Tse-tung and Lin Piao, except in the self-evident sense that weapons were said to be effective only to the extent that they were effectively used by men, hence created their own exacting demands for discipline, loyalty, political consciousness and motivation. Realistic assessment of the Vietnamese situation led relentlessly to the conclusion that all conceivable sources of strength, whether material or spiritual, should be utilized to the fullest possible extent and to a belief that men and weapons, human factors and technology, popular participation and military professionalism, guerrilla war and regular war, could be combined in a synthesis of greater power than any selective approach could produce. The Resistance legacy was a commitment to preparation for total war.

The main elements of this legacy generally have been reconciled, but military development has required their redefinition and events sometimes have made them appear contradictory. It is a measure of Vietnamese pragmatism and flexibility that they have not held the lessons of the Resistance or any single interpretation of them sacrosanct. This genius helps explain the harmony and spirit of accommodation that usually have prevailed in the DRV's civil-military relations as well as the PAVN's capacity for adaptation to changing battlefield conditions, though transformation from a sophisticated guerrilla force to a modern conventional army has produced exceptions to this rule.

Modernization and Regularization

Because of the priority given to reconstruction, revolution, and Party consolidation, military regularization and modernization were not begun in a systematic way until 1957, when Soviet military assistance helped make a program feasible. In 1958, a spate of directives created the specialized branches and laid the organizational groundwork of a modern, conventional army. The keystone was the Law Establishing a System of Service for Officers, passed by the National Assembly on April 29.[23] During the Resistance, officers had been designated by function e.g., regimental commander, battalion commander, company commanders. This law established a formal hierarchy of conventional ranks, systematized evaluation and promotion procedures and inaugurated the wearing of epaulets and rank insignia. The regular officer corps thus created was very much like those of the other people's democracies. Although the law was very similar to the Regulations on the Service of Officers of the Chinese People's Liberation Army,[24] it did not provide ranks of Marshall or mention compulsory military service (though a modified system was soon to follow). Also unlike the PLA, the PAVN never has abolished the conventional rank system and reverted solely to functional designations except for pragmatic political purposes in the special circumstances of the war in the South.[a] The importance of the Law for the PAVN was that it marked the end of the Resistance army, even if the Resistance ethos survived, and created the patterns of hierarchy and rigidity of procedure common to modern, conventional forces. The objective was to make the PAVN a more "professional" army and the officer corps a more "expert" profession:

The system clarifies the duties, powers and rewards of cadres in the army, raises their spirit of responsibility and strengthens cadres and soldiers' awareness of organization and discipline. Thus it will make the relationship between command and compliance more clear and guarantee unified, centralized direction over the various units, branches and services in their daily work and combat.... Conferring of rank on cadres must depend on political quality, professional ability and service achievements in the army as well as contribution to the revolution. These regulations will motivate officers to make every effort to study

---

[a]PAVN units operating south of DRV Military Region V, which is under the direct command of the general staff in Hanoi, adopt the insignia and functional rank designations of the People's Liberation Armed Force of South Vietnam (PLAF).

and raise their military, political, professional and cultural levels in order to keep up with the requirements of the Party and be worthy of the responsibilities and honors which the Party and State have given them. Cadres will go deeply into their professions and adopt their work and military service as their long-term occupation.[25]

In brief, the law, through manipulation of a predictable career structure and fixed rewards system, created incentives for the officer corps to fulfill the prevailing conception of what a "regular and modern army" should be.

That conception was based primarily on the familiar notions of "red" and "expert," or high political consciousness and loyalty combined with high professional standards and technical expertise. In the Vietnamese context, "redness" for many officers and political leaders who had served through the Resistance also implied the qualities of élan, voluntarism, imagination, initiative, self-sacrifice, egalitarianism, and decentralization that were characteristic of the pre-modernization revolutionary army. However, because modern, regular armies need routine, strict obedience, elaborate rules, centralization and hierarchy, it did not take long for the modernization program to produce contradictions. In addition to disgruntling old cadres who had a "guerrilla mentality," there was potential for conflict between those who benefited most by the Resistance definition of "red" and those who stood most to gain by greater emphasis on professional expertise. Since many military cadres retained strong ideological preference for "redness" and many politicos acknowledged the need for professionalism, while most leaders regardless of organizational affiliation believed the two could be reconciled, the line of cleavage did not fall between Party and army or between clearly demarcated groups within either. The contradictions did not create polarization. They clearly demonstrated, however, that modernization would change the PAVN's political role and character.

The first and most authoritative analysis of the problem was coauthored by Generals Vo Nguyen Giap and Nguyen Chi Thanh on the PAVN's anniversary in December 1958.[26] Giap, Minister of Defense and Commander-in-Chief, and Thanh, head of the army's General Political Directorate and the only man ever to hold rank equal to Giap's, may privately have disagreed on the issues they discussed, if the divergent points of view which emerged later during the war in the South (see below) had earlier roots. But they shared common ground on the fundamental principle that in some degree both political and professional values should be promoted. Disagreement was constrained by the fact that all DRV leaders subscribed to an analytical framework which predicted and condemned the phenomena Giap and Thanh described and were well informed of similar problems faced earlier in China and the Soviet Union. Since a consensus was achieved among top political and military leaders as to the nature of the problem and how to treat it, conflicts created by the first stage of modernization were mainly between the leadership and ranks, between generations of cadres,[27] and between new specialists and old generalists.

Giap and Thanh pointed out that the PAVN was especially vulnerable to modernization's enticements because "an absolute majority of our cadres and soldiers are peasants or from the petit bourgeoisie," two elements which were similar in their inclination to adopt "individualism" and "covetousness of position." Both of these groups attached excessive importance to patterns of deference and authority derived from Vietnamese traditional society, undercutting Party leadership and the ideological preference for "workers"; and the skills on which modernization placed highest value still were possessed mainly by the urban bourgeoisie. Many officers considered themselves a privileged class, relied excessively on rules, regulations and "commandism" to get things done, affected imperious deportment and in general were "militarist." Such tendencies were said to be incompatible with the popular, democratic character of a people's army and destructive of the voluntarism and willing obedience believed essential to military effectiveness. Giap and Thanh also noted that modernization had encouraged some officers to belittle "the role of man and the political factor" and to neglect political studies in favor of technical studies. These tendencies could lead to separation of political and military affairs, of civil and military authority:

In the army . . . there is a deviation which holds that while the army is becoming regular and modern the problem of building the army politically and ideologically is not as important as before and which does not give sufficient stress to the revolutionary and class characteristics of the army.

Marxism-Leninism teaches us that in a society that still has classes and class struggle, politics must have a supremely important position—the position of leadership . . . [B]ut in some places the election of comrades who are strong politically for party committees has not been advocated because it is believed that someone weak in a specialty cannot lead the unit, and they want to change the Party committees into committees of 'technicians' . . .

Political work in substance is the work of the Party; the Party leads the army, especially in political and ideological respects, therefore any tendency to weaken or neglect political work in reality weakens or neglects the leadership of the Party.

Excessive attention to technology in the present time is a weakness which must be overcome; excessive emphasis on technology and neglect for politics and thought is an error. This is not an ordinary error, it is a fundamental error—because it will lead us away from the path of revolutionary struggle.

This analysis foreshadowed all subsequent discussion of military modernization. Frequent references in following years to the insidious effects of regularization on the "revolutionary class consciousness" of officers, the tendency of specialized technical and professional training to produce "purely military points of view," and repeated "political retraining" campaigns for military cadres and technical training for political officers assigned to "modern" branches indicated the intractable nature of the problem. Never was it suggested that either "redness" or professionalism be sacrificed in order to achieve perfection in one or the other. Contradictions were bridged ideologically by the principle that political consciousness should enhance professionalism by providing the dedication and spirit of self-sacrifice which inspired greater effort to master one's specialty and by preserving the distinctive qualities of a people's army that made it a more effective military force than if it were isolated from its social environment by occupational separatism and excessive specialization. However, as it became increasingly clear that war on a large scale would resume in the South, the need for accelerated training in basic combat skills came to have special urgency.[28] General Thanh's departure from the General Political Directorate in 1961 may have signalled a drift from the orthodoxy of 1958 in favor of the growing professional and conventional orientations of General Staff officers. Yet, whatever the differences over how best to prepare, the fundamental faith in the adequacy of people's war as practiced in the Resistance, refined by improvements in weapons or tactics introduced during modernization, was not challenged. The resumption of the war in the South and the extension of the air war to the North, however, did bring into question some basic assumptions and opened the way for adaptations appropriate to a war which was most notable, from the military viewpoint for the huge volume and sophistication of technology employed by the interventionist foreign power.

The Impact of the Second Indochina War

The army's development during the period of direct American involvement must be viewed in the context of the DRV's general strategy and the material exigencies of each stage. The decision to pursue the struggle in the South regardless of American actions, evidently made at the Ninth Conference of the Central Executive Committee of the Party in December 1963, put the Party in an awkward position in respect of Khrushchev's line on peaceful coexistence and placed a premium on self-reliance.[29] In 1964, the introduction of American troops into combat and the "reprisal bombings" against the North confirmed fears of a protracted conflict involving American forces, possibly in the North as well as South, while the PAVN was still quite primitively equipped. Military techniques which stressed the "human factors" to compensate for physical weakness and to minimize the need for sophisticated technology and foreign assistance therefore enjoyed a revival.

If the prospect of confronting American firepower outside the PAVN's home base raised protests that the army was unprepared,[30] these objections were overridden by the seeming inevitability of American escalation, the need for a strategic defense of the North and residual confidence in the Resistance ethos. The introduction of "Kuo Hsing-fu's training method," a regimen of political training and consciousness raising which had appeared in the CPLA at the height of a campaign exalting men over weapons,[31] signalled the shift in emphasis. Either in testimony to his own change of position or on assignment to provide a mask of collegiality, General Hoang Van Thai wrote the article which introduced the program.[32] The modernization and technological improvement of the army continued as far as material resources allowed, but there was discernible enhancement of commitment to "revolutionary awareness" and of Party leadership organs in the army including its specialized technical components.[33] Fear of the enemy's superior weapons, including nuclear weapons, and the corollary of demand for more and better armament than the DRV could then obtain, were called rightist tendencies, "bourgeois and reactionary arguments." This posture was of course entirely sensible in respect of territorial defense, mass mobilization, and para-military organization in the North, but the war in the South posed somewhat different problems for the regular army and was not contemplated with unlimited confidence by all officers.

It is helpful here to recall the basic characteristics and periodization of the war as seen from Hanoi. DRV strategy in each stage[34] had as its main objective the frustration of whatever strategy or tactics the Americans employed (which sometimes required only to survive them) and thus to prove the futility of trying to "win" in Vietnam, leaving withdrawal the only sensible course. Each engagement which helped teach the Americans this lesson was a "decisive victory," regardless of its immediate results. Thus, to win the war, it was not necessary to win battles in the traditional military sense (though of course this was desirable and an objective of each engagement). It was conceded early that the PAVN and the PLAFSVN (People's Liberation Armed Force of South Vietnam) could not physically eject the American army. The purpose of military action was to produce political effects by stalemating the enemy. In relation to this objective, victory could be claimed in each period of the war,[35] regardless of purely military considerations.

In 1960-64, the period Hanoi calls the "special war," destruction of the strategic hamlet program and defeat of American-trained and equipped ARVN (Army of the Republic of Vietnam) units, especially at the battle of Ap Bac in My Tho (January 2, 1963) and confirmed at Bia Gia in Quang Ninh (May 31, 1965), demonstrated the inadequacy of American efforts to nurture indigenous counter-revolutionary forces or to supplement their leadership with "advisors." In 1965-68, the period of Johnson's "limited war," successful resistance to American bombardment of the North, frustration of American "search and destroy" missions and pacification programs, and the "Tet Offensive" of 1968 proved that the revolutionary forces were ineradicable, that they could concentrate with impunity for attack even on cities, and that stalemate was the best the Americans could hope to achieve, compelling them to seek a negotiated settlement. During the next period, of "Vietnamization," the inability of ARVN troops to destroy liberated areas, the repeated defeats or inconsequential results of ARVN operations in Cambodia and Laos, and the frustration of ARVN pacification especially in the central lowlands (mainly Quang Tri) proved that nothing could be gained by "changing the color of the corpses" or by widening the war to all of Indochina. Finally, the Spring Offensive of 1972, "a key turning point" and "the largest and most comprehensive strategic offensive ever opened on the battlefield," proved decisively the inadequacy of Vietnamization and the fundamental strength of the revolution which made continued American support of Saigon untenable.

The tactics employed in each period were adapted to immediate political objectives and the revolution's resources in relation to them, but always in such a way that coordinated resources or political and tactical advantages in the South's "three strategic regions": the mountains, lowlands, and cities.[36] The interrelationship of these regions is held to be a major cause of the "unique features" of the war. In the cramped geography of Vietnam, unlike that of China, space cannot be traded for time. Protection of base areas and maintenance of offensive capability both require keeping the better-armed enemy dispersed or off balance, and these needs can be met only by building political and military capabilities in all three regions. With such capabilities, sufficient force can be concentrated anywhere, anytime, to tax and deplete a much larger, more mobile force or to create "turning points" at moments of political opportunity or necessity such as the offensives of 1968 and 1972.

In addition to the three regions concept, great importance is attached to having three types of military force: local guerrillas, regional forces, and main forces.[37] The division of labor among these forces, particularly the assignment of the main force, has been a subject of controversy, but it is agreed that the main force has a special role in dealing the "annihilating blows" which lead to "turning points" in the war. Thus, whereas the guerrillas and regional forces employ rather static and long-used organizational forms and tactics, it is primarily the main force which must cope with innovations in enemy mobility and firepower. The main force nonetheless is expected to retain ability to launch "dispersed, small-scale attacks to create conditions for guerrilla war to develop." The mutual support and parallel activities of all types of forces and all three regions—in forms appropriate to the constantly changing tactical strategic and political requirements which give the war its "seething" (sôi nôi), not sequential or schematic, quality—is called "coordinated struggle." In the terminology of Western military science, this strategy seeks to harmonize the "defensive-offensive" of guerrilla-style people's war with the "offensive-defensive" of modern, conventional warfare.

As presented here, these ideas are the DRV's retrospective interpretation of the war. In practice, of course, strategy evolved through many experiments and adaptations, and in this process disputes often occurred. In the early stages of American escalation, the "men over weapons" mentality that was prescribed for defense of the North also was applied in the South, where the PAVN launched large-scale assaults at close quarters against entrenched American positions.

Although these tactics may have dashed American hopes for quick and easy victory, they also involved high human and material costs and caused considerable controversy. This controversy has been portrayed as having separated the advocates of more cautious tactics, who gathered around Vo Nguyen Giap, from Nguyen Chi Thanh, by this time a member of the Party Central Committee's Central Office for South Vietnam, a regional Party committee secretary, and political officer and military commander of forces in the South, who favored main force frontal assaults, relying on superior troop motivation to overcome larger, better-equipped American units.[38] In addition to his faith in the ability of men and proper tactics to compensate for material weakness, Thanh believed the cost of this approach was counterbalanced by the greater hope it held out of creating political conditions which would compel the Americans to withdraw in a short period of time. This portrayal of the debate, (which waned as high losses and continuing American escalation compelled all leaders to reappraise their positions and to seek greater flexibility of tactics[b]), is basically correct, but some contextual circumstances need to be examined to place it in proper perspective.

In 1965 it was the conviction not only of General Thanh but of a majority of the Party leadership that the PAVN could hold its own against American firepower. Thanh was merely the Central Committee's agent in the South to implement a line of which he was acknowledged to be a leading exponent; his authority to determine strategy and tactics unilaterally was limited if it existed at all. He was, in fact, a "political general," charged with tightening up political organization and cadre policy among armed forces in the South, and his contribution to the debate on strategy and tactics was largely a side-effect of analyzing what were conceded to be problem areas at that time anyway.[39] Furthermore, theorizing on the war in the South often conflicted with questions of defense in the North. Disagreement therefore was diffuse, alliances cross-cutting. However, awareness of these disagreements and combat experience stimulated reflection and criticism on the part of military commanders and political officers throughout the army.[40]

The line on frontal assaults, by placing a premium on both conventional military formations and "human factors," did not choose between competing conceptions of what kind of army the PAVN should be but expressed faith in what the existing army could do. Both better military modernization and greater revolutionary awareness and motivation were sought. Thus one former officer recalled that one of the critical "test" battles against American forces was said to have proved the PAVN had mastered techniques of modern warfare adequately to employ new weapons beginning to arrive from the Soviet Union, while also under Thanh's command political criteria for recruitment and promotion of military cadres were tightened up.[41] This two-pronged approach to military

[b]Thanh's death in July 1967 may have simplified matters, as McGarvey suggests, but there is no evidence that it was an important factor in changing policy.

development helped mollify all doctrinal persuasions by conceding something to all of them, although it also held out the possibility that energetic, simultaneous application of both principles would only demonstrate more clearly the areas of their incompatibility. In any event, during the period of "limited war" the issue was not the intrinsic merit of men or weapons—denigration of the *enemy's* weapons never was intended to mean the DRV did not want better weapons for itself—but over whether the PAVN was sufficiently "mature" a military force to cope with American firepower while it was materially weak and compelled to use compensatory tactics and spirit.

The predominant conviction in 1965-66 that the PAVN could handle American units in direct assaults was based partly on Resistance hubris and partly on concrete experiences early in the period of "limited war," especially the battle of Van Tuong. Le Duan, Party first secretary, claimed that this battle was as important a turning point in the war in Vietnam as the battle of Stalingrad had been to the defeat of Germany:

(W)e can regard the battle of Van Tuong as a turning point testifying... *that the southern liberation army is fully capable of defeating U.S. troops under any circumstances, even though they have absolute superiority of ... firepower compared with that of the liberation army.* Indeed, the Battle of Van Tuong in August 1965 for U.S. troops is just like the battle of Ap-Bac by the end of 1963 for the puppet army. U.S. troops took the initiative in choosing Van Tuong, a coastal battle ground in their favor. They mobilized 8,000 troops with the coordination and support of Air and Navy units in an attempt to destroy one force of the southern liberation army seven or eight times smaller than their force. But just as in Ap-Bac, the helicopter-supported tactics and armoured car-supported tactics of the U.S. imperialists were defeated and more than 900 Americans were buried together with the bulk of iron and steel which the U.S. military used to brag about.[42]

As subsequent battles and continued American escalation raised the cost of persisting in these tactics (even Le Duan, the "flame of the South," acknowledged that "the revolutionary forces have had to withdraw temporarily," and "the revolutionary forces have suffered heavy losses"), conviction gave way to reappraisal. For a while, PAVN units were used on more carefully selected targets, the potentials of guerrilla and regional war were more fully explored, and tactics were developed to neutralize American advantages in airpower and artillery. However, these efforts were insufficient for achieving the strategic objective of proving to the Americans that substitution of American troops for the ARVN could at best produce stalemate. The "Tet Offensive" of 1968 was necessary to induce this realization so that the war could progress to its next stage. This victory, however, also proved the necessity of concentrating large numbers of troops to strike heavy blows against the enemy's most entrenched positions including cities in order to create key "turning points."[43] This fact and the observation that the victory of 1968 only presaged evolution into a new type of war—a "prolonged de-escalation" fraught with unpredictable perils—gave new urgency to military development. The Americans were obdurate, and there was a distinct possibility that they would transform the war into a "general war" throughout all of Indochina involving larger forces and greater increments of equipment. The PAVN still could not achieve the totality of its objectives and it could not indefinitely hold points the enemy valued. A former senior captain and assistant in the operations section of staff headquarters for Interzone V (mainly northern provinces of the RVN) observed that the condition of the infantry and the disparities of armament in the 1968 Offensive "placed limits on the victories the army could achieve," and "we could not stand up against such conditions."[44] Such perceptions in the army paralleled the weaknesses of resolution, tendencies to shrink from action and unrealistic expectations of quick results that were noted among Region and Province Party committee members by a COSVN Conference in July 1969.[45] In this environment it was natural for reappraisal to take the form of reassessing tradition and the comparative merits of human factors and weapons, yet retain the framework of a strategy which had achieved most of its objectives and to which there was no viable alternative.

Whereas Giap and Thanh had agreed in 1958 that experiences from the Resistance were applicable to a modernizing PAVN and to the DRV's defense, Thanh in 1965 castigated those who still worshipped that past, and by 1969 there was seemingly unanimous willingness to depart from tradition in search of greater effectiveness:

We should not apply old experiences mechanically or reapply outmoded forms of warfare.[46]

The practical conditions of our fight . . . constantly change and, therefore do not permit us to mechanically utilize our own combat experience which is no longer practicable.[47]

The lengthy articles in which these passages appeared and a companion piece by Lt. Gen. Song Hao[48] did not identify which old experiences were outmoded or what would take their place, but for the most part elaborated on the components of Vietnamese people's war best suited to that stage of the struggle. The character of the army in 1969 was portrayed as a modern army "with numerous branches and services modernly equipped,"[49] but one that simultaneously had strengthened its class character, that is, enlarged the proportion and improved the quality of military cadres from the worker-peasant class, in spite of "tendencies to divert from class policy, to neglect the task of improving outstanding persons from the worker-peasant class, and narrow-minded sectarianism."[50] In assessing the balance of forces, more importance was attached to the enemy's material strength than in the past as a factor which enabled him to stay in the battlefield.

Taken together, these elements reaffirmed faith in the basic principles of a people's war (though with flat assertion that specifics of implementation were subject to revision), confirmed that tight Party control and political criteria to improve class character would continue to be highly valued (against some opposition), and admitted that certain difficulties had been created by the sheer force of material and numerical factors which nonetheless could be overcome in the passage of time. As always, the line was an amalgamation of values held to be complementary, not a choice between alternatives, either in respect of overall strategy, combat tactics or conception of what the army's character should be. But the greatest potentials for development and innovation were recognized to be in accelerated technical modernization, better mastery of "modern forms of warfare" (usually meaning coordinated attack by larger, more specialized units), and further professionalization of the officer corps.

The implications of these themes were demonstrated forcibly in the spring offensive of 1972, in which PAVN units employed their most conventional tactics and modern weaponry of the war in coordination with political and local armed struggle to create another "turning point." In a book published the same year,[51] General Giap made the main themes of 1969 more explicit and placed them in broad historical perspective. Much of the inheritance of the past remained relevant, he said, because the distinguishing characteristics of the current war—vast disparity of numbers and matériel between the DRV and its enemies—probably also would characterize the DRV's wars in future. However, perfection and adaptation of a people's war were to be conducted mainly by improving the technical competence of cadres and troops, acquiring better equipment and technology and consolidating procedures to permit more effective, centralized coordination of units. "Modernization" had made great strides in the army but in relation to the army's present and future tasks still was insufficient:

Actually, by comparison with many countries on our side and around the world, our army's level of modernization is still not high. Between our army and the enemy's army there still exists a disparity of equipment and technology. The present anti-U.S. national salvation resistance as well as our long-range national defense require that we make much greater efforts to modernize our army.[52]

Modernization was complicated, however, by the fact that the DRV would need to expand its industrial base and communications network to support it. Defense needs were drawing the army and society into a different kind of relationship than that which had been established during the Resistance or even in the peacetime agrarian economy. The effectiveness of the main-force increasingly would depend on the DRV's ability to sustain its economy and infrastructure without reciprocal support from the army for civil construction, political mobilization or management. Although Giap did not not explicitly say so, it is reasonable to surmise that these lines of development were held to be more capable of realization after the Americans had withdrawn from the war (which they were then expected soon to do) and the air raids would end permanently.

In pursuit of "modernization," the PAVN also would have to accelerate "regularization":

Regularization is a necessary step for any army whose organization has achieved a certain level of perfection. Not only in the present but also in the past, in our country and in many others around the world, military regularization has been proposed and achieved. The more an army modernizes the greater is the need to integrate [or centralize—tâp trung] and unify, and the more the regularization problem must be emphasized.[53]

By 1972 the army had grown in organizational complexity, and would continue to do so to a degree that required more detailed elaboration of basic routines under tighter central direction. Giap's definition of regularization was unrepentantly bureaucratic:

Regularization is the realization of army unity in respect of organization based on systems, ordinances and regulations in order to place all army activities on a uniform foundation, to improve its character in organization, integration and science, and to achieve resolute and unanimous actions and close coordination of all parts of the army in warfare. Regularization is closely related to the promulgation of systems, ordinances and regulations and to their implementation.[54]

The steps outlined for implementation in the near future also were consistent with the bureaucratic construction of the term "regularization."[55] Although experience in a protracted people's war may make some officers more "red," this war seems to have compelled the forces of revolution to attempt a remarkably thorough (the Vietnamese would say "creative") amalgamation of "red" and "expert" values, guerrilla and conventional forms. As Giap observed while reviewing the previous fifteen years of regularization: "The practice of war has helped us make improvements on necessities and rectify irrational points, and it has furnished us with extremely rich experiences with which to build and develop regulations."[56]

But what was to be the role of politics, specifically of the Party, in this program of military development which combined political education, revolutionary zeal, and class ascription with technical education, bureaucratism, and merit rewards? Was there to be a quiet separation of politics and professionalism, of the Party and the army? Giap treated these questions rather briefly but made it clear that accelerated modernization and regularization programs were to be supplemented by more rigorous application of the "ideological task" and of democratic centralism in the Party apparatus in the army, not only to infuse the army with the proper political consciousness but also to help in a practical way to solve the PAVN's discipline problems.[57] Cadre policy would increase recruitment and promotion of persons from the worker-peasant class. Political cadres were expected to study technology to improve their ability to lead politically, technical and military cadres were expected to study politics, and both were to work alongside older revolutionaries who were deeply imbued with the revolution's spiritual values. On balance, however, a slightly greater degree of importance was attached to development of technical cadres with the hope that they would remain politically "steadfast."[58]

In anticipation of the stress further modernization and regularization would place on the existing political apparatus, new guidelines were issued on Party organization in the army.[59] The functional divisions of the army that caused the most concern were obvious in the distribution of Party membership among the various parts of the army by Lt. Gen. Song Lao, who as head of the General Political Directorate has primary responsibility to implement the new regulations:

> The proportion of Party members in the modern technical services and branches must be larger than in the other units in order that there may be close, firm party leadership. The proportion of Party members in the agencies must be higher than in the units because the agencies are the elements which directly help guide and command the organizations in implementing Party leadership . . . [60]

The Party was not immediately able to satisfy these requirements, however. "The need for political cadres is very large but the source of these cadres has not been developed to any great extent"; cadre reserves had been depleted by the war and the modernization program outstripped capacities to prepare new ones.[61] Moreover, the rich experience and "political education by practice" that many Party members had received during the war was considered inadequate for the demands that modernization in future would make on them. Successful completion of formal studies would be adhered to as the basic criterion of appointment and promotion of political cadres.[62]

Although the intensification of Party-building in the army in 1972 was part of a continuing modernization program, it also had direct application to and was affected by temporary circumstances arising from the ferocity of the war in both the North and South during that year. The deployment of all but one division outside the DRV and the December bombing strained manpower reserves in the Party as well as the army, and Party cadres were of necessity recruited or promoted without adequate training or experience. This problem was most marked at the company level, where young Party cadres were said to have "high revolutionary spirit" but lacked leadership capabilities.[63] The war also prevented effective implementation of routine training and development. Party chapters (chi bô), through which most Party instructional activities are conducted, "made excuses about how busy they were and did not pay enough attention to education and training of Party members during combat or emergencies . . . "[64] Prolonged deployment in conventional combat reduced the quality of Party cadres and eroded the effectiveness of Party leadership, and it stimulated demand for modernization and regularization which created doubt as to the relevance of political work. This circular relationship between intense combat, modernization and Party-building had been observed in the past, and the issuance of guidelines on Party organization in the army two months after the beginning of the Spring Offensive doubtless was timed to counteract negative side effects of this, "the largest and most comprehensive strategic offensive ever opened on the battlefield" and to prepare the army for the political settlement then being negotiated. But because of the expectation that the war would become even more conventional and "modern," requiring at some point the destruction of large, well-armed ARVN units,[65] the guidelines and Party-building programs also were a basic element in the long-term construction of the army.

Obviously, an effective Party presence in the army was highly valued and there was no intention of relieving the army of its political obligations to allow it to focus more assiduously on modernization. The belief that Party political work enhances technical and conventional combat competence by providing properly directed motivation is too deeply rooted and the propriety of Party leadership too widely respected to permit renegotiation of basic principles. Also, the PAVN continues to operate in areas and employ tactics which create need for political liaison and instruction. However, it was implicit that accelerated modernization was expected to promote preoccupation with technical competence, narrow definitions of professionalism, and "purely military points of view." The campaign to strengthen Party organization in the army thus testified to the maturation of the PAVN as a modern, conventional, bureaucratized armed force and the gradual relegation of its guerrilla origins to history, myth and tradition.

A Note on the Army and the Paris Agreements

Since the Paris Agreements signified a strategic if partial victory that removed American forces from the battlefield and altered the PAVN's responsibilities, repercussions in the army and in DRV political processes may be expected. On the one hand, American withdrawal could be interpreted as permitting a quick military solution to the unification problem prior or parallel to reconstruction in the North; on the other hand, political conditions in the South and the devastation of the North were reasons for restraint, rebuilding, and consolidation. Evidence of the Agreements' impact on the army's internal affairs and role in the post-Paris period is ambiguous, but some general patterns are discernible.

The Agreements and subsequent army assignments appear to have received a mixed reception in the military. According to an authoritative military commentator writing in December 1973 under the pseudonym of "Chien Thang" (Victory), "expeditious and continuous political education" had been necessary to bring about a realization in the armed forces that a great victory had been achieved and to promote awareness of "subsequent tasks, favorable conditions and difficulties . . . " Development of the "revolutionary offensive spirit" and criticism of "erroneous ideas" were needed to "overcome all manifestations of negativism and self-complacency."[66] Such remarks suggest that the Agreements created apathy, both in the sense that they seemed to justify relaxation and that the terms did not satisfy those who felt they had sacrificed most for it.

Aside from the Agreements themselves, there evidently was chagrin over the emphasis given to economic reconstruction and the army's role in it while the battlefield situation was unresolved. At the National Assembly meeting in February 1974, only Le Thanh Nghi's long report on the economy was reproduced in the press. The report of the Ministry of Defense was not even discussed in the army newspaper. In speeches to military units at Tet, both Le Duan and Truong Chinh described the army's role in the current phase only in terms of training, participation in economic construction, assistance to the people in recovering their means of livelihood and reducing the burden of garrisoned forces on the civilian economy.[67] Underscoring the economic task, Le Duan in a speech before the Vietnam Trades Union Congress observed argumentatively that the war had destroyed all economic progress previously achieved and that postponement of large-scale socialist construction would endanger the future of socialism itself; this speech was reproduced in full in the monthly journal of the General Political Directorate in the army.[68] In the spring of 1974, a special unit to assist in economic reconstruction was created for the first time in Hanoi.[69] Military leaders might be irritated by assignment of their units to economic work, which could lead to military opposition to the overall policy of reconstruction.

The one value the military leadership clearly seeks to protect at all costs is the modernization program, specifically training in tactics which combine different branches and services in large operations and acquisition, use, and maintenance of sophisticated weapons.[c] When Le Thanh Nghi's economic report appeared in the army journal, it was followed on the next page by an article (by Tran Sam, the specialist on foreign military assistance) which applauded the role of modern military science and technology in the war against the United States and argued for a small but technologically proficient force.[70] The modernization program is not in dispute, but rather the army's insistence on it and the preference for technical quality and selectivity of recruitment are suggestive of the PAVN's maturation as an occupational group with increasingly professional interests and values. These patterns are not necessarily evidence of "factionalism" in the leadership or of disabling internal problems, but they do indicate an accumulation of commitments throughout the political system, with the army often in the lead, to technocratic modes of development.

---

[c]This program is essential to the defense of "points" and mounting of strategic offensives that have come to characterize clashes between the PAVN and ARVN.

Conclusion

Since its founding in 1944, the PAVN has evolved from a simple organization composed entirely of infantry performing a variety of civil as well as military tasks, and assimilated to civilian society, into a complex organization with many functionally-specific units capable of operating without direct civilian support. At each stage of this process, the army's character has been determined by the exigencies of the social environment and the political prerequisites of Party goals. The Resistance placed a premium on building an armed force from the most meager of human and material resources, hence upon integration with the population and participation by all social classes; therefore political work emphasized education, civilian mobilization, and recruitment irrespective of class origins. After 1954, the need to maintain military loyalty and discipline during revolutionary reforms in society at large and to fulfill promises to the "worker-peasant" class required intensified political education parallel to enforcement of class criteria in recruitment and promotion of cadres. Subsequently, modernization, professionalization, and occupational separatism fostered ideologically unpalatable values and behavioral traits. These problems have required that political work be focused still more exclusively on the internal affairs of the army and on Party organization in it. All of these elements have been present in all stages, but the distribution of emphasis has shifted in accordance, first, with demands of the social environment and, second, with structural and material changes in the army itself. At present, since the proportion of "worker-peasant cadres" has grown large under an entire generation of Party rule[71] and the basic revolutionary reforms of society have been accomplished, the main source of political problems in the army is modernization. While these problems have been confined to the military, they may have consequences for the army's future political role. The army has become sufficiently distinctive in its values and interests and coherent as a profession to advance effectively a "military viewpoint" in the political process.

In view of this potential, it is significant that PAVN commanders have not seriously challenged political requirements and that the army has not become a setting or source of political upheaval.[d] Compromise and incrementalism have been the hallmarks of the PAVN's political role, and the reasons for this are fairly clear. The top military leadership since the earliest days of the Revolution has been well integrated into the political process: two officers are members of the Political Bureau, nine are Central Committee members and eight are alternates. Dissidence has been muted further by the constancy and intensity of

---

[d]Of course dissension exists and disputes have occurred, but the DRV has not had such contests of power as have occurred in other Communist systems and no member of the Chiefs-of-Staff or Ministry of Defense has ever been purged or demoted. I am assuming there are no "secret army papers" similar to those of the PLA that might lead to a different conclusion, and this is a reasonable assumption given the greater opportunities during the war for such evidence to come to light.

external threat. Unity in the face of adversity is strengthened by the popular support and stability of the government and by the tremendous disparity of resources created by American intervention and support for the RVN. According to estimates of the Defense Intelligence Agency, between 1966 and 1973 the United States spent twenty-nine times as much on the war as the DRV received in aid from the USSR and China,[72] and the ARVN still has a four-to-one advantage in number of field guns.[73] Military doctrine and tactics designed to "use weakness to defeat strength" therefore have a degree of authority they otherwise might not have had, and arguments that they are the only course open to the DRV short of surrender are persuasive (though this factor recedes as the PAVN achieves parity with the ARVN).[74] Moreover, in comparison with China's PLA, fractionalization and sharp conflict are less likely to occur because of Vietnam's small scale. Whereas the PLA is subdivided into five field armies which are the basis of competition for personnel assignments and influence on policy,[75] the PAVN has a unified structure which obstructs development of independent bases of power in the army and prevents its internal politics from being injected into the national political process. More important, the state and Party are not undermined by regional pulls to such an extent as in larger systems, consequently there is less need for the kind of order that the PLA has been called upon to provide in China. Finally, the DRV's military doctrine does not postulate mutually exclusive methods of waging war but seeks to combine all of them in a synthesis of great subtlety and flexibility. The objective of policymakers always has been to do more of everything, so that no point of view has ever been completely excluded and no interest completely frustrated. This framework has endured not only because of tradition but also because it has been the most practical approach to the DRV's defense problems. Consequently, the sense of collective endeavor and habituation to low-key conflict resolution is strong.

Notes

1. "VPA," for Vietnam People's Army, also is an acceptable translation of the Vietnamese, *Quan doi Nhan dan Viet-nam.* "North Vietnamese Army (NVA)" is not a translation of any term used in the DRV but rather an attempt, in which journalists and common usage unfortunately have acquiesced, to label organizations in a way consistent with official American and Saigon interpretations of the war.

2. *Ten Years of Fighting and Building of the Vietnamese People's Army* (Hanoi: Foreign Languages Publishing House, 1955), pp. 7-8, 15.

3. "Decision of the Revolutionary Military Conference of North Viet-Nam Held from April 15 to 20, 1945," *Breaking Our Chains: Documents of the Vietnamese Revolution of August 1945* (Hanoi: Foreign Languages Publishing House, 1960), p. 35.

4. "Resolutions of the Viet Minh Conference Held on June 4, 1945," *Breaking Our Chains: Documents of the Vietnamese Revolution of August 1945* (Hanoi: Foreign Language Publishing House, 1960), p. 55.

5. "Decisions of the Revolutionary Military Conference," p. 34.

6. *Chinh tri vien trong Quan doi* (Hanoi?: Moi, 1945?). There was no publication date on the copy of this eighty-page booklet at the Bibliotheque Nationale in Paris since the cover was lost and there was no date on its title page, but the approximate date of writing can be established by internal evidence, especially in the discussion of the balance of Vichy, Gaullist and Japanese forces in Indochina and the footnote on page 56.

7. Ibid., p. 73.

8. Ibid., pp. 67-68.

9. Ibid., p. 73.

10. Decrees on military ranks (116/SL of January 25, 1948 and 131/SL of February 15, 1948) are cited in article 47 of the 1958 regulations on officers' service. *Quan doi Nhan dan*, 443 (May 2-5, 1958), p. 3.

11. PAVN officers who fought in the Resistance and who were interviewed in 1972-73 by the author in Saigon all agree on the above points. These interviews, conducted while the author was in Vietnam as a Ford Foundation Southeast Asia Research Associate, are collected in three volumes as *Interviews with PAVN and LDP Defectors: Officers, Men and Political Cadres*, Morris Library, Southern Illinois University. In particular, see interviews I, a captain and battalion commander who said political officers during the Resistance were merely "helpers," pp. 4-5; and VII, an assistant zone political officer and colonel who viewed the matter from the perspective of one who was alternately a military commander and political officer in the Resistance, pp. 28-29. (Hereinafter cited as *Interviews.*)

12. Ibid., VII, p. 31.

13. Ibid., VII, pp. 14-15.

14. Ibid., I, pp. 3, 8-9.

15. Ibid., VII, p. 30.

16. Van Tao, "Qua trinh phat trien cua giai cap cong nhan Viet-nam trong Cach mang xa hoi chu nghia" (Developmental Process of the Vietnamese Working Class in the Socialist Revolution), *Nghien cuu Lich su*, no. 145 (July-August 1972), p. 38.

17. *Interviews*, i, pp. 7, 10-11; VII, p. 23.

18. Ibid., I, pp. 10-11; VII, pp. 17-19. Interviewees all mentioned the delicacy and caution with which the weeding and culling process was conducted.

19. Van Tao, "Qua trinh phat."

20. For an analysis of historical continuities in Vietnamese military thought, see Georges Boudarel, "Essai sur la pensée militaire vietnamienne," *Tradition et Revolution au Vietnam*, edited by Jean Chesneaux, Georges Boudarel, and Daniel Hemery (Paris: Editions anthropos, 1971), pp. 460-95. A brief but illuminating introduction also is provided by Boudarel to General Giap's *Banner*

of People's War, The Party's Military Line (New York: Praeger Publisher's 1970), pp. xi-xxvi.

21. For a colorful presentation of the Vietnamese perception of the strength to be drawn from weakness, see Nguyen Khac Vien, "La lecon de judo," *Experiences vietnaminennes* (Paris: Editions sociales, 1970), pp. 11-14.

22. Van Tien Dung, "Ban ve nhung kinh nghiem xay-dung luc-luong vu-trang cach-mang cua Dang ta" (On Experiences in Building the Revolutionary Armed Strength of Our Party), *Hoc Tap* (September 1964), p. 9.

23. "Luat qui dinh che do phuc vu cua si quan quan doi nhan dan Vietnam," *Quan doi Nhan dan*, 443 (May 2-5, 1958), p. 3.

24. Adopted February 8, 1955. *Current Background*, no. 312 (Hong Kong: American Consulate General, February 15, 1955). Since the Chinese system was based on that of the Soviet Union, it is impossible and irrelevant to determine which of these models the Vietnamese drew upon.

25. "Che do phuc vu cua Si quan Quan doi quy dinh ro nghia vua cua si quan trong thoi binh va thoi chien," *Nhan Dan*, 1, 515 (May 6, 1958), p. 1.

26. "Duong loi quan su Mac-sit la ngon co chien thang cua quan doi ta" (The Party's Marxist Military Line is the Banner of Victory of Our Army), *Quan doi Nhan Dan*, special issue and no. 519 (December 22 and 23, 1958).

27. Those recruited early in the Resistance during the height of the national front policy, those recruited later under preferential class criteria, and the newest cadres recruited since Geneva. On the concept of military generations, see William V. Whitson, *The Chinese High Command* (New York: Praeger Publishers, 1972), pp. 416-35.

28. In particular see Lt. Gen Hoang Van Thai, Assistant Chief of Staff, *Quan doi Nhan dan* (26′ November 1959), *Hoc Tap* (December 1960), and *Quan doi Nhan dan* (August 20, 1963).

29. See the Resolution of the Ninth Conference, "World Situation and Our Party's International Mission," *Viet-Nam Documents and Research Notes*, no. 98 (Saigon: U.S. Mission, 1971); and Le Duan's speech, "Some Questions Concerning the International Tasks of Our Party" (Peking: Foreign Languages Press, 1964).

30. The consistent advocacy earlier by staff officers such as Hoang Van Thai, *supra* fn. 30, of greater professionalism and the tenor of the Ninth Conference Resolution suggest that such protests indeed were raised, as did criticism after the basic decisions were made of those who continued to "praise and worship the role of weapons" (Song Hao, *Hoc Tap*, December 1964).

31. *Quan doi Nhan dan* (May 28, 1964).

32. *Quan doi Nhan dan* (May 26, 1964).

33. Tran Quy Hai, "May y kien ve van de chi bo lanh dao chuyen mon" (Some Ideas about the Specialized Technical Leadership Cells), *Hoc Tap* (April 1964), pp. 40-44.

34. A more detailed analysis is presented in David W.P. Elliott, "NLF-DRV

Strategy and the 1972 Spring Offensive," International Relations of East Asia Project Interim Report, no. 4 (Ithaca: Cornell University International Relations of East Asia Project, 1974).

35. See "Nhung that bai to lon cua de quoc My trong chien tranh xam luoc Viet Nam" (The Great Defeats of the American Imperialists in the War of Aggression in Vietnam) *Tuyen Huan* 11-12 (Nov.-Dec. 1972), pp. 62-70.

36. Huy Nghiem, "Van de 'ba vung chien luoc' trong chien tranh cach mang mien nam" (The Problem of the 'Three Strategic Regions' in the Revolutionary War in the Sourt), *Tuyen Huan*, 11-12 (Nov.-Dec. 1972), pp. 33-36.

37. Dinh Tuc, "Ba thu quan voi nhieu cach danh phong phu" (Three Types of Forces with Many Rich Methods of Attack), *Tuyen Huan*, 11-12 (Nov.-Dec. 1972), pp. 37-40.

38. Patrick J. McGarvey, *Visions of Victory: Selected Vietnamese Communist Military Writings, 1964-1968* (Stanford: Hoover Institution Press, 1969).

39. *Interviews*, I, pp. 36-37.

40. A large minority of Party cadres, even in the South where support for armed struggle seems to have been strongest, had long had misgivings about confronting American firepower, according to a former member of the Tay Ninh province Party committee. See Jeffrey Race, interview with Vo Van An (Chicago: Center for Research Libraries, 1968), p. 34. The colonel and assistant zone political officer cited earlier, who defected in 1968, held a grudge against Thanh and called his line boastful babbling. *Interviews*, VII, pp. 8-10. A battalion commander with six years in combat before his defection in December 1972, however, maintained that motivated men were superior to any amount or kind of weapons. Ibid., I, Passim. All former officers interviewed were aware of the central issue and the main protagonists. In addition, a senior captain who had served in staff headquarters of Military Region V (mainly northern provinces of the RVN) claimed that "many" generals who held field command in the South during this period "demanded" material improvements and changes in tactics. A leading member of this group was Maj. Gen. Nguyen Don, who was commander and Party secretary in MRV from 1962 to 1967, when he returned to Hanoi to become Vice-Minister of National Defense, a Deputy Chief of Staff, and to be elected to the Fourth National Assembly from Nghe An province. *Interviews*, II, p. 80.

41. *Interviews*, I, pp. 41, 46.

42. Letter from Le Duan, March 1966, marked "absolute secret," *Working Paper on the North Vietnamese Role in the War in South Vietnam: Captured Documents and Interrogation Reports* (U.S. Dept. of State, May 1968), Item 302, p. 16. Emphasis in original.

43. Huy Nghiem, "Vande 'ba vung chien luoc'," pp. 34-36.

44. *Interviews*, II, p. 81.

45. *COSVN Resolution No. 9, July 1969* (Saigon: U.S. Mission, undated), p. 9.

46. Vo Nguyen Giap, "The Party's Military Line is the Ever-Victorious Banner of People's War in Our Country," *Viet-Nam Documents*, no. 70.

47. Van Tien Dung, "Under the Party's Banner, Viet-Nam's Military Art Has Constantly Developed and Triumphed," *Viet-Nam Documents*, no. 71, p. 15.

48. "Party Leadership is the Cause of the Growth and Victories of Our Army," *Viet-Nam Documents*, no. 72.

49. General Giap, *Banner of People's War, The Party's Military Line* (New York: Praeger Publishers, 1970), p. 20.

50. Ibid., p. 26.

51. *Vu trang guan chung cach mang xay dung quan doi nhan dan* (Arm the Revolutionary Masses and Build the People's Army), (Hanoi: Su That, 1972). This work first appeared in the form of articles published serially in various periodicals beginning in December 1971. Giap undoubtedly had completed most of the book by that time. Part IV, concerning the modernization and regularization of the armed forces, probably was revised or written in the spring of 1972.

52. Ibid., p. 218.

53. Ibid., p. 209.

54. Ibid., pp. 209-10.

55. Ibid., pp. 211-12.

56. Ibid., p. 211.

57. Ibid., pp. 214-15. Discipline was one of the few weak points specifically cited. Although the PAVN undoubtedly has the best discipline of any army in Southeast Asia, frequent references to the unruliness of recruits accustomed to the work habits of "small-scale production" in "a backward agrarian country" identify the source and nature of problems considered to be regrettable hindrances of the DRV's social, economic, and military progress.

58. These aspects of cadre policy in the army were identical to themes of the "New Cadre Policy" which appeared in 1973 to promote economic reconstruction. See William S. Turley, "The Democratic Republic of Vienam and the 'Third Stage' of the Revolution," *Asian Survey* 14, 1 (January 1974): 83-85. DRV development policies strive for uniformity of procedure in all institutions and usually are implemented in a carefully orchestrated fashion. This pattern of organizational development is of course one result of central planning, but it also indicates the stability of consensus on basic values and the absence of autonomy for any single institution aside from the Party.

59. "To chuc, nhiem vu, nguyen tac lanh dao va che do cong tac dang uy" (Organization, Functions, Leadership Principles and Systems of Party Committee Work), *Quan doi Nhan dan* (June 20-22, 1972). To my knowledge the regulations on Party organization in the army had never before been published in their entirety as a single document, although decrees and commentary in the press conveyed essential information on the system to a fairly broad audience. Comparison with particular details of past practice is difficult. One interesting aspect of the 1972 guidelines was their complete non-use of the terms "political

officer" and "military commander," which are nonetheless the terms used in everyday discourse, and their replacement by "responsible political and military cadres" (cán bô phu trách quân chính).

60. Song Hao, "Dang vung manh nhan to quyet dinh su truong thanh va chien thang cua quan doi" (A Strong Party Is a Decisive Factor in the Maturation and Victory of the Army), *Tap chi Quan doi Nhan dan*, 184 (February 1972).

61. Tran Nguyen Phi, "Ta Ngan Military Zone Builds and Trains Cadres," *Tap chi Quan doi Nhan dan* (January 1973).

62. Editorial, *Quan doi Nhan dan* (April 9, 1973). This may be a matter of dispute. Tran Nguyen Phi, "Ta Ngan Military Zone," held the practical experience of cadres who had risen through the ranks in particularly high esteem. Of these two sources, however, the QDND editorial is the more authoritative.

63. Editorial, *Quan doi Nhan dan* (June 16, 1973), p. 1.

64. Editorial, *Quan doi Nhan dan* (April 9, 1973), p. 1.

65. A directive on political reorientation and training of Party cadres and dated February 5, 1974 conceded that "The enemy temporarily has the upper hand" and took note of the ARVN's large size and "abundant equipment." *Viet-Nam Documents* no. 117, p. 7. Although the document predicted that American aid to the ARVN would continue to decline with effect on its strength, the PAVN is explicitly described in the DRV press as preparing for positional and for high-mobility tactics, which suggests what forms the "annihilating blows" will take in future, e.g., Le Ngoc Ha, "Stepping up Conventional Training to Heighten the Level of Combat Coordination Among Various Branches," *Tap chi Quan doi Nhan dan* (April 1973), pp. 36-44, 52.

66. "Heighten Revolutionary Struggle," serialized in *Quan doi Nhan dan* (November 26-December 7, 1973). *Viet-Nam Documents*, no. 116, pp. 32, 34, 37.

67. *Quan doi Nhan dan* (29 and 31 January 1974), 4.

68. *Tap chi Quan doi Nhan dan* (March 1974), pp. 1-19.

69. Ha Van Xa and To Cong Dinh, *Hanoi Moi* (June 13, 1974), p. 1.

70. "Nang cao trinh do khoa hoc—ky thuat cua can bo, gop phan tang cuong suc manh chien dau cua quan doi ta" (Raise the Scientific and Technical Level of Cadres, Contribute to the Combat Strength of Our Army), *Tap chi Quan doi Nhan dan* (February 1974), pp. 1-18. Even military historians seek justification in the tenth to eighteenth centuries for a compact, technologically advanced, functionally-specific armed force of selected, highly-trained men. Nguyen Ngoc, "Tim hieu mot so tu tuong tien bo trong xay dung quan doi cua to tien ta" (Seeking Progressive Ideas in Building the Armies of Our Ancestors), *Tap chi Quan doi Nhan dan* (January 1974), pp. 67-73.

71. The proportion of worker-peasant cadres in the army continues to grow under preferential recruitment and education policies, and most recently large numbers of these elements were promoted from reserve forces to fill vacancies in

the cadre ranks of the regular army created by the 1972 offensive. Such deliberate efforts to enable worker-peasants to "undertake greater responsibilities" indicate that non-worker-peasant cadres still are relied upon to some extent. Tran Nguyen Phi, "Ta Ngan Military Zone."

72. Reported by Representative Les Aspin in a press release (Washington, D.C., June 3, 1974).

73. Senate Committee on Foreign Relations, Staff Report, "Vietnam: May 1974" (August 5, 1974), p. 6.

74. PAVN and PLAF forces now have as many tanks as the ARVN, the smaller number of field guns is compensated by longer range, SA-7 anti-aircraft batteries which have been introduced on the Cambodian border and in ARVN MR III near Saigon, and an improved road network has given the PAVN excellent interior lines of communication for the first time in the war and enables the DRV to move men and supplies into the South four times faster than before. "Their overall effect is to diminish significantly the logistical advantage which the South enjoyed in the past . . . " Ibid., pp. 5-7.

75. Whitson, *The Chinese High Command*, pp. 498-517.

7

Political Integration in North Vietnam: The Cooperativization Period

David W.P. Elliott

Theories of Political Development and the DRV Model

Over a decade of devastating warfare and preoccupation with the military potential of North Vietnam have largely obscured the constructive efforts of the DRV regime to reintegrate a polity shattered by colonial rule. Heavy U.S. involvement with South Vietnam resulted in an intensive but unsuccessful attempt to find a model of political development which would bring some order into a chaotic political environment and provide a justification for the heavy U.S. commitment in an area only marginally connected with its national security needs. The crowning irony of this quest is that one of the most impressive models of political development in Asia was near at hand. As an a priori villain in the U.S. view of the "Asian Drama," however, North Vietnam was not considered a suitable model for either emulation or academic analysis.

This prejudgment is reflected in the writings of most American developmental theorists, who either ignore the North Vietnamese case or relegate it to a general category of totalitarian "mobilization" regimes. Yet by using the analytic framework of one of the foremost theorists in this field, Samuel Huntington, a strong case can be made for considering the DRV as a highly successful model of political development. The DRV case demonstrates the usefulness of Huntington's analytic scheme and also raises some problems inherent in the Huntington approach.

As Huntington has noted, the most basic element in political modernization is a widespread participation by social groups in politics beyond the village and town level.[1] In this view, the key to political development is the creation of effective political institutions capable of absorbing the newly mobilized "participants" in the political system. It is important that those institutions be adaptable rather than rigid, complex rather than simple, and relatively autonomous from the interests of particular social groups. Huntington also points to the importance of the linkages between the urban leadership and the peasantry, and concludes that the way in which this relationship evolves has a decisive impact on the shaping of the political future of developing countries.

This approach is a valuable aid in analyzing the struggle of the DRV to modernize, because it focuses on two critical and related concepts: (1) the relationship between political participation and political institutionalization, and (2) linkages between urban and rural areas—in other words, political integration. There are, however, several important deficiencies in the Huntington theory, which are revealed by its application to the specific problems and history of the DRV. The most important shortcoming is that this approach along with most other current theories of political development does not explore at length the causes for the rapid expansion in political participation, whether they are internally or externally generated, and what the consequences of different causal factors on political institutionalization might be.[2] The fact that the DRV "captured" the Nationalist movement and came to power as the victors in a prolonged anticolonial war, while the nucleus of the Saigon government was largely made up of the *collaborateur* elite is of vital importance in understanding the relative degree of success each leadership had in integrating city and countryside, and channeling political participation toward constructive ends.

Another deficiency of the Huntington analytic framework is its over-concentration on the role of the political party as the major instrument of political integration, and the assumption that "in one party states, the modernizing elite typically attempts to impose controls upon the peasantry and to permit them to become politically active only insofar as they accept the modernizing values of the political elite."[3] North Vietnam's cooperativization program had the political goal of reconstituting local communities which had been disrupted by the impact of the colonial rule. It was recognized that cooperativization could not be an effective program of economic development unless it enlisted the full participation of North Vietnam's peasantry. This could not be done by mobilization efforts imposed from above or by administrative fiat of a small party elite representing less than 2 percent of the rural population.

Prior to the advent of colonial rule, some 30 percent of North Vietnam's land was owned communally by the village. French rule was accompanied by a growing commercialization of agriculture and concentration of land in the hands of a few owners. By 1930, 2 percent of the rural population owned 40 percent of the land. The Vietnamese emperor was forced to concede his right to dispose of the land to the French administration, which parcelled out land abandoned by peasants fleeing the colonial armies to French *colons* or Vietnamese collaborators. While allocation of communal lands had never been done in the scrupulously impartial welfare fashion that the ideal prescribed, during the colonial occupation these lands were alienated from the village community and transformed into private property.

It was not, therefore, private ownership of land that represented the traditional ideal, but equality of access to it. From an economic point of view, cooperativization was considered an indispensible step toward rationalizing the utilization of North Vietnam's scarce natural resources, of providing effective technical inputs into agriculture, and accumulating a surplus to fund the state economic plans. This would break the cycle of poverty by building an industrial base that could be applied to raising agricultural productivity. The political aim was to restore a sense of security and dignity to the peasantry, a sense of community in the villages and hamlets of the countryside, and an outlet for peasant initiative that would complement these goals.

Absolute equality in the rural economic domain was never a goal of the DRV leadership. It was recognized that failure to relate rewards and performance would have adverse effects on production, while the attempt to enforce an absolutely egalitarian system of distribution was beyond the administrative capacity of Party, state, and local institutions. Cooperativization was an attempt to establish a framework for reconciling the interests of the individual, the community, and the state. Individuals would be guaranteed equal access to the "factors of production" (land, tools, water pumps, credit, seed, and fertilizer) but would receive an income based on their actual contribution to production. This involved a welfare floor, or guaranteed minimum income, supplemented by a second division of the cooperative's production based on a complicated work point measurement of labor performed. This, in turn, was augmented by private plots which account for approximately half of peasant income.[a] Once established, the cooperative would be run by its members, who would devise production plans with general guidelines from above and, most importantly, determine the criteria for distributing cooperative income. Party leadership was directed toward regulating the smooth functioning of this system. Ironically, it was the Party that was called upon to protect the interests of the minority of higher income peasants from the egalitarian demands of the majority of cooperative members. Cooperativization provided a formula for reconciling individual interests and equality by establishing a structured process of political participation which allows the individual to influence decisions made about the matters which most directly concern him in his daily life, in Huntington's terms "institutionalizing participation."

"The achievement of political community in a modernizing society," says Huntington, "involves both the 'horizontal' integration of communal groups and the 'vertical' assimilation of social and economic class."[4] He views the political party as the primary instrument of this integration, and acknowledges that parties emerging from a prolonged revolution have a valuable "inheritance from the past" (he eschews the terms "legitimacy") but concludes that while it can "coast for a while on its inheritance from the past" a monolithic party will ultimately find it difficult to retain its vitality in the absence of political competition. Huntington is generally critical of one-party systems, since they made their leaders "less sensitive to the needs to expand and organize participation in the system." The one-party system also "multiplies and diversifies the groups seeking to participate in the system."[5]

---

[a]Throughout the period under discussion, income from private production comprised between 40 and 60 percent of peasant income, while the cooperative sector provided the rest.

The North Vietnamese leaders, however, have shown considerable sensitivity to the question of political participation, and they have devoted great energy to finding ways of integrating groups into the framework of the DRV political system. The agricultural cooperatives in North Vietnam are not state organizations or Party instruments for mobilizing an inert peasantry. They are local organizations woven out of the economic and social networks of village communities. Perhaps the best characterization of the organizational principles of the cooperatives is the example of the TVA which, "constantly searched for, defined and refined a unifying purpose that could be understood by all participants and demonstrated by day-to-day leadership," while it "sought constantly to decentralize decision making and action into the smallest possible units of activities and human energies."[6]

The Revolutionary Aftermath—Problems
of Integration

During the colonial period, class differences were intensified and social antagonisms sharpened. The Resistance War further exacerbated social tensions by deepening the split between the *collaborateurs* and the revolutionaries. French manipulation of religious and ethnic minorities further fragmented the social fabric of the constituent parts of the future Democratic Republic of Vietnam. Overall French strategy was to erode the Vietminh united front by fostering separatism, regionalism, and religious and ethnic particularism.

This policy had some success, particularly among the Catholic minority. Moreover, the long period of division between French and Vietminh controlled areas created serious problems of political integration for the DRV after 1954. These problems were not limited to the reintegration of city and countryside, but also involved the absorption of some French controlled rural areas into the framework of the new state.

Paradoxically, the legacy of French control offered some advantages in integrating these areas into the post-liberation DRV framework precisely because the Vietminh united front had not been allowed to develop, and the revolutionary movement in these provinces was not firmly entrenched among a broad cross-section of the population. In strong Vietminh resistance bases, on the other hand, the revolutionary movement included patriotic landlords and other elements whose devotion to the revolution flagged when it was transformed from an independence movement to a social revolution. Many cadres with meritorious service in the resistance fell victims to the land reform movement in the old resistance areas. Despite the reinstatement of most of these cadres in the following "Rectification of Errors" campaign, the Land Reform had caused even more serious problems in the traditional areas of Vietminh strength than in the former French-occupied zones.

All these problems of political integration faced the DRV leadership as they embarked on a comprehensive program of collectivization of agriculture—an indispensable step along the road to socialism. A major problem of political integration had already had an important impact on cooperativization. In the hope that the Geneva Accords would be implemented, the DRV had delayed moving from land reform to cooperativization, fearing that the social and political differences between North and South Vietnam would become increasingly more difficult to bridge when unification came. When it became apparent that the Geneva Accords would not be implemented, North Vietnam moved cautiously toward cooperativization, setting up a three-year transitional plan (1958-60) to lay the groundwork for a comprehensive five-year state program of socialist construction (1961-65).

A growing realization that delaying cooperativization would result in increasing disparities in income and welfare led the DRV to accelerate the move toward cooperativization in early 1959. In a report to the National Assembly in 1959, Truong Chinh reported that, "Capitalist tendencies appeared relatively strongly in the rectification of errors period, that is from late 1956 to the end of 1957."[7] The reemergence of these "capitalist tendencies," if left unchecked, would lead to a return to the class divisions that had been an important cause of the revolution. Cooperativization was a necessary step to check this disintegration process.

On a broader social scale, cooperativization was designed to serve as an instrument of political integration by revitalizing the unity of the basic social groupings in Vietnam—the neighborhood, the hamlet, and the village. The colonial period had intensified a split between ordinary villagers and the village elite that had been developing during the Nguyen dynasty.[8] Village unity, symbolically expressed by the communal house (the dinh) and the participation in village rites had been dissipated by the hardening of class antagonisms as inequality in land ownership grew, and political power gravitated to the *collaborateur* notables, representing the French administration and protecting their own interests rather than those of the village. In the phrase of a French scholar, Vietnamese society was "thrown off balance" by the impact of colonial rule.[9]

In many ways an elitist pattern of leadership was preserved during the Resistance—though directed toward quite different goals. The hierarchical requisites of clandestine organization meant that the ordinary villager was still subject to the dictates of an elite leadership. Generally speaking, the rural populace saw the necessity of this system, and supported its goals. Most important, the revolutionary movement revived participation in village activities and solidarity among the peasants that had been conspicuously lacking during the French period.

Still this participation, though generally voluntary, was instrumental—participation as a cog in the revolutionary machine, whose goals demanded the rejection of immediate self-interest for the "consumatory" goal of national independence. The revolutionary leadership acted on behalf of the people, but not always "for the people," since revolutionary action by definition involved considerable short-term sacrifice for long-term interests. Although instrumental participation was compatible with the Resistance struggle, it was not suitable for the post-Liberation period.

Despite its recognized adverse consequences, the Land Reform was the first step in the transition from instrumental participation to what might be called community participation. Whereas the instrumental participation of the Resistance period was national in scope, the integrative problem of the post-1954 period was the linkage of national and community interests. Local interests would clearly not be served by perpetration of an economic and political structure which concentrated power and wealth in the hands of a local elite. Land reform was a form of direct political participation that had an immediate impact on the local community.[b]

Excesses committed during the Land Reform campaign also had a negative impact on political participation. Many Resistance cadres were attacked during this period and removed from power. Some subsequently refused preferred reinstatement during the Rectification of Errors campaign. This object lesson may have had a dampening effect on potential political activists, particularly since the youths who had been promoted during the high tide of the Land Reform for their activist zeal were, in many cases, placed in more modest positions later on. Nonetheless a major lesson had been learned in North Vietnam's villages; that active community participation could break the grip of elitist rule in local communities. This served also as a cautionary note to cadres who became "commandist," rested on achievements of the Resistance period, and hoped to obtain rewards of position and honor in a traditional sense for their exploits. And despite the upheavals of the land reform period older cadres remained in the majority. In 1959, it was found that "the vast majority of Party members and cadres are people who have joined the Party for ten years or more, and are over thirty years old. Party members under twenty five are very few."[10]

Revolution inevitably entailed social dissonance. Class, ethnic, religious, and generational conflicts were the legacy of an extended colonial occupation and a protracted revolution. Moreover, the problem of finding new modes of social and political participation for women had been intensified by the widespread participation of women in the revolution. Cooperativization had to deal with these issues as well as the ownership of the means of production. In many ways,

---

[b]It is clear from accounts of the Land Reform that participation in the denunciations of the land reform was hesitant and tentative at first, and that excesses at the height of the campaign created a backlash of sympathy for the victims. Nonetheless, most villagers clearly subscribed to the goals of the campaign, and it was the Land Reform that transformed political participation from patriotic national sacrifices to an active restructuring of the local community. It was this latter aspect of participation that was unprecedented in Vietnamese history.

the social impact of cooperativization was more important than its economic impact.

Cooperativization and the Task of Social Integration

The political system that the DRV set out to construct as it embarked on a program of agricultural cooperativization was a combination of three elements; (1) highly centralized state institutions, (2) local communities based on mutual social and economic interests, and (3) the Party which linked the two. While the Party played a key role at all levels, its linkage role most clearly sets it apart from the other sectors of the political system.

Cooperativization was based not on a party-led attempt to impose an institutional structure on an inert society, but an attempt to revitalize a system of community action in the countryside. It was clearly recognized from the outset that any system not based on the interests of the local community would founder in "bureaucratism" and "commandism." The challenge faced by the DRV was not only how to use the Party to mobilize the pesantry for a major social and economic transformation, but how to create a set of institutions and procedures that would elicit self-motivated participation.

Even as late as 1963, Party membership in many provinces constituted a mere 1-2 percent of the population, and in some provinces it was less than 1 percent.[11] Clearly a system that relied on the Party as the sole agent of mobilization in the rural areas would be doomed to failure. Political integration required harmonizing individual, collective, and national interests. The necessary self-motivated behavior at the individual and community level could only be achieved by structuring a system of extensive political participation in the villages. As Ho Chi Minh had already observed during the Resistance, "Democracy, initiative and enthusiasm are closely interconnected. If you have democracy, only thus can the cadres and people have initiative."[12] Political integration was thus seen to be dependent on effective political participation.

Despite the existence of elected local governments, "democracy" in the sense of formal voting for elected officials was little more than an exercise in symbolic political action.[13] Democracy in its broader sense means the involvement of the members of the village community in the decisions that most directly affect their lives. This political participation is accomplished in a number of ways. First, there is recruitment of local community members into positions of authority. It is important to stress that this does not mean only Party positions, or even positions of local government, but also positions of production leadership within the cooperatives. Since these latter activities most directly and continuously involved villagers, it is natural that leaders within the agricultural cooperatives would play a major role in village political life. The relatively small number of rural Party members, and the significant number of hamlets and villages without a Party organization, underline the importance of non-Party positions of leadership.

In addition, the organizational format of the cooperative both encourages and requires participation in decisions concerning the economic welfare of both individuals and the collective. Work assignments and distribution of income are determined by the collective within the general guidelines laid down by the state. Because the scale of the lowest level decisionmaking units is small, a traditional social unit, the hamlet or neighborhood, is generally the forum for discussion and decision. By 1963 the recommended size of the smallest agricultural unit, the production team, was thirty to forty persons.[14] In 1965, the cooperative (the parent unit of the production teams) became coterminous with the hamlet, averaging from 150 to 200 families.[15] During the war years in North Vietnam, the size of cooperatives was expanded, partly due to the drain of the war on manpower.

Needless to say, decisions concerning economic welfare were not always made in a smooth and harmonious way. The importance of broad participation in decisionmaking, in fact, is underlined by the necessity of arriving at the proper balance between individual and community interests so that the results are viewed as fair and legitimate. It is this problem that is the basic restraint to an all powerful "mobilization party" that would penetrate the local rural society and brush aside community (and individual) interests to serve the goals of the leadership. The experience of the first years of cooperativization demonstrated that the most successful cooperatives had fully implemented the recommended system of "democratic management" (quan ly dan chu) while those which had not encouraged wide participation in decisionmaking had the worst economic performance.[16]

The program of cooperativization, in fact, was not an uninterrupted line of successes. By a malicious turn of nature, 1960-62 were exceptionally bad years for agriculture throughout Asia. The first year of consolidation, 1960, was particularly disastrous. Despite this severe challenge, and momentary periods of confusion and disarray, cooperativization was successfully completed by the end of this period, and standards of living had not only been maintained but raised in some areas.

In the process, the DRV had made remarkable progress toward the reintegration of the rural village communities, which had been increasingly "thrown off balance" by colonialism, war, and the resulting disruption of a social revolution. This integration was not accomplished by administrative fiat, or by an all powerful Party, but through the structuring of popular participation. The elaboration of a strong organization framework, and the widespread impact of the Lao Dong Party in the village were important and indispensible prerequisites for reintegration. However, it was the establishment of a process of community participation—not orders and organizational structures—that channeled the energies of the rural society in a direction that mutually benefited individual, collective, and state.

Instruments of Integration: State, Party, Mass Participation

There are fundamentally three strategies for integrating the individual, society, and the state. The first is the creation of an elaborate state structure that confines individual activities within the sphere acceptable to the state. Second is the need for a large and powerful party which can channel the individual energies in the direction desired by the state. And, finally, is the institution of processes of behavior by regulations and incentives that will mediate between the interests of the individual and the state.

In a largely agricultural society the creation of state institutions that will engage the entire population is clearly an impossibility. The heavy burdens of a swollen bureaucracy would defeat the main goal of state policy—rapid economic expansion. Moreover, the availability and training of personnel posed obstacles to a major expansion of the state bureaucracy. Continuous efforts were made to counteract the concentration of trained personnel at the central level of the bureaucracy, but lack of available cadres limited the effect of these measures.[17] Moreover, the dispersed and non-specialized nature of agriculture makes it impossible to rely solely on state institutions, such as technical assistance and credit facilities, and the regular village, district, and province governmental machinery to organize economic life in the countryside.

For this task, a political Party would be more appropriate. But despite its long experience and effective organization, the Party, too, was relatively weak at the actual production level. The overall ratio of Party members to population in North Vietnam was about 2 percent at the outset of cooperativization. Moreover only 40 percent of Party members were at the village level.[18] Unlike China and North Korea, there had not been a major expansion of the Party during the land reform period, as evidenced by the statement, cited above, that "the vast majority of Party members and cadres are people who have joined the Party for ten years or more and are over thirty years old."[19] Even by 1962, the situation had not significantly changed. The major reason was that, unlike China the Party had been built up during the pre-Liberation period and was relatively evenly spread throughout the country, and unlike China (and North Korea) the first major expansion of the Party came with cooperativization—not land reform.[20]

As late as 1964, key populous agricultural provinces in North Vietnam still lacked a strong Party presence at the production level.[21] The initial problems of cooperativization created difficulties in expanding the Party. These difficulties were a reflection of the strains in a society undergoing basic transformation. A 1964 report by the Party's organizational expert noted that "we must acknowledge that 50% of the Party members in the countryside (including the average and poor Party members) have not yet definitively resolved the question of 'who emerges victorious' with respect to ideological matters touching on their own selves."[22] Ideological laxity was noted in some places, which resulted in the tacit condoning of inadequate performance. The report also noted that, "There are, at present, a number of Party infrastructure organizations which are lacking unity and solidarity in their internal affairs . . . in some places to a serious degree. In these places, Party members are split along family, factional or neighborhood lines . . . "[23]

These ideological and organizational problems were a reflection of the society which produced the Party. An elite group, no matter how strongly motivated, cannot transcend the social context in which it operates. Vertical integration of social and economic class, and horizontal integration of regional or local interests could theoretically be accomplished by allowing these incipient splits to take concrete form in a multiparty system. In a social and economic setting where the management of scarcity is the basic problem, such a system often exacerbates the basic divisions, and dissipates scarce organizational resources. It also complicates the problem of long-range planning to break out of the cycle of poverty.

A single "mobilization" party is an obvious alternative and has been used in many third world contexts as a means of avoiding the problems multiparty systems in societies with a thin resource base. The DRV case shows that "mobilization" by itself is not sufficient, and that the single Party must perform an integrative function as well. It does this by trying to reflect the major groups of society in its own composition.[24] It also serves as the linkage between the collective (and its component individuals) and the state.

Primary emphasis was placed on ideological and material incentives (normative and remunerative) for the peasants to join the cooperatives. It was recognized that heavy-handed measures would defeat the goal of reintegrating the rural community, which was a prerequisite for economic development. Needless to say, violations of this policy took place and frequent official admonitions to local cadres for exerting too heavy pressure on villagers to join the cooperatives indicate that the principle of voluntarism was not always strictly observed. Nonetheless the bulk of evidence shows that cooperativization succeeded because the regime was able to establish conditions in which the vast majority of peasants saw an advantage in joining the cooperatives.

The Initial Phase of Cooperativization

Far from being a forced draft rural mobilization, cooperativization in the DRV was a gradual systematic process which progressively enveloped North Vietnam's peasantry with a network of institutions and procedures that fundamentally restructured the rural economy without major upset to rural living patterns. During the early period of cooperativization (in late 1958 and early 1959) some local efforts by overzealous cadres to push the program too fast were reigned in. *Nhan Dan* editorialized that it "is absolutely necessary for us to set our course for every action in a more exact way, and to eliminate confusion in understanding which would lead to trying to cut short the two stages and attempting to jump over stages (dot chay giai doan)."[25]

In some rural areas district cadres, attempting to impress, neglected their subsidiary responsibilities (water conservancy and drought prevention, for example) in an effort to gain impressive results in enrolling peasants into cooperatives. The Province party secretary of Thai Binh (the largest rice-producing province in the North), a man of long experience in the province, attempted to dampen the ardor of his subordinates. The district cadres fought back, publicly accusing their superior of adversely "affecting the determination" of the District Committee. The major point at issue was whether the district cadres were responding to mass demand for cooperatives or whether they were pushing the peasants faster than organizational resources and peasant acceptance of the new program would permit.[26]

The issue was debated for several months. District cadres expressed their irritation at inadequate and "timid" (rut re) support from the province, while the province committee criticized the district for being "over hasty" (nong voi).[27] The province secretary replied, "I know we are slow, but if you don't have conditions for a leap, you might break a leg."[28] Despite the opposition of the province secretary to a faster paced mobilization campaign, the debate dragged on for three months until a final resolution was made and published in the Party newspaper.

This early debate over cooperativization offers important evidence on the way in which policy decisions are made in the DRV. The essence of this decisionmaking style is a deliberate, pragmatic sifting of evidence, and tolerance of competing views until the final decision is made. The publication in March 1959 of two lengthy articles pointedly supporting lower level criticism of province leadership gave added weight to the District Committee's position, and forced the province committee to fully justify its own stand. Not until May 1959 did a definitive resolution of the issue take place, as the province secretary's self-criticism and rebuttal was published. To underline the point that the Province Committee view (amended by concessions to its critics) was now official policy, it was published on the same day as the Central Committee Resolution summing up the first phase of cooperativization and setting the goals for the forthcoming period.[29] Noting that the number of cooperatives had expanded "rather quickly" while the quality had lagged behind, the Central Committee endorsed the view that the pace of cooperativization should be slowed.

Friction over the pace of cooperativization also developed in areas like Thanh

Hoa province, with the largest population of any DRV provincial area and the most Party members. Unlike Thai Binh, which had been under varying degrees of French control during the Resistance, Thanh Hoa had been a solid Vietminh base area throughout the First Indochina War. As a consequence of its size and history, the social composition of its Party members and cadres was mixed, reflecting the society from which they emerged to positions of leadership. Cadre ambivalence, and the fact that Thanh Hoa had national attention focused on its program from the start resulted in an early decision to slow down the pace of cooperativization. A major national conference in Thanh Hoa on the programs of cooperativization concluded that some middle and lower level cadres had been "hot headed" and wanted to "skip over things" (luot qua). Only 70 percent of the Party members in the province joined, setting a bad leadership example. The conference noted that there are "still some upper middle peasant party members who didn't enthusiastically participate in the cooperatives."[30]

This situation was probably more prevalent in old Resistance areas where many people had joined the Party primarily out of patriotic motivations and at an early stage of the Resistance, before the question of social reform became prominent. Ho noted that "in the old days we needed Party members who could fight the enemy and engage in guerrilla warfare; now we need Party members who can build socialism and construct factories, and be farmers."[31] Ho did not suggest discarding or purging the Resistance party members who only had military skills, but urged them to devote greater efforts to studying "politics, culture and technology."[32] The rectification of errors campaign had acknowledged the heavy cost of a radical change in the rural leadership.

But the social composition of the Party in the rural areas—especially the old base areas—posed a problem of integration *within* the Party itself. In Ha Tinh province, for example, some Party members "asked why they always had to rely on the poor peasants" and why poor peasants must have a fixed percentage of positions in the Party Committees. There was friction between middle and poor peasant Party members.[33] Ironically, the vanguard role of the Party was hampered by its deep social roots. The case of "Comrade Chiem" was singled out in the Party press as an example of the problem. Chiem had been an outstanding cadre during the Resistance, but was unenthusiastic about joining the cooperative. This problem exemplified the fact that "Most Party members and specialized cadres in our Party are people who came from all classes in the countryside, and at present most have many close ties with their families in the countryside in many ways."[34] Chiem was only an illustration of a larger and troublesome problem. In Ha Nam province, some province cadres went home to sell off some of their ricefields (before they were cooperativized) and some district cadres urged their families to sell off their buffaloes.[35]

Thus the Party could not plunge ahead, dragging the peasantry behind it, precisely because it was a reflection of the society it wanted to transform. To be successful in building socialism the Party would itself have to be transformed in the process. This meant that "commandism" and coercion could not serve as effective instruments of leadership in cooperativization, even if the Party leadership had been inclined in that direction. The mass line and popular participation were not empty slogans, but indispensable aspects of a social and political process that was the key to laying the groundwork for economic development.

Rural Cleavages and the Problem of Integration

The first pressing matter that had to be addressed was how to forge bonds of mutual interest among the social classes in the countryside during the period in which class and income differential were still a major facet of rural society. The Party guideline on classes in the countryside during cooperativization was: "Rely completely on the poor and lower middle peasants, unite closely with the middle peasants, restrict and finally eliminate the rich peasant economy, be on guard against the landlords raising their heads, and open the way for landlords to reform and become new persons."[36] The basic regulation for carrying out the cooperativization program instructed that, as a ground rule, class categories determined during the Land Reform should not be altered, but that this should not be applied in a mechanical way.[37]

The major problem of the integration of classes in the countryside was the growing income differential in the countryside. In a report to the National Assembly on cooperativization, Truong Chinh explained that cooperativization had to be undertaken because, "the situation in the countryside in the past few years has proved that if individual farming is permitted to drag on, the land will gradually become concentrated in the hands of a few people, and classes in the countryside will become fragmented in a serious way."[38] Thus the decision to cooperativize was not taken for doctrinaire ideological reasons, but because a continuation of unchecked growth in income disparities would shatter the fragile existing balance between social classes in the countryside. If the Party acquiesced in this, it would be in danger of betraying the purpose of the Revolution. As Truong Chinh put it, "If we let a small segment of the population exploit and become rich and distinct from us, the majority of peasants will become impoverished and fall into decline, and *will be resentful of us* (italics added) and the worker peasant alliance will suffer."[39]

Approximately 90 percent of North Vietnam's rural population was in the "rely on" and "unite with" categories.[40] Moreover, there is some indication that the relatively small percentage of rich peasants was the result of a policy decision to restrict the size of this group by assigning the better off peasants into the "upper middle" category.[41] The editor of *Nhan Dan* stressed that the difference between the middle peasants that Lenin and Stalin discussed and the Vietnamese middle peasants is that in Vietnam this group was also oppressed by imperialism and feudalism. Therefore, unlike the case in Europe and Russia, "the middle peasants in our country are close to the poor peasants and workers."[42] But while upper middle peasants were to be "united with," they were not to be "relied on." In Hai Duong province after the Rectification of Errors, many of the Labor Exchange Teams were led by upper middle peasants (presumably because they had superior entrepreneurial and technical skills). The leadership of the teams had to be reshuffled to bolster middle and lower peasant leadership.[43]

Income statistics underline the differences in standard of living among DRV peasants. A post-Land Reform study of thirty-four villages in five North Vietnamese provinces revealed the following:[44]

	Food Surplus	Just Enough	Underfed
Landlords	19.8%	51.3%	28.8%
Rich Peasants	41.3%	45.8%	12.8%
Middle Peasants	27.9%	55.9%	16.7%
Poor Peasants	19%	52.6%	27.5%

While the landlords had been reduced to almost exactly the living standard of the poor peasants, the rich and middle peasants still had an appreciably higher standard of living. The income differential between the upper middle and poor peasants was over 30 percent.[45] The Land Reform had left the rich and middle peasants with a sizable advantage over the poor peasants in land, tools, and buffaloes, so their superior economic performance was hardly surprising.

The middle peasants posed the difficult problem in the early phases of the cooperativization program. Because the lower stage cooperatives provided for shares to be allotted according to the amount of land contributed, and rental payments for buffaloes and farm implements, the middle peasants' income within the cooperatives was substantially higher than that of poor and landless peasants.[46] Moreover, because of their past standard of living, middle peasant families tended to have more working members, and thus accumulated more work points than poor peasants. It was therefore imperative to find an income formula that would reconcile the interests of both.

There had apparently been some backlash from poor peasants directed at "some comrades" who were "only worried about resolving problems of the middle peasants, while ignoring those of the poor and landless peasants," during the Rectification of Errors campaign.[47] In many cases, cooperativization resulted mainly in increasing the incomes of middle peasants. Some peasants commented that "there is real benefit in joining the cooperatives—but only for the middle peasants."[48] Despite this political pressure, the Party stressed that the treatment of middle peasants during cooperativization would be different from the Land Reform. Whereas the Land Reform injunction was to "rely completely on the poor and landless peasants," the cooperativization slogan blurred this line of demarcation by adding the lower middle peasants to the "rely upon" groups. Criticisms were directed against allowing upper middle peasants to take too prominent a leadership role in the cooperatives, but it was also noted that some places had forced them to move too fast toward the higher stage (where income differentials would be reduced) and to take a lower percentage of cooperative profits than they were entitled to by the Central Committee Resolution on the subject.[49]

Again it took pressure from the center to restrain the poor peasants from alienating the middle peasants.[50] A Party examination of the problem noted that in some areas cooperatives were criticized as "entirely composed of water-drinkers" [e.g., too poor to afford tea]. Some people were reputedly worried that if they entered the cooperatives they would be constrained "like a bird in a cage, and would have to ask permission every time they wanted to go to the market or go out for pleasure, and would have other people directing their work."[51] *Nhan Dan* took this occasion to remind local areas that voluntary action is the key, and warned against using coercive measures.[52] Party policy was to stress three basic principles to be observed during cooperativization; (1) voluntary entry, (2) mutual benefit, and (3) democratic discussion. "We must not only guarantee the principle of voluntarism but in all things relating to carrying out of tasks in the cooperatives," was the instruction of a *Nhan Dan* editorial. "Some comrades and cadres have not yet understood this, and therefore there have been times when there has been commandism and coercion of the peasants into the cooperatives. And in the cooperatives, little attention has been paid to educating the peasants, and there has not been a zealous consolidation of the cooperatives to make the peasants ever more self-instructed and enlightened and closely linked to it."[53]

Since the poor peasants generally saw it in their interests to join, it was the middle peasants who were the real test case of how faithfully the principles of voluntary entry, mutual benefit, and democratic discussion would be observed. At the outset of cooperativization the "administrative ability and production experience of middle peasants—upper middle peasants in particular—made them natural candidates for leading positions in the cooperatives." In some cases so many upper middle peasants were elected to the Cooperative Administrative Committees that reelection had to be held to ensure that they be kept to the prescribed ratio (one-third or less) of leading positions.[54] This restriction on the class composition of the Cooperative Administrative Committee was felt to be necessary because some middle peasants were "reluctant to carry out the Party's class policy and transmit it to the cooperative members," which resulted in a high concentration of upper middle peasants in leadership positions.[55] The one-third figure was an exact reflection of the 30 percent middle peasant proportion of total rural population.[56] The purpose of this quota system was not to discriminate against the middle peasants, but to bring the poor peasants into active participation in the cooperative's affairs.[57]

Integrating the poor peasants into full participation in village life required a twofold policy which would provide basic guarantees for the middle peasants, so they would not be alienated from the cooperative (which would then lose the benefits of their draft animals, tools, and production experience), while at the same time building a solid base of poor peasant leadership which, once firmly established, could then take in rich peasants, and subsequently even landlords. A bad spring harvest in 1960 further added weight to the argument for giving additional consideration to middle peasants, since skilled labor and draft animals were getting increasingly scarce and expensive.[58] Thus the cooperatives were urged to "overcome the equalitarian mentality" and assign work on a contract (piece work) basis.[59]

Expanding Participation and Increasing Incentives

By 1961, the first stage of cooperativization had been completed. A major reformulation of agricultural policy was issued at the fifth Plenum of the Lao Dong Party Central Committee in July 1961, noting that 88 percent of peasant households had joined the cooperatives, and nearly one-quarter of those were in higher level cooperatives (where income was divided mainly according to work points). (Land shares and buffalo rentals were eliminated by full collectivization.)[60] After the initial period of consolidation, the quota system was not retained for leadership positions. The major social and political aim was to strengthen the integration of lower and middle peasants, and to eliminate the income differentials which separated them. In the words of the Party directive, "We must lay stress on uniting poor peasants and middle peasants under one roof" and "we must not discriminate among Party members between poor and middle peasants, but judge everyone according to his ideological stand." It added that "any of them who have won the confidence of the cooperative members and have been appointed by the Village Party Committee can hold key positions in the cooperatives."[61] To encourage participation of middle peasants, the fifth Plenum directed cooperatives to "apply the principle of distributing income according to work done; apply the system of bonuses and penalties and combat egalitarianism."[62]

By 1963, the income differential between poor and middle peasants had "sharply diminished" and about 30 percent of poor peasant families had raised their income to the level of upper middle peasants—a major goal outlined by the 1961 fifth Plenum.[63] Nonetheless, a 30 percent average difference still remained between the incomes of the groups.[64] Because of the three successive years of bad crop weather, the overall rural standard of living rose only slightly over the 1959 level (which, it should be remembered, was the second of two good harvest years).[65]

	Food surplus	Just enough	Underfed
1959:	22.08%	53.39%	23.83%

	Good living standard	Average living standard	Suffering some deprivations
1963:	25%	56%	19%

Since the poor peasants showed a 30 percent rise in a relatively constant economic "pie," it must be assumed that there was a drop among the middle peasants as a result of the cut-off of land and buffalo rental income. Nonetheless, in the face of severe natural calamities, it must be considered an achievement to hold gross income levels at the pre-calamity level, in the face of an extremely high rate of population growth (3.4 percent).[66]

But while income levels were stabilized during the first years of cooperativization despite natural calamities; the anticipated material gains were not achieved, and the superiority of the cooperatives was not made convincingly apparent to some skeptical peasants. A DRV economist later wrote, "if, in 1962, this superiority was still not plain to everyone, the principal reason was bad management of the cooperatives."[67] In 1962, only 25-30 percent of cooperatives were considered well managed. By the end of 1964 a survey of eighteen delta provinces found the percentage of well-managed cooperatives was raised to 36 percent and satisfactory cooperatives to 48 percent.[68] Diversification into secondary crops increased total food production, but placed an additional strain on cooperative management, possibly contributing to relatively static productivity in rice growing.[69]

Recognizing the seriousness of the managerial problem, which included both inexperience in leadership and petty corruption, the Party made major changes in agricultural policy at the 8th Plenum in April 1963. The year 1963 was particularly disastrous because of typhoons and drought. Moreover there had been a drop in fertilizer production (in part due to the mismanagement of animal raising, which affected the principal source of fertilizer during the early stage of cooperativization). In addition, the application of available fertilizer was increasingly shifted from rice to dry food crops.[70] Despite the drop in rice production, *total* agricultural production rose an average of 4.8 percent per year from 1961 to 1964.[71] This reflects an increase both in industrial crops and dry food crops which were encouraged as a diversification measure to decrease reliance on the vulnerable rice crop.[72]

Acknowledging that production had dropped during 1962 in the case of planted crops and animal raising, the Politburo issued a directive initiating a major campaign to improve management of the cooperatives.[73] A key aspect of this campaign was a reemphasis on the importance of material incentives. "If there are too many monks, no one will close the pagoda door" and "If everyone has the same father, no one will feel like mourning for him," were proverbs in currency that reflected the difficulty of building a collective spirit on ideological grounds alone.[74] It had been stressed from the outset that socialism could not be built "by sincerity alone."[75] Hence it was again emphasized that, "if you don't bring the principle of material benefit into play, you will become divorced from the masses and won't be able to encourage their enthusiasm in production."[76]

This stress on material incentives did not mean a return to free enterprise agriculture. One of the greatest concerns of the eighth Plenum was to "fully realize the principle of democratic management."[77] This meant giving more scope to the cooperative Administrative Committee, expanding participation in its decisions, and strengthening the Supervisory Committees to oversee its activities. The dilemma of employing material incentives was that it would require even more managerial resources and skills than a standardized and "equalized" system of remuneration.[78] Party cadres were still not numerous enough to supervise all aspects of cooperative activities. It was estimated by the Party's organization section that to lead a cooperative of from 70-80 to 150-200 families, establishment of a cooperative Party chapter would be required, and that if the production teams were to satisfactorily fulfill the "three contracts" every team must have a strong Party cell.[79] But "because in the past several years, the local areas have not fully recognized this requirement, and have not resolutely overcome narrow mindedness in the task of Party expansion . . . at present there are very many cooperatives without a Party chapter, and very many production teams with no Party cell. In many places one Party chapter has to lead two or three cooperatives, and one Party cell two or three production teams. Some cooperatives don't have any Party members. In many places the Party organization isn't meshed with the production organization."[80]

In some cases, the Party leadership of cooperatives was itself a problem.[81] In Bac Ninh province, singled out for strong criticism for its leadership deficiencies in the 1960-62 period, the failures were ascribed to the "rightist character" of province leadership in carrying out the Party's class policy.[82] Apparently Bac Ninh had encountered serious problems in the Rectification of Errors campaign, which resulted in a decision to restrict admission to the Party to those who were "reliable" and would not rock the boat.[83] Instead of selecting youths who had shown zeal and initiative during cooperativization, "a number of Party Chapters took in (new) members with insufficient qualifications on the basis of family or neighborhood attachments."[84] The poor peasant youths were considered "too eager to struggle and were viewed as an obstacle to orderly leadership."[85] The only way of overcoming the rigidity and stratification in Party leadership was to expand popular participation in the management of cooperatives in order to encourage and identify new leadership talent. Equally important was the increasing of representation from the overlapping categories of youths, women, and poor peasants, who were not being adequately represented in leadership positions, as a means of integrating the community.

Expanding popular participation was viewed as the major integration strategy in the countryside. It would supplement the Party's overtaxed resources and eventually add to them. But it was clearly recognized that the Party could not and should not do everything. Furthermore, it was apparent that the fate of Party leadership in the countryside was directly related to its performance in solving the basic problems of rural poverty. Poor Party leadership in agricultural production, it was felt, not only affected the living standard of cooperative members, but had a debilitating impact on Party organization itself, since "Party members and cadres in the countryside and the families of these comrades are tightly linked to the fate of the cooperatives."[86] This close linkage of Party and society suggests that Huntington's generalization that in one-party states "the modernizing elite" impose controls upon the peasants and only allow their political participation when peasants accept the "modernizing values" of the elite[87] does not apply to the case of North Vietnam. The DRV recognizes that the Party's organizations in the countryside are a reflection of rural society and that their effectiveness in spreading "modernizing values" depends on their success in solving the basic problems of the peasant's daily life.

Even during the colonial period, when rice surpluses from the South were available to match food deficits in the industrial North, economists like Gourou concluded that there was no way out of the cycle of poverty and misery of the North Vietnamese peasants. Gourou raised the specter of stark tragedy which would arise if "modernizing values" were imposed on the peasantry.

What would become of a people when poverty would stare in the face and who would concentrate their thoughts on it . . . for they would have no other preoccupation than material ones—who while considering material welfare as the only possible form of happiness would contemplate their horrible misery, who would be convinced of the absolute impossibility of improving their lot, for a change in the social and political regimes would be powerless against population overcrowding?

In this overpopulated country where the land cannot give much more to the peasants than it does now, it is not to be hoped that material welfare may reign some day. . . . Only traditional civilizations . . . can give a sympathetic and wretched people the share of happiness to which they are entitled; outside this there would be only chaos and despair.[88]

In the light of this dire forecast, the DRV must be credited with a substantial success in simply holding rural income steady and overcoming potential calamitous weather conditions during the first years of cooperativization.

The Political Consequences of Cooperativization

Despite the slow economic progress of the early phases of cooperativization, the DRV was able to solve most of the numerous problems outlined above. Party membership had increased from 500,000 (1960) to nearly 800,000 (1966).[89] It could be argued that this increase came from those who had "accepted the modernizing values of the political elite." But this is an inadequate and incomplete description of the political and social change that occurred during the cooperativization campaign.

The basic premise of "accepting the ideals of a modernizing elite" is that they are somehow different, if not opposed to, the ideals of the peasantry. This, in turn, is based on an explicit contrast between the party of a "modern organization" and the "traditional countryside."[90] In the DRV, however, the Resistance had fostered the spread of political organization and revolutionary ideas over an extended period, most notably from 1945 on. But these "revolutionary" ideas were not distinctively "modern." The main focus of these ideas was an expulsion of the colonial power, the raising of living standards, and a reduction of political, social and economic inequality. These aspirations were supported by traditional ideals as much as by "modern" ideology.

As Huntington notes, "At some point . . . even in one party states the needs of stability require that the political system confront and resolve the issue of rural political participation."[91] Rural participation was an essential factor of the 1945-54 Resistance, the Land Reform, and Cooperativization. But it was only the cooperativization program that sought to institutionalize procedures of participation that would endure on a long-term basis. This was done in explicit recognition of the fact that the Party could not serve as an instrument of political integration unless it was deeply rooted in rural society. If it operated as a "modernizing" force, disembodied from its social context, it would wither at the bottom, and prove unable to regenerate itself.

In order to breathe political life and social meaning into the cooperatives, they had to engage the active participation of the peasantry. To this end, the cooperatives were constructed not as a village "institution" but as a network of social, political, and economic relationships. Participation in the activities of the cooperatives was accomplished through an incentive system. It was more profitable to join than to remain outside because of the subsidization of necessities of life through the cooperatives, while they remained considerably more expensive on the outside. Cooperatives also got first priority on items in limited supply. Despite an early tendency toward egalitarianism, the local community was bound together in the cooperatives by a shared interest in increased production.[c] And once the majority of the village was enrolled in the cooperatives, social ties made it difficult to stay on the outside. Cooperativization was achieved by a subtle interplay of social, political, and economic factors. It was fitted onto rural society like a glove—with some tugging and pulling—rather than a Procrustean frame distending existing social institutions out of joint.

---

[c]This integrative aspect of cooperativization was greatly strengthened in 1963 when a ceiling was fixed for compulsory sales to the state, as an incentive to cooperatives to increase production (since they could retain the bulk of the surplus).

Cooperativization in North Vietnam not only provided the basis for economic development, it also was the instrument of political integration. Political integration was accomplished by establishing procedures for popular participation in basic decisions affecting individual welfare. Because the personnel resources of the Lao Dong Party were limited, its role in cooperativization was to provide the main guidelines, and the impetus for the campaign. It could not oversee the details of the daily workings of the cooperatives. Thus it was necessary to enlist community participation in support of the regime's goals, since the ultimate success of cooperativization depended on the self-motivated and self-perpetuating involvement of the peasants.

Integration had social, economic, and political dimensions. The class discrimination of the early phase of the cooperatives, often viewed as a deliberate and divisive ideologically motivated attempt to encourage class struggle, was actually aimed at ensuring the political rights of the large body of poor and middle peasants who had been previously excluded or restricted from participation in the basic decisions concerning their welfare. When their participation had been firmly guaranteed, the formal class restrictions were dropped, and rich peasants (and even landlords) taken into the cooperatives. Thus the distribution of authority in the countryside was restructured not to limit, but to extend political participation and to eliminate the inequalities that were the source of class antagonisms.

With respect to Party leadership in the countryside, the cooperativization campaign revitalized Party membership by inducting a new generation of young members, and increasing the representation of women. Pressure from above prompted local Party organs to alter their "narrow minded" attitudes about accepting new members. The infusion of younger members into the Party alleviated a serious problem of an aging local leadership. This rejuvenation of the Party's local leadership was subsequently partially checked by the mobilization of youth demanded by the DRV war effort. But this mobilization also had the effect of dramatically increasing the number of women in positions of local leadership, and accelerating the integration of women into full participation in community leadership that had begun during cooperativization.[92]

Perhaps the most important lesson to be drawn from the North Vietnamese experience in political integration during the cooperativization campaign was that integration requires more than the development of formal institutions. The linkages between state and society cannot be accomplished by a political Party (or Parties) in the absence of a widespread supporting basis of popular participation in political, economic and social affairs. Far from constituting a threat to political integration and the "art of associating together," the development of political participation was a prerequisite for the binding together of North Vietnam's political community.[93]

North Vietnam's developmental experience provides a notable exception to the basic problem of third world countries, in which "The primary problem of politics is the lag of development of political institutions behind social and economic change."[94] Huntington notes the high and effective levels of political institutionalization in the DRV. Comparing the political systems of North and South in Vietnam and Korea he finds the North with "well organized, broadly based, complex political systems" and the South with "unstable, fractured, narrowly based personalistic regimes. . . ."[95] The Communists' challenge to modernizing countries is not their ability to overthrow governments, but rather to "create governments that can govern."[96] By this criterion, North Vietnam must be considered a successful example of political development.

One of the major contributions of Huntington's writings to the theory of political development is his observation that "the most important political distinction among countries concerns not their form of government but their degree of government."[97] An important shortcoming of Huntington's work is a persistent inclination to see the expansion of popular participation as a threat to political development, a tidal wave that will either swamp the fragile dike of political institutions or lead to autocratic rule. The DRV case illustrates that expanded participation can be an instrument of integration, rather than a threat to it and that it is social, economic, and political integration rather than a simple "enhanced control" that the DRV has strived to achieve by expanding participation.

The shortcomings of the DRV in its efforts to achieve political and economic development are many, and usually freely admitted. It is, in fact, the focus on problem-solving that is the most outstanding feature of the DRV political system. Given a narrow resource base, a complex social structure, and unremitting hostility from powerful international forces which challenged its very survival, the North Vietnamese leaders were obliged to make a very careful appraisal of the realities of their environment, and to correct their errors when they strayed from these realities. In the light of these problems, it is not the relatively modest pace of economic development which is noteworthy, but the reintegration of a society shattered by poverty, colonial rule, and destructive warfare. The most profound observation in Huntington's book may serve as a post-script to the DRV experience in political integration in the first decade of its existence.

The truly helpless society is not one threatened by revolution but one incapable of it. In the normal polity the conservative is devoted to stability and the preservation of order, while the radical threatens these with abrupt and violent change. But what meaning do concepts of conservatism and radicalism have in a completely chaotic society where order must be created through a positive act of political will. In such a society who is then the radical? Who is the conservative? Is not the only true conservative the revolutionary?[98]

Notes

1. Samuel P. Huntington, *Political Order in Changing Societies*, (Yale University Press, New Haven, 1968), p. 36. In a subsequent article Huntington

questions the utility of the term "modernization." "The Change to Change; Modernization, Development, and Politics," *Comparative Politics* 3, 3 (April 1971): 283-98. Limited space does not permit a lengthy consideration of this issue, but this chapter accepts as a point of departure the perspective of political development, with its focus on political participation and political institutions, as proposed by Huntington.

2. "By focusing largely upon variables relating to indigenous aspects of social structure and culture, modernization theorists have either underestimated or ignored many important external sources or influences upon social change. . . . Any theoretical framework which fails to incorporate such significant variables or the impact of war, conquest, colonial domination, international political and military relationships, or of international trade and the cross-national flow of capital cannot hope to explain either the origins of these societies or the nature of their struggles for political and economic autonomy—struggles, it should be added, which all societies face, though perhaps in varying degrees and contexts at different historical moments." Dean C. Tipps, "Modernization Theory and the Comparative Study of Societies: A Critical Perspective," *Comparative Studies in Society and History* 15, 2 (March 1973): 212. Huntington explicitly limits the causal source of participation to an apparently internally generated process. "The fundamental source of expansion of political participation is the nonpolitical socioeconomic processes identified with modernization." *Comparative Politics*, p. 314.

3. Huntington, *Political Order*, p. 434.

4. Huntington, *Political Order in Changing Societies*, p. 397.

5. Ibid., p. 427. Huntington points to the difficulties of assimilating new groups in a one-party system since they will weaken the party by watering down its unity. This assumes that groups emerging during the modernization process (presumably technicians, skilled workers, etc.) will behave as similar groups in pluralist systems and push their own interests at the expense of those of other groups. The possibility of an overriding commitment of emerging groups to the welfare of the political system itself is not considered.

6. Eugene Staley, *The Future of Underdeveloped Countries* (New York: Praeger, 1961), pp. 235-36.

7. *Nhan Dan*, May 22, 1959. Truong Chinh implied that the failing of the Land Reform was that it was not done within the context of an overall plan of economic development and political integration. "We didn't completely grasp the importance of cooperativizing the countryside after the Land Reform. When errors in the Land Reform were discovered and the organization was revised, we lost a period of more than a year in completing the Land Reform well. . . . During the Rectification of Errors, at the beginning we divorced the task of mobilizing for Labor Exchange Teams and Cooperatives from the Rectification of Errors campaign; it was not until phase 3 of the Rectification of Errors that it was coordinated with the reorganization of the Labor Exchange Teams and the Cooperatives." Ibid.

8. Cf. Ngo Vinh Long, *Before the Revolution* Harvard University Press, 1973).

9. Mus has pointed to this impact in eloquent terms: "The traditional village could not survive. It continued to look the same, at least in Tonkin and Annam . . . but it became an empty shell, void of the social substance it once had which had kept life constantly renewed. With the heart gone out of it, even the appearance of the village was in a precarious position unless there could be a complete reversal in direction back to the lost equilibrium of life." John McAlister, Jr. and Paul Mus, *The Vietnamese and Their Revolution* (Harper, 1970), p. 36.

10. *Nhan Dan*, November 28, 1959.

11. *Nhan Dan*, March 23, 1963.

12. *Nhan Dan*, February 2, 1959.

13. James R. Townsend concludes that in China, "The most important aspect of mass participation in basic level government now appears to be the education function, broadly defined to include the encouragement of attachment to, and understanding of, new levels of political community as well as transmission of information on laws and policies." *Political Participation in Communist China*, (University of California, 1968), p. 143. In the DRV mass participation in local government is also largely educative in function and symbolic in form, though unlike the PRC, the DRV has retained the village level of government as an important level of administration.

14. *Nhan Dan*, July 31, 1963.

15. *Nhan Dan*, December 10, 1965.

16. This view was frequently repeated from the very beginning of the cooperativization program, and was reaffirmed in an editorial summarizing the experience of democratic management of cooperatives. *Nhan Dan*, December 14, 1965.

17. Vu Canh, "Dieu chinh can bo, tang cuong cho co so va dia phuong" (Reassign Cadres and Strengthen the Lower Level Infrastructure and Local Areas), *Hoc Tap*, February 1963, p. 27. "At present, there is an irrational situation in our [administrative] machinery, that is, the organizations of central level are too large and the local and infrastructure organizations are too small. About 65% of the cadres are concentrated in professional [specialized] and administrative organs. . . . The job of arranging cadres from top to bottom is still feeble. . . . So the main task is to reassign cadres to increase the [number of] cadres in the production infrastructure . . . and particularly in the agricultural production infrastructure, to put an end to the present situation in which cadres are lacking at the lower level as soon as possible." Ibid.

18. *Nhan Dan*, September 25, 1961.

19. *Nhan Dan*, November 28, 1959.

20. In the Democratic People's Republic of Korea, the Party had already reached a figure of 800,000, or about 8 percent of total population in 1949. The figure rose to 1,000,000 in 1952 (9 percent) and increased only slightly (to 10 percent) in 1956 during the late stage of cooperativization. Robert A. Scalapino

and Cheng Shih-Lee, *Communism in Korea, Part II: The Society* (Berkeley, 1972), p. 712. The DPRK is a much more appropriate example of integration through a mobilization Party than the DRV, with almost one out of four adults belonging to the Party. Ibid., p. 714.

21. In Thai Binh, for example, only 50 percent of the APC production teams had a Party cell, and the number of team leaders who were Party members was only 40 percent. Pham Bai, "May kinh nghiem xay dung Chi Bo Dang trong quoc van dong cai tien quan tri Hop Tac Xa san xuat nong nghiep," (Some lessons in building up Party Chapters in the movement to strengthen administration of Agricultural Producers Cooperatives), *Hoc Tap*, August 1964, p. 34. In Hai Duong the ratio of Party members to population was only 2 percent and in some districts as low as 1.3 percent. Nguyen Chuong, "Kay dung Dang manh la nhan to guyet dinh moi thang loi" (Building up the Party is the decisive factor in gaining victories), *Hoc Tap* August 1964, p. 28. In Son Tay, a French-controlled area during the Resistance, almost every village had a Party chapter after 1955, but the average number of Party members was small, 11 to 25 in a Party chapter or 7 for every 1,000 peasants. Some had no Party members (39 out of 382 hamlets in Quoc Oai district had none, and in Phu Tho district 15 percent of the hamlets had no Party representation). The average of "poor" quality Party members was high—27.4 percent. Almost no Party members were recruited after the Land Reform, May 21, 1959.

22. Vu Oanh, "Tang cuong suc chien dau cua to chuc coso cua Dang," (Step up the combat strength of the Party's infrastructure organizations), *Hoc Tap*, August 1964, p. 18.

23. Ibid., p. 20.

24. In comparison with China and North Korea, however, the DRV has shown itself relatively less concerned with class background than with leadership performance. The Party has opposed "class backgroundism" (thanh phan chu nghia), largely because it recognizes that in the light of Vietnamese history and the social makeup of Vietnamese society, it was inevitable that the Party would not have an orthodox proletarian or even predominantly poor peasant base. Vo Canh, "Ra suc lam tot cong tac phat trien Dang," *Hoc Tap*, November 1962.

25. *Nhan Dan*, February 23, 1959.

26. *Nhan Dan*, March 30, 1959.

27. Ibid. Possibly an implied criticism of the mobilization style of the Great Leap in China. It should be recalled that it was at precisely this time that China itself was reorienting its agricultural policies, and that its early mistakes may have been a cautionary experience for higher level DRV cadres.

28. *Nhan Dan*, March 31, 1959.

29. *Nhan Dan*, May 15, 1959.

30. *Nhan Dan*, May 22, 1959.

31. *Nhan Dan*, June 3, 1960.

32. Ibid.

33. *Nhan Dan*, April 10, 1959.

34. *Nhan Dan*, February 23, 1959.

35. Ibid.

36. *Nhan Dan*, February 27, 1959.

37. *Nhan Dan*, May 23, 1959. In fact there was some readjustment of class categories. *Nhan Dan* on October 14, 1959 noted that this had been overdone and that "some places have taken in landlords and rich peasants who have recently changed their class" as well as some counter-revolutionary elements. The greatest readjustment appeared to be in the minorities areas. *Nhan Dan*, July 21, 1960.

38. *Nhan Dan*, May 22, 1959.

39. Ibid.

40. Rural Work Department statistics show that at the outset of cooperativization, North Vietnam's rural class composition was (a) rich peasants: 0.6 percent of the total rural population, (b) upper middle and ordinary middle peasants: 30 percent, (c) poor and lower middle peasants: 60 percent. *Nhan Dan*, June 6, 1959. During the Land Reform, the number of landlords comprised about 2 percent of the rural population. Tran Phuong, *Cach mang ruong dat o Viet-Nam* (The Land Revolution in Vietnam), (Hanoi, 1968), p. 162.

41. Unlike the Chinese, the North Vietnamese did not consider the rich peasants a major problem since they were "very weak." This is cited as an important factor in the success of the first three years of cooperativization. Cf. 5th Plenum Resolution (July 1961) in *Vietnamese Studies*, February 1964, p. 155.

42. *Nhan Dan*, June 6, 1959.

43. *Nhan Dan*, April 4, 1959.

44. *Nhan Dan*, May 22, 1959.

45. *Nhan Dan*, April 1, 1963. By 1963 it was 30 percent and was evidently higher before the move toward higher level cooperatives.

46. Middle peasants owned an average of 4 *sao* (1 sao = 360 square meters) of land, as against 3 *sao* (about 1/4 of an acre) for the poor peasants. *Vietnamese Studies*, No. 13 (Hanoi, 1967).

47. *Nhan Dan*, June 6, 1959.

48. *Nhan Dan*, August 7, 1959.

49. *Nhan Dan*, August 7, 1959.

50. *Nhan Dan* October 14, 1959, noted that "many places have not fully understood the matter of uniting with the middle peasants," and that in some places middle peasants had been targets of criticism (da kich) and victims of prejudice.

51. *Nhan Dan*, May 15, 1959.

52. Ibid. *Nhan Dan* again stressed that it was up to the Party members to join and set a good example for others, but that there was still reluctance among some Party members to do so.

53. *Nhan Dan*, August 3, 1959. It is hard to estimate the extent to which coercion took place. One province investigation (Phu Tho) revealed that 7 percent of those joining cooperatives had been coerced. (*Nhan Dan*, August 13, 1959.) It is unlikely that the magnitude of reluctant entrants was much greater in other areas, since the option of withdrawing remained. As will be discussed below, some withdrawals did take place during the bad crop years of 1960-62.

54. *Nhan Dan*, February 26, 1959. The cooperative regulations are translated in *Vietnamese Studies*, No. 13. The quote is mentioned on page 89.

55. *Nhan Dan*, February 26, 1959.

56. *Nhan Dan*, August 11, 1960.

57. Vo Nhan Tri, *Croissance Economique de la Republique Democratique du Vietnam, 1945-1955* (Hanoi, 1967), p. 276.

58. *Nhan Dan*, August 18, 1960.

59. Ibid. As a concrete example of mutual concessions between middle peasants and the cooperative, the practice of regarding "people cheaper than buffaloes" and paying a flat rental fee for buffaloes prior to totaling and allocating labor points was criticized (that is, a guaranteed profit even if the crop failed), but cooperatives were warned not to overlook the question of compensation for buffalo rentals.

60. Cf. "Resolution of the 5th Plenum of the Party Central Committee (July 1961) on the Development of Agriculture in the First Five Year Plan (1961-1965)," *Vietnamese Studies*, November 2, 1964, pp. 154-177.

61. Ibid., p. 159.

62. Ibid., p. 160.

63. *Nhan Dan*, April 31, 1963.

64. *Nhan Dan*, April 1, 1963.

65. The 1959 figures are extrapolated from *Nhan Dan*, May 22, 1959, and weighted according to figures cited in Tran Phuong, *Cach Mang ruong dat o Viet-Nam*, p. 162. The 1963 figures are from a National Assembly report, *Nhan Dan*, April 31, 1963. It is assumed that food surplus or sufficiency is closely correlated with the measure of living standards, making the two sets of figures roughly comparable.

66. Population in the DRV increased from 14.5 million in 1955 to 18.4 million in 1964. Doan Trong Truyen and Phan Thanh Binh, *L'edification d'une economie nationale independante au Vietnam (1945-1965)*, (Hanoi, 1966), p. 169.

67. Vo Nhan Tri, *Croissance Economique*, p. 416.

68. Ibid., pp. 416-417.

69. Figures on rice and dry crop production for 1957, 1960, and 1964 may be found in *Vietnamese Studies*, "Agricultural Problems" (Vol. 2), "Rice," (Hanoi, 1967), p. 8-9.

70. Vo Nhan Tri, *Croissance Economique*, p. 424.

71. Ibid., p. 421.

72. Ibid.

73. *Nhan Dan*, April 7, 1963.

74. *Nhan Dan*, April 17, 1963.

75. *Nhan Dan*, July 18, 1959.

76. *Nhan Dan*, April 17, 1963.

77. *Nhan Dan*, April 7, 1963.

78. Ibid.

79. In a critique of the Bac Ninh province leadership of cooperatives, cited below, it was determined that "lack of democracy in Bac Ninh cooperatives has become rather serious. In many cooperatives everything is decided by the management committee. Many (production) targets are not known to cooperative members. The production plan is not discussed. . . . In many cooperatives there are currently manifestations of egalitarianism (binh quan chu nghia), that is, anyone can do as he wishes, and in the distribution of the fruits of this labor everyone receives about the same benefits." *Nhan Dan*, March 26, 1962.

80. *Nhan Dan*, April 7, 1963. Party bylaws require a minimum of three Party members in a basic organization to set up a Party chapter. In practice, the minimum number seems to be somewhat higher.

81. *Nhan Dan*, April 5, 1963. The target set for 1965 was that every cooperative should have a Party chapter and every production team a Party cell in delta areas; in every cooperative a Party cell, every team a Party member in highland minorities areas.

82. *Nhan Dan*, March 26, 1962. "Bac Ninh was a province that had encountered many difficulties during the Rectification of Errors campaign."

83. Ibid.

84. Ibid.

85. Ibid. This was apparently a persisting problem. *Nhan Dan*, September 9, 1959, noted that some Party organs felt that they should only accept "well behaved" types, and reject those who "struggled and criticized the leadership."

86. *Nhan Dan*, April 5, 1963.

87. Huntington, *Political Order*, p. 434.

88. Pierre Gourou, *Les Paysans du Delta Tonkinois*, cited in *Vietnamese Studies*, No. 2 (Hanoi, 1964), p. 183.

89. *Nhan Dan*, April 19, 1966.

90. Huntington, *Political Order*, p. 434.

91. Ibid., pp. 434-435.

92. The number of new Party members in 1965 under the age of thirty was 81 percent of the total new enrollment (as opposed to 71 percent in 1961) while women joining the Party constituted 20.8 percent of new recruits (9.4 percent in 1961). *Nhan Dan*, February 4, 1966.

93. Huntington observes that, "The political instability in Asia, Africa, and Latin America derives precisely from the failure to meet this condition: equality of political participation is growing much more rapidly than the 'art of associating together'." *Political Order*, pp. 4-5.

94. Ibid.
95. Ibid., p. 343.
96. Ibid., p. 8.
97. Ibid., p. 1.
98. Huntington, *Political Order*, p. 263.

Part II:
Communism in Cambodia

8

The Khmer Resistance: External Relations, 1973-1974

Sheldon W. Simon

Introduction

Cambodia was the last of the four Indochina states to become fully involved in the war and is now the only country in the region for which not even a theoretical armistice has been signed. In the two years since the Paris negotiations, which stipulated there should be no further foreign intervention in Cambodia, hundreds of people were still being killed or wounded daily in continued fighting made possible through aid from outsiders.

The persistence of hostilities in Cambodia reflects the fact that since the 1973 American bombing halt a relative military equilibrium has developed between a U.S.-funded and -trained republican army of approximately 60,000 combat troops (out of an estimated 200,000 soldiers) and a Khmer Rouge adversary of approximately the same number. As of Autumn 1974, on the ground, Phnom Penh controlled most of the cities, large unbroken tracts of land such as those bordering Thailand (including the provinces of Battambang and Pursat), and perhaps 60 percent of the population, three million of whom (half the Cambodian population) are refugees. The Khmer Rouge controlled a somewhat larger area, and the status of the remainder of the country was perhaps best classified as "under contention."[1]

Although most of the Vietnamese Communist forces left Cambodia after the 1973 Paris Agreement, parts of eastern Cambodia remain under their control and continue to serve as bases for operations in South Vietnam (the Parrot's Beak) and as transit routes for supplies into the Mekong Delta region. Hanoi also continues to serve as the Khmer Rouge chief supplier of weapons, primarily of Chinese origin, as well as providing military advisors and certain special units.

For its part the United States has assigned approximately one hundred officers in Phnom Penh to supervise military aid and observe the course of the war. U.S. economic aid pays for the transport ships which supply Phnom Penh via the Mekong and Tonle Sap Rivers. American military transport planes airlift supplies to republican troops when they are surrounded.

This study covers the period primarily from the fall of 1973 to the end of 1974. For an analysis of the Cambodian conflict from its 1970 inception through the cessation of U.S. bombing in August 1973, see the author's *War and Politics in Cambodia: A Communications Analysis* (Durham: Duke University Press, 1974).

The continuation of American involvement in Cambodia should be seen in the context of Washington's "interlocking parts" interpretation of the Indochina War and its belief that Hanoi is pressing to obtain the hegemonic position among the four countries. Only in Cambodia could the United States bring direct military pressure to bear on the North Vietnamese (at least until the August 1973 bombing halt) without immediately endangering the cease-fires in Laos and Vietnam. Moreover, Cambodia's possible fall was foreseen as a severe psychological shock to South Vietnam, in addition to presenting Saigon with a serious military problem if the port of Kompong Som (Sihanoukville) were to be reopened to Communist traffic. By providing the Lon Nol government with the capability for sustaining its own defense, the United States hoped to create a political and military stalemate conducive to a negotiated settlement, leading to a neutralized Cambodia which would not upset the status quo in either Vietnam or Laos.[2] By 1974-75, however, it had become problematical whether the U.S. Congress would provide the wherewithal to sustain the government's strategy and whether, in any event, the non-Communist political structure in Cambodia was effective enough to utilize even the minimal aid provided.

It is the primary task of this chapter to examine the character of the Khmer Resistance's relations with its external backers, particularly North Vietnam and China, and to assess the insurgents' potential for politico-military success as well as their proclivity to accept the compromise, negotiated settlement desired by the United States. There will also be some discussion of Lon Nol's government and its American backer in order to present the complete political context in which the Resistance is operating.

The Politics of External Support in the Cambodian Insurgency

Components of the Insurgency

The 1970 Indochinese People's Summit Conference formally linked the "liberation movements" of the three non-Communist states to North Vietnam for the first time since the 1951 Indochina Communist Party conference. But, unlike their counterparts in Laos and South Vietnam, the Khmer insurgents had neither a long history of operations in the countryside nor the advantage of North Vietnamese control mechanisms dating back to the 1950s. Rather, the Khmer insurgents consisted of a somewhat disjointed combination of (a) Sihanoukists (Khmer Rumdo); (b) those intellectual and middle class elements who became increasingly disillusioned with the corruption of Lon Nol's regime; (c) peasants who were either cajoled or coerced into the insurgency with appeals to their national pride against the American and South Vietnamese "invaders"; and finally the only two true Communist elements of the coalition—(d) the Khmer

Rouge, who had fought against Sihanouk for two decades, and (e) a cadre of perhaps 6,000 Cambodians who had gone to Hanoi in 1954 with the Vietminh and returned with them in 1970-71.[3]

Each of these coalition components brought to the insurgency its own motivation, group organization (or lack thereof), and attraction to (or repulsion from) its North Vietnamese mentors. The Khmer Rouge and dissident intellectuals were said to be influenced by the French Communist Party, with Soviet sympathies; the Hanoi-trained cadres were seen as the DRV's spokesmen; and the Sihanoukists were simply nationalists and perhaps even anti-Communists. According to U.S. government observers, by 1973 severe dissension had broken out in Southern Cambodia between the Khmer Communists and Khmer Rumdo over the former's successful takeover of FUNK (National United Front for Cambodia). Specifically, several bloody clashes were reported by refugees who fled into South Vietnam because of the Khmer Rouge's forced population relocation; its denigration of Sihanouk (who still remained popular in the countryside); its land collectivization and forced rice purchasing program; and its overall effort to assert rigid controls over the life styles of the people in the areas under its control. Refugees told, for example, of the prohibition of travel beyond one's village without Khmer Rouge permission, forced membership in mass organizations, and the requirement of wearing Viet Cong-style black pajamas instead of traditional, colorful Cambodian garb.[4]

There is general agreement that most North Vietnamese forces withdrew from Cambodia—with the exception of the eastern provinces bordering South Vietnam—in early 1973. The withdrawal was an earnest sign of Hanoi's willingness to abide by the Paris Agreement (at least in Cambodia) and perhaps also to decelerate the insurgents' military progress which, from North Vietnam's perspective, could have led to the premature fall of Phnom Penh and created an onerous administrative responsibility for governing Cambodia before either the unification of Vietnam or the establishment of effective control over the Khmer insurgent movement. An additional consideration, encouraging a reduced North Vietnamese profile, may be found in numerous accounts since 1972 of friction between North Vietnamese advisors and their Khmer associates near the Vietnam border as well as between Khmer Rouge hardliners and Sihanoukists mentioned above. Indeed, Kenneth Quinn concluded, after conducting numerous refugee interviews over several months in 1973 at the South Vietnam-Cambodia border, that a primary goal of the Khmer Rouge was to drive the Vietnamese Communists out of Cambodia. Thus, a major reason for the forced Cambodian population movement away from the border regions was to reduce Vietnamese influence in Khmer Rouge-occupied areas. By contrast (and in conflict with many reports other than Quinn's) the Khmer Rumdos were actually seeking Vietnamese Communist aid against their supposed Communist compatriots.[5]

Publicly, North Vietnamese media and high level government statements have consistently purveyed the line of "militant solidarity of the three Indochinese peoples ... fighting side by side and coordinating with and assisting one another" as the formula for "final victory." Heaping scorn on Western efforts to effect compromise settlements in Indochina, the DRV military press branded them "perfidious, bankrupt schemes" designed "to divide the Indochinese people."[6] Reassuring its Cambodian allies, the Vietnam People's Army paper declared that "the people and army of Vietnam will do all they can to assist the fraternal Cambodian people till total victory is won for their just struggle."[7] These attestations coincided, however, with the above-mentioned stream of reports over friction between the North Vietnamese and the Khmer liberation forces.[8]

Sihanouk's Viewpoint

Sihanouk expressed his own disillusion with the North Vietnamese in the fall of 1973, when he complained to T.D. Allman, of the *Far Eastern Economic Review*, that active support from Hanoi had ceased for over a year and that Hanoi was encouraging negotiations with the Americans and Lon Nol. The Prince attributed DRV reticence to fear that an insurgent victory in Cambodia could bring American retaliation on Hanoi.[9] Whether the prince's explanation was genuine or designed rather to embarrass the North, this author's view—as stated above—differs. Hanoi's reduced support is probably attributable more to its overall Indochina plan (which subordinates Laos and Cambodia to Vietnam) than to any apprehension over renewed American military intervention in Indochina, especially after the U.S. congressional injunction which halted American bombing in August 1973. Indeed, Sihanouk acknowledged this interpretation himself when he pointed out "that the transport of arms between the two Vietnams does not require the taking of Phnom Penh."[10] Moreover, Hanoi's support for the rejection of a negotiated settlement by the Resistance in 1974 either gives the lie to Sihanouk or else demonstrates that the DRV changed their position and became more optimistic about a long-run military victory.

In the course of 1974, Sihanouk's discontent with North Vietnamese strategy has continued. He has unfavorably contrasted the "huge military and financial aid from the United States" sent to Lon Nol with the "lack in arms and ammunition ... of our peoples army." Insisting that he remains the spokesman of the RGNUC (Royal Government of the National Union of Cambodia) and that his presence in Cambodia "would be very useful" to the liberation front, he has averred, nevertheless, that the Khmer Rouge fear him because of his popularity among the peasants and opposition to the Communization of his country.[11] Once again, it is difficult to determine which portion of Sihanouk's analysis of both insurgent and North Vietnamese attitudes and behavior is accurate and which represents a self-serving attempt to thrust himself upon U.S. decisionmakers as the essential component of any Cambodian solution. As he rhetorically posed the issue in a letter to the *Far Eastern Economic Review*: "But the question remains of whether the Cambodian problem can be resolved, and, above all, if an authentic independence can be restored to the country without the participation of myself."[12] Clearly, the prince has not yet excluded himself from a key political role in Cambodia's future. Moreover, the longer the war continues without a definitive victory, the more attractive he probably hopes to become to the Americans, especially if he can separate himself and the liberation front from Hanoi and if events demonstrate that Lon Nol's regime is decreasingly viable over time.

The Khmer Rouge Gains Some Independence

Sensitive to allegations that they were merely North Vietnamese puppets, Khmer Rouge leaders increasingly stressed their independence from Hanoi. FUNK's Minister of the Interior, Hou Youn, was even reported to have insisted that "the Vietnamese must respect our rights."[13] Moreover, the top-level insurgent government, created in November 1973 to provide an alternative to Phnom Penh in the United Nations and located in the northeastern part of the country, included neither Hanoi-trained cadre nor Sihanoukists among its listed ministers. Ieng Sary, the number two man on most lists and a Hanoi-style Communist, chose only those leaders outside Sihanouk's personal entourage to move from Peking to the "liberated area" of Cambodia, effectively separating the prince from the politics of the movement. There was little more than a Khmer Rouge diplomatic corps remaining in Peking. Khmer Rouge propaganda leading up to the fall of 1974 United Nations vote insisted: "We are a complete state, totally independent politically, militarily, and economically. We have power, an army and sufficient finances. In brief, we have a complete administrative regime . . . without being dependent on any foreign country."[14]

The FUNK particularly began to stress its own independence in January 1974, while congratulating itself over the CPLAF (Cambodian Peoples Liberation Armed Forces) dry season military performance. FUNK soldiers opened a series of military fronts around Phnom Penh, while abandoning the siege of the capital itself. Pointing up the lessons of its "victories," five of FUNK's six points emphasized the Front's independence from outside manipulation, insisting that "they are masters of their own destiny."[15] Concurrent with this emphasis on self-reliance came reports of large streams of refugees leaving Khmer Rouge zones and complaining of a much more rigorous discipline imposed by the Cambodian Communists than by their North Vietnamese counterparts who had withdrawn months before.[16] Khieu Samphan indirectly acknowledged this unwanted exodus when he railed against Phnom Penh "spies, pacification agents, pirates, agitators and commandos that the CIA has sent to the liberated zone to rally the inhabitants."[17]

Many of the fighting forces who defected from the insurgents in the spring of 1974 were Sihanoukists (Rumdos) who had had enough of both North Vietnamese influence within the Front and the heavy-handed indoctrination and terror of the Khmer Rouge.[18] There was even a report of armed clashes between Khmer Rouge and North Vietnamese forces near the South Vietnamese border over distribution of food supplies and command areas in Cambodia.[19] Nevertheless, it is unlikely that large numbers of disenchanted revolutionaries found the Lon Nol regime's corruption and ineptitude an attractive alternative to Resistance factionalism and terror.

While friction continued both within the insurgent movement and between the insurgents and their North Vietnamese allies, important changes occurred which reflected leadership conflict inside the FUNK. The changes, initiated by the Khmer Rouge, were designed to separate Sihanouk from his external backers in Peking, while strengthening the image of an independent—if pro-Hanoi—Front orientation. The origins of these maneuvers go back to the ostentatious November 1973 RGNUC (Royal Government of the National Union of Cambodia) shift from Peking to the "liberated region" of northeast Cambodia (where, incidentally, it would be much more susceptible to North Vietnamese influence). The purpose of the shift was at least partly diplomatic/propagandistic: to refute the claims of Lon Nol's defenders that the Front operated a government-in-exile and hence was unworthy of consideration for Cambodia's U.N. seat. The proclaimed transfer of ministries to the Cambodian jungles, however, served not only the FUNK's diplomatic ends but also the political desires of Deputy Premier and Defense Minister Khieu Samphan—the actual leader of the Resistance. Throughout 1974, reports from insurgent-held territory described the systematic removal of pro-Sihanouk cadres from local leadership positions and their replacement by Khmer Rouge stalwarts.[20]

Sihanouk's monopoly over diplomatic representation abroad was broken when a Front delegation, led by Khieu Samphan and consisting entirely of Khmer Rouge (with no Rumdo representation), embarked on an extensive tour of socialist and third world states in the spring and summer of 1974. The tour was given extensive publicity by both Peking and Hanoi; and although Khieu Samphan dutifully referred to Sihanouk as head of state, it was apparent where actual insurgent decisionmaking resided. *People's Daily* itself referred to Khieu Samphan's visit as "the first important delegation to China from the interior part of Cambodia," implicitly discounting earlier visits from pro-Sihanouk individuals.[21] One report went so far as to claim that Sihanouk had been reduced to the role of part-time interpreter during Mr. Samphan's visit and did not participate in the talks held by Premier Chou with the Khmer Rouge leader.[22]

Khieu Samphan's visit to Peking extended over almost two months during which an agreement on China's gratis provision of military aid for 1974 was reached.[23] Extensive talks were held to "clarify the policy of independence, neutrality, and nonalignment which Cambodia pursues . . . ," in which Sihanouk apparently did not participate, according to the namelist released by NCNA.[24] When specifically queried by a Western reporter over how Cambodia could retain nonalignment given its heavy dependence on both Hanoi and Peking, Mr. Samphan replied that Cambodia must make sacrifices—not to "be dominated by those who are our friends"—but to be completely independent and "not the slaves or the satellites of anybody."[25] In the joint communique with the DRV on April 1, 1974, just before its visit to China, the RGNUC delegation insisted on the self-sufficiency of its armed forces as a "solid base of the Cambodian revolution."

Beginning in 1974, then, it appeared that the Khmer Resistance leadership was concentrating increasingly on establishing the legitimacy of its independence from its backers and on the exclusion of Sihanouk from even a significant diplomatic role. Insofar as the Khmer Rouge could promote their own predominance in Cambodian politics to the leaders of sympathetic countries, they could render Sihanouk's exile role redundant and perhaps even undermine his last bastion of support in Peking.

Military Aspects of External Support

Any definitive political settlement for Cambodia depends to a large extent on the relative military successes of the antagonists. The steadily improving military fortunes of the insurgents have precluded interest in a negotiated settlement on their part. And the reduced participation of Vietnamese Communist cadre in the fighting since mid-1972 has certainly diminished Hanoi's ability to influence either the military tactics of the Resistance or its political decisions.

Although the insurgents have issued no complaints against their Vietnamese allies, Sihanouk has not hesitated to point out deficiencies in Hanoi's supply of weapons, claiming on more than one occasion that "our North Vietnamese friends are no longer willing to help us by transporting supplies from the Chinese to the borders of Cambodia."[26] Such revelations must be viewed cautiously, of course, given Sihanouk's distrust of both the North Vietnamese and Khmer Rouge and his desire to promote the indispensability of his own participation. At the same time, allegations of insufficient supplies proved a convenient (and plausible) explanation for insurgent inability to take and hold any major Cambodian city in over four years of fighting. Moreover, the prolonged presence of an RGNUC "financial and economic delegation" in both Hanoi and Peking during the months of October and November 1974 suggested that the insurgents may have been pressing their case on both allies for the kind of material support necessary to win total victory.

Limited North Vietnamese supplies have probably been a major determinant of Khmer Resistance tactics. These alternate between sporadic attacks on such major centers as Kompong Chom, Takeo, Kompong Speu, Oudong, and Phnom Penh (in the last half of 1973 and the spring of 1974), when artillery can be concentrated, and the more normal guerrilla style of interdicting supply routes into the capital and other government centers, which entails dispersal of weapons and personnel over several fronts. In some cases the inadequacy of North Vietnamese supplies has been partially compensated by captured U.S. weapons taken from FANK (National Cambodian Armed Forces) forces. Captured U.S. artillery, for example, was used in the sieges of Kompong Chom and Phnom Penh. Nevertheless, the North Vietnamese reportedly refused to come to aid of their Cambodian allies when the latter's siege of the capital stalled, suggesting once again that Hanoi was unenthusiastic about the implications of Cambodia's military collapse before either a political or military settlement in Vietnam.

The North Vietnamese explain the protracted character of the Cambodian War and rationalize slow insurgent progress by referring to the "massive introduction of weapons and war material to the Lon Nol clique at a rate of $1 million a day" from the United States plus American orders to secretly send so-called volunteers to Phnom Penh.[27] According to Hanoi:

Under American officers, the Lon Nol army is doing all the combat tasks while Thai mercenaries have to see to the transportation by air of weapons, gas, and food to the Lon Nol army, and the training of spies and commandos, and the defense of certain places along the northwestern borders, and the Saigon mercenaries are given the tasks of protecting the Sihanoukville port, helping Lon Nol troops in holding some frontier areas, and escorting convoys on the Mekong River.[28]

In sum, Hanoi depicts the insurgents as fighting not merely a weak, demoralized, and disorganized Phnom Penh army but also a broad sampling of American strength in Southeast Asia, including contingents from South Vietnam, Thailand, and even Taiwan. The FUNK has also accused the United States of building up from 3,500 toward a total of ten thousand U.S. military and civilian personnel in Cambodia, who "are directly in command of military operations on all battlefields."[29] Peking has repeated these allegations.[30]

Unlike Sihanouk, Khieu Samphan and the Hanoi-oriented Khmer Rouge leadership have displayed no reservations about the adequacy of North Vietnamese backing. Mr. Samphan has publicly praised the DRV on several occasions for its "continuous support" and has promised that the liberation forces will "persist ... whatever the difficulties."[31] The disparity between the postures of Sihanouk and Samphan reflect their differing constituencies. The Khmer Rouge, lacking a popular base in Cambodian society and dissociating themselves from Sihanouk in the occupied areas—though not yet in international diplomacy— need the North Vietnamese to supply material and advisors despite some local suspicion about long-term Vietnamese Communist ambitions for Cambodia. Sihanouk, on the other hand, has displayed his distrust of the North Vietnamese from the early days of the rebellion in 1970. If the prince has any future in Cambodia, it will be derived from his charismatic relationship to the peasantry, his symbolic personification of national unity, and his ties to a Chinese government, which is probably unenthusiastic over the prospect of a Khmer Rouge regime closely tied to North Vietnam.

In 1974, however, even the Chinese began to hedge their bets through their effusive reception for Khieu Samphan and his exclusively Khmer Rouge delegation from the Cambodian interior. Sihanouk—as mentioned above—was absent through much of the visit. The warm reception in Peking coincided with reports of an intensification of Communist (as distinct from nationalist/anti-American) indoctrination in Resistance-occupied areas.[32] This onerous new regimen has accounted for the relatively large number of recent "political" refugees moving into provincial centers controlled by FANK and should be distinguished from those who fled earlier in order to escape the fighting.[33] Refugee accounts from those who fled Khmer insurgent areas in 1974 reveal extensive atrocities by the Cambodian Communists who appear more sanguinary, doctrinaire, and vindictive than their Vietminh predecessors.[34]

External Economic Aid for the Antagonists

Economic dislocation resulting from more than four years of warfare has afflicted both sides in Cambodia. As mentioned previously, conflicts over distribution of rice harvests between the Vietnamese Communists and Khmer Rouge have reportedly led to limited military clashes between the ostensible allies.[35] On the other side, the Lon Nol regime is heavily dependent on U.S.-funded air and river transport to supply the centers under its control with food and fuel. As one exasperated American diplomat put it: "You cannot imagine how much time we spend just seeing that barges full of rice and gasoline make it up the Mekong to Phnom Penh."[36]

Control over economic resources has become increasingly important to the insurgents as they have seen their offensives stall from lack of supplies even as their responsibilities increase as more territory and population have come under their aegis. Thus, in mid-1974, the RGNUC nationalized foreign-owned rubber plantations for the first time, offering to sell the latex "to anyone who desires to purchase it . . . in conformity with the present and future market."[37]

FUNK propaganda has claimed not only that the economy in the "liberated areas" is thriving but that agricultural products are produced "in more than sufficient quantities for [our] own consumption and even for export to our neighbors and brothers of liberated South Vietnam and Laos."[38] If the Khmer insurgents are exporting rice and other foodstuffs—voluntarily or otherwise—to their Indochinese cohorts, this may well alleviate some of the pressure on North Vietnam which has an annual grain deficit of around one million tons. Over the long run, access to Cambodia's rice-rich Battambang province could render Hanoi "self-sufficient" in grain. Both the Khmer Resistance and China are undoubtedly cognizant of this possibility and its implications for future Cambodian economic independence.[39]

Economic warfare is also an important component of the insurgents' overall struggle against Phnom Penh. By cutting supply routes at the same time as large numbers of refugees streamed into government centers, the Resistance triggered a severe inflation which has wiped out the economic security of the salaried middle classes who had been the Lon Nol regime's original base of political support. Prices were estimated to have risen in government-controlled areas by 275 percent in 1973 and an additional 40 percent in the first quarter of 1974.[40] In more meaningful terms to a Cambodian consumer, between early 1970 and the end of 1973, the cost of rice shot up twenty times; pork twenty times; chicken thirty times; eggs fifteen times; and bananas twenty times. On the pay front the picture was equally bleak. A construction worker who earned 18 U.S. cents a day before the war earned only 54 cents at the end of 1973; and an office girl at Khmer Airlines increased her pay in the same period from around $30 to only $100 per month.[41]

Cambodia's import bill more than doubled between 1970 and the end of 1973 to $214 million—a situation made possible only through the U.S. PL-480 Commodity Import Program and contributions to the Exchange Support Fund both of which were drastically reduced for fiscal 1975.[42] In short, the Khmer Republic was surviving economically only through U.S. airlifts into government centers and armed convoys up the Mekong and Tonle Sap Rivers. American aid for fiscal 1974 included $325 million in military supplies, $170 million in food, and $75 million in other economic support.[43] The food aid included some 265,000 tons of rice, accounting for more than two-thirds of Cambodia's needs.[44] Much of the economic aid found its way into Phnom Penh's military budget via the Food for Peace program which permitted the Cambodian government to sell U.S. commodities on the commercial market and transfer some 80 percent of the proceeds into the military budget.

By the end of 1974, however, the patience of the U.S. Congress seemed to have reached its limit. The fiscal 1974 total Cambodian authorization of $688.5 million was almost halved to $377 for fiscal 1975. (This of course, does not even take reduced purchasing power into account.) Military aid was slashed from just under $400 million to $200 million. Only $20 million was made available for refugee assistance, $63 million for commodity imports, $15 million for exchange support, and $2 million for technical assistance and training. An additional $77 million could be provided through PL-480 commodities.[45] There was a pervasive belief in U.S. governmental circles that this sum would be nowhere near sufficient for the Phnom Penh administration to retain even its current low level of popular support. Food riots and possible military mutiny were foreseen by some. Neither the insurgents nor their backers were unaware of this evidence of the political and economic limitations on the Americans.

Prospects for a Diplomatic Settlement

A negotiated settlement to the war would seem to depend on *both* Cambodian antagonists' beliefs that no end to the protracted conflict is in sight and that each side's external allies are willing to continue only the level of support necessary to keep their Cambodian counterpart in the contest. The growing unacceptability of a prolonged stalemate to the Cambodians (though not necessarily either to the North Vietnamese or Chinese as explained below) could lead to a search for a Laotian-type coalition settlement rather than the continuation of what is essentially a civil war with outside assistance.

Reflecting its relatively weak position, the Phnom Penh government, under several prime ministers, sought a negotiated settlement beginning in April 1973. Each time its conditions have been progressively reduced until in July 1974, Lon Nol offered unconditional negotiations.

While Phnom Penh—with U.S. backing—has been seeking a negotiated end to the war, there is scant evidence to suggest any comparable interest on the parts of its Khmer Rouge, North Vietnamese, Chinese, and Sihanouk opponents. The Khmer Rouge and their North Vietnamese mentors would be unenthusiastic about any settlement which would give Sihanouk an independent government role. So long as the insurgents are able to consolidate control over the areas they have occupied and progressively isolate the Phnom Penh regime, there is little need to share political authority with either Lon Nol or Sihanouk. And, as mentioned above, for the North Vietnamese, *any* settlement in Cambodia before an ultimate disposition of South Vietnam would be viewed as a liability. Military victory for the insurgents would both drain North Vietnamese administrative resources and enhance tendencies toward political independence on the part of the Khmer Rouge. Although a negotiated settlement might not entail the same drain on North Vietnamese political and administrative expertise, it would still encourage a less dependent relationship for the Khmer Resistance. The status quo possesses distinct advantages from Hanoi's viewpoint: it sustains military dependency for the Khmer Rouge, while continuing to provide North Vietnam unimpeded control over the eastern Cambodian access routes and supply depots for Hanoi's primary objective—South Vietnam.

Sihanouk's own discontent with the North Vietnamese and Khmer Rouge has been demonstrated through his numerous interviews and explanations of his preferred outcome for Cambodia. The prince has stated that he wishes to see Cambodia's buffer role in Indochinese politics restored and that he would not be averse to the maintenance of American forces in Thailand.[46] He has indicated a willingness to negotiate directly with the Americans if Washington abjures Lon Nol and establishes diplomatic relations with the RGNUC.[47] But the FUNK itself has indirectly disavowed Sihanouk's feelers by recalling other statements of his denying "the right of any foreign power to become involved in the affairs of the Cambodians. . . ."[48]

For the Khmer Rouge and the North Vietnamese, Sihanouk's primary utility—as Khieu Samphan somewhat exaggeratedly put it—was "to promote broad international solidarity for our just combat and help us win the *de facto* and *de jure* recognition of the great majority of the world's countries and peoples."[49] But as discussed previously, even the role of roving diplomat was circumscribed for the prince in 1974 as Khieu Samphan himself led a combined FUNK/RGNUC delegation on an extended tour to drum up international support to replace Phnom Penh in Cambodia's United Nations seat.

The ostensible movement of the exile RGNUC from Peking to a "liberated region" in November 1973 was designed to dramatize its independence for purposes of international recognition and the forthcoming U.N. vote. Phnom Penh managed to retain its seat in 1973 by a narrow 53-50 margin (with 21 abstentions); and it is noteworthy that China was the only Asian U.N. member supporting the insurgents' candidacy. The major diplomatic campaign undertaken in 1974 by Khieu Samphan who, unlike Sihanouk, has fought the war on Cambodian soil rather than from a safe, comfortable exile, was calculated to reverse the 1973 U.N. vote. In visits to eleven countries, spanning Asia, Europe, and Africa, timed to coincide with the Front's military offensives during the 1974 dry season, emphasis was placed on the inevitability of an RGNUC victory and the futility of Lon Nol's continued occupation of Cambodia's seat in the United Nations.[50] Both Chinese and North Vietnamese media provided extensive coverage of the tour, perhaps in part because of the important diplomatic precedent which could be set if the United Nations voted to replace an incumbent by an insurgent government before a civil war had been terminated. Such an event would have important implications all the way from Northern Ireland through the Palestine terrorist movements to the PRG in South Vietnam. In the specific case of Cambodia, Sihanouk argued, acquisition of the U.N. seat would render it increasingly difficult for the U.S. Congress to appropriate funds for a government no longer recognized in the world's most prominent international forum.[51]

Nevertheless, after an arduous U.N. General Assembly session in the fall, replete with arcane American parliamentary maneuvering and a good deal of political arm-twisting, Lon Nol's government managed to survive for one more year in the world's primary international body by a vote of 56 to 54 with 24 abstentions. The General Assembly appeal for negotiations by both sides was once more rejected by the insurgents and their backers—Peking, for example, insisting that the issue was strictly an internal matter for the Cambodians to resolve without outside interference.[52] Sihanouk, this time from Pyongyang, declared that his compatriots were "firmly determined to continue the armed struggle against the enemies for five years or ten years, or even for 20 years, if necessary."[53] His bitter condemnation of non-Communist Asian states' opposition to the RGNUC in the United Nations interestingly was excised from NCNA's version of a mid-October statement, demonstrating that the Cambodian issue took second place to Peking's current bridge-building efforts to non-Communist Asia.[54]

Efforts by Phnom Penh, with American support, to arrange face-to-face negotiations with the Resistance remained as elusive in 1974 as they had in the previous year. Part of the frustration from Phnom Penh's perspective was an inability to identify those who could speak for the Resistance as a whole rather than isolated, disaffected units, some of which (Khmer Rumdo) were willing to negotiate a transfer of allegiance.[55] Moreover, it was apparent that top level Resistance leaders remained unwilling to consider either a ceasefire in place or a reactivation of the International Control Commission in Cambodia to monitor the activities of outsiders, as proposed by Prime Minister Long Boret toward the end of 1973.[56]

Reports persist, however, of attempts to contact the RGNUC in a variety of locales, ranging from former premiers Son Sann and Cheng Heng in Paris to an alleged anti-Lon Nol liberation front formed in Phnom Penh and willing to exclude Lon Nol and his advisors if the insurgents agree to discuss a Laotian-style coalition settlement—thus turning the clock back to Sihanouk's own early proposals for a restoration of unity back in 1970.[57] There is no evidence that any of these attempts have borne fruit.

Sihanouk has demonstrated some sensitivity to charges by a few governments (such as Thailand) that the Resistance is at fault for being unwilling to halt Indochinese bloodshed even after the Laotians had agreed to a cease-fire and there was at least a semblance of an international monitoring presence in South Vietnam.[58] He has countered by insisting that only Washington can end the Cambodian war by withdrawing its support from Lon Nol. Hanoi has backed this position.[59]

Khmer Rouge leaders have sustained their insistence on a military victory, citing their ability to besiege the capital at will and the alleged flight of "thousands of persons" from the cities to the liberated zone.[60] The Khmer Rouge's unyielding attitude partly explains U.S. Secretary of State Kissinger's unwillingness to meet North Vietnam's Le Duc Tho. Meetings had been scheduled for March and June 1974 but were reportedly cancelled because of the intractable Khmer insurgent posture. Presumably the talks would have focused on U.S. reconstruction aid to North Vietnam as well as the situation in South Vietnam.[61]

Although Sihanouk is once again reported to be willing to see Kissinger (unlike his ostentatious absence from Peking in November 1973) he at least publicly refuses to consider either a physical division of Cambodia or the formation of a coalition government—the only two bases for a *negotiated* settlement. Such adamancy has consistently characterized the Resistance public posture since 1971, although it may no longer have Peking's enthusiastic endorsement, judging from reports of Chou En-lai's conversations with visitors. The Chinese premier may believe that the only real chance for Sihanouk to retain some influence in a postwar government is through a coalition which offers him a linkage role between the antagonists.[62] Sihanouk himself has demonstrated an awareness of his utility to his erstwhile allies on a number of occasions—most recently when he pointed out: "The Khmer Reds are very clever. They know that without Sihanouk, they are regarded by many just as rebels against Lon Nol. But with Sihanouk, they have legitimacy. They have a monarchy."[63] On the other hand, the prince has consistently refused to consider any alternative to a military victory and has insisted that neither Peking nor Hanoi will attempt to alter that strategy.[64] Thus, Lon Nol's July 1974 appeal for absolutely unconditional negotiations has not only been rejected but also interpreted by the insurgents as yet another sign of the progressive deterioration of his regime.

Even the Soviets—who have played their cards very cautiously by maintaining contacts with both antagonists, despite their October 1973 "recognition" of the RGNUC—have increasingly publicized Khmer Rouge victories. And by late summer 1974, the Russians appeared to conclude that the insurgents' victory, under Khieu Samphan's leadership, was only a matter of time. Sihanouk, moreover, was rarely mentioned in Soviet dispatches.[65]

As for North Vietnam—the insurgents' key outside backer—carefully controlled support for the Khmer Rouge will undoubtedly persist, given Hanoi's view of its mission as driving the United States out of Southeast Asia, despite the latter's detente with the major Communist powers:

The United States is prolonging the war of aggression in Cambodia and sabotaging the Lao revolution, pursuing its scheme to form a regional alliance among the reactionary forces of Indochina. It maintains more than 200,000 U.S. troops in the Southeast Asia and Western Pacific region as a deterrent, trying to threaten and contain the revolutionary movement in this region—primarily in Vietnam and in the other countries of Indochina.

The Nixon administration is also pursuing the so-called policy of detente and the strategy of achieving a balance among the big powers, resorting to insidious and crafty political, diplomatic, and economic tricks to alienate our people from the forces of peace, national independence, democracy and socialism in the world.

Obviously, these U.S. schemes and acts have been carefully calculated and premeditated, and the United States began to consistently carry them out well before it had to sign the Paris agreement on Vietnam.[66]

Thus, the analyst is left to contemplate the continuation of a political and military stalemate which appears likely to be broken only if (a) the United

States abandons the non-Communist side, as desired by Sihanouk; (b) North Vietnam succeeds in incorporating South Vietnam and subsequently agrees to back a Khmer Rouge military victory; (c) North Vietnam agrees to help the Khmer Rouge obtain a military victory prior to an ultimate disposition of South Vietnam in exchange for the Khmer insurgents' pledge not to interfere with the Vietnamese Communist occupation of eastern Cambodia; or (d) because of its own corruption and inefficiency as well as the absence of sufficient U.S. support, the regime in Phnom Penh collapses, leaving a political vacuum which elements of the Resistance would fill simply because there is no other organized political alternative. Such a development would upset the DRV's timetable but would give Hanoi little choice other than to provide support for the new insurgent regime.

Note that none of these alternatives envision prospects for either a Lon Nol victory or a negotiated settlement which would provide Cambodian anti-Communists with a significant political voice. Although the above four alternatives appear to this author to encompass the most plausible outcomes in the long run, only the last seems likely to occur before the 1976 U.S. presidential election, for the Khmer Republic has demonstrated neither the political nor military capability of moving beyond population enclaves and the few safe Western provinces it currently controls. And both its adversaries and supporters seem prepared to bide their time while awaiting the ultimate collapse.

Notes

1. Sydney Schanberg, "Cambodia's Little War: 600,000 Casualties," *New York Times—Week In Review*, September 8, 1974.

2. U.S. Senate Committee on Foreign Relations, *Thailand, Laos, Cambodia, and Vietnam*: April 1973; A Staff Report for the Subcommittee on U.S. Security Agreements and Commitments Abroad (Washington, D.C.: U.S. Goverment Printing Office, June 11, 1973), p. 2.

3. For a good, brief background discussion of the group composition of the Khmer insurgency, see Elizabeth Becker, "Who Are the Khmer Rouge?" *Washington Post*, March 10, 1974.

4. Ibid. See also the detailed report by Kenneth M. Quinn, "The Khmer Krom Program to Create a Communist Society in Southern Cambodia," (an unpublished State Department paper) February 19, 1974, especially pp. 1, 4, 7, 30, 33, 34.

5. See, for example, Fox Butterfield, "Reds Still Clash Inside Cambodia," *New York Times*, September 9, 1973. See also Kenneth M. Quinn, "Khmer Krom Program," pp. 1, 5, 32.

6. *Quan Doi Nhan Dan*, November 30, 1973.

7. Ibid., December 11, 1973.

8. Cf. footnotes 4 and 5.

9. *Far Eastern Economic Review*, October 1, 1973, p. 13. Needless to say, the author found no evidence of any North Vietnamese encouragement of negotiations in Hanoi's own media output as presented in the Foreign Broadcast Information Service, *Daily Report: Asia/Pacific.*

10. Sihanouk interview in *Le Monde*, October 27, 1973.

11. Sihanouk interview in the *Far Eastern Economic Review*, January 7, 1974, pp. 22-23.

12. Ibid., January 28, 1974, p. 6.

13. From a Cambodian book by a former Phnom Penh teacher who spent part of 1972-73 with the Khmer Rouge, cited in Elizabeth Becker, "Who Are the Khmer Rouge?"

14. Khieu Samphan Interview with the Cambodian Information Agency (AKI) September 27, 1974.

15. Voice of FUNK in Cambodian, January 19, 1974.

16. Philip McCombs, "Life With Cambodian Rebels: Short Hair and 'Cheap Stuff'," *The Washington Post*, February 3, 1974; Elizabeth Becker, "Who Are the Khmer Rouge?", March 10, 1974; and Kenneth M. Quinn, "Khmer Krom Program."

17. Khieu Samphon address carried by AKI in French, October 1, 1974.

18. Mike Snitowsky, "The Dividends of Defection," *Far Eastern Economic Review*, March 18, 1974, pp. 10-11; the *Christian Science Monitor*, March 13, 1974; and Kenneth M. Quinn, "Khmer Krom Program."

19. *The Washington Post* March 29, 1974; and the *Christian Science Monitor*, March 11, 1974.

20. *New York Times*, April 30, 1974; and Kenneth M. Quinn, "Khmer Krom Program," pp. 4 and 6.

21. Editorial in *People's Daily*, April 1, 1974.

22. *Far Eastern Economic Review*, May 13, 1974, pp. 26-27.

23. NCNA, May 26, 1974.

24. NCNA, May 24 and 27, 1974.

25. *Christian Science Monitor*, April 9, 1974.

26. *The Guardian* (London) September 18, 1973; *Agence France Presse* (AFP) (Hong Kong) September 20, 1973.

27. Radio Hanoi in Vietnamese, January 9, 1974.

28. VNA, February 18, 1974.

29. RGNUC Propaganda and Information Ministry statement broadcast by the Voice of FUNK in Cambodian, March 22, 1974. See also the KCNA (Pyongyang) report of Khieu Samphan's speech in North Korea, April 7, 1974.

30. NCNA, March 24, 1974.

31. Khieu Samphan interview carried by Radio Hanoi, March 30, 1974.

32. James M. Markham, "Cambodia's Military Situation Worsening, With No Peace Talks in Sight," *New York Times*, April 28, 1974.

33. *Far Eastern Economic Review*, May 27, 1974, pp. 26-27; and Kenneth M. Quinn, "Khmer Krom Program."

34. Donald Kirk, "Khmer Rouge's Bloody War on Trapped Villagers," *Chicago Tribune*, July 14, 1974.

35. Cf. footnote 5.

36. *New York Times*, March 3, 1974.

37. RGNUC deputy prime minister's office communique, carried by the Voice of FUNK in Cambodian, July 20, 1974.

38. Sihanouk statement broadcast by the Cambodian Information Agency (AKI) in French, July 12, 1974.

39. Kenneth P. Landon, "The Impact of the Sino-American Detente on the Indochinese Conflict," in Gene T. Hsiao (ed.), *Sino-American Detente and Its Policy Implications* (New York: Praeger Special Studies in International Politics, 1974), p. 221.

40. *New York Times*, April 28, 1974.

41. Mike Snitowsky, "The Cambodian Way of Life," *Far Eastern Economic Review*, January 21, 1974, p. 43.

42. Personal communication with Mr. Norman Sweet of the United States Agency for International Development, December 26, 1974. See also Nayan Chanda, "The Cambodian Nightmare," *The Far Eastern Economic Review*, September 20, 1974, pp. 42-43.

43. *Christian Science Monitor*, February 4, 1974.

44. *Washington Post*, December 15, 1973. Prior to the war, Cambodia was a rice exporter.

45. Congressional authorization figures were obtained through the courtesy of Norman Sweet of the United States Agency for International Development, December 26, 1974.

46. Sihanouk interview in the *Bangkok Post*, September 29, 1973.

47. Reported by AFP (Hong Kong), October 14, 1973.

48. FUNK statements carried by AKI in French, October 18 and November 1, 1973.

49. Khieu Samphan birthday greeting to Sihanouk, carried by AKI in French, October 30, 1973.

50. Voice of FUNK in Cambodian, July 7, 1974, for a summation of the purposes of Khieu Samphan's tour.

51. Sihanouk interview in Roumania reported in the *Lexington* (Ky.) *Herald-Leader*, August 25, 1974.

52. CPR delegate Huang Hua's speech to the UN General Assembly, NCNA, November 27, 1974.

53. Sihanouk speech carried by the *Korean Central News Agency* (KCNA), December 3, 1974.

54. Compare the versions of Sihanouk's speech carried by NCNA on October 19 and AKI on October 21, 1974.

55. See the press conference with Khmer Republic Information Minister Trinh Hoan on the difficulty of making contacts with the FUNK, Phnom Penh Domestic Service, January 10, 1974.

56. Long Boret's proposal was made in an address to the Cambodian parliament, carried by Phnom Penh Domestic Service on December 28, 1973. It was rejected by Sihanouk two days later (AFP, Hong Kong).

57. *New York Times*, January 13, 1974, and *The Nation* (Bangkok) March 1, 1974.

58. Sihanouk speech in Sam Neua to the Pathet Lao, Radio Pathet Lao, March 17, 1974.

59. Sihanouk banquet address in Canton, NCNA, March 23, 1974, and the *Nhan Dan* editorial of the same day.

60. Speech by RGNUC Special Missions Minister, Chau Seng, in Paris, carried by AKI in French, March 30, 1974.

61. *Far Eastern Economic Review*, July 15, 1974.

62. Ibid., May 13, 1974, p. 31 and AFP (Hong Kong) July 9, 1974.

63. *Lexington* (Ky.) *Herald-Leader*, August 25, 1974.

64. AFP (Hong Kong) report of a Sihanouk statement in Peking, August 5, 1974.

65. Malcolm Browne, "*Pravda* Asks Cambodian Government to Step Aside for the Insurgents," *New York Times*, August 9, 1974.

66. "The New U.S. Strategy Will Surely Fail," *Tap Chi Quan Doi Nhan Dan* (Hanoi) June 1974.

Revolution and Political Violence in Cambodia, 1970-1974

Donald Kirk

Legacy of Terror

Political violence occurs frequently in the protracted conflict for control of the Khmer countryside. Hundreds of peasants were killed during the revolt in Battambang Province in 1967 as Cambodian government troops swept through the region in support of the interests of well-to-do landlords. Prince Norodom Sihanouk, before his overthrow on March 18, 1970, ordered the secret executions of a number of his opponents—including at least three Khmer Rouge leaders who escaped in the *maquis* and then fought nominally in his name after his fall. Certain Cambodian army commanders, soon after the onset of full-fledged war in mid-1970, ordered their troops to behead North Vietnamese prisoners with their bayonets—or to decapitate the bodies of North Vietnamese already slain in combat. At the same time, American warplanes, flying in support of Cambodian troops until August 15, 1973, devastated villages and pockmarked the countryside.

It was in this atmosphere of intermittent violence that the Khmer Rouge, as Sihanouk began calling the Communist forces in the late 1960s, opened a campaign of forced labor and killing ranging over much of the land. The specter of violence, whoever was responsible, seemed to fit in more naturally with the war in Cambodia than with the fighting in Laos and Vietnam. The combatants in Laos were less warlike than the superficially placid Khmer, noted since before the French colonial era for their propensity for fighting when sufficiently motivated or adequately led. And the combatants in Vietnam, despite the long history of warfare in both North and South, seemed much better disciplined and coordinated than the Khmer—and more attentive to the interests of the civilian populace. Indeed, one might argue that field leaders in Cambodia displayed a marked degree of amateurism in their often indiscriminate use of tactics that could hurt their cause. Certainly, the Khmer Rouge, by pursuing the path of political violence, induced thousands of peasants to flee their areas for the relative safety of Phnom Penh and lesser provincial enclaves still held by Cambodian government troops. The Vietnamese Communists, by contrast skilled professionals, carefully discerned and singled out their specific enemies and did not alienate the populace.

Beyond the overall nature of the war, however, certain factors were involved

215

in the decision to advocate the use of violence as a means to ideological and political ends. In order to win decisively, Khmer Rouge leaders knew they had to impose iron-tight discipline over a reluctant, lethargic populace. "This side here is not weak enough to give up and the other side is not strong enough to achieve a real victory," was the comment of a Western ambassador to Cambodia in a conversation with the writer in June 1974. The Khmer Rouge appeared to have scored a notable triumph in March 1974 when they captured the old royal capital of Oudong, twenty-four miles northwest of Phnom Penh. Yet Phnom Penh forces finally reoccupied it three and a half months later in the kind of back-and-forth fighting that epitomized the tragedy of the conflict—all that were left of Oudong after the battles for the town were the ruins of what had been Buddhist wats and other monuments to Khmer history and culture.

The battle for Oudong also dramatized the policy of indiscriminate violence by which the Khmer Rouge hoped to topple the regime of the ailing President Lon Nol. After conquering Oudong, Khmer Rouge cadres led the populace of 20,000 persons into the nearby jungle, killed some 200 school teachers and government officials, according to Phnom Penh diplomatic and military sources, and deliberately razed the town, setting buildings on fire or tearing them down. Confirmation of this killing lay in reports from those who had escaped and freely told their stories to anyone who was interested. During a visit in June 1974 to Kompong Chnang, northwest of Oudong on the Tonle Sap, a girl named Chan Socheat told the writer of her experience while serving as a cook at a nearby Khmer Rouge outpost. "They treated wounded people before the crowd, but they killed them later," said the girl. "Some they shot, and some they beat with sticks." The girl, whose unit was guarding a crossing of the Tonle Sap at a point at which Khmer Rouge soldiers were herding groups of civilians captured in the battle, estimated that about 100 persons were executed—sometimes just because the Khmer Rouge were reluctant to "waste their medicine" on the wounded.

The frustration of the Khmer Rouge, as reflected in recourse to violence, resulted in part from a shift in strategy of the North Vietnamese, on whom the Khmer Rouge relied for arms, advice, and sometimes combat support. In the period preceding the signing of the Paris Agreement in early 1973, the North Vietnamese began to give the Khmer Rouge increasing independence in field operations. Khmer Rouge units, only half Khmer in many instances until that time, became truly Khmer in the latter months of 1972 and in 1973. Although North Vietnamese cadres advised them on tactical matters and provided radio operators and other technical assistance, the Khmer Rouge, for the most part, fought alone. The North Vietnamese remained in their traditional base areas in the northeast provinces and along the South Vietnamese border down to the sea. Their primary interest clearly was the war in Vietnam; in Cambodia, their central concern was to maintain the level of security required for holding their bases and supply routes.

Another factor in the North Vietnamese decision to decrease combat activities in Cambodia was persistent conflict all along the frontier between Khmer Rouge and North Vietnamese troops. The conflict, reflecting traditional Khmer and Vietnamese hostilities, provided complications that could only be resolved by top-level agreement on areas of operational control and responsibility. Besides, North Vietnamese troops—or rather those who directed North Vietnamese units in senior command positions—may not have wanted to accept the burden that would have been imposed on them by complete military victory in Cambodia while the war was still very mucy alive in Vietnam. How could the North Vietnamese possibly rule Phnom Penh and other towns before they had finished the fighting in what they regarded as their own country, all Vietnam, North and South?

For these reasons, then, the Khmer Rouge, limited numerically to probably no more than 50,000 combatants, assumed the main combat role against the Cambodian army—badly led, demoralized, but still well equipped by American arms and ammunition. Headquartered in or near the town of Kratie, on the Mekong River north of Phnom Penh, the Khmer Rouge were organized in a complicated network of military regions and independent units for what they hoped would be the crushing final series of attacks. Their toughest military leaders no doubt had been among the several thousand Khmer trained in North Vietnam in the 1950s after the signing of the Geneva Agreement. It was this core cadre that was mainly responsible for the conduct of the war on the Khmer Rouge side.

Leadership and Organization

The question of whether or not Prince Sihanouk, as chief-of-state in exile of the Peking-based Royal Government of National Union of Cambodia, should exercise any influence in his own country assumed paramount importance in the 1973-74 period. As the Khmer Rouge failed to achieve quick victory, even after the halt in American bombing, Khmer Rouge field cadres inevitably grew impatient with the specter of a profligate prince remaining the figurehead leader of a revolutionary movement. The top-level field leadership of the Khmer Rouge—notably Khieu Samphan, who held the titles of "deputy prime minister" and "minister of defense"—doubtless shared and encouraged this sentiment. Khieu Samphan—one of the three "leftist" national assembly deputies whose execution Sihanouk had ordered several years earlier—may himself have been responsible for the decision to eliminate Sihanouk entirely as a "leader" of the Khmer Rouge inside Cambodia. The feeling, by late 1973, was that Sihanouk represented so regressive an influence in Khmer society that he would set a poor example among the populace whom the Khmer Rouge needed to convert.

The most convincing evidence for this point lay in the experiences of refugees from a wide range of Khmer Rouge areas. In a series of interviews refugees told the writer that Sihanouk was no longer a leader in any sense, that his name was not mentioned in statements, speeches or local propaganda of any kind. "In April of 1973, they stopped talking about Sihanouk," said a village chief named Meak Sam Hon, who had fled a Khmer Rouge area for the relative safety of Kompong Thom, a provincial enclave still held by Cambodian government troops some eighty miles north of Phnom Penh. "They said that he was 'not the only man' and that he was 'no good now' and that 'we do not need him any more'. If you still use his name and support Sihanouk, then you will be sent away and you will never return. They told us to support Khieu Samphan and no others." A woman in a refugee camp along a riverbank outside Kompong Thom told much the same story. "Before they wanted all of us to say, 'we want Sihanouk'," said the woman, "but now no more." Like the others, she had no idea what lay behind the new directive. "They just stop, that is all," she said. "Before you can say anything about Sihanouk, but now you cannot show his picture any more." Nor could villagers ask questions regarding the shift in policy. "They will kill you if you ask to see the leader," she said.[1]

A Khmer Rouge defector, interviewed at a refugee camp near Phnom Penh, cited the middle of 1973 as the point in time at which the Khmer Rouge had begun to downgrade Sihanouk. "They told us, 'we do not talk about Sihanouk any more'," said the defector, named Nong Chin. Unlike civilian refugees, Nong Chin knew that Sihanouk had visited northeast Cambodia in March of 1973 and had encouraged soldiers to "unite to oppose the imperialists." He had even seen photographs of Sihanouk addressing a rally in Rattanakiri province. Nonetheless, he could understand why Khmer Rouge cadres had not approved of him despite the international propaganda value of Sihanouk's "inspection tour of the Cambodian Liberated Zone," as a supplement to *China Pictorial* had called the visit.[2] "Sihanouk never came and helped us fight," said Nong Chin, speaking intensely. "He never joined the army. He did not care about weapons and ammunition. He came from Peking only. He did not spend time with the soldiers." At the same time, Nong Chin indicated there was less than complete unanimity in Khmer Rouge ranks on the topic of Sihanouk. He himself had joined another much smaller force, the Khmer Blanc, still operating in Sihanouk's name in the eastern provinces of Svay Rieng and Prey Veng, after a quarrel with his Khmer Rouge commander, before deserting the insurgent side entirely and returning to Phnom Penh.[a]

This campaign against Sihanouk contrasted with the glorification of his image in the weeks and months after his overthrow—a period in which Khmer Rouge forces claimed to have been fighting in Sihanouk's name in order to restore him

---

[a]The Khmer Blanc, like the Khmer Rouge, obtained arms from the North Vietnamese, who allied for a time with the former as a result of continuing disputes with the latter. The Khmer Blanc, operating mainly along the Vietnamese border near North Vietnamese base areas, were not a factor in the basic conflict between Cambodian government and Khmer Rouge forces.

to power. It also contrasted with the image that Sihanouk still projected in interviews in Peking in which he protested that he and the Khmer Rouge in Cambodia were in agreement with each other. Sihanouk claimed that he wanted to give up his title of chief of state but that the Khmer Rouge did not want him to do so. He said he would keep the title of chief of state while not assuming the responsibility: "My position will be somewhat like that of the king of England."[3]

Sihanouk's remarks coincided with Khieu Samphan's assumption of power over the Khmer Rouge. He made his international debut in a lengthy journey from Hanoi to Peking to North Korea, back to China and then to eastern Europe, Algeria, Egypt, and Syria. He had an audience in Peking with Chairman Mao Tse-tung on April 2, 1974, and appeared in a highly publicized photograph sitting on the right hand of Mao while Sihanouk sat on Mao's left. An article disseminated by the New China News Agency on the same day reported in the first paragraph that Khieu Samphan and Ieng Sary, "special adviser to the office of the deputy prime minister" and actually the liaison between Sihanouk's Peking entourage and the Khmer Rouge, had met with Mao. Then, in the next paragraph, the article added that Sihanouk and the "prime minister" of his government, Penn Nouth, had also been "present at the meeting. . . ."[4] If Sihanouk's relegation to a secondary, ceremonial position was now well known, however, there was no clear indication of the extent and efficiency of the campaign against him inside Cambodia. Only those who had lived in Khmer Rouge areas could verify Sihanouk's de facto expulsion from the movement in his own country. Although he still served a useful function "in the diplomatic domain," as he asserted in his conversation with the French journalist, he was not merely irrelevant but distinctly distasteful to the men waging the war on Cambodian soil.[5]

Dishonored though he was in his native land, Sihanouk still served the purposes of the Khmer Rouge as an international spokesman in Peking. Thus, in keeping with this role, it was Sihanouk who went through the pro forma motion, on behalf of his government, of formally rejecting a proposal for peace talks issued by Lon Nol in early July. From the viewpoint of Khmer Rouge activities inside Cambodia, Sihanouk's statement was most significant in his protestations of unity with his Khmer Rouge comrades. In the opening section he noted his "capacity as the legal head of state of Cambodia recognized by the whole Cambodian resistance (including the Red Khmers, the most outstanding of whom is Khieu Samphan)," and added that his government, the united front, the armed forces and he himself "together embody the state of Cambodia, the state of independent and non-aligned Cambodia."[6] The phraseology suggested the pervasive doubts regarding Sihanouk's place in the movement. If the attitudes of the Khmer Rouge offer any clues to the future, Sihanouk might not be able to return to Phnom Penh even after a Khmer Rouge victory. At this point in the struggle it did not seem likely that he could assume more than an honorific position in a Khmer Rouge government.

The denigration of Sihanouk indicated the desire of Khmer Rouge leaders not only to gain complete control over their own movement but also to instill a new revolutionary order. Sihanouk was identified with the old order—with a way of life repugnant to the men who had endured the hardship of the *maquis*, in some cases since the period of early revolt against the French after World War II. The core of the Khmer Rouge organization, as might have been expected, was not its government per se but rather the Khmer Communist Party, sometimes known as the "Communist Party of Kampuchea," which emerged in clearly identifiable form in 1972. The Khmer Communist Party was the direct descendant of the former Revolutionary Party of the Cambodian People, formed in 1951 with the strong encouragement and support of the Vietminh organization. In April 1951, a provisional government, known as the National Liberation Committee of Cambodia, was also formed—followed by the creation of a government of Khmer resistance.[7]

It was during the period of calm after the signing of the Geneva Agreement in 1954 that the Khmer Communist organization coalesced into a viable underground movement. Some of the Khmer Rouge went to Hanoi for training while others formed cells in the forests in preparation "for a long period of hot war." Still others participated in the formation of the People's Party or Kanapak Pracheachon, a Front organization that sponsored candidates for the National Assembly in the 1955 and 1958 elections and functioned openly until Sihanouk ordered the arrest of some of its members in 1966.[8] The period from 1954 to 1967 was marked by a dual strategy of overt "political struggle" through "the press, in parliament, in the various quasi-governmental institutions" and preparation for "armed struggle." Young intellectuals "were repeatedly sent to the *maquis* to form combat cells," according to one account of a Party history. "The clandestine disappearance of young intellectuals explains this tactic of the party."[9]

Then, beginning with the Battambang revolt in 1967, "the Party resumed the armed struggle," the account continues. "The events ... were prepared in advance and gave new impulse to the struggle." Finally, on September 30, 1972, according to the account, the Khmer Communist Party "proclaimed its existence from 1951 and its rights of leadership through all vicissitudes of the struggle." The Party on that date held an anniversary ceremony marking the end of twenty-one years of activities—and displayed for the first time a flag "which has as emblems a hammer and sickle in the center of a blood-red field." The central committee of the Party, at this point, included not only Khieu Samphan and Ieng Sary but, perhaps more significantly, two others who had vanished from Phnom Penh several years before them. They were Suloth Sar, a well-to-do, Paris-educated member of the Phnom Penh elite, who disappeared in 1963, and Son Sen, a Vietnamese-born Khmer who disappeared at the beginning of the 1960s and was responsible for military operations. Described as "second-rank personages" on the committee were Hou Yuon and Hu Nim, the two other deputies whose executions Sihanouk had purportedly ordered, along with that of Khieu Samphan, in 1967. Hou Yuon was minister of interior and Hu Nim minister of information—titles that seemed to have exaggerated their importance in the Khmer Rouge organization.[10]

Building on the organizational base established in the latter 1950s and early 1960s, the Khmer Rouge divided the country into five tactical regions whose commanders served as "both vice ministers and members of the party central committee." From the regional level the administrative line of authority ran through the *srok* to the *khum* to the *damban*, a lower-level subdivision, and finally to the *phum* or village. "Each zone is administered by a committee assisted by various associations: Patriotic Youth Association, Association of Young Democrats (molding the cells of the Party), Association of Patriotic Women," according to the same account. "The number of members of the committee varies with the importance of the zone. The committee is composed of a President, a Vice-President, members charged with supply and the economy, instruction and education, health services, etc." Leaders of local committees of the National United Front of Cambodia, the increasingly meaningless organization set up to wage the war in Sihanouk's name immediately after his overthrow, "are members of the Party and cell leaders" as "are most of the leaders of FUNK Committees for Khums," said the account. And if a committee of a khum—subdivision of a srok or district—did not "have the party's trust," it was "flanked by one or two representatives of the party."[11]

Interwoven with this organizational framework were village militia units, regional forces, and the regular army, as the report noted, as well as regular cadre selected from Party cells. "From company level, the commander of each unit is helped by a Political Commissar whose authority over combatants is indisputable," said the report. "The Party seeks to give command over each unit to sons of peasants, sympathizers and faithful to the movement." At the same time, the report noted, "the term 'monarchy' has passed into silence." The Khmer Communist Party, "in methodically getting rid of pro-Sihanouk cadres, has *carte blanche* over the direction of the country," the report went on. "Under the veil of FUNK and with the complicity of the Chinese and Vietnamese Communist Parties, it has followed and respected only its own program not as yet revealed to the public."[12] It was, in fact, quite difficult to discern the extent of "complicity" by the Chinese and Vietnamese Communist Parties, but Khieu Samphan's itinerary through Hanoi and Peking meant that his emergence had their full support. Nor was it absolutely clear whether or not the Khmer Communist Party had a well-defined program of its own—or rather was operating on a pragmatic day-by-day basis, resorting to violence as a means of asserting authority.

Techniques of Operation

Quite aside from Sihanouk's formal rejection of peace proposals put forth by what he called "the traitorous Lon Nol clique under U.S. instigation," the nature of the fighting in the countryside indicated there would be no room for compromise of the sort engineered by peace agreements covering Vietnam and Laos. The Khmer Rouge, confident of victory, were determined to accomplish their revolutionary goals by coordinating political violence with propaganda attacks against the Lon Nol regime and by fostering student unrest in Phnom Pehn. The decision to resort to political violence reflects the difficulties of motivating the rural Khmer populace, much less the elite of the capital. While peasants in every civilization have exercised strong resistance to change, those in Cambodia may have been more intractable than most. Cambodian society, in terms of agricultural techniques and education beneath the upper level of petty officialdom and mercantile interests, was one of the most backward of Southeast Asia. Not since the Angkor era had Cambodia exercised real power in the region. Unlike the Vietnamese, who had been struggling southward for centuries, the Khmer had lived calmly in their rich land—seemingly without national ambition or purpose other than the right to hold what was theirs by birth.

For all the obvious oversimplification inherent in these observations, they may help to explain why the Khmer Rouge seized upon extreme tactics to move the inert peasant mass. Despite the lack of documentary evidence of a rationale for violence by the Khmer Rouge, one can gain insight into the overall technique of Khmer Rouge cadres from refugee interviews. A group of Khmer Rouge prisoners discussed what they had seen and heard during their captivity some fifty miles south of Phnom Penh. The prisoners, five or six of them in all, had had their hair closely cut except for tufts by which they could be identified if they escaped. One of them, a farmer named Nou Seng, said that he had left the camp along with 150 others after they had killed their guards, and then he had spent a week or so walking to Phnom Penh through jungle regions at night. Every day, he said, fifteen or so prisoners died—some of them victims of starvation, others killed by Khmer Rouge. The Khmer Rouge "arrested the people, collected their rice and belongings and put them into the camp," he said, "they gave speeches to the people in the camp telling us to unite with them" and ordered them to "dig the ground" in order to construct "a new capital" of the country. "The people do not believe them," Nou Seng explained, "because they kidnap them, and they hurt them, and they also shoot them or kill them with clubs. And when they are working they tie the necks of the people together so they cannot escape." Another escapee said the prisoners were also tied up at night—and displayed rope marks on his arms and legs. They had gotten away, he said, by jumping on their guards at lunchtime.

Nou Seng then provided a summary of the shift in Khmer Rouge attitudes toward the peasants:

From 1970 until the end of 1973 they were not so bad. They did not begin killing people until 1974. We do not know why they changed, but they kill people who do not follow their instructions or ideology. We were afraid if we stayed in the camp any longer, the Khmer Rouge would also kill us. They accuse the people of betraying their program, and then they kill them. They asked five people to carry a boat, and if the five could not lift up the boat, they asked three people to do it, and when the three could not do it, they killed them. There was no explanation.

Nou Seng pointed out that the Khmer Rouge preferred to kill older people rather than young ones—and had made plain that they hoped to build "a new society with the young people." In fact, he said, the Khmer Rouge had expressed the desire for a "new generation" entirely different in outlook from the old, inculcated with the odious teachings of an irrelevant religion, Buddhism, and a corrupted leader, Prince Sihanouk.[13]

Thus, the Khmer Rouge, in the midst of their terrorist acts, claimed to be fighting for libertarian, egalitarian goals and values. In the tradition of Communist movements in other nations, they were seeking to make over the society and the culture whatever the cost in lives—if the lives were already corrupted by conflicting, debasing traditions. Nou Seng supported this impression with an observation on the method by which the Khmer Rouge in some instances had selected officials for local administrations. "The people who do not know how to write are appointed as Khmer Rouge chiefs," he said, "because the Khmer Rouge believe they are honest men. The people who have no knowledge, no education must always be the chiefs." Those who already knew how to read and write presumably had been corrupted by the old system of education. "Usually the rich man dominates the poor man," said Nou Seng, talking quickly, excitedly to the writer during much of the interview, "but the Khmer Rouge think the poor man should dominate." Nou Seng added, with a kind of simplicity often reflected by Khmer peasant farmers, that he thought the Khmer Rouge were "honest" even if they did "use force, dictate and kill the people." He estimated that they had killed approximately 1,000 persons from his region. "They have black blood," he said, "because they want to kill the old men and convince the young of their ideology."

Other interviews invariably revealed the same combination of revolutionary aims and violent techniques among the Khmer Rouge. During my visit to the town of Kompong Thom, I talked to the commander of Cambodian government forces in the region, Brigadier General Teap Bin, who was constantly deploying his troops to confront Khmer Rouge attacks from all sides. He listed half a dozen factors that he thought explained the influx of some 45,000 refugees into the town in February 1974, at a time when Khmer Rouge units were diverted from their areas to support a campaign against Phnom Penh. "The Communists force them to work without rest," said the general. "The Communists make the villagers give them all they have. They force villagers to do the farming—and give the harvest to the Communists. They force people to fight without pay. They do not care about health—about whether a man is sick or dying." The general, like many others, seemed especially surprised by Khmer Rouge antipathy toward religious institutions. "Religion is very important to the Khmer people," he said. More than anything else, however, it was the brutality of the Khmer Rouge that surprised him the most. "If they want to kill," he told me, "they just kill."[14]

While General Teap Bin was necessarily a biased source, the refugees sequestered in and around Kompong Thom outlined much the same set of factors. "We were forced to work very hard and got nothing," said Meak Sam Hon, the former chief of a village in the Khmer Rouge region. "They hit and shot people. They killed anyone they suspected as an 'agent' of the government army." An aging woman interrupted to say that the Khmer Rouge had led away her four sons to fight in the Khmer Rouge army. "They were forced to go," she said. "If they do not go with them, they will be killed." Despite their harshness, however, Khmer Rouge cadres display the same drive for egalitarianism noted earlier. "They take away the clothes of the people and tell them only to wear black cloth," said the woman, named Chieu Lod. "They say the capitalists and imperialists wear good clothes." The chief of the village, reentering the conversation, substantiated the view that Khmer Rouge cadres deliberately selected those who were "poor and ignorant to be head of something." Those who knew how to write and had "so much to eat," he said, were likely to be executed. "I saw whole families killed—the wife, the children, the husband," he added.

A combination of food shortages and political violence increased the desperation of villagers to get to the provincial center at the earliest opportunity. "I left most of my belongings behind me," said Meak Sam Hon. "I got out of the Khmer Rouge area with all five of my children and all we could carry on one ox-cart. It took me two days to travel 30 miles from my village to this place." The stream of ox-carts moving from Khmer Rouge area to Kompong Thom stretched for miles during the interval of several weeks in which Khmer Rouge forces were consolidating for what they thought would be a decisive thrust against Phnom Penh. At the time of my visit, refugees still arrived every day despite the efforts of the Khmer Rouge to tighten their authority after failing in the drive on Phnom Penh. On the edge of town refugees occupied huts built in front of the foundations of houses bombed or shelled to the ground more than a year previously. "We never have enough food," said a woman, noting that each refugee was allotted 300 grams of rice a day. "When we were in the Khmer Rouge region, we did not get that much. They made everyone work, and gave us only rice soup every day and nothing more." The woman elaborated on other reports of mass killings. "You cannot talk the wrong way. You can only do what they tell you to do. This year they have killed a lot of people. They accuse you of providing information to the other side," she said hurriedly. "Sometimes they kill one member of a family or the whole family. They bring people to the forest in chains. They put five people in one grave. You have to dig the ground yourself."

This picture of Khmer Rouge techniques was corroborated wherever the writer met those who had lived under Khmer Rouge control. At a refugee camp near Tuol Sampeou, six miles northwest of Phnom Penh, villagers said that Khmer Rouge soldiers had invaded the camp in January, burning many of the houses. A man named Lach Pech, who had spent two years in a Khmer Rouge region near the Mekong River ferry-crossing town of Neak Loeung, southeast of the capital, said the Khmer Rouge had promised to win the war in 1974—and also "to destroy Phnom Penh." While building up for this denouement, the Khmer Rouge imposed the same rigorous discipline in his area as they had elsewhere. "All the rice was gathered into common barns, and they gave away very little to each family," he said. "The monks were forced to dig up big trees, and the trees were made into firewood, and the holes for the roots were turned into places to bury the dead. The monks sometimes get food from people who are religious, but those who are busy working have no time to give food to the monks. Many hundreds of people who were captured want to come here."[15]

The negative impact of the Khmer Rouge tactic of violence was perhaps most graphically evident in the account of a young refugee named Sanguon Preap, a former Khmer Rouge soldier who was prompted to flee regardless of the risks:

I was very frightened when I saw the Khmer Rouge saw off the neck of a civilian with sugar palm leaves. They sawed little by little and made the victim stand up, and on the last day they sawed strongly until his head fell off. They sawed for three days, at seven in the morning and at nighttime. They did it in front of hundreds of people. The victim cried out until he was too weak. Everyone was frightened. I saw only one case like that. Then the next night I ran away. They called the man a traitor. They did not say what he did. The Khmer Rouge have killed hundreds of people.

Sanguon Preap had served with the Khmer Rouge for a year, mostly along Route 4 running west and south of Phnom Penh, before his escape a couple of weeks before our meeting. He still seemed to quiver with fright as he recited his story.

Beyond interviews with refugees, statistics on the movement of the populace during the war bore out the state of panic induced by Khmer Rouge policies. In the ten-month period between the cessation of American bombing in August of 1973 and my interviews with refugees in June of 1974 the refugee populace had increased by more than 200,000, according to official reports. "A large number of people have moved from enemy territory," said a diplomatic source, while "only small numbers are moving back to their homes." During more than four years of fighting, by official estimate, approximately 1.2 million persons had become refugees—not counting Vietnamese residents of Cambodia, many of whom had fled to South Vietnam as a result of atrocities and threats perpetrated by Cambodian government troops. The actual movement of population resulting from war may have been much higher than indicated by these figures.[16] It is significant to note, however, that the halt in the bombing, previously regarded as the major factor in the refugee flow, did not mark a statistical turning point. Since the Cambodian army was not aggressively pursuing Khmer Rouge anywhere, one could only attribute the continued movement to the desire of villagers to escape the Khmer Rouge. Ironically, the level of violence perpetrated by the Khmer Rouge seems to have increased after the bomb halt—further indicating the Khmer Rouge plan to galvanize the populace and muster all resources for the climactic moments of the war.

Besides consolidating control over the countryside, moreover, Khmer Rouge strategists hoped to undermine the Lon Nol regime in its central base area, Phnom Penh, by exploiting political differences and discontent stemming from economic problems and corruption. Popular revolt inside Phnom Penh, resulting in Lon Nol's overthrow, would inevitably ease the military task confronting Khmer Rouge units besieging the capital from distances ranging from five to fifty miles. This goal appeared attainable in view of the moral weakness of the Lon Nol establishment—and the resulting outrage of increasing numbers of non-Communist urban critics. There were daily stories of exaggerations on the number of men on military payrolls, which commanders then used to increase their own bank accounts or private investments, and there were still more disturbing reports of the sale of arms and ammunition to the Khmer Rouge.

In this setting, Khmer Rouge political operatives could appeal to the ideals of young students and teachers not only through propaganda broadcasts but also through personal approaches imploring them to fight with them in the *maquis*—or to lead protests in the capital. Summarizing the attitudes of Phnom Penh youth, Kun Thon Thanarak, secretary-general of the Association of Students of the Khmer Republic, remarked in an interview with the writer that students today "know that death is a meaningless thing and do not want to die for corrupt commanders." Since the outset of the war, he observed, with considerable accuracy, "the majority of military officers have obtained their own villas by stealing money, by lying about the number of soldiers in their units, by selling gasoline on the open market and selling arms to the enemy." If the government "does not resolve the corruption affair and does not punish the corrupted officers," he said, "the other side will win." Nor did he seem dismayed by this prospect. "Among the members of the other side are some who were here during Prince Sihanouk's time," said Thanarak. "Sihanouk denounced them as 'red' or Khmer Rouge, so they are not corrupted." "In general," he went on, "the leaders of the other side are clean." When asked to comment on the violent tactics employed by the Khmer Rouge, he turned the question around: "In the B-52 time there were many bombs and shells—is this cruel?" When students talked with refugees, he conceded, they realized "the other side" sometimes imposed "severe discipline." Nevertheless, he said, in comparing the two opposing forces one had to conclude that the Khmer Rouge "has a lot of discipline and no corruption but the Phnom Penh government has a lot of corruption." Therefore, he said, "this side is worse."[17]

Although Thanarak himself may have had no direct association with Khmer Rouge agents, his pattern of thought fit in exactly with the outlook of the

Khmer Rouge in its efforts to influence Phnom Penh youth. In this phase of operations, in fact, Khmer Rouge leaders may have been more effective than they were in their program for winning over the peasantry. All the key members of the central committee of the Khmer Communist Party, after all, had emerged from the same Phnom Penh elitist milieu as Thanarak—and all had presumably joined the Khmer Rouge for many of the same reasons. Thus Khmer Rouge broadcasts, focusing to a large extent on the venality of the Lon Nol "clique," were skillfully pitched to the sentiments of the students.

Ideology and Doctrine

A current of ideology ran through all day-to-day Khmer Rouge operational activities despite the contradiction between lofty ideals and political violence. In whatever arena they were operating, whether with students or with peasants, Khmer Rouge cadres evinced the longing for a total revolution by which they could reverse centuries of tradition culminating in the neo-colonialism of Prince Sihanouk—a non-leader whom they now recognized would only jeopardize achievement of this aim. The National United Front, at a meeting in Peking shortly after Sihanouk's overthrow, drafted a political program that still provides the theoretical framework within which the Khmer Rouge functions on a daily basis. "The Cambodian society, which will be established in the liberated zone and then in the whole country, will be rid of all defects impeding its rapid and full bloom," says one passage, citing "elimination of depraving customs, corruption, all sorts of illicit trading, smuggling and means of inhuman exploitation of the people." The same passage promises "democratization of Cambodian society. . . ."[18]

The program also calls for freedom of religion, "the right of ownership of the land the peasants cultivate," "the freedom of vote"—all promises more honored in the breach than in the observance. Khmer Rouge cadres, however, could refer to the same program if the necessity ever arose to explain some of their tactics. "The mission of the NLA [National Liberation Army] is to destroy to the maximum the enemy armed forces and to defend and expand the liberated areas, the solid rear for our struggle," says a passage in part one of the program. "In the course of struggle the NLA must develop the spirit of patriotism, raise its political level and foster utter devotion to the cause of the people." If necessary, the passage goes on, "Severely punish the reactionaries guilty of crimes against the people, but show leniency to those criminals who have sincerely repented." The victims of political violence, then, presumably were those who had not "sincerely repented"—or at least had not shown sufficient interest in the program.

Despite the exigencies imposed by the constant fact of war, Khmer Rouge leaders were sincerely interested in explaining and propagating their doctrine. A review, *Revolutionary Young Men and Women*, stated in its first issue that its purpose was "to educate to inculcate in youth political principles and a revolutionary conscience following the direction of the party in order that youth might be even more committed, more courageous." The review called for "class conscience," "a just revolutionary morale," "a sense of necessary struggle both against the enemy and against nature and for personal fulfillment for the good and maximum success of all the party's work," "a spirit of serving the nation and people, especially the little people" and "a spirit of collectivism, abandoning personal interest for the common interest."[19]

The problem, as the new publication indicated, was how to synthesize ideology and doctrine with practical realities. "In a society divided into dominating and dominated classes as is ours, each class had its own particular interests and therefore special points of view, principles and activity," said another article in the same publication. "They are convinced that foreign aggression and domination over worker-farmer classes is just." At the same time, the article argued, "the youth and people have their own viewpoint and position" which demand "struggle to recover independence and democracy and to do that which is necessary" under the direction of the Khmer Communist Party. "In the cities, especially the capital, young workers and laborers, students are the pivot and the fuse of the struggle through demonstrations and meetings," said the article. "In the countryside after educating the young poor farmers and lower middle class cultivators, the party gives them the job of village defense, communes, cadres and the rooting-out of traitorous agents. Despite difficulties the party uses all legal and clandestine means to educate youth."[20]

Therein lay perhaps the best explanation for the Khmer Rouge policy of promulgating its ideology through a program of political violence unprecedented in scope in the Indochinese conflict. The zeal with which the Khmer Rouge espoused its ideology, the toughness with which it attempted to put it into practice, would not permit the existence of the Lon Nol regime in uneasy coalition. "We want all foreigners to withdraw aid, we do not want the United States to provide weapons," said Kun Thon Thanarak, the student leader, in our conversation. The United States should "let the Cambodians discuss together to resolve all problems without aid from foreigners," he went on, convinced that Khmer Rouge leaders would "come and talk to the uncorrupted people" though "not to the others," the members or representatives of the Lon Nol government. In other words, the Khmer Rouge would agree to negotiate only after the defeat of Lon Nol—and then with those who already supported their ideology and their program.

By 1974, the war in Cambodia had indeed entered a new phase—in the sense that both the use of political violence and the denigration of Sihanouk were "new" for the Khmer Rouge. Complementing this shift in Khmer Rouge strategy, young leftists in Phnom Penh seemed more than ever to prefer the revolutionary promise of the Khmer Rouge to the drab daily reality of unparalleled corruption in the milieu in which they lived. There was, in the end, a definite correlation between the shift against Sihanouk, the upsurge in student activity and the turn toward violence as a means of completing the "revolution" in a nation resistant to deep change for centuries. By dissociating themselves from Sihanouk inside Cambodia, the Khmer Rouge made clear they would not tolerate him in a permanent figurehead position in Phnom Penh. They were much too intent on spreading their ideology—and accruing power for themselves—to suffer such a compromise.

Yet the use of violence by the Khmer Rouge—and the corruption of leaders in Phnom Penh—may reflect a tragedy about Cambodia that transcends that of daily battles and killings. Perhaps Sihanouk's one-time "oasis of peace," a term he was wont to use while pursuing some semblance of a "neutral" foreign policy in Phnom Penh, was really in the throes of its own destruction, exacerbated by regional and global factors beyond the control of the combatants. "This country," a foreign diplomat in Phnom Penh once told me, "could ultimately disintegrate into history and fade from view." It was a fate that Sihanouk had always feared as he confronted Thailand on the west and Vietnam on the east before his demise. Perhaps, in order to avoid this fate, a "revolution" of this conservative society was indeed unavoidable whatever techniques the "revolutionaries" chose to accomplish their aims.

Notes

1. The writer visited Kompong Thom on June 16, 1974.

2. "Samdech Sihanouk's Inspection Tour of the Cambodian Liberated Zone," Supplement to *China Pictorial*, No. 6, Peking, June 1973.

3. *Le Monde*, April 12, 1974, interview with Alain Bouc.

4. New China News Agency dispatch, April 2, Peking, published in *Peking Review*, 17, 14 (April 5, 1974): 3-4. The photograph of the meeting with Mao appears on pp. 4-5.

5. *Le Monde*, April 12, 1974, interview with Alain Bouc.

6. *New China News Agency*, Peking, July 10, 1974.

7. Tan Kimhuon, "Le Parti Communiste Indochinois," a succinct résumé of the conference held on November 30, 1972, in the Tchenla Cinema, Phnom Penh, distributed in typewritten form.

8. Ibid.

9. Ith Sarin, "A Report on 9 Months with the Maquis," distributed in Phnom Penh in 1973. Ith Sarin, former inspector of primary schools in Phnom Penh, defected to the Khmer Rouge on April 19, 1972, and then returned to the government side nine months later.

10. Ibid.

11. Ibid.

12. Ibid.

13. The writer interviewed the escapees on June 14, 1974, the morning after their arrival.

14. The writer interviewed General Teap Bin in his headquarters before visiting refugee homes.

15. The writer interviewed refugees at Tuol Sampeou camp on June 18, 1974.

16. Figures supplied by the American Embassy, Phnom Penh, in June 1974. Other knowledgeable sources estimated the number of refugees at between two and three million.

17. Interview with Kun Thon Thanarak, June 20, 1974, Phnom Penh University. Student unrest in this period reached a crescendo on June 4 with the killing of the education minister and his assistant, held as hostages for the release of five students and four teachers arrested earlier. The assassin escaped. Phnom Penh officials believed the Khmer Rouge were responsible but could never prove the point.

18. "Political Programme of the National United Front of Kampuchea (NUFK)," Peking, May 3, 1970, distributed in English translation in leaflet form.

19. *Revolutionary Young Men and Women*, published by the Khmer Communist Youth, August 1973.

20. Ibid.

10 Norodom Sihanouk: A Leader of the Left?

Milton Osborne

More than four years after he was overthrown as Cambodia's chief of state, Prince Norodom Sihanouk continues to fascinate journalists and scholars. His extended political commentaries and personal reminiscences have formed the basis for two books, while he has provided almost countless column inches of copy for journalists who have interviewed him both in China and in the course of his travels abroad.[1] The continuing preoccupation of writers and commentators with Prince Sihanouk's role, and his own readiness to talk in detail of his past, present, and future, leave him at the center of much discussion of developments in Cambodia. Whether this attention is justified and the extent to which a transformed Sihanouk has become a leader of the Left will be the concern of this chapter. At the very least, an analysis of Sihanouk's role, both before and after the March 1970 coup d'état, should contribute to our understanding of the forces which have come so close to bringing down the Republican regime in Phnom Penh.

The problems of information and focus that were associated with discussion of Sihanouk's pre-1970 regime have persisted following his downfall.[2] As two examples, until very recently, little attention has been given to such a key left-wing figure as Ieng Sary,[3] and many commentators have been ready to dismiss the possibility of an emerging *Cambodian* resistance movement distinct from Vietnamese Communist forces operating in the Indochinese region.[4] An additional problem crops up in reviewing Sihanouk's current association with a left-wing political and military movement. Some assessment of his earlier political attitudes is essential, but to what extent may this be made on the basis of his own statements? The following rule of thumb seems useful, if not infallible: Sihanouk means what he says *when* he says it. A man of volatile personality, Sihanouk is subject to changes of mind on matters of greater and lesser importance. Whether his statements are accurate, unwise, perceptive or calculated, he seldom speaks publicly or for publication without expressing his thoughts as they exist at the time.[a]

Whether Sihanouk's views accord with "reality" in a particular situation is

---

[a] I acknowledge the problems, both psychological and methodological, associated with this presumption. Clearly my assertion depends on the assessment of there having been a congruence between Sihanouk's statements and his actions, and on the degree of consistency which marks his view of a range of political problems.

231

quite another matter. Before he was deposed, for instance, the prince genuinely seemed to believe that the benefits of education had been extended broadly to his countrymen. In fact, the best evidence shows that the educational system existing before 1970, and the problems associated with it, played a significant part in promoting rather than eliminating social tensions.[5] As another example, talking in Peking, in his post-1970 mood, Sihanouk may well believe that his actions against left-wing forces in the years between 1966 and 1970 were less a reflection of his personal wishes than of the anti-Communism of his advisers. The record seems to suggest otherwise. If, in the past, Sihanouk showed a distinct lack of sympathy for the advance of the Left in Cambodia, this underlines the importance of looking carefully at the part he is now playing in conjunction with those whose left-wing sympathies are beyond dispute. Is there a "new Sihanouk"? And if so, what importance does he have within the forces opposing the Lon Nol regime?[6]

Sihanouk Before 1970

The importance of Sihanouk's experiences during his youthful years, when he enjoyed the fruits of royalty while increasingly chafing against the control of his French mentors, cannot be overemphasized. The effects of the period between 1941, when he mounted the throne, and 1955, when he abdicated in his father's favor, were varied. He was left with a deep distrust of the factionalism of Cambodian political life.[7] He came to resent those who claimed to have played an earlier or more significant role than he in ending French colonial control of Cambodia.[8] Finally, he was left ill-disposed to accept views that ran contrary to his own.[b]

Prince Sihanouk's attitude toward those who disagreed with his policies in the later 1950s and 1960s can be understood as easily as stemming from personal resentment as from the existence of some form of philosophical underpinning. Whether the challenge came from the Left or the Right, it was the fact of challenge that most excited Sihanouk's wrath and moved him to action. Sihanouk had little time for political theory and its application to solving Cambodia's problems. When he said of himself that he did "not give a rap about political economy, political science or other subjects," and that he did not, in any case, read books, he was being no more than frank.[9] As a leader and a politician he reacted instinctively; so he was instinctively opposed to those on the Cambodian Left who threatened *his* status quo.[10]

There is every reason to believe that Sihanouk was revealing his true feelings when he argued, throughout the 1960s, that both the Right and the Left were a threat to Cambodia's survival.[11] In circumstances of disintegrating national

---

[b]Even if the French did not always act as Sihanouk desired, particularly after 1949, they treated him with great courtesy and deference, addressing him as "Your Majesty" or "Sire."

unity, however, the Right rather than the Left gained the advantage in the arena of overt Cambodian politics. It could scarcely have been otherwise. So long as Sihanouk depended on such men as Lon Nol to bolster his position there was no opportunity for significant, let alone radical, transformation of Cambodia's society. The Left, in brief, faced a grave choice. Whereas men of the Right could enjoy the opportunities for advancement and gain provided by the existing political system without in general having to pay too high a personal price, those committed to the Left could only survive in politics through a very considerable compromise.

Some Cambodian leftists were not prepared to compromise and never chose the option of working in the political arena after 1954. Among the younger generation, some, Ieng Sary notably, chose clandestine resistance as early as 1963, while for others, including the famous "three missing deputies," Khieu Samphan, Hou Yuon, and Hu Nim, the opportunities for compromise did not disappear until 1967.[12] The causes and chronology of the antigovernment activity of 1967 that began with the Samlaut rebellion require much more detailed study. In terms of the evolution of a Cambodian left-wing movement and Sihanouk's view of it, however, the significance of developments during that year is already clear. The possibility of compromise gave way to the necessity for clandestine organization. As Sihanouk saw his personal political interests increasingly linked with the forces of the Right, the Left entered a period of intense difficulty.

This is not the picture Prince Sihanouk has presented since his transfer to Peking. His account of the events following the outbreak of the Samlaut rebellion is, at best, ambiguous—even though he may believe it. He denies that the suppression of antigovernment activity, in Battambang province and else-where, resulted in heavy casualties,[13] arguing that peace returned to the Cambodian countryside as the result of his personal intervention.[14] In a surprisingly naive assertion, Sihanouk has repeatedly argued that his actions during the tense years from 1967 until his overthrow were understood by those whom he repeatedly condemned in speeches and whom his security forces pursued with vigor.[15] The accumulated evidence contradicts Sihanouk's general account of developments.[16] As for the claim that his left-wing opponents "understood" his actions, this seems much more an indication that, as sophisticated politicians, men such as Khieu Samphan and Ieng Sary continue to see benefit in using Sihanouk than a reflection of the true feelings of the Cambodian Left in the late 1960s.

In short, irrespective of whether a "new" Sihanouk has risen from the ashes of his destroyed pre-1970 regime, any suggestion that the prince was secretly well-disposed toward the Cambodian Left before the March 1970 coup d'état can be discounted.

The Cambodian Left Before 1970

Considerable research will be necessary before a detailed and satisfactory description emerges of the Cambodian Left in the period before Sihanouk's deposition.[17] Its clandestine nature and its diversity are two of the more obvious factors standing in the way of analysis. Some broad features of the Left may, however, be noted. Of considerable importance is the fact that there is a substantial history of left-wing action and involvement among educated Cambodians—a much longer history than most analysts suspected when they wrote on these matters in the 1960s. The tendency in the past has been to argue that the Cambodian Left was insignificant because it was small.[18] But the fact that the Cambodian Left was small when the First Indochinese War ended was less important than the fact that it existed and formed a nucleus for at least one element in later developments. Although many of those who sided with the Vietminh in the period before July 1954 were of mixed Cambodian-Vietnamese ancestry, and it was from this group that cadres were selected for training in the Democratic Republic of Vietnam (DRVN), a more clearly Cambodian left-wing movement emerged later.[19] Developments up to the Geneva Accords truce of 1954 suggest that the Cambodian Left was in an early stage of development and heavily dependent on outside assistance.[c]

In the years after 1954 the Cambodian Left developed along several lines, by no means all of them clear today. Most shadowy of all is the Cambodian Communist Party, which with its overt Front organization, the Pracheachon, maintained a fragile existence during the 1960s. A more readily discussed group of leftists emerged among those Cambodians who studied in France in the fifties and sixties. Sihanouk was particularly preoccupied with these visible critics of his regime.[20] The extent to which he understood the dissent of those exposed to Western society is, again, a matter for debate. One thoughful commentator has suggested that Sihanouk's readiness to condemn all opponents on the Left as Communists was, in part, an astute way of gaining both domestic and international support.[21] Of equal importance was Sihanouk's judgment that the Left could be a danger to his highly personal regime. Despite this judgment, however, Sihanouk may well not have fully grasped how deeply the Paris

[c]The preoccupation of many commentators with the degree of independence of Cambodian or Laotian left-wing movements—independence from the DRVN in particular—is striking, but it involves a continuous risk of distortion and the application of a double standard. Concern about the independence of left-wing forces has frequently not been matched by the recorded recognition of the lack of independence on the part of regimes opposed to the left. As for distortion, there should be no surprise that revolutionary political movements, of whatever affiliation, are dependent in their infancy on some form of "outside" assistance. This is a worldwide and long-term phenomenon. The whole concept of "outside" assistance depends on the viewpoint from which a situation is regarded. Does Prince Souphanouvong, from his perspective, look upon DRVN assistance to the Neo Lao Haxat as "external" in character? The answer may even be "yes," but this does not necessarily mean that he regards the assistance as illegitimate.

experience affected young Cambodians. In noting as he once did that Hou Yuon and Hu Nim had associated with Son Ngoc Thanh in France,[22] Sihanouk seems not to have understood the motivations that inspired opposition from the Left. Whether or not Hou Yuon and Hu Nim did meet with Son Ngoc Thanh is not the vital point. What was important to Sihanouk was opposition to or criticism of his rule, from whatever source it came. Because of this he failed to comprehend that a section of the Cambodian Left emerged, during the 1950s and 1960s, which had reached political decisions about Cambodia's society and its future on the basis of study and conviction.[23]

The dissatisfaction felt by educated Cambodians that led to the adoption of "progressive" or left-wing views has frequently been discounted. The myth still survives of Sihanouk's pre-1970 Cambodia being a society essentially untroubled by social inequality,[24] but substantial qualification can already be made to the picture of an untroubled, eupeptic peasantry and a settled, socially stable urban community. For too long observers of Cambodian affairs have depended on French accounts and judgments of Khmer rural society, without giving sufficient thought to the framework within which those assessments were made. The judgments of Jean Delvert have been accepted uncritically as reflecting a rural social system unmarked by any significant abuse.[25] Even Sihanouk, it appears, gave broad credence to the picture of Cambodia's peasants being untroubled by major economic or social problems.[26]

The fact that less than half of Cambodia's arable lands were cultivated was not an index of rural contentment. Reliable statistics are difficult to obtain, but in the case of Battambang province the existence of widespread rural indebtedness has now been generally accepted as one factor in the unrest that broke out in that province during 1967.[27] Strikingly, some of the most detailed analysis of the major social and economic problems lurking beneath the surface calm of Cambodian rural life has been provided by three of the best known leaders of the Left, Khieu Samphan, Hou Yuon, and Hu Nim. The information they provide seems convincing in its emphasis on widespread usury, a proportionately declining share in the holdings of cultivated land among poorer peasants, and the reinforcement of old and inflexible social relationships.[28] This set of circumstances affected a population that continues to suffer staggeringly high public health problems, and which as a matter of course faces the risk of hunger and even famine should the crops fail.[29]

If social conditions in the rural regions could evoke a critical and left-wing response, the same was also true for Cambodia's urban society which, by the end of the 1960s, began to show cracks in the facade. Because the discontent of those making up the urban elite was vital in bringing about Sihanouk's fall, much attention has been focused on the attitudes of this group. Deserving at least as much attention were other urban elements, most particularly those with some education who had not found a place within the bureaucracy, and those who had moved from rural regions to Phnom Penh in the hope of finding employment only to face bitter disappointment.[d]

Inequality and corruption were widespread in Phnom Penh. Perhaps in their pervasiveness these features were more easily ignored or discounted by foreign observers who sought to gauge the pulse of Sihanouk's Cambodia. If unemployment or underemployment did not lead to riots or agitation, there was a tendency to minimize the seriousness of these problems. At the same time, too few observers walked through the sewerless shanty towns on the edge of Phnom Penh or talked with men who were, in their own eyes, the victims of the system that prevailed.[30] If the existence of left-wing feeling is thought to depend upon genuine social grievances, there need be no doubt these were present in Phnom Penh.

Finally, the Cambodian Left before 1970 was extremely diverse in composition. When Sihanouk was overthrown the key figures in the Cambodian Left were scattered geographically and divided in terms of ideology and personal character.[e] We know least about that section of the Left that linked its fortunes with the combined anti-French efforts headed by the Vietminh in the First Indochinese War. The number of these men, their actions after 1954, and their degree of participation in events since 1970 are all open questions.[31] Less shadowy are those Cambodian exiles who chose to remain in France in the 1950s and 1960s rather than return to the threat of action against them by Sihanouk. Two brothers, Thiounn Mumm and Thiounn Prasith, are among the best known names in this group. Because of their absence from Cambodia in the final years of Sihanouk's governance they have been given little attention, but, as events since the coup have shown, they continue their left-wing interest in developments.

Then there is the largest identifiable group: the men headed by Khieu Samphan, Hou Yuon, and Hu Nim, whose names are known and whose adherence to left-wing ideas was also well known before March 1970. To write of these men as a "group" should not be taken to imply a lack of diversity within their proclaimed adherence to left-wing positions. A few examples emphasize this point. Prominent among those of the pre-1970 Left who have rallied to the United National Front (FUNK) is Chau Seng, a former minister in many of Sihanouk's governments and a former head of the prince's private secretariat.[f] Chau Seng came to Sihanouk's attention when, after his return from study in France in the fifties, he prepared a private report on the problems of

---

[d]These could be one and the same. Three years secondary schooling and complete fluency in French could end in no other opportunity than health-breaking toil on a *cyclo-pousse* (bicycle rickshaw). This comment is made on the basis of personal observation in Phnom Penh.

[e]My own judgment is that factions do exist in the FUNK and that these reflect, in part, the diverse political origins of its members. To date, however, the existence of factions does not appear to have qualified the FUNK's capacity to function.

[f]Chau Seng was appointed as Minister for Special Missions of the GRUNK, resident in Paris.

secondary education in Cambodia.[32] Despite his apparently genuine concern for social and educational problems revealed in this report, and his links with French left-wing organizations through his French wife, Chau Seng's image in Phnom Penh during the 1960s was not that of a dedicated man of the Left. He was seen as deeply concerned with the pursuit of personal wealth and was an object of contempt in at least some left-wing circles.[33]

If Chau Seng is a prominent name, others in this group are less well known, but probably of greater importance. Such a figure is the Royal Government of Khmer National Union (GRUNK) "ambassador" in Paris. He is Ok Sakun, a former railroad union official whose efforts at industrial action led to a sharp conflict between him and Sihanouk, and to Ok Sakun's flight into clandestine opposition to the prince. Others are Poc Deuskoma and Phouk Chhay. The first worked in unhappy tandem with Chau Seng during 1966 producing editorial material for *La Dépêche*. The second was a leader of a student union in Phnom Penh before being imprisoned during Sihanouk's regime in 1967. Ieng Sary, to whom reference has already been made, differs from those others just noted because of his relatively less known public posture before his disappearance in 1963.

The members of the Cambodian Left before Sihanouk's overthrow were not totally unknown personalities, however much our knowledge of their political persuasions was restricted, and despite the need many of them felt to work clandestinely, fearing the pursuit of men who acted in Sihanouk's name. Lack of knowledge about these leftists led to misestimations of their importance, just as the clandestine role they pursued made it difficult for any Western analyst to chart the nature and course of the Left's progress. As knowledge of the Left's role before 1970 grows, however, there is little justification for the dismissive attitude once held toward it.

Sihanouk and the Left since 1970:
The First Phase

More than four years after the event, there may be some difficulty in recalling the confusion attendant upon Sihanouk's downfall in 1970. The confusion encompassed some of the actors and most of the external observers. Attention continued to focus on Norodom Sihanouk, a man who, as he confronted the unexpected, revealed his own uncertainties about how to face the future.[34] A brief survey of the two months following the coup d'état suggests that this was a vital time for the Cambodian Left, a period when long-term contingency plans were put into effect and when some decision was made to work with a man whom they had for some years regarded as an enemy.

The public record is reasonably clear. Having arrived in Peking on March 19, 1970, Sihanouk issued a "Message and Solemn Declaration" on March 23. This document denounced the new regime in Phnom Penh and emphasized Sihanouk's readiness to work for its overthrow. He called on his compatriots, regardless of political affiliation, to join him in this task, and noted that he would soon establish a new government in exile to coordinate the battle against General Lon Nol and his associates. All would work within the framework of the FUNK, which was now established. On March 26, 1970, a statement was released in Hanoi, over the names of Khieu Samphan, Hou Yuon, and Hu Nim, indicating their readiness to work with the FUNK.[35]

The next major development involving Prince Sihanouk was his participation in the Summit Conference of the Indochinese People, held in southern China between April 24 and 27, 1970.[36] This was followed, between May 3 and 5, by the formation of the GRUNK and the publication of a political program.[37] With the formation of the GRUNK a list of members of both the FUNK and GRUNK was published and it became possible, for the first time, to make some assessment of the balance of political forces within the ranks of those who were committed to bringing down the Phnom Penh regime.[38]

Because many commentators doubted that Khieu Samphan and his colleagues were still alive, and because of a lack of knowledge concerning some other members of the FUNK and GRUNK, too little attention was paid to the individuals listed in the various documents that were now circulated. At the same time, descriptions of developments by writers with well known left-wing views, such as Wilfred Burchett, appeared so marked by propaganda intent as to merit little credence.[39] As for Sihanouk's own comments, during the first eighteen months following his deposition these suggested a wide range of moods, from a conviction that he still had a major role to play in a future Cambodian government, to admissions that "Khmer Rouge" forces dominated both the FUNK and GRUNK.[40]

In retrospect, there is little doubt that the FUNK or GRUNK has been dominated by the Left. Men of the Left are clearly dominant in the Political Bureau of the Central Committee of the FUNK, with six of the twelve members possessing a long record of left-wing identification.[g] In the original listing of members of the GRUNK no less than half of the twenty-two ministers and vice-ministers were of the Left, while left-wing personalities are clearly dominant in the public listing of the leaders of the anti-Lon Nol military forces (FAPLNK).[h] By comparison with these left-wing individuals, many of those whose names appear as members of the GRUNK and FUNK, and whose capabilities are clearly known as the result of public life before March 1970, are little more than ciphers, men who served Sihanouk and clung to him since there was no other route open to them. Individuals such as Huot Sambath and General Ngo Hou fall readily into this category.

[g]Thiounn Prasit, Thiounn Mumm, Khieu Samphan, Hou Yuon, Hu Nim, and Chau Seng.

[h]Note should be taken of the manner in which key figures hold appointments in the FUNK, GRUNK, and FAPLNK (Khmer National People's Liberation Armed Forces). Khieu Samphan, for instance, is a member of the FUNK's Political Bureau, Vice-Premier of the GRUNK, and Commander-in-Chief of the FAPLNK.

Reluctance to give serious consideration to the FUNK and GRUNK and Sihanouk's own ambiguous comments on his relationship with the Left have led some commentators to discount the importance of *Cambodian* left-wing forces in the continuing struggle. Such assessments do not take account of the growth of the Left before the March 1970 coup, nor of the Left's capacity to develop after Sihanouk's downfall. The speed with which the Left organized itself and came to terms with the problems posed by Sihanouk seem a positive comment on its efficiency. Within less than a week formerly exiled Cambodian leftists in Paris had departed for Peking with a clear understanding of the duties they were to perform once they arrived in the Chinese capital.[41]

Sihanouk himself found great difficulty in understanding how circumscribed his position was to be. His vacillation between his vision of a de Gaulle-like role and admission that there might be little further part for him to play if the Left won its battle makes this clear.[42] By November 1970 he had come to speak, on some occasions, of retiring to France once the Lon Nol regime was defeated.[43] During 1971 and 1972 the apparent sudden shifts in Sihanouk's feelings and the readiness with which he filled unexpected roles made judgment of his position difficult in the extreme. How was one to assess a man who acknowledged the failure of "Sihanoukism," praised the achievements of Chairman Mao in terms that seemed to be borrowed directly from his Chinese hosts, and yet, on occasion, still seemed to think that his personality was the chief rallying point for resistance within Cambodia?[44]

Most probably Sihanouk was himself uncertain about his position until early 1973. If, as argued earlier, Sihanouk believes what he says when he says it, his first three years of exile were ones in which he could still think in terms of being a leader and possessing followers—even if his followers were now men of the Left. Ambivalence was a feature of these first three years of exile and is a dominant feature of the two compilations of his memoirs, which were produced during this time. By early 1973, in contrast, this first phase of the exiled Sihanouk's relations with the Left was coming to an end and the new and more difficult second phase was about to begin.

Sihanouk and the Left since 1970:
The Second Phase

Doubts about the extent to which Sihanouk was under the political supervision of the Left quickly dissipated during 1973. During that year his role as an international legitimizer was made clear. To write of his role as a legitimizer should not be taken to mean that the Left has no legitimacy of its own. But in circumstances in which the FAPLNK could not look confidently to any quick victory over the Republican armed forces, backed by the United States, the diplomatic battle that had been proceeding ever since May 1970 became more and more important. Critical attention was given to gaining the Cambodian seat in the United Nations for the GRUNK.

This aim was clearly behind the decision that Sihanouk should visit some of the liberated zones under the control of the FUNK in February and March 1973.[45] This visit and the decision announced in late 1973 that all important ministerial positions in the GRUNK were held by men or women based in Cambodia itself, rather than in Peking, clearly mattered as much in external terms as for the gaining of advantage within Cambodia.[46] In pursuit of wider international recognition for GRUNK, Sihanouk, during 1973, traveled abroad, outside the restricted sphere of Asian Communist states. His visits to East European countries in June and July of 1973 took place in company with Ieng Sary and this fact, taken with Ieng Sary's readiness to qualify Sihanouk's commentaries on the policies of the FUNK, hinted at tensions of even greater proportions than had been revealed before. No one with a knowledge of Sihanouk's personality can imagine that he took kindly to having to accept Ieng Sary's explanation of the "nuance" involved in a message sent from Khieu Samphan.[47]

The tensions apparent in June and July 1973 seem to have led to Sihanouk's determination in the second half of 1973 to assert himself, and hence to the spate of interviews he accorded Western journalists in which he spoke bitterly of his left-wing associates and pessimistically of his own future. His interview with Alain Bouc of *Le Monde*, published on October 27, 1973, is typical. Sihanouk noted his estrangement from the Left, whom he still described as the Khmer Rouge, using the term he relied on before 1970. He was critical of their "Stalinism," and he gave broad hints of conflicts between himself and the Left as to what future policies should be followed. He offered the same story, with greater or lesser variations, to other journalists. To T.D. Allman, in September 1973, Sihanouk revealed the depth of his personal antipathy for Ieng Sary.[48] To both Sylvana Foa of UPI and the Italian freelance journalist Oriana Fallici, Sihanouk used the same phrase to describe the Left's vision of his future. The Left, Sihanouk insisted, would eventually "spit me out."[49]

Although, in 1973, Sihanouk revealed disillusionment with his comrades in arms and risked some form of estrangement from them, there was little public criticism of the prince from his left-wing colleagues. Ieng Sary was an exception. When Sylvana Foa interviewed Sihanouk in Peking, in September 1973, she was told by Ieng Sary that "Sihanouk is one of those aspects of Cambodian tradition, like Buddhism and the monarchy, which we believe unnecessary for the larger union." In the future, Ieng Sary continued, "We will phase out those aspects we do not consider to be progressive and revolutionary." This frank commentary did not evoke public echoes from other leaders of the Cambodian Left. As 1973 drew to a close there were indications that some efforts at rapprochment were being made by the Left in an effort to soothe Sihanouk's clearly ruffled feelings. The messages sent to the prince on the occasion of his fifty-first birthday were notably warm, particularly that coming from Khieu Samphan. The decision, noted earlier, to place all GRUNK ministries in the hands of persons within Cambodia, met one of the points of criticism that

Sihanouk had persistently offered in September and October. Furthermore, the start of a dry weather offensive—the first to take place after the end of American bombing in Cambodia—seems to have brought a realization among the members of the FUNK that public quarrels should be avoided at a time when they might have to face the heavy demands of administering a larger area of Cambodia.[50]

If hopes for success on the battlefield, in the Phnom Penh sector, and at the United Nations were indeed held by those of the FUNK, these were unrealized. The effort to seat Sihanouk's representatives failed narrowly in New York and the Republican forces managed to maintain their defense perimeter about Phnom Penh. It was against this background that Khieu Samphan finally emerged into the public spotlight to further the international cause of the FUNK and GRUNK. The explanation for Khieu Samphan's emergence provided by the FUNK was that he needed to consult Prince Sihanouk in Peking. With this visit planned, the opportunity was taken to visit those countries that had extended recognition to the GRUNK.[51]

The high point of Khieu Samphan's international tour was his visit to Peking beginning on April 1, 1974. He was received with courtesies usually reserved for heads of state, accorded a meeting with Mao Tse-tung, and given the opportunity to hold a press conference at which Sihanouk filled the role of translator.[i] The whole tone of the visit greatly enhanced Khieu Samphan's prestige and provided, at very least, considerable and visible qualification to Sihanouk's role.

Yet Sihanouk's role continues. He has shrewdly insisted on the extent to which he provides legitimacy for the FUNK's efforts, and this appears to be still accepted as the case by the dominant left-wing personalities within the FUNK. Prince Sihanouk's position as leader of the GRUNK is important for some of the states that have accorded recognition to this government in exile. In the same fashion, the nearly successful effort to seat GRUNK representatives at the 1974 General Assembly of the United Nations might well have been a less close run affair if Sihanouk's name could not have been invoked. As the siege about Phnom Penh tightens in mid-March 1975, Sihanouk continues to insist that he will not play any significant role in Cambodian politics should the anti-Lon Nol forces triumph. There seems little reason to doubt that here, once again, Sihanouk believes what he says, at least for the moment.[52]

Sihanouk, the Left, and the Future

There has been no attempt in this chapter to make a detailed review of the character of left-wing groups associated with the FUNK. Probably divergences on matters of policy and theory—some possibly substantial—do exist between

---

[i]I do not accept the suggestions that the fact Sihanouk acted as Khieu Samphan's translator indicated that the world was not seeing the "real" Khieu Samphan. Quite apart from the symbolic significance of Sihanouk's filling the role of Khieu Samphan's tranlator, it would appear that the Cambodian insurgent leader was only following a practice used by many others, including Chou En-lai. Use of a translator gave him extra time to formulate answers to questions posed in a language (French) he knows.

those in the FUNK who have had long-term links with established Asian Communist parties and others whose leftist commitment is less clearly connected with one or other of the various forms of national Communism. Yet to devote excessive amounts of time to attempts at deciding who is "pro-Hanoi" and who "pro-Peking" is likely to be as misleading as an uncritical acceptance of Ieng Sary's assertion that there are no significant frictions within the FUNK.[53] Short of an unrealistic belief that the FUNK is nothing more than a creation of either the Vietnamese or the Chinese, or both together, the truly significant fact seems to be that a front organization has been established that is dominated by a left-wing group but which continues to have within it a substantial number of men and women whose political affiliations before March 1970 were certainly not of the Left.

With the Left dominant, what then will be Sihanouk's future, and that of other non-leftist Cambodians aligned against the Republican regime in Phnom Penh, should the FUNK eventually gain power? Several times throughout this chapter I have noted Sihanouk's own judgment on his future, that he will play no significant internal role in a future Cambodia dominated by the Left. In any long-term perspective there seems little reason to disagree with this assessment. One forceful reason to share Sihanouk's own view of his future is the history of his relations with the Left before 1970. Can the men whom he persecuted run any risk, however slight, that if they gain power Sihanouk should be allowed a political base within Cambodia, one that he might turn to his advantage once again? This comment does not preclude the possibility that the Cambodian Left will agree to the prince's returning to live in Cambodia, following the downfall of the Lon Nol regime, perhaps even to assume an honorific title. From the Left's point of view, however, Sihanouk would need to be prevented from causing difficulties or making threats. More immediately, there is the possibility of Sihanouk's playing a role in negotiations should these take place with the aim of facilitating the FUNK's accession to power.

In short, Sihanouk's significance for the future of Cambodia may well be much less than that suggested by the amount of attention he still receives. Indeed the Left's concern with Sihanouk's future may well be less than the broader concern that leftists must feel about the future role of others associated with the FUNK, persons often described as "Sihanoukists," but perhaps more satisfactorily described as "Nationalists" or Khmers Rumdos. In terms of individuals whose names are known from the past, there are certainly many who are not likely to make a contribution to the long political and military struggle in which the FUNK has been engaged. There are many others, however, about whom it is much less easy to make assessments. The various members of the Cambodian royal family who have aligned themselves with the FUNK provide a case in point. Despite the routine messages of support sent by these one-time princes to Sihanouk in the troubled times that have followed March 1970, some of these royal insurgents have long histories of uneasy relations with him. Such past difficulties, on the basis of the available evidence, did not lead to these members of the royal family becoming men of the Left.[j] Other, non-royal public figures from the pre-1970 period have political backgrounds suggesting energy and competence but not, of necessity, complete acceptance of the broad policies of the Left. On the basis of his past record, for instance, a man such as Sarin Chhak is dubiously described as a "progressive."[k]

A Speculative Conclusion

Considered in historical perspective, Sihanouk's current role is one he fills despite the past and in spite of continuing basic political differences between him and those who work most actively to overthrow the Cambodian Republican regime. His personal sympathies are not for the style of regime he believes the Cambodian Left seeks to establish should it be victorious. Enough is known of his post-1970 attitudes to be sure that at least some of the Left's leaders offend his susceptibilities. Yet he remains important, not for reasons associated with political philosophy, but because of his symbolic importance within Cambodia and for the world of international politics.

That the Left seeks to use Sihanouk is clear enough, but the question remains as to whether Sihanouk wishes, or is able, to use the Left. To predict Sihanouk's total disappearance from the future of Cambodian politics would be rash. So, too, would be a suggestion that, in the event of the FUNK's success, he would not try to assert himself, to fly in the face of the future he has predicted for himself in which the Left "spits him out," whether this predicted expectoration comes rapidly or over a period of time. For the moment, however, as a temporary "leader" of the Left through a combination of unexpected circumstances, Sihanouk continues to fill another role, and here to some extent one may say that he uses the Left. He is, as was so often the case in the past, at the head of an organization dedicated to bringing down his enemies. In a complete reversal of the pre-1970 years, he now waits to see his left-wing allies bring down Lon Nol, the man whom he once unleashed to become the scourge of his left-wing enemies.

When seeking to understand why Sihanouk has continued to work in association with the Cambodian Left, despite the difficulties of this relationship,

[j]One example is Prince Sisowath Dussady. He has no record of left-wing identification and he has offered routine assurances of support to Sihanouk since joining the FUNK. He was, on the other hand, a private critic of the prince in the years before March 1970.

[k]There have been suggestions that Sarin Chhak should be described as a "progressive." Whatever may have happened to his views since 1970, such a description does not seem appropriate on the basis of his public life and private statements before the March 1970 coup. In the middle 1960s, for instance, he was one of those who privately urged Sihanouk against too ready acceptance of DRVN and National Liberation Front guarantees of Cambodia's frontiers. This information comes from a private Cambodian source.

one would be wrong to dismiss his sense of patriotism, his strong feeling of identification with his country. He is clearly deeply concerned about the destruction of those positive contributions which were a feature of the earlier years of his rule. Equally, however, due account should be taken of his sense of personal outrage following his deposition. His political association with the Left is more than a matter of practical politics, therefore, and more than an uncomplicated testimony to his patriotism. In his sense of outrage and deep personal affront one may find the cement binding his various motivations together. This highly personal involvement in Cambodia's affairs guarantees Sihanouk a place in the developments of the present. It provides no certainty of his involvement in the future. If there should be a place for Prince Sihanouk in a future Cambodia dominated by the Left, one must doubt, on the basis of events since 1970, that the role he plays will be, essentially, of his own choosing.

Notes

1. See Norodom Sihanouk, *L'Indochine vue de Pékin: Entretiens avec Jean Lacouture* (Paris, 1972), and Norodom Sihanouk (as related to Wilfred Burchett), *My War with the CIA* (New York, 1973).

2. See my recent *Politics and Power in Cambodia: The Sihanouk Years* (Camberwell, Vic., 1973), Chapter 1. David Chandler's review of this book has accurately noted those areas in which a lack of information handicapped analysis. See *Journal of Asian Studies* 33, 4 (August 1974): 742-43.

3. Another neglected figure is Salath Sar, who may be, according to some commentators, "the top military strategist" among the resistance leaders. See Robert Shaplen, "Letter from Indochina," *The New Yorker*, January 28, 1974, p. 91.

4. David E. Brown, "Exporting Insurgency: The Communists in Cambodia," in J.J. Zasloff and A.E. Goodman (eds.), *Indochina in Conflict: A Political Assessment* (Lexington, Mass.: Lexington Books, D.C. Heath and Company, 1972), pp. 125-36. My own analysis in the first eighteen months following Sihanouk's deposition certainly gave insufficient consideration to the possible rapid growth of a Khmer resistance to the Lon Nol regime.

5. See *Politics and Power in Cambodia*, pp. 61-2, 71-72, and passim.

6. The concept of a "new Sihanouk" or "another Sihanouk" is discussed in *L'Indochine vue de Pékin*, pp. 116-17.

7. P. Preschez, *Essai sur la démocratie au Cambodge* (Paris: Fondation Nationale des Sciences Politiques, Centre d'Etude des Relations Internationales, 1961). This essay still provides one of the most useful accounts of the political factionalism.

8. For perceptive discussion of Sihanouk's denigration of the part played by Son Ngoc Thanh and Pach Chhoeun in opposing the French in 1942 see David

Chandler's review of *L'Indochine vue de Pékin*, in *Journal of the Siam Society* 61, 1 (January 1973): 358-59.

9. Radio Phnom Penh, March 10, 1967.

10. The italicization is important, for it was as much *his* as *the* status quo that Sihanouk saw threatened. Hence his revealing comment in 1967: "had I been born to an ordinary family, I would have been on the leftist side. . . . But I was born a prince and have the royal family around me. I cannot detach myself." Radio Phnom Penh, March 10, 1967.

11. See, for example, *Agence Khmère de Presse*, May 16, 1964, reporting Sihanouk's speech at Kep of May 15, 1964, and Radio Phnom Penh, April 3, 1967.

12. I am now certain the three deputies were not executed in 1967. For comment see *Politics and Power in Cambodia*, p. 107, n. 11.

13. See *L'Indochine vue de Pékin*, pp. 89-93. Sihanouk notes on p. 90 estimates that as many as 10,000 died in clashes with government forces but claims (p. 92) that no more than three hundred were killed.

14. In *My War with the CIA* Sihanouk avoids discussing the numbers killed. Rather (pp. 62-69), the emphasis is on his role in bringing the resistance to an end.

15. *L'Indochine vue de Pékin* and *My War with the CIA*, passim.

16. See D. Lancaster, "The Decline of Prince Sihanouk's Regime," in Zasloff and Goodman (eds.), *Indochina in Conflict*, p. 52; J.-C. Pomonti and S. Thion, *Des Courtisans aux partisans: Essai sur la crise cambodgienne* (Paris, 1971), pp. 122-25; C. Meyer, *Derrière le sourire khmer* (Paris, 1971), pp. 192 et seq.; Osborne, *Politics and Power in Cambodia*, p. 100. My personal judgment also relies on interviews in Cambodia during visits in 1967, 1968, 1970, and 1971.

Sihanouk's estimate of casualties in government action in the provinces does not accord with such figures as were published in the *Agence Khmère de Presse* daily bulletin. (See as a single example a report of April 21, 1968, noting Khmer Rouge casualties of eighty-nine killed during a two day operation in Battambang.) Nor does his current description of his attitudes in the 1967-70 period sit well with his repeated assertions, from 1967 onwards, that he would be merciless to those who opposed him. (Typical authorized reflections of this view may be found in *Les Paroles de Samdech Preah Norodom Sihanouk*, April-June 1967, Phnom Penh; n.d., Radio Message to the Nation, April 7, 1967, pp. 111-15; and *Les Paroles*, January-March 1968, Phnom Penh, n.d., Speech of March 4, 1968, p. 170.)

17. Pomonti and Thion, *Des Courtisans aux partisans*, pp. 112-25; Meyer, *Derrière le sourire khmer*, pp. 185-201; J.L.S. Girling, "The Resistance in Cambodia," *Asian Survey* 12, 7 (July 1972): 549-63; Elizabeth Becker, "Who Are the Khmer Rouge?" *Washington Post*, March 10, 1974, has interesting detail, but the information from a defector, Ith Sarith, needs to be treated with reserve. A more recent newspaper assessment is provided by Sydney H. Schanberg, *New York Times*, March 13, 1975.

18. M. Laurent, *L'Armée au Cambodge et dans les pays en voie de développement du Sud-Est Asiatique* (Paris, 1968), pp. 43-7, and pp. 283-84 for the Annex, "Deux notes du General Séta (C.R.) . . ."

19. In 1968, Sihanouk, even though he designated his left-wing opponents as "Khmer Viet-Minh," made clear his realization that a new generation of the Left had emerged. *Les Paroles*, January-March 1968, passim.

20. *Agence Khmère de Presse*, May 16, 1964.

21. Laura Summers, "Cambodia: Model of the Nixon Doctrine," *Current History*, December 1973, p. 254, n. 5. As an example of Sihanouk's practice see, "How Fares Cambodia in the Changing Indochinese Peninsula?" *Pacific Community* 1, 3 (April 1970); particularly pp. 351-52. This article was written before Sihanouk's overthrow but published subsequently.

22. Sihanouk over Radio Phnom Penh, September 18, 1967.

23. This conclusion is made on the basis of having consulted Hou Yuon, "La Paysannerie du Cambodge et ses projets de modernisation," Paris, 1955, thèse de droit, and Khieu Samphan, "L'Economie du Cambodge et ses problèmes d'industrialisation," Paris, 1959, thèse de droit. I have not had an opportunity to consult the academic critiques of Cambodian society provided by Hu Nim and Phouk Chhay in their theses prepared for the University of Phnom Penh. For a most valuable synthesis of the analysis provided by these four men see Laura Summers, "The Cambodian Liberation Forces: Political and Economic Doctrine," *Indochina Chronicle* 17 (July 1972): 1-6.

24. See, for instance, the observations on Cambodian rural society in Sheldon W. Simon, "Cambodia in the Vortex: The Actors' Perceptions, Goals and Settlement Prospects," in M. Zacher and R.S. Milne (eds.), *Conflict and Stability in Southeast Asia* (Garden City, N.Y., 1974), p. 151, and the same author's *War and Politics in Cambodia: A Communications Analysis* (Durham, N.C., 1974), p. 3.

25. M. Delvert's massive book, *Le Paysan cambodgien* (Paris, 1961), remains most valuable. But there is need to reconsider the views he expresses in his "Conclusion," where he writes, ". . . Everywhere, in effect, they [the peasants] are masters of the soil. Smallholders working the land directly with the aid of their family. A true peasantry therefore. A rural democracy, rare in Asia. Dominated by the businessman, it is true, but also served by him and in a less onerous fashion than one believes. A victim of usury, certainly; but the usurer here is not the great landowner and he is thus more easily borne." M. Delvert concludes the paragraph from which this quotation is taken with the observation: "Happy, the peasants are poor" (pp. 652-63).

26. Sihanouk's concern before 1970 was more with "modernization" than social transformation. This is revealed in his emphasis on the number of students in schools rather than on the quality of education, and on the number of kilometers of railroad built rather than on the economic significance of the railroad to the areas through which it ran. Even post-1970 he still speaks of the

past in Cambodia as if the peasants lived in an Arcadian idyll. See his interview with Oriana Fallici, *New York Times Magazine*, August 12, 1973.

27. Osborne, *Politics and Power in Cambodia*, pp. 99-100 and 106, n. 6. On conditions in Battambang province, see Delvert, *Le Paysan cambodgien*, pp. 639-40.

28. See n. 23 above and the summary of the analysis provided by Khieu Samphan, Hou Yuon, and Hu Nim, in Laura Summers, "The Cambodian Liberation Forces, Political and Economic Doctrine."

29. For an excellent summary of the fragile limits of existence for a member of the Khmer peasantry see, David Chandler, *The Land and People of Cambodia* (Philadelphia, 1972), pp. 97-99.

30. I do not suggest that all the disadvantaged Cambodians in Phnom Penh embraced left-wing ideals as a response to their circumstances. Further, even when men of some education adopted left-wing positions, this did not necessarily mean that the level of comprehension of left-wing theory was notably high. I make this comment on the basis of personal interviews in Phnom Penh with a later senior member of the FUNK on April 28 and May 7, 1966.

31. Meyer, *Derrière le sourire khmer*, pp. 180-201, and particularly pp. 185-88, provides valuable discussion.

32. Roger M. Smith, "Cambodia," in G.McT. Kahin (ed.), *Governments and Politics of Southeast Asia*, 2nd edn. (Ithaca, N.Y., 1964), pp. 438-39.

33. These judgments reflect private information communicated to me in Cambodia from 1966 through 1970, including information from men now associated with the FUNK.

34. Consider Sihanouk's initial expectation of assistance from both Peking and Moscow. See *New York Times*, March 23, 1970.

35. Sihanouk's message of March 23, 1970 may be found in *Documents publiés à l'occasion de la Journée Nationale du 23 Mars* (Paris, 1971), a collection published by the FUNK. An English translation of the response from Khieu Samphan and his colleagues, of March 26, 1970, is Appendix 6 in Malcolm Caldwell and Lek Tan, *Cambodia in the Southeast Asian War* (New York, 1973), pp. 394-98.

36. See *Documents publiés à l'occasion de la Journée Nationale du 23 Mars.*

37. *Political Program of the National United Front of Kampuchea (NUFK) (adopted unanimously by the Congress held in Peking on Sunday, May 3, 1970)*, undated and without place of publication, a copy distributed by the GRUNK office in Paris.

38. See Caldwell and Tan, *Cambodia in the Southeast Asian War*, Appendix 3, pp. 384-86, for a listing of the leadership of the FUNK and GRUNK.

39. Wilfred Burchett, *The Second Indochinese War* (New York, 1971).

40. Sihanouk's changing views are usefully set out in Meyer, *Derrière le sourire khmer*, pp. 384-88.

41. Information on the exodus of Cambodian leftists from Paris, led by Thiounn Mumm, comes from private sources in the French capital.

248

42. Sihanouk compared his position with de Gaulle's during the Second World War in an interview with the French journalist François Debré on July 17, 1970. See also Sihanouk's article, "The Future of Cambodia," *Foreign Affairs* 49, 1 (October 1970): 1-10.

43. *New York Times*, November 20, 1970.

44. *L'Indochine vue de Pékin*, pp. 158-59. Radio Peking, February 22, 1971, broadcast Sihanouk's comment on Mao made in Shanghai.

45. See the *Bulletin d'Information*, No. 161/74, published by the GRUNK office in Paris for details.

46. *Far Eastern Economic Review*, December 10, 1973, for a summary.

47. *New York Times*, July 1, 1973.

48. *The Guardian*, September 18, 1973.

49. UPI news service, September 9, 1973; *New York Times Magazine*, August 12, 1973.

50. *Bulletin d'Information*, February 1, 1974, published by the GRUNK office in Paris, provides the FUNK communique of January 17, 1974, indicating an expectation that Phnom Penh would fall. I judge this expectation to have represented more than a propaganda exercise.

51. Earlier in 1974 Sihanouk had indicated his own wish to revisit areas under the control of the FUNK in Cambodia. He stated, however, that the "Khmer Rouge" did not desire such a visit and that his mother's ill-health, in addition, was a further factor in keeping him in China. See *Far Eastern Economic Review*, January 7, 1974.

52. *New York Times*, March 1, 1975; *Newsweek*, March 10, 1975.

53. *L'Indochine vue de Pékin*, pp. 121 and 124.

11 Communism and Ethnic Conflict in Cambodia, 1960-1975

Peter A. Poole

In Vietnam, the war was fought over the issue of who would rule, but in Cambodia the conflict was between opposing strategies for national survival. The irony could not be more bitter, because the longer the fratricidal war between right and left factions of the Khmer elite continued, the more likely it would mark the end of the Khmer people's distinctive race and culture. This is not to deny the important role of the United States and other outside powers in provoking and prolonging the war in Cambodia. But as Cambodia makes the transition from war to peace, its future seems to depend mainly on internal political forces—that are only superficially similar to those in South Vietnam or Laos.

Throughout the 1960s, Prince Sihanouk and his ministers tried to keep Cambodia as isolated as possible from the Vietnam War. Although they are known to have disagreed bitterly among themselves over the correct approach to take toward the various parties in the struggle, Sihanouk remained the final arbiter of Cambodian policy. However, from the early 1960s—when he broke with the United States and Saigon, then recognized the Vietnamese Communists, and later (in 1969) resumed relations with America but not Saigon—Sihanouk's foreign and domestic policies were increasingly attacked by members of the Phnom Penh elite. This small, interrelated group was divided into several factions, which Sihanouk necessarily played upon to maintain his ascendancy.

Older members of the civil bureaucracy and senior army officers, whose careers began in the French colonial service, generally saw Vietnamese encroachment as the greatest threat to Cambodia's existence. Hence, Cambodia's strategy, they believed, should be to ally itself with whatever power was capable of containing the Vietnamese threat. The United States seemed an ideal successor to France (which they viewed as having protected Cambodia in the colonial period), because America was believed able to control Saigon by tightening the pursestrings, and the United States seemed determined to contain Hanoi with its firepower.

This older faction of the Khmer elite, which we can call "rightist," believed (probably correctly) that the Indochina Communist Party and successor groups, such as the *Pracheachon* in Cambodia, had always been dominated by ethnic Vietnamese. With less reason, they believed that only those Cambodians who had some Vietnamese blood or who had lived in Vietnam could possibly be

249

susceptible to Communism. Before the recent war, if a Cambodian had openly supported the aims of the Vietnamese Communists, he would certainly have been regarded by many older Cambodians as disloyal to his Theravada Buddhist culture. While admitting that some Communists might not be Vietnamese and some Vietnamese might not be Communist, the rightists believed that Communism and Vietnamese encroachment were virtually one and the same thing.

The Khmer rightists found themselves in an agonizing position in the mid-sixties as a direct result of Sihanouk's rupture of relations with the United States. Without its U.S. subsidy, the Cambodian army was reduced to selling transportation and other services to the hated Viet Cong. This collusion, which mocked the basic ideology of the rightists, also made many Cambodians fear that the United States might allow the Saigon army to attack Viet Cong bases in eastern Cambodia. However, each president until Nixon resisted the pressure of his generals to do this.

A younger, more leftist group of the ruling Khmer elite (often educated in French universities) was brought into the government in the early 1960s by Sihanouk, who hoped to harness their skills and energy and silence their criticism of his policies. These young men tended to identify with the Vietnamese tradition of resistance to French colonial rule and to support, at least morally, the Vietnamese Communist struggle against the United States and Saigon forces in South Vietnam.

The leftists decried the Saigon regime's alleged policy of forced assimilation of the Khmer Theravada Buddhists living in South Vietnam and sought to present themselves as the true defenders of Cambodian culture. The issue of Saigon's treatment of the Khmer Krom residents of South Vietnam produced some overlap in the Khmer leftist and rightist positions: both groups saw the Khmer Krom as threatened by Vietnamese racism; both groups regarded it as America's duty to restrain its Saigon ally. However, such overlapping views became increasingly rare as tensions rose.

To the Khmer leftists, history was obviously on the side of the "liberation" forces in Vietnam (as elsewhere in the world), and it would be a grave mistake for Cambodia to align itself against them. The Khmer leftists saw the Vietnam War as part of a worldwide battle of the colored races against white imperialism.[a] This reversed the Khmer rightist view that Cambodia's greatest danger was Vietnamese racism. The leftists argued that Cambodia could survive only by working *with* the Vietnamese Communists *against* the United States, their common enemy.

This split in the Khmer elite showed itself in regard to the Vietnamese minority in Cambodia, who probably numbered around 400,000 in the late

[a]The Democratic Republic of Vietnam has often claimed that white racism was what caused the United States to support France rather than the Vietminh after World War II, and has been the basis of U.S. policy in Indochina ever since. See recent statements of the DRV and Provisional Revolutionary Government about U.S. motives in airlifting Vietnamese orphans to the United States.

1960s. This group had long been resented by the Khmer elite because they had been used by the French administration and private French firms as overseers of the supposedly less energetic Cambodians. Even after Cambodia regained its independence, the French (and Vietnamese) presence in Cambodia continued to grow, partly because of Sihanouk's close ties with Gaullist France. The Vietnamese seldom made much effort to disguise the fact that they regarded Cambodia as an extension of their homeland.[1]

In the 1960s, the Khmer rightists began to see the Vietnamese community in Cambodia as a fifth column, controlled and manipulated by Hanoi through the DRV and PRG diplomatic missions in Phnom Penh. From time to time, Sihanouk added his own voice to the criticism, apparently on the principle of keeping all groups in the country a little on edge. His criticisms of Viet Cong encroachment became more pointed and more specific after he resumed diplomatic relations with the United States in 1969.

There seems to be no doubt that Sihanouk developed very intimate links with the U.S. government in the late 1960s, exchanging intelligence data on the Vietnamese Communists in eastern Cambodia and sanctioning U.S. bombing in the region. One result was that both Sihanouk and Lon Nol became overconfident to the point of recklessness in their dealings with the Vietnamese Communists in late 1969. Both of them probably also believed that the chances of military stalemate in South Vietnam were greatly improved by 1969.

However, internal politics probably also played a major role in determining Sihanouk's new attitude. Sihanouk was engaged in a struggle to keep the initiative in foreign and domestic affairs from passing into the hands of his cousin, Sirik Matak, a younger, more intelligent, and very determined leader of the rightist faction. (Sihanouk had appointed Sirik Matak deputy premier in the summer of 1969, but this may have been because Sihanouk felt his cousin would be less of a political threat if he held a responsible government post.)

As for the Khmer leftists, they thought they knew exactly where the talk in Phnom Penh about a "Vietnamese fifth column" was leading, and their suspicion turned out to be correct: the talk was preparing the ground for a rightist coup that could be led only by Lon Nol, who controlled the army. The Khmer leftists had good reason to believe that they would be summarily jailed or shot in such an event. After a rightist electoral victory in 1966, some of the more prominent Khmer leftists, including Khieu Samphan, were denounced by government leaders and they quickly dropped out of sight. As it turned out, they apparently all joined the Khmer Rouge insurrection against Sinahouk's regime.[b] A short time later, Lon Nol's heavy-handed suppression of the Samlaut rebellion, which had leftist overtones, was supported or at least condoned by Sihanouk.

Ironically, Sihanouk reached the height of his international acclaim as the "indispensable" preserver of Cambodian neutrality in the final year before he

---

[b]The term *Khmer rouge* was coined by Sihanouk in the late 1950s to describe those leftists who rejected his one-party rule. Rightist dissenters were dubbed *Khmer bleu*.

was overthrown. His kingdom was invariably described by foreign journalists as an "oasis of peace" and a model for its chronically unstable neighbors. Yet anti-Sihanouk bitterness was bubbling just beneath the surface in both the leftist and rightist camps. The main thing that held it in check was Lon Nol's belief that Sihanouk, by some diplomatic magic, might evict the Vietnamese Communist intruders from Cambodia without jeopardizing Lon Nol's small, poorly equipped army.

In March 1970, Sihanouk (who was resting in France) probably stumbled into a trap laid by Sirik Matak to prove to Lon Nol that Sihanouk had lost his magic powers. Hearing that rightist-provoked demonstrations against the Viet Cong in eastern Cambodia had spread to Phnom Penh and had gotten out of hand, Sihanouk decided not to fly home and try to restore order. Instead, he went to the leaders of France, Russia, and China asking for help in containing the Vietnamese Communists—and he was publicly refused by all three governments. They all quite simply lacked the influence to persuade a small, ruthless Communist power to stop violating its neighbor's territory.

Lon Nol probably failed to realize their impotence and interpreted the powers' refusal to help as proof that Sihanouk's influence was gone. (It was not; he was still the Cambodian with whom all the major powers preferred to deal.) At any rate, Lon Nol finally gave his support to a rightist coup. He also issued an ultimatum to the Vietnamese Communists to leave their border sanctuaries, and he condoned and encouraged attacks against the helpless Vietnamese residents in Cambodia. This dual provocation raised the question of which Vietnamese army would be first to overrun Cambodia and reap revenge.

The United States could have chosen to restrain its Vietnamese ally, and it could have abstained from pushing the Vietnamese Communists deeper into Cambodia. Expecting Nixon to adhere to this relatively restrained policy, General Abrams did not urge a great incursion. But Nixon proved even more eager than his commander to seize the transitory military advantage.

Since the immediate public outcry in America prevented the use of American ground forces in Cambodia after June 30, 1970, Lon Nol was then forced to rely on ARVN divisions. The Khmer Rouge also depended initially on their Vietnamese supporters. Thus, until North Vietnam's Easter 1972 invasion of South Vietnam, Cambodia served as the main battleground of the Vietnam war. Along with the foreign invaders and the rightist Khmers, the leftists must share the blame for the wholesale destruction of life and property that followed—and for the annexations of Khmer territory by Vietnam.

Sihanouk, meanwhile, adopted the basic position of the Khmer leftists, whom he had so recently excoriated as traitors. He made full and frequent use of the Chinese propaganda media, which Chou En-lai placed at his disposal, to argue that U.S. air attacks (begun, evidently, with his consent) justified an alliance of Khmer leftists with the Vietnamese Communists. However, Sihanouk sometimes spiced his broadcasts with praise for the excellent fighting qualities of DRV units in Cambodia; this was a jibe at Hanoi and the Khmer Rouge, who publicly maintained that no DRV forces were in Cambodia.

In Phnom Penh, meanwhile, Sihanouk was being condemned to death in absentia and portrayed by political cartoonists as a demon for the double treachery of selling services to the Viet Cong before being deposed and welcoming Communist units onto Cambodian soil after March 18. As for the leftists, their grooming of Khieu Samphan to replace Sihanouk in dealings with foreign powers seemed to prove their deep distrust of Sihanouk.

If five years of war in Cambodia have proven anything, they have shown that neither the rightist nor the leftist strategies can save Cambodia unless they are sharply modified. Having defeated their rivals, the Khmer leftists are now presumably faced with the problem of negotiating with Communist South Vietnam to regain the eastern provinces of Cambodia, which have been in Vietnamese hands for the past five years. Even during the war the Khmer Rouge and Viet Cong reportedly clashed over territorial issues (just as Lon Nol's troops and ARVN were involved in bitter scrapes). With peace, the facade of Khmer-Vietnamese solidarity may not last long.

The collapse of the rightist forces, after the Khmer Rouge blocked their Mekong River life-line, has inevitably led many rightists to charge that they were abandoned by America in their hour of peril. Only a few are sophisticated enough to realize that there was never any clear moral commitment to their survival by the war-weary American leadership or public. President Nixon's decision to send U.S. and ARVN troops into Cambodia in 1970 was designed to gain a breathing spell for the Saigon regime and thus make it possible to withdraw U.S. forces from Vietnam without toppling that house of cards. Congress must share the blame for this shabby and cynical abuse of a weak country, because its members let themselves be beguiled by the hope of disengaging "with honor" from Vietnam; they allowed enough military aid to reach Cambodia to keep the war going but refused to let the executive branch make any firm commitment to the Phnom Penh government. This is surely one of the most dishonorable passages in American diplomatic history.[c]

Apart from their faith in U.S. support and their opposition to Sihanouk's return, the Khmer rightists had little in the way of a common program or ideology. During the first year of the war, they rallied strong support among the Phnom Penh elite for the slogan of "republicanism," mainly because the elite knew they would lose the increased freedom and influence which they as a class enjoyed under Lon Nol's loose autocratic rule if Sihanouk were restored to power.[d] The rightists never followed any ideological line in economic affairs, although Sirik Matak clashed with Sihanouk in 1969 because he (Sirik Matak)

[c]The only redeeming aspect of American policy was Ambassador John Gunther Dean's gallant effort to produce a "Laos-type" coalition in Cambodia in spite of the almost unbelievable confusion of aims of the Nixon and Ford administrations.

[d]Sihanouk's constant concern had been to limit the urban elite's influence over policy; he felt that their love of factional debate was a luxury no developing nation could afford. He also knew that many of the elite members were brighter and better educated than he was. His main political technique was to mobilize the peasant masses—through the prestige of his royal lineage and charismatic personality—to offset the power of the urban elite. He also played on the factional rivalries of the elite, as noted earlier.

wanted to abandon Sihanouk's experiment with socialist planning and enact laws to attract western investment capital.

The leftists, as already noted, were given a chance by Sihanouk to run a centrally planned economy in the 1960s; most observers agree that this led to stagnation and massive bureaucratic corruption. During the recent war, stories of brutal Khmer Rouge efforts to collectivize "liberated" villages were circulated in Phnom Penh by refugees.[e] Sydney Shanberg and other foreign journalists who witnessed the Khmer Rouge takeover in Phnom Penh reported the forced evacuation of all urban dwellers to the countryside to engage in farming and revolutionary purification of their minds.[2] Initial statements by the new regime indicated that agriculture would continue to form the basis of Cambodia's economy, but that the country's industrial base would also be rebuilt and expanded. As regards foreign aid, the new leaders announced in early May that they were prepared to accept foreign aid as long as there were no strings attached.

It remains to be seen whether sheer necessity or other considerations will cause the Khmer leftists to modify the harsh, simplistic, and xenophobic program they seem to have evolved during the five-year war. There was a notable contrast between the behavior of the Khmer Rouge army in the first weeks after their victory and the far more flexible and sophisticated behavior of the Vietnamese Communists. During the war, there were also refugee reports of Khmer Rouge efforts to eradicate Buddhism in the "liberated" zones. Sydney Shanberg's observations suggest that these reports may have been untrue or that the Khmer Rouge have already changed this aspect of their program.

An important indicator of the new Khmer regime's evolving policy will be whether it decides to align itself with any of the regional and multilateral organizations that have shown an interest in Cambodia. Such institutions include ESCAP (the UN regional body), the Asian Development Bank, the Association of Southeast Asian Nations, and the IMF/IBRD. Alternatively, an economic federation of Vietnam, Laos, and Cambodia might be formed, with or without links to these regional and multilateral bodies.

The American military disengagement from Indochina and the possible divergence of interests between Khmer and Vietnamese Communists might lead, in time, to some form of reconciliation between the two main factions of the Khmer elite. This is undoubtedly necessary if Cambodia is to survive for long as a distinct cultural and political entity. Cambodia has no surplus of talented leaders, and it faces graver internal and external problems now than at any time in its recent history. The events of the last five years have surely proved that the more extreme views of both Khmer factions are not viable.

The initial public statements of the new regime seemed to point to a warmer regard for China than Vietnam and a sullen disregard for the Soviet Union; the

[e]For a summary of refugee reports, in many cases based on first-hand interviews, see Donald Kirk's chapter in this volume.

Russians waited until 1973 to recognize Sihanouk and kept a caretaker staff in Phnom Penh until they were expelled by the victorious Khmer Rouge leftists. It would be logical for the new Cambodian regime to turn to China and eventually Thailand as the countries most interested in helping them avoid complete Vietnamese domination. (Thailand is currently trying to normalize its relations with China and the Indochina states, while maintaining good relations with the Western powers.)

As for the United States, I believe the chaotic spectacle of the collapse of our Khmer and Vietnamese allies need not signal the end of American influence in East Asia. Our major allies, Japan and the NATO countries, expected the Indochina debacle sooner or later, and they have indicated that they regard it as a unique case. Looking ahead, the new focus of our policy in Asia should be on improving relations with Japan by pursuing our economic interest rather than on propping up marginal states with military power.

The Communist victories in Indochina have divided Southeast Asia into two natural subregions: the *maritime* countries (including Thailand and the insular states), whose combined rapid development depends on foreign trade and investment; and the other *mainland* states, who are more likely to follow China's example of socialist development with very limited foreign aid or other foreign contacts. There is no reason why continued close economic ties between the maritime countries and the United States, Japan, and Western Europe should disturb China or the other mainland states; and there is no reason why such mutually beneficial economic ties should involve any of the major powers in new military adventures in the region.

Notes

1. See Peter A. Poole, "The Vietnamese in Cambodia and Thailand: Their Role in Interstate Relations," *Asian Survey*, April 1974.

2. Sydney Shanberg's extraordinarily fine dispatches, describing the arrival of the Khmer Rouge in Phnom Penh and their initial treatment of the local population and remaining foreigners, were published in the *New York Times*, May 9, 1975.

Part III:
Communism in Laos

12

The Pathet Lao and the Politics of Reconciliation, in Laos, 1973-1974

MacAlister Brown and **Joseph J. Zasloff**

Introduction

Like its Indochinese neighbors, Laos has been divided by a Communist revolutionary segment of its society fighting against an anti-Communist right-wing government, with each side leaning heavily upon external support during a long, destructive war. Yet Laos enjoys special features which support an accomodation. In Laos, the king served as a unifying symbol accepted by both sides. Buddhism, the dominant religion among the lowland Lao, contributes to unity, and other factors within the political culture have produced a tendency towards harmony and tolerance. Family ties, despite bitter political differences, cut across political lines—e.g., the relationship of Prince Souvanna Phouma and his half-brother Prince Souphanouvong—and the elite of both sides share not only family relationships, but many have gone to school together and served together in earlier coalition governments. Thus, once the major external powers supporting the war in Laos—the United States and North Vietnam—had reached an accommodation in Paris, there was a strong possibility that the disputing Lao factions could achieve a durable solution.

The Cease Fire Agreement and Protocol

The war in Laos ended February 21, 1973, after four months of negotiations in Vientiane between the Pathet Lao (PL) and the Royal Lao Government (RLG). The initiation of these talks reflected the progress made in the secret Paris negotiations on Vietnam between Kissinger and Le Duc Tho, but the issues at Vientiane related specifically to the Laotian past experience with two aborted coalition governments, two separate zones of administration, and the dominating

A Note on Sources. This study draws principally upon interviews conducted by the authors during July, 1974 in Vientiane and Luang Prabang with Pathet Lao and Vientiane-side officials in the new coalition government, as well as with foreign embassy officials and others with knowledge of Lao politics. The authors also made field trips to southern Laos, meeting with Lao government civilian and military personnel, and with students, merchants, peasants, refugees, and U.S. government officials. In addition, the authors examined translations of the Lao press and radio broadcasts from Vientiane, Sam Neua, and Hanoi.

influence of outside powers. The PL entered the Vientiane talks in a military position far superior to the 1956, 1961, or 1964 negotiations, and the ultimate agreement reflected this advantage, as well as the PL's greater organization and negotiating skill.[1]

Despite their insistence for two years upon complete cessation of American bombing as a precondition for the negotiation of a "political settlement," the PL suddenly, on September 22, 1972, informed Prime Minister Souvanna Phouma, through their permanent emissary in Vientiane,[a] that full-scale talks should begin immediately, without preconditions, in the RLG capital. (With the American presidential election pending, the North Vietnamese had made their crucial private concession to the United States in Paris ten days earlier and were within two weeks of presenting Kissinger with their draft peace agreement for Vietnam.[2]) The PL's concession to Souvanna caught his government not at all prepared for serious negotiations, and even the U.S. Embassy did not apply itself thoroughly to the process until after Kissinger's "peace is at hand" statement on October 26.

The PL moved fast and effectively in the preliminary stages, and formal talks were opened on October 17 (after one day's protest over certain arrangements in the hall). The chief PL delegate,[b] General Phoun Sipraseuth, seized the initiative by explicating the PL's Five Points, which Souvanna had agreed to accept on July 24 as a basis of discussion. The main thrust of the PL position was: (1) the American imperialists and their lackeys must cease all military interventions in Laos; (2) a *new* national provisional coalition government and political council must be established pending definitive national elections.

Subsequent PL speeches at weekly formal meetings repeatedly branded the war as brutal, illegal aggression waged by the "United States imperialists." Further, they maintained that the Tripartite government of National Union established in 1962, had been destroyed by assassination and *coup d'état*. Therefore, two negotiating delegations were meeting as equals rather than as a constitutional government delegation and a penitent splinter group returning to its previously allotted seats in the cabinet, as the RLG would have it. The PL held that the National Assembly elected after the 1963 breakdown, was illegitimate.[3] They further maintained that a provisional coalition government

[a]Throughout the war the PL made no attempt to establish a separate state, and they maintained a mission in Vientiane, even after coalition government broke down.

[b]The PL delegation consisted of: General Phoun Sipraseuth (1961–Chairman of LPF cease-fire delegation), Tiao Souk Vongsak (1974–Minister of Information), Maha Kou Souvannamethi (1974–Minister of Religion), Sot Phetrasy (1974–Minister of Economy and Planning) Pradith Thiengtham, Cheng Sayavong, Bousbong Souvannavong, Phao Bounnaphol, Khamsome Vannavongsa.

Unlike the previous negotiations toward reunification, Souphanouvong did not participate directly, nor did Souvanna. The RLG delegation was chaired by Pheng Phongsavan (Minister of the Interior), and filled out by Ngon Sananikone (Minister of Public Works), four generals, two intellectuals (PhD's) and one other minister–with two observer deputies from the National Assembly.

should resume the tripartite pattern of 1962, with the PL contributing one-third, the rightists of Vientiane one-third, and the "patriotic neutralists" (PL) and personalities approving of peace, independence, and neutrality making up the other third.

One week after the opening meeting, a ruthless attack by North Vietnamese troops hit previously sacrosanct areas (Kheng Khoc) in the south. Phoumi Vongvichit, the most sophisticated PL leader next to Prince Souphanouvong, was then dispatched to Vientiane to deal directly with the willing Souvanna Phouma. With an October 31 agreement on Vietnam apparently in the offing, the North Vietnamese had an interest in achieving a cease-fire in Laos, which would spare their forces there any greater punishment from American power redirected from Vietnam. The PL, however—unlike North Vietnam, the U.S. government and, the Laotian rightists—had greater interest in a political settlement than a simple cease-fire. In this respect they agreed with Souvanna's main goal.

When the October 31 agreement in Paris did not materialize, the weekly Vientiane talks settled down to rhetorical salvoes. Nonetheless, on December 12, after an eight-day visit by their three top leaders to Sam Neua via Hanoi, the PL delegation presented a draft Agreement. The Vientiane government responded the following week with one of their own. The two drafts were more alike than dissimilar, and as the Paris talks resumed in January (concluding on the 23rd), Kissinger obtained a private assurance from Le Duc Tho that a cease-fire would follow in Laos within twenty days. Kissinger publicly declared that it was "clearly understood that North Vietnamese troops are considered foreign with respect to Laos and Cambodia."[4]

Phoumi Vongvichit soon returned (February 3, 1973) to Vientiane for daily private negotiations. Kissinger passed through en route to Hanoi a week later, and American "strategic power" rained evermore heavily in support of RLG forces attempting to expand their ribbon of territory along the Mekong River and the bulge toward the Plain of Jars which constituted the 20 percent of Laos that they still controlled. North Vietnamese regulars were apparently not moved in from Vietnam, as many feared would happen, and Vientiane hard-liners were discreetly dissuaded by the Americans on February 15 from expecting U.S. air power to improve their positions. Souphanouvong was apparently pressured, in turn, by Hanoi to propose on February 18 an immediate cease-fire, without prejudice to the peace talks. Within three days the combined political and military agreement which both he and his half-brother preferred, was worked out and signed in Vientiane. Unlike the 1954 and 1962 agreements on Laos at Geneva, this was signed by simply the two Lao parties, at home.

The major stumbling blocks to the Vientiane Agreement were political, not military. The PL gave ground in accepting a provisional government composed of equal numbers from the Vientiane and PL sides, plus only two personalities chosen by common agreement. They abandoned early their pressure for obligatory return of refugees to their villages of origin. Explicit references to American bombing were jettisoned in the final text. The RLG plenipotentiary, Pheng Phongsavan, had to sign, however, for the "Government of Vientiane," (or as he explained it, the "Government at Vientiane"), while Phoumi Vongvichit signed for the "Patriotic Forces."

The PL insisted that all paramilitary organizations be withdrawn or disbanded but agreed that *all* foreign military personnel and bases (not simply those associated with American military activity) be required to withdraw. They agreed that these provisions be fulfilled within sixty days after the establishment of a provisional government rather than simply within ninety days of the agreement. They summarily refused the RLG proposals to return to the cease-fire positions of 1962. The PL gained grudging agreement to a National Political Consultative Council to assist the provisional government and prepare for "general elections to set up the National Assembly." Some diplomatic observers had wrongly thought that the Council was a "throw-away" bargaining point for the PL. The fate of the existing National Assembly, which the government had offered to enlarge, was left in limbo, since the Agreement does not mention it. The PL proposal of a joint commission to control and supervise the cease-fire, with the aid of the existing International Control Commission (ICC), was accepted by the government, but the withdrawal of foreign troops was not put under ICC jurisdiction. The PL proposed neutralization of Vientiane to assure the security of the coalition government, and when the government countered by proposing it for the royal capital at Luang Prabang, the PL insisted upon both, and won. Two other critical provisions won by the PL were the principle of the unanimity of the two sides in the functioning of the provisional government and political council, and the maintenance of two separate areas of administration pending general elections. Remaining issues were left for further negotiations.

Within hours of the signing, the town of Pak Song, west of the lower Ho Chi Minh Trail, was seized by North Vietnamese troops, and U.S. B-52's were brought to bear in response. Within a week, however, serious seizures of territory had petered out, and American air power was unleashed only once more, in April, to help stabilize the lines south of the Plain of Jars.

The PL delegation in Vientiane stalled for a month on the formation of the government, then announced that a Protocol to the Agreement must first be negotiated. After the Vientiane side (with American help) had drafted a proposal, Souvanna Phouma accepted Phoumi Vongvichit's counter draft late in April as the basis for discussion.

The equal allocation of ministerial posts was complicated by the importance attached to Defense, Finance, Interior, and Foreign Affairs, and the PL's desire to hold the Vice-Premiership. They eventually conceded all of these but Foreign Affairs to the Vientiane side, however, and accepted two equal vice-premiers, one from each side, under a neutral prime minister (expected to be Souvanna Phouma).

Not so easily resolved were the neutralization of the two capital cities, the demarcation of a cease-fire line, and the differences over the political council. Souvanna Phouma was far more pliable than the right-wing generals and powerful families in these matters, but his government was not ready to sign the Protocol until September 14, 1973, after an attempted coup, jumping off from Thailand, had been suppressed with American diplomatic help, and the Russian Embassy had brought the former rival generals together socially. The PL made concessions by scaling down the number of troops to be stationed by each side to neutralize the capital cities,[c] and by accepting ambiguous language concerning the possible legislative role of the National Political Consultative Council (NPCC). They insisted, however, upon the right to take part in the control of immigration, emigration, and airport protection in the two capitals, and refused to fix a date for general elections. The cease-fire line was to be demarcated in twenty-seven specified disputed areas by temporary markers, to be fixed exactly by the Joint Central Commission to Implement the Agreement (JCCIA).

Thus the PL achieved, after initially dilatory negotiation, contractual establishment of equal participation in the provisional government in two physically neutralized cities, and the maintenance of two zones of control for an indefinite period. The actual formation of the Provisional Government of National Union was delayed another half year, during which the two sides jostled over the conditions of entry of Pathet Lao police and military forces into the seats of the royal government, and the provision of satisfactory living quarters.

PL in the Provisional Government of National Union (PGNU)

On April 5, 1974, the new Provisional Government of National Union (PGNU) was promulgated by Royal Decree (see Figure 12-1). It contained many of the major personalities on both sides who had served in the 1962 coalition government (although Souphanouvong is preoccupied elsewhere in the NPCC). All of the posts nominated by the Pathet Lao went to lowland Lao (Lao Loum), and all but one of the nominees of the Vientiane side (Touby Lyfoung, a Meo leader) were also lowland Lao.

The PL membership in each ministry is generally no more than four persons: the minister or secretary of state, a *chef de cabinet*, an aide, and perhaps a private secretary, bringing the total PL personnel in the PGNU to little more than fifty. All the PL personnel who have come to Vientiane and Luang Prabang are without their wives and children, except for a few whose wives have official appointments. PL members of the government say that time is not propitious for them to bring families, since they must devote their energies to their new jobs and getting installed. Security conditions for them in Vientiane were unknown

[c]In Vientiane, each side may station 1,000 police and one battalion (1,200) of troops; in Luang Prabang, 500 police and 2 companies (600) of troops.

Prime Minister and President of the Council of Ministers

Prince Souvanna Phouma

From the PL Side	From the Vientiane Side
Vice President of Council of Ministers	**Vice President of Council of Ministers**
Phagna Phoumi Vongvichit	Phagna Leum Insisiengmay
Foreign Affairs	
Minister Phagna Phoumi Vongvichit	Secretary of State Tianethone Chantharasy
Education, Sports, Youth and Fine Arts	
Secretary of State Oun Neua Phimmasone	Minister Phagna Leum Insisiengmay
Interior	
Secretary of State Deuane Sounnarath	Minister Phagna Pheng Phongsavan
Finance	
Secretary of State Bousbong Souvannavong	Minister Ngon Sananikone
Information and Tourism	
Minister Tiao Souk Vongsak	Secretary of State Phagna Ouday Souvannavong
National Defense and Veterans Affairs	
Secretary of State Kham Ouane Boupha	Minister Chao Sisouk na Champassak
Public Works and Transport	
Minister Singkapo Sikotchounamaly	Secretary of State Houmphanh Saignasith
Economy and Plan	
Minister Sot Phetrasy	Secretary of State Somphou Oudomvilay
Religion	
Minister Maha Kou Souvannamethi	Secretary of State Soukan Vilaysarn
Public Health	
Secretary of State Khamlieng Pholsena	Minister Phagna Khamphay Abhay
Justice	
Secretary of State Sensathit	Minister Phagna Khamking Souvanlasy (Qualified neutral nominated by Vientiane side)
Posts and Telecommunications	
Minister Phagna Khampheng Boupha (Qualified neutral nominated by PL side)	Secretary of State Touby Lyfoung

Figure 12-1. Provisional Government of National Union

at the outset. (Right-wing critics of the PL claim that families are kept in the Sam Neua zone as hostages, to discourage those who might be inclined to any swerving from the Party line, or even defection.)

PL authorities insisted upon their perquisites. As their opponents noted maliciously, they were demanding air-conditioned offices, handsome villas and Mercedes cars. PL spokesmen insisted that they had no desire for luxury—they had clearly demonstrated their ability to lead a Spartan life—but they simply were seeking the dignity of equality with their right-wing counterparts.

The new coalition government in Laos has provided a distinct advantage to the Pathet Lao. Under the Agreement, which recognizes the existence of "two zones and two separate administrations," the PL maintain strict control of what they call their "liberated zone," administering it from their headquarters in Sam Neua and permitting no access to members of the Vientiane side. Nevertheless, their personnel in Vientiane and Luang Prabang participate in policing these neutralized cities, and within the PGNU they take part in the sole governmental instrument of the Vientiane side. A wry observation was repeated in Vientiane, that the PL now can say "what is ours is ours, and what is yours is half ours." This morbid humor captures an essential truth reflecting the outcome of the war. If the PL were not totally "victorious," they were winning, and the peace arrangement reflects their ascendancy.

The PL Vice Premier, Phoumi Vongvichit, set a tone of cooperation and concord at the inaugural PGNU session in laying out ten workmanlike and noncontroversial tasks for the future. "As for the routine functioning of each ministry," he added, "that will proceed as usual."[5] And it has, to a great extent. The addition of an average of four PL persons to each Ministry, even though at top-level positions, has not seemed to affect the day-to-day work of the administration, nor altered the basic operating assumptions of the Vientiane-side civil servants.

The tone of moderation and continuity has been expressed by PL ministers throughout the government. At the Ministry of Plan, Sot Phetrasy, has continued business as usual. Several high level delegations of Vientiane-side officials, who had been preparing to seek resources from the United States and Canada, and international agencies, were sent out with his encouragement. (The PL have not presented plans to direct foreign aid resources to their own zone, no doubt tied to their reluctance to permit outsiders access to the zone.) The new Minister of Public Works, General Singkapo, has shown a pragmatic approach by prudently requesting a prolongation of U.S. technical assistance in airport operation and roadbuilding.

At the Ministry of Information, now headed by PL Minister Prince Souk Vongsak, the official spokesman for the PGNU continues to be a Vientiane-side official. The press releases and radio output are sometimes stated rather obliquely. For example, when a letter was written to the International Red Cross by North Vietnamese prisoners of the Royal Army appealing for release the spokesman announced simply that an appeal for release had been received, written in *quoc ngu* (Vietnamese script), from soldiers claiming to be members of the Lao Liberation Army, thus avoiding any contradiction of the North Vietnam's denial that its forces fought in Laos.

In foreign affairs, under PL Minister Phoumi Vongvichit, routine administration continues and new ambassadorial appointments have gone to Vientiane-side officials in accordance with previous expectations. Without opposition from the Vientiane-side, a personality from the PL-side, Khampay Boupha (of the "genuine patriotic neutralists") was named as Ambassador to the DRV. While both sides profess a commitment to "neutrality," as enshrined in the Agreement, there are moderate differences in their orientation. The PL have insisted that Laos should not participate in any regional organizations, while Vientiane-side officials believe that, while avoiding involvement with *military* organizations such as SEATO, Laos should look positively toward regional *economic* organizations. From the start, however, Phoumi Vongvichit announced his support for continuation of FEOF, the institution through which the United States and other donor countries (including Great Britain, France, Japan, and Australia) provide support for the stability of the Lao currency.

A divergence on foreign policy emerged with the PL proposal for recognition of the Provisional Revolutionary Government (PRG) in South Vietnam and its counterpart (GRUNK) in Cambodia. The PL argued that true neutrality required that Laos recognize both sides in these neighboring countries, rather than only the regimes in Saigon and Phnom Penh. At cabinet meetings, PL members were accused of showing their subservience to the North Vietnamese while the PL labeled their opponents "American lackeys." In view of the requirement for unanimity in the cabinet, and his own predisposition against recognition, Prime Minister Souvanna accepted a tabling of the issue. (This intense debate, along with a severe altercation over the future of the National Assembly, surely contributed to Souvanna's heart attack, which occurred July 11, 1974, the day following bitter exchanges on these two issues.)

There is the least evidence of cooperation—indeed there is sharp hostility—between the two sides within the Ministry of Defense. The PL charged that the right-wing minister of defense, Sisouk na Champassak, has denied his PL Secretary of State for Defense, Kham Ouane Boupha, access to data concerning the Royal Lao Army. Sisouk ripostes that the PL do not permit access to their zone, nor do they provide information about their army. The PL have made Sisouk a major target of denunciation in their radio broadcasts, charging him with plotting with Americans and Thai to subvert the Agreement, and he, in turn, publicly flays the Pathet Lao as agents of North Vietnamese aggression.

The Protocol and Agreement require that the PGNU (and NPCC) function in all important matters on "the principle of unanimity of the two sides." Despite apprehension that this provision would rapidly produce stalemate, the coalition cabinet has proceeded at a reasonable Lao pace, though the harmony has been sometimes strained. Prime Minister Souvanna Phouma has played a critical role by transforming his position from chief of the Vientiane side to national leader "above" the partisan conflict of each faction, a role known in French as *arbitre*. In hotly contested issues Souvanna has wielded his influence to keep up the momentum of cooperation within the coalition, even if it has meant conceding certain arguments to the PL. This is designed to inspire their confidence and bring them more rapidly into the national fold. Such moves brought heavy criticism upon Souvanna from his former followers. Not only has his shift deprived the Vientiane side of its most effective leader, but before his heart attack some right-wing officials even complained that Souvanna "is not really *un arbitre*—he has been kicking the ball into our goal!"[6]

Souvanna has not resolved every impasse so clearly in favor of the PL as his critics contend. At times he has maneuvered to achieve compromises, and, on some issues he has challenged the PL position. For example, he countered the PL-inspired Eighteen-Point manifesto in its call for support of all national liberation movements, by suggesting that this refers only to anti-colonial struggles. He squarely opposed the PL resolution calling for recognition of the PRG and GRUNK.

The PL, understandably, are silent about Souvanna's role, but they seem to see him as a valuable, if not indispensable, leader of the PGNU at the current stage. The PL seemed genuinely concerned at Souvanna's heart attack, and immediately requested medical assistance from socialist allies. (The total number of doctors converging to look after Souvanna Phouma peaked at seventeen: seven—Lao, three—Thai, one—U.S., one—French, two—Soviet, three—Chinese.)

During Souvanna's convalescence in France, from August 26 to late November 1974, Phoumi Vongvichit, the more senior of the two vice premiers, assumed the role of acting prime minister, though Leum Insisiengmay, of the Vientiane side, signed all cabinet matters. This did not prevent Phoumi from delivering an address at the United Nations General Assembly that was harsher toward the "capitalist-imperialists" than the version that the cabinet had authorized. Phoumi explained that the "draft" had been revised and Souvanna Phouma had initialed every page when the two conferred in France before Phoumi reached New York.

PL Decisionmaking Process

A notable PL strength in the new coalition arrangement, particularly in contrast to their Vientiane-side competitors, is their discipline and unity. The PL organization, strongly influenced by the North Vietnamese during its developing years, has followed the Communist practice of democratic centralism and it has employed criticism and self-criticism to guide its cadres. There is ample opportunity for the PL leadership in Vientiane and Luang Prabang to prepare a common front within the government, since many live in the same villas and take their meals, it appears, in the central PL compound.

Although there is no clear-cut documentation, nor are there insiders' memoirs describing how the PL achieves this unity and makes its decisions, the following description seems a reasonable summary of the existing evidence. The People's Party of Laos (Phak Pasason Lao, or PPL), the semi-secret Communist Party of Laos, estimated in 1968 to have some 14,000 members, is the ruling instrument of the movement. Meetings of the PPL politburo (whose membership has never been publicly announced), presided over by Kaysone Phomvihan, reach policy positions on the basis of democratic centralism. Party decisions are binding upon Party members, who apply them with loyalty and discipline. PPL members, following the practice of other Communist systems—particularly that of North Vietnam—are distributed throughout the key organizations of the society, and have the duty to enforce Party directives.

Although Party directives provide the framework of PL policy, the leaders have a certain measure of autonomy in their functional fields. In view of the poor communication lines within the PL zone and also between PL headquarters in Sam Neua and their missions in Vientiane and Luang Prabang, this functional autonomy is of major importance in day-to-day operations. Experienced, disciplined, high-level leaders can confidently make most decisions with relative independence, following, of course, the basic Party guide lines. Major decisions, however, must be referred back to Party headquarters in Sam Neua, which often explains the PL delay in reaching a decision in Vientiane. In a few cases, decisions made by PL leaders in Vientiane appear to have been countermanded by instructions from Sam Neua. The PL cabinet members, for example, agreed at first to participate in a ceremony to open the National Assembly in 1974, then withdrew and began a successful denunciation against the opening.

It seems quite clear that the primary Party leadership remains in Sam Neua. Kaysone Phomvihan appears to be the highest-ranking Party member with Nouhak Phoungsavan number two, followed by Prince Souphanouvong and Phoumi Vongvichit, although there is disagreement as to who takes precedence. The other names most frequently listed are Phoun Sipraseuth, Khamtay Siphandone, and Singkapo Sikotchounamaly. Phoun's role seems to be to provide a liaison between the PL headquarters in Sam Neua and the PL leaders in Vientiane and Luang Prabang. Although clearly a powerful figure in the Party, Phoun has no official post in the coalition government, which leaves him free to travel regularly, by plane, between Sam Neua and Vientiane. Prior to the formation of the coalition government, during his assignment as a key negotiator, the PL and Hanoi Radio transmissions show that he stopped for consultation in Hanoi intermittently. It is not clear how PL meetings are organized in Vientiane, but apparently Phoun, when in town, presides. Written guidelines and instruction from Sam Neua to the PL delegations in Vientiane and Luang Prabang are presumably delivered from time to time, but regular radio communication seems unlikely.

It is worth speculating whether factions exist within the PL leadership. Prince Souphanouvong insisted in an interview "we are one bloc, totally unified."[7] He was unwilling to discuss the role of the PPL within the PL decisionmaking process, stating that this subject was a PL internal affair. He asserted that the LPF, of which he is chairman, makes the decisions for the PL movement—a statement which masks the leading role of the PPL. The possibility of divergence between hard-liners and moderates clearly cannot be ruled out. The leaders in Sam Neua may be more intransigent toward an accommodation with the right-wing elite of the Vientiane side, more suspicious of the Americans and the Thai, and more inclined to rely upon the support and guidance of the North Vietnamese than upon their counterparts in the coalition.

A critical question regarding PL policy, then, is the extent to which their decisionmaking depends upon the DRV. On most issues, the PL leadership does not appear to be under heavy North Vietnamese influence. However, access to South Vietnam through Laos has been of critical importance for the DRV. They are further concerned that ethnic minorities in Laos, all of whom are found in adjacent North Vietnamese regions, not be manipulated to make trouble in North Vietnam. The present PL policy of closing their zone to outsiders alleviates this concern. As for the political progress of the Pathet Lao movement, the North Vietnamese have reason to be satisfied, and they have supported the Agreement.

On a few issues, there may have been strong North Vietnamese pressure. For example, recognition of the PRG is of secondary importance to Lao national interests, even though the PL leaders, understandably, have sympathy for the liberation movement in South Vietnam. In pressing this point so zealously against determined opposition in the PGNU, the PL opened themselves to charges that they were agents of the North Vietnamese. The PL could not hope to make political gains in Laos with this issue. In fact, it strained relations with their Vientiane-side counterparts, which they had been taking pains to cultivate, and even contributed to the Vientiane side's determination to develop a more united front. The PL radio's constant denunciation of U.S. Air Force bases in Thailand, notwithstanding Laotian dependence on Thailand for access to the sea, may be another example of North Vietnamese encouragement.

Military and Police Forces and the JCCIA

During the six month delay in forming the PGNU, PL military forces moved into the two neutralized cities by means of a Soviet airlift to Vientiane, and a Chinese airlift to Luang Prabang. As these troops settled into the buildings allocated to them and began to take up their tasks, the PL political leadership completed arrangements for their own arrival. Although it appears that all PL personnel for both police and military assignments were drawn from the PL military forces, each force retains a separate function, and they do not appear to be interchangeable.

The police groups are assigned joint patrol duty with the Vientiane-side counterparts, though joint operations are more in evidence in Luang Prabang than in Vientiane. These patrols perform normal security functions, the guarding of residences, offices and foreign embassies (when necessary), but technical tasks such as the direction of traffic are retained by the professional police of the two cities.

The primary mission of the military elements is to defend each city against possible external attack or internal coup d'état. The military patrol the exterior perimeter of the city, and each side has a responsibility for particular zones within the city. During off-duty hours the PL soldiers appear to be confined to quarters. One might wonder if the boredom attached to little work, plus the isolation to which they are committed, will not erode the morale of these country boys, who have been taken from their families, their normal environment, and a greater freedom of movement. However, PL officials note that their soldiers, besides the tasks of patrol and security-maintenance, have ample sessions of training, exercise, study, and barracks maintenance. In addition, these officials see their troops as well-disciplined and uncorrupted, an observation which finds widespread agreement among the population of Vientiane and Luang Prabang.

The instrument established by the Protocol and subsequent agreements to oversee fulfillment of the Agreement is the Joint Central Commission to Implement the Agreement (JCCIA). The JCCIA consists of fourteen members, seven drawn from each side, with a total staff on each side not to exceed one hundred. All the PL staff are military, while the Vientiane side is mixed. Among the JCCIA tasks are general direction of the joint police, implementation of other provisions for neutralization of the two cities, guaranteeing the exercise of democratic freedoms of the people, and generally supervising the cease-fire. The priorities established by the JCCIA are, first, to complete its tasks in consolidating the cease-fire (including the establishment of the landmarks delimiting the two zones); next, to verify the withdrawal of foreign troops; next, to deal with the return of military and civilian prisoners and the gathering of information regarding the missing-in-action; and finally, to oversee the implementation of the provisions regarding refugees.[8] Although the work of the JCCIA, by Western standards, seems slow—by January, 1975 only four of the twenty-seven landmarks had been definitely agreed upon—there have been no severe altercations that seem to threaten a continuing consideration, if not early action, in regard to these responsibilities.

In conformity with the requirement that all foreign troops be withdrawn from Laos within sixty days of the formation of the new government, the United States announced the completion of the withdrawal of its own advisors, as well as the Thai troops it had been supporting. Yet, there is little doubt, despite the official denials of both PL and North Vietnamese spokesmen,[d] that North Vietnamese troops continue to be present in Laos, primarily in the Ho Chi Minh Trail area in the south. The upper limit in U.S. intelligence estimates of NVA troops in Laos during 1974 ranged from 28,000 to 40,000. Since the PL spokesmen deny the presence of these troops, one can only speculate about their attitude toward them. The PL recognize the North Vietnamese abiding interest in winning control in South Vietnam, and probably consider the passage of North Vietnamese troops through Lao territory to be both reasonable and inevitable. (For those who might be inclined to oppose this passage, they must realize that their option to refuse is hardly a realistic one.) The relatively small numbers of North Vietnamese military posted outside the Trail, on the other hand, assure a critical logistic and advisory support to the PL, and, with their implicit threat to the Vientiane forces and their allies, can be seen by the PL as a reassuring deterrent and political asset.

Still, many PL leaders, as Lao nationalists, must feel some discomfort at NVA on their territory. The Lao have traditionally been suspicious of the Vietnamese, whose historic westward expansion has been regarded as a threat. NVA presence in Laos is a violation of the Agreement, and the necessity to deny the truth is awkward for some PL leaders.[e] Nevertheless, while some may feel uneasy about the NVA presence, most would feel nervous if it were abruptly removed.

The National Political Consultative Council (NPCC)

Following his emotional reunion with his half-brother, Souvanna Phouma, and a wildly-cheered entry to Vientiane on April 3, 1974, Prince Souphanouvong astonished Western observers by opting for the presidency of the National Political Consultative Council (NPCC)[f] rather than the foreign ministry and vice-premiership. The Protocol designates the NPCC as independent and equal to

[d]In an interview at the North Vietnamese Embassy in Vientiane in July 1974, a North Vietnamese diplomat declared, "There are no North Vietnamese troops in Laos—that is the official position of my country."

[e]Several foreign embassy sources report that certain PL leaders will artfully dodge the question, to show that they will not blatantly misinform their diplomatic colleagues.

[f]Various sources render this title in different ways, which suggest slightly different political meanings. In the earliest French version of the peace agreement it appears as *Conseil Nationale Consultatif Politique*. More recently U.S. government translations have referred to the Joint National Political Council (JNPC) or the National Political Council of Coalition (NPCC), and National Coalition Political Council. If the National Assembly is finally dissolved, the consultative aspects of the Council may well be minimized in favor of a legislative role.

the PGNU, which accounts for Souphanouvong's not really so surprising choice.[9]

The forty-two man Council, which is to meet every six months for sessions to last not more than a month, gathered in Luang Prabang after each side designated sixteen members, and the PL selected ten independent, neutral personalities from a list submitted by the Vientiane side. Twelve of the PL's sixteen members are lowland Lao, notwithstanding the customary PL emphasis on ethnic equality.[10] Only two beside Souphanouvong are important enough to have served on the Central Committee of the Neo Lao Hak Xat, as of 1964, and Sanan serves with Souphanouvong on the PPL Central Committee. The non-Communist elements in the PL, the Santiphab (Peace and Freedom) Party and the Patriotic Neutralist Forces are also represented. Five NPCC members from each side form a Standing Committee, headed by Souphanouvong and the "patriotic neutralist" Khamsouk Keola on the well-coordinated PL side. Their VS counterparts include three volunteers who are native to the royal capital. As one Vientiane member ruefully observed, "No one from Luang Prabang will ever oppose his Highness" (Souphanouvong).

The Vientiane Agreement gives the NPCC responsibility "to discuss and present its views concerning the major questions of domestic and foreign policy to the PGNU," to promote and help them in the implementation of the Agreement. It will "join the PGNU in organizing general elections to set up the National Assembly and a definitive National Union Government." Concerning the general line and orientation of foreign and domestic policy there must be discussion with the Government and unanimous approval by the NPCC or its Standing Committee.

With this amount of constitutional clay, Souphanouvong set to work in May, 1974, constructing a quasi-legislative forum and converting the disorganized Vientiane members into prophets of a new doctrine and era. Capitalizing on the vanity and political variability of the Vientiane-side's vice president, and the lassitude of its delegation,[g] the PL leader readily seized the initiative. At the third meeting, in a long address garnished with anti-imperialist rhetoric, the prince launched his Eighteen-Point program "for the current construction of the fatherland." Within two weeks the various substantive committees (headed by standing committee members) had discussed the points until unanimous agreement was achieved. Even the hard bitten former army chief of staff, General Ouan Ratikon, expressed extravagant praise at the ratifying session for what he called a coherent program, unlike those of the past. In addition, Souphanouvong pushed through his "Provisional Regulations on Guaranteeing the Democratic Freedoms of the Lao People," as a step toward general elections.

[g]The Vice-President designated by Vientiane, Prince Sisoumang Sisaleumsak, seems to have associated himself, at various times since 1945, with almost every political faction. In 1974, he aired both anti-colonialist (U.S.A.) views in a radio Sam Neua interview (May 27) and solidarity with Souvanna Phouma in an interview with the authors (July 13, 1974).

The president of the NPCC has dominated its brief proceedings by force of his royal presence, his reformist reputation, his intellect, organization, and energy, and the use of rules which he fashioned. His non-partisan seating plan and the unanimity principle specified in the Agreement have also contributed to the atmosphere of democratic centralism which he has created. The discussion in the committees has been described by a VS member as uninhibited and intense, "even with severe criticism," but if a committee member is "stubborn" the others repeat and explain until he understands what is correct.[11] Committee suggestions are received by the Standing Committee but may be returned for reconsideration, and Souphanouvong himself may chair such sessions, sometimes in his house. Even a modern, well-educated member with the temerity to pose questions at such a gathering has allowed that the prince "replied calmly, and was not at all annoyed."[12] No staff or offices were available to the Vientiane-side members, and when Souvanna Phouma privately consulted with them at his house on weekends he was not inclined to counsel a stand on issues in dispute.

There is little for the right-wing to quarrel with in the Eighteen-Points, which Souphanouvong considers an engineer's blueprint for peace and national concord. They became controversial only in respect to the foreign policy section, certain rhetorical flourishes, and to the extent that NPCC joint member teams began explaining the program in Luang Prabang and Vientiane[h] (and the foreign minister sent it to Lao embassies abroad) before the cabinet had approved or published it. References to "U.S. neo-colonialism" and "ultra-rightist reactionaries," and "support for the struggles of people in Indochina . . . for peace, national independence, democracy" prevented the cabinet from reaching agreement upon first consideration.

On the domestic side the program speaks to the economic development and national unification of a poor agricultural society, with scarcely a hint of socialism,[13] aside from the conventional areas of state responsibility for infrastructure. In their emphasis on equality of nationalities and the sexes, while promoting Lao nationhood and language, respecting and maintaining religion, attacking vice, and supporting the kingdom, the Eighteen Points could easily have sprung from the pen of a Western liberal. The "Democratic Freedoms" are equally uplifting in tone, with the exception of a prior-censorship provision for newspapers and potential restrictions on political meetings and associations. The right of citizens to own private property is guaranteed, and freedom of enterprise "must be" guaranteed.

The major controversy surrounding the NPCC, however, has not been its

---

[h]Following the first NPCC adjournment, seven mixed four-man member teams set out to "consult" (in accordance with the Protocol) the people concerning the eighteen Points, in whatever meetings they could organize in Vientiane and Luang Prabang. They were seconded at times by Pathet Lao members of the Joint Police, or JCCIA, but occasionally these unsolicited visits to homes, schools or organizations provoked resentment, and increasingly the visitors were asked about the presence of North Vietnamese troops in Laos after the June 4 deadline for withdrawal.

output but rather whether it will supplant the National Assembly, as the PL have intended from the start. When existing Assembly president, Phoui Sananikone, imprudently sent a letter to the cabinet for transmittal to the king in early May 1974 requesting his traditional presence at the re-opening of the National Assembly, the PL seized the opportunity to prevent action under the unanimity rule. Prior to this windfall the PL serving in the PGNU seemed to have had no interference in mind. In July, when a petition against the continuing presence of North Vietnamese troops in Laos was opened to public signature by seven assemblymen in the vacant National Assembly building, the prime minister sought to abort controversy by cordoning off the grounds. Following a day of smoldering confrontation between a few assemblymen and youthful critics, Souvanna declared that the "two sides" in the PGNU were unanimously agreed to ask for dissolution of the National Assembly, even though Ngon Sananikone, the Minister of Finance, reportedly opposed. A day later the harried Souvanna suffered a near fatal heart attack, and the dissolution question was frozen during his four-months' convalescence. Since the Constitution calls for a new National Assembly within ninety days of a dissolution, and the PL is yet unwilling to hold national elections, some political equivalent may be sought, such as a "limited popular consultation" to enlarge the NPCC into a sixty-member National Assembly. Until such time the NPCC, under Souphanouvong's guidance, will attempt to translate the Eighteen Points into specific policies for each ministry, a rather unlikely achievement for such a body sitting in isolation from the administrative and budgetary realities faced by the government in Vientiane.

Critical Problems Ahead

Refugees

The final settlement of the estimated 750,000 persons in the Vientiane zone who were displaced by the war is an economic as well as political issue for the PL. Their Five Point Peace Proposal of March 6, 1970, declared that the "pro-American forces must . . . resettle in their native places those people who have been forcibly removed from there," and pay compensation for damages. However, the final Agreement simply stipulated that "assistance shall be given to people who were forced to leave their native villages during the war to help them return there freely to earn their living according to their desire." During the negotiations, the PL spoke vividly of forced separation from ancestral homes and fields, forced enlistment of the youth into special forces, "concentration camps," and the destruction of economic and social systems in the "liberated zone." These accusations reflected operations such as the U.S. airlifting of 15,000 residents out of the Plain of Jars in 1970 prior to its B-52 bombing, and the recruitment by the Central Intelligence Agency of thousands of mountain people into the Irregular Army, or Special Guerrilla Units.

The refugee rolls grew during the war as the Force Armée Royale (FAR) and CIA-supported forces were pushed westward, bringing their dependents with them. Many refugees moved to avoid military operations and American bombing and also to get subsistence provided by U.S. agencies. The number receiving U.S. subsistence has declined since the peak of 378,801 in October 1973, but the 1974 cost was nearly $15 million, almost a third of the American economic aid to Laos. (Refugee aid is admnistered directly by the United States, despite dissatisfaction registered by the PL vice minister of the interior. This arrangement originated years earlier, after U.S. recognition of scandalous local corruption.)

Unlike the government in Vientiane, the PL cannot look forward to large-scale American assistance when refugees return for resettlement. The Vientiane-side policy is not to discourage refugee return to the PL zone, and even to provide a one month's food supply and packet of tools if a family wishes to leave. Most refugees harbor some inclination to go back, if conditions are right. The PL reportedly have been providing three months' subsistence at the receiving end, but they want the movements across the line to be irrevocable. Some refugees have sent family members back to their former villages to undertake cultivation of their old land and to test the political water. Those few who have tried and returned usually complain that their former land was occupied by others, or that they were pressed into labor corvées. Rice is not as plentiful in the PL zone and taxation and restrictions on private animal raising are considered onerous. Nonetheless, increasing numbers of refugees are expected to depart for the PL areas after the November 1974 harvest.

The most agonizing disincentive for refugees to return home is past association of a family member with the Special Guerrilla Units or General Vang Pao's Irregular Army. Even the lowest ranking veteran's family fears retribution from the PL, and they are not likely to return home until their former patrons assure them that they should. Meanwhile, the once fiercely independent Meo mountain people, to whom the U.S. government has incurred such a moral obligation, presently find themselves in refuge in north central Laos, with a high susceptibility to disease at unaccustomed low altitudes, and a surplus population of 105,000 relative to the cultivable land available. A generous PL program of re-acceptance, as dependence on the Americans grows more difficult for both Parties, might respond to Meo preferences at the time. Acceptibility of such a program would depend upon how much economic autonomy the PL is willing to allow and the trust they could generate in a promise of no retribution. The political impact of such a movement could be impressive, either as a symbol of reconciliation or of political attraction in competition with the Vientiane side.

Even though the distribution of refugee population might heavily influence the outcome of national elections, these elections may not come soon. Thus, the PL need not force the refugee question, so long as it does not embarrass them politically.

Freedom of Movement

The Agreement notes that "both sides will promote normal relations between the two zones, setting up favorable conditions for people to travel, earn a living, visit one another, carry out economic, cultural and other exchanges and other activities in order to develop national concord and build national unity quickly" (Article X, Section B). The later Protocol is silent on the question. Notwithstanding the Agreement, the PL have been adamant in maintaining the seclusion of their zone. Delegations from socialist and friendly third world countries were received from time to time during the war period and since the cease-fire, French, British, and Australian diplomats have been invited to visit PL headquarters at Sam Neua for highly-structured, limited-observation tours. But requests to travel to the PL zone are put off with explanations that the cease-fire must first be consolidated, landmarks sited, and other pressing priorities dealt with, before the zone can be opened.

Why has the PL guarded entry to their zone so tightly? Perhaps the most important reason is their habitual suspicion of outsiders, developed over long years of struggle against both Lao and foreign enemies. Stringent limitation of access to outsiders has been a common practice among revolutionary regimes such as the USSR or China, which felt besieged from without and within. Freedom of access by outsiders also tends to stimulate the desire of insiders to travel. Permitting such freedom of movement in a society so tightly controlled for so long would violate the PL leaders' habits and instincts.

Secondly, the PL zone is populated by a myriad of minority peoples whose loyalty to a largely lowland Lao political leadership in Sam Neua must be regarded, despite frequent protestations to the contrary, as fragile. PL radio broadcasts suggest that PL leaders are apprehensive that right-wing elements on the Vientiane side, serving the American imperialists, will make mischief in the "liberated zone." Special guerrilla units still exist under the FAR.

Perhaps a sense of discomfort about the primitive level of development of their zone (compared to the more developed Mekong River plain controlled by the Vientiane-side) also contributes to the PL refusal to open their territory. PL leaders do not wish to invite comparisons by people on either side, nor leave them with a freedom of choice at this stage. Even prior to the war, the highland zone of Laos controlled by the PL was the most backward in a country little developed overall. Its highland minorities were the least literate, the least technically developed peoples of Laos. The long and destructive war, with heavy bombings, further retarded the development of this area. Although this backwardness is not the fault of the PL system, they nonetheless shun comparisons.

The presence of North Vietnamese troops, especially in the Ho Chi Minh Trail area of southern Laos, is another important reason not to open their zone. North Vietnamese presence elsewhere in the PL zone appears relatively sparse, but reports of it would equally be evidence of violation of the Accords. A NVA commander, surreptiously interviewed in the Pak Kading area, near the Mekong River, stated that his troops were helping the Lao and Khmer people in their fight against the American imperialists and they would not depart as long as there are U.S. troops in Laos and Thailand.[13] A counterpart to PL reluctance to open their zone may be North Vietnamese resistance to such a development, which would allow hostile elements to use adjacent Lao territory as a "springboard" for making trouble in North Vietnam.

Of course, travel could be eased in certain sectors, and the importance of the Ho Chi Minh Trail will diminish with a PRG-NVA victory in South Vietnam. Yet any partial openings may be resisted, because the PL leaders realize that opening one area leads to pressures for access elsewhere, difficult to withstand once the barrier is broken.

Economic Viability

Given the fundamental economic weakness of Laos, with a per capita income of less than $100 and more than half its national budget devoted to the army and police, the instability of the kip is a continuing threat. For the past ten years the Foreign Exchange Operations Fund (FEOF) has operated to compensate for the extraordinary budget deficits run by the RLG as the war mounted. It helped dampen the potential inflation, and financed most of the country's supposedly essential imports. These have included many luxury items acquired by privileged commercial families. In July 1974, with the government deficit running at about $1 million per month, and the shock of Souvanna's illness contributing to a run on foreign currency, the International Monetary Fund recommended a devaluation of the kip. While the Government hesitated and sought less painful remedies, the Vientiane press singled out the nearly $1.4 million (out of a budget of about $40 million) spent by the PGNU in refurbishing houses and providing vehicles for the new PL officials in Vientiane and Luang Prabang. The cost of rice imported to feed Vientiane had also been increased by the PL's closing of the overland connections between Vientiane and the southern provinces, above Thakhek on the Mekong River. The proper remedy, the press argued, was to obtain donations from the socialist countries, comparable to FEOF's assistance. Foreign Minister Phoumi Vongvichit called privately instead at the U.S. Embassy, seeking a larger contribution, while Pathet Lao Radio denounced the rumors of devaluation as a deliberate campaign to discredit the PGNU and the NPCC. The ultra-rightist and unscrupulous "big shot" businessmen, they said, had helped create unfavorable conditions by hoarding goods and converting their kip to dollars.

With no additional foreign currency forthcoming, and with the PL unwilling to bear the onus for further inflation through devaluation, the government had to settle for the dubious remedy of stricter controls over foreign exchange and "essential imports." The PL ministers insisted, as before, upon austerity, opposing a government pay increase and favoring the closing of bars and nightclubs at midnight. They called for increased productivity and self-reliance, while their radio explained the issue in terms of ending the economic dependency created by twenty years of U.S. imperialist intervention.

The mixed team dispatched to seek aid from socialist countries in the fall of 1974, under Planning Minister Soth Pethrasy (PL), managed to secure a $25 million commitment from China, largely in long-term commodity loans. Hanoi announced a grant of $3.5 million and will assist in the reconstruction of Routes 7 and 8 to the North Vietnamese port of Vinh, giving Laos an alternative to Thailand for access to the sea. (The roadbuilding agreement might serve to legitimize North Vietnamese troop presence in Southern Laos.) In Western Europe a second mixed team under Defense Minister Sisouk na Champassak achieved some small commitments, but the United States, as of the end of 1974, was yet to be reached. The question of distribution of aid between the two zones has not yet been squarely faced, even though the economic planners in Vientiane have pressed the PL for basic planning data.[i] Admission of aid administrators into the "liberated zone" is still a stumbling bloc, but Souvanna has suggested that three quarters of foreign economic aid go to the PL areas to help them catch up.

Since July 1974 the rate of inflation did not accelerate, thanks in part to inventories and perhaps to tighter import controls, but the foreign currency and marketing systems have not encouraged the needed import substitution or increased domestic rice cultivation. Meanwhile labor unrest and strikes began to plague the government.

The first successful strike, against the contract guards service working for the U.S. Embassy, set a pattern for successive controversies. Subsequent walkouts hit the air services, the Government electric company, a slaughter house, a hospital, and telecommunications. In addition, rebellious tribal soldiers, who were formerly CIA-supported irregulars, occupied the northern town of Ban Houei Xay and took hostages to demand back pay and legislative reforms. In the South, restless students occupied the sole bridge out of Pakse to issue demands for provincial anti-corruption reforms, approval of the Eighteen-Point program, and dissolution of the National Assembly. These organized protests, unusual for Laos, seem not to have arisen simply from PL machinations. Indeed, PL ministers were involved as respondents in some of the negotiations. Clearly, there is a growing mood in recent months, especially among youth and workers, that is self-assertive, xenophobic and reformist.

---

[i]In July 1974, Nouhak Phoungsavan proudly launched a Three-Year Plan for the reconstruction and development of the "liberated zone," and pointed to its value as a model for "the zone under the control of the Vientiane side." While he saw the development of his zone as a potential benefit for the other, he made no mention of eventual merger.

Theories of PL Behavior

The political future of Laos naturally depends a great deal on the post-war behavior of the PL in Vientiane and Luang Prabang. What are the possible interpretations of their actions thus far?

First, one might assume that the Pathet Lao are a well-organized, cohesive Communist revolutionary movement whose aim is to seize power as soon as possible. They would then install a political system throughout Laos modeled on the "liberated zone," which, in turn, has been strongly influenced by the North Vietnamese, with whom they have long had an intimate, even dependent, relationship. To this purpose, according to this interpretation, they aim to demolish or neutralize the principal institutions of their adversaries while shaping the new institutions to suit their objectives. Already they hold half the posts in the PGNU.

Prince Souphanouvong has masterfully shaped the NPCC into a body which, so far, has propounded programs initiated only by the Pathet Lao. The National Assembly was crippled by the calculated ambiguities of the Agreement and the Protocol, and subsequent political maneuvers will probably render it a coup de grace. With the positioning of their police and military in Vientiane and Luang Prabang, the PL have a capability to gather political and military intelligence not only to nullify possible right-wing coups but to plan, if necessary, their own coup de main. A PL minister presides over the Ministry of Religion giving them potential influence throughout the wats in a devoutly Buddhist society. The powerful families of the Vientiane side, such as the Sananikones, are being subjected to denunciatory radio broadcasts from Sam Neua. The Royal Army, which is a latent political element, is a foremost target of the Pathet Lao. They will attempt to weaken it through the cabinet by demanding reduced national military expenditures on the grounds that the war has ended and severe economic needs require priority.

Inasmuch as the U.S. advisors and Thai troops withdrew from Laos within sixty days of the formation of the PGNU, the continuing presence of North Vietnamese troops has diminished the self-confidence of the rightists. In the postwar political atmosphere of neutralization the PL can more easily work at "revolution from below," the strategy of building a base for support among the Lao public. Certain political assets, such as the PL image as a noncorrupt movement dedicated to fundamental reform in the interest of the poor, and against the "phou yai" ("big people") will be traded upon. Many people, particularly the youth are tiring of the same old crowd in power. Thus, the PL can be seen as moving from a position of strength toward an early political take-over.

A second theory of Pathet Lao behavior assumes a holding action on their part. They are giving priority to the security and development of the "liberated" zone, in recognition of its weakness. Located principally in the highlands, it is sparsely populated and economically backward; its population is principally highland minorities (Lao Theung), the least developed of the peoples of Laos, with few trained personnel competent to manage the tasks of development. Further, during their long and difficult struggle living in caves under U.S. bombing (1964-73), the PL leaders were conditioned to see their imperialist enemy, the United States, manipulating the Vientiane side, and utilizing Thailand as a puppet. In their continuing perception of reactionary cliques in Vientiane plotting the destruction of the coalition government, they feel bound to concentrate upon building and securing their liberated zone, husbanding their limited trained and politically reliable people within their own areas. Only as they gain in strength in their zone can they venture into an active role within the Vientiane side's zone. In keeping with this strategy, it is argued, the PL have sent only a small group of, primarily, second-level leaders, while the top echelon of the Party under the leadership of Kaysone Phomvihan and Nouhak Phongsavan, operate from Sam Neua, relying heavily on the North Vietnamese.

This thesis assumes that the upper level of the PL cadres is so thin that they lack sufficient skilled administrators for their own territory, and could hardly consider undertaking full national responsibility at this time. Although giving first priority to their own area, the PL may utilize their presence in the coalition to draw upon government resources for their zone. Since it may take years for the PL zone to develop, one can expect them to maintain the de facto partition in the near term, cautiously testing the experience of the coalition government, and, perhaps most importantly, waiting for guidance from their North Vietnamese mentors, whose interests in Laos will be determined primarily by developments in South Vietnam.

A third interpretation starts from the assumption that the PL is essentially a nationalist movement and that most of its leaders are neither doctrinaire nor strongly ideological. Although committed to fundamental reform, they are capable of pragmatic accommodation and wish to move toward a genuine reconciliation. Once wartime emotions cool and reasonably free electoral conditions can be assured, they will abide by the democratic process called for in the Agreement, expecting to win a majority in the National Assembly. This interpretation provides a satisfactory explanation for the cautious but sustaining role the PL have been playing within the PGNU. As PL leaders gain experience in their jobs in the coalition, and a sense of security living in Vientiane and Luang Prabang, they will grow more accommodating with their political competitors and more pragmatic in their relations with foreign powers, as they realize their needs and dependence. Some of their adversaries even predict that as the PL "cave mentality" erodes, a process of "bourgeoisification" will mellow their revolutionary zeal, as they accustom themselves to the "good life" in Vientiane and Luang Prabang.

Prince Souvanna Phouma embraces this third theory, and his own recent political strategy has been founded upon the conviction that compromises must be made to bring the PL nationalist leaders back into the national family. His interpretation allows for differences within the PL leadership, with those in Sam Neua assumed to be the more dogmatic, suspicious Communists. The process of time, some believe, may either split the "Nationalist" PL leaders from the more intransigent doctrinaire Communists in Sam Neua, or create a process by which the Vientiane group will draw the Sam Neua group toward greater moderation.

Yet it seems unlikely that Souvanna can ever resume his previous level of active political leadership. After his convalescence, he announced plans to retire following national elections, which he estimated for the end of 1975. (Few others predict such rapid movement toward elections, which the Agreement simply stipulates must be held "as soon as possible.") As for prospective candidates to succeed Souvanna, Souphanouvong is thought to be the choice of his half-brother. Souphanouvong unquestionably possesses a driving ambition for the post and has impressive attributes for it. At sixty-three, he is still vigorous, widely experienced in political life and, as a Luang Prabang prince, has traditional appeal. His astute political performance as President of the NPCC has probably enhanced his chances for succession. However, he would not be readily acceptable, at this juncture, to the Vientiane-side political elite because of his Communist affiliation. Moreover, it is not known conclusively that he would be the PL organizational choice.

In any case, the prospects for continued peace in Laos seem good. No group prefers war to peace, and the major external powers, so influential in the past, are supportive of the peace arrangement. The Pathet Lao may be subject to the logic of each of the three interpretations above. What revolutionary movement of such long standing would not seize the opportunity to take charge of the national destiny (as the first theory holds)? Yet they must remain wary of another intervention to prevent their consolidation of power, and they must be hesitant about their capabilities to rule the entire country at this time. Thus, while awaiting more propitious future conditions, they can do much to improve their capabilities and conditions of life in the "liberated zone" (as the second theory suggests), while continuing, even expanding, their influence within the coalition. Once committed to moving slowly toward gaining control, however, they must share power, and certain social processes (third theory) may moderate their Marxist revolutionary zeal.

As peace persists the PL leaders will experience greater difficulty defending their military blockage of road traffic along the Mekong and the prohibitions on access to their zone. The PL serving in the PGNU will confront problems within the national context, and they are likely to see value in extension of services such as posts and telegraph, roads, and public health on a nationwide basis. The Pathet Lao has championed the goal of reconciliation, and if Laos can be left sufficiently to itself, cautious movement toward national integration will probably continue.

Notes

1. The major sources for this account of the negotiations are interviews with Lao and foreign government officials with knowledge of the talks, as well as the record of formal speeches by the delegates at the weekly Vientiane meetings.

2. Tad Szulc, "Behind the Vietnam Cease-fire Agreement," *Foreign Policy*, Summer 1974, pp. 48-52.

3. The most explicit formal expression of this idea, which later became politically critical, is found in the PL draft agreement presented December 12, 1972, which states: "In the period when the *National Assembly* and the official government of national union *do not yet exist*," (i.e., during the period of the proposed provisional government and political council) "each side will manage the zone under its control." (italics added)

4. T. Szulc, "Behind the Vietnam Cease-fire Agreement," p. 63, and H.A. Kissinger, *Press Conference*, January 24, 1973.

5. Vientiane Domestic Service Radio Broadcast in Lao, April 10, 1974, in *FBIS*, April 11, 1974, I-4.

6. Interviews by authors in Vientiane, July 10 and 11, 1974.

7. Interview with the authors, July 23, 1974, Vientiane.

8. Interview with PL representative on JCCIA, July 18, 1974, Vientiane.

9. Interview of Prince Souphanouvong by the authors, July 23, 1974.

10. Members chosen on the PL side in probable order of political standing within the PL (except for the initial listing of officers), were: (1) Prince Souphanouvong (President); (2) Phagna Khamsouk Keola (Vice President and Secretary General); (3) Sanan Southichak; (4) Phao Phimphachanh; (5) Maha Khamphan Virachit; (6) Mrs. Khamsouk Vongvichit; (7) Lo Foung Pablia; (8) Thammasing; (9) Y Bottaphanith; (10) Visit Southivong; (11) Pao Vanthanouvong; (12) Souvandy; (13) Maha Boutdi Soulingnasak; (14) Mrs. Phaiboung Pholsena; (15) Thiep Litthideth; and (16) La Soukan. Although highland minorities probably comprise well over 70 percent of the PL zone population, their limited representation in the PL delegation to the NPCC was explained by two PL NPCC members as due to their relative lack of education (Interview, July 16, 1974, Vientiane). Prince Souphanouvong explained it as being due to the need for ethnic leaders to handle administrative tasks in the PL zone. (Interview, July 23, 1974, Vientiane).

11. Interview, July 16, 1974, Vientiane.

12. Interview, July 17, 1974, Vientiane. This Member estimates that only 10 of the non-PL members understand the issues with any thoroughness.

13. *Xat Lao*, July 2, 1974. Reprinted in *Vientiane News*, July 7, 1974.

Index

Index

Abrams, Creighton, 252
Action committees, 11
Agriculture, x, xii, 20, 166-168; in
Cambodia, 205-206; collectiviza-
tion, 58, 59, 169, 171, 254; in DRV,
117, 124, 143, 149, 158
Alliance of National Democratic Peace
Forces, 29, 52
Allman, T.D., 200, 240
An Ping-sheng, 123
ANDPF. See Alliance of National
Democratic Peace Forces
Angkor era, 222
Annam, 9, 188
Anti-Communist Denunciation Cam-
paign, 36
Ap Bac, 147
Armed Propaganda Brigade for the
Liberation of Vietnam, 30
ARVN. See Army of the Republic of
Vietnam
Army of the Republic of Vietnam, 36,
66, 77; and Cambodia, 253; collapse,
x, xi, 71, 111, 112; conscription, 64,
65; and PLAF, 69, 76, 147-148, 155,
156n, 158
ASEAN, 128
Asian Development Bank, 254
Assassination, 19, 21, 22, 41, 260
Association of Former Resistance
Members, 47
Association of Patriotic Women, 221
Association of Students of the Khmer
Republic, 226
August Revolution, 18, 21, 22, 30, 138
Australia, 117, 129, 266, 276
Aviation School of Leningrad, 9

Bac Ninh Province, 182, 192
Bac Son uprising, 13, 14
Ban Houei Xay, 278
Banmethuot, 71
Bao Dai, 16, 18
Battambang, 167, 197, 206, 220, 233,
235, 245
Ben Tre Province, 44
Bia Gia, 147
Bien Hoa, 7

Big Minh. See Duong Van Minh
Binh Dinh Party Conference, 70
Binh Xuyen, 35, 41, 48
Borodin mission, 4
Bouc, Alain, 240
Bourgeois parties, 4, 6, 10, 11, 23, 58
Bousbong Souvannavong, 260n
Buddhists, 51, 119, 223, 250, 254,
259, 279
Buddhist Struggle Movement, 51
Bui Quang Chieu, 5, 11, 19
Burchett, Wilfred, 238
Bureaucrats, 173, 249

Cadres, xiii, 139, 161, 162, 170; in
Cambodia, 199, 217, 221, 222, 227,
234; casualties, 42-43, 47, 111;
combat, 36, 44; Laos, 268; political,
154; recruitment, 47, 49, 137,
140-141, 153, 163, 185; rural, 175,
176, 182; training, 29, 43, 144-145,
149, 154-155; Vietnam, 7, 13, 15,
29, 32-34, 36-37, 41
Cambodia: ARVN in, 147; bombing
in, 225; border, 67, 118, 164, 199;
and China, 128, 201, 202-203, 210,
240, 252, 254-255; collapse, ix;
Communism, x, xi, 231-232, 234-
244; and DRV, 109, 110, 112, 119-
120, 197, 199-200, 204, 205, 207,
210-211, 254; and Laos, 254, 266;
military policies, 202, 203; negotiations, 207-211; and South Vietnam,
210, 252, 254-255; and Thailand,
204, 229, 255; and US, ix, 96, 197-
198, 210-211, 225, 249, 250, 252,
255. See also Sihanouk; Khmer
Rouge
Cambodian Front of National Union
(FUNK), 120-121, 125, 199, 201,
204, 205, 208, 236, 237-239, 241;
Central Committee, 238; internal
division, 241-242; and Sihanouk,
240, 243
Cambodian People's Liberation Armed
Forces, 201
Can Tho, 52
Canada, 265

About the Editors
and Contributors

Joseph J. Zasloff is professor of political science at the University of Pittsburgh. He was Fulbright Professor of Political Science at the University of the Philippines in 1972 and Smith-Mundt Professor of Political Science at the University of Saigon in 1959-1960. Dr. Zasloff is the author of *The Pathet Lao: Leadership and Organization* (Lexington Books, 1973), coauthor of *North Vietnam and the Pathet Lao* (Harvard University Press, 1970), and coeditor of *Indochina in Conflict* (Lexington Books, 1972). He has contributed to journals such as *Asian Survey, Pacific Affairs, Pacific Community*, and *Commentary.*

MacAlister Brown is professor of political science and chairman of the Political Economy Program at Williams College. He was Fulbright Lecturer in Public Administration in Nepal in 1968-1969 and a budget examiner for the International Division of the U.S. Bureau of the Budget in 1963-1964. Dr. Brown has contributed articles to *Asian Survey, Nepal Review, Pacific Community*, and other scholarly journals.

William J. Duiker is assistant professor of history at the Pennsylvania State University; in 1964-1965 he was a foreign service officer in Saigon. He is the author of *Prelude to Revolt: The Rise of Nationalism in Vietnam* (Cornell University Press, forthcoming) and has contributed to such journals as *Southeast Asia, Modern Asian Studies, Journal of Asian Studies, China Quarterly, Philosophy East and West*, and *Journal of Southeast Asian Studies.*

David W.P. Eliott is a candidate for the Ph.D. in the Department of Government at Cornell University. He is the author of "NLF-DRV Strategy and the 1972 Spring Offensive" (International Relations of East Asia Project, Cornell University, 1974) and numerous RAND studies on the Vietnamese Communist movement.

Allan E. Goodman is an international relations research fellow at the Hoover Institute of War and Peace, and chairman and associate professor of government and international relations at Clark University. Dr. Goodman is the author of *Politics in War: The Bases of Political Community in South Vietnam* (Harvard University Press, 1974) and coeditor of *Indochina in Conflict* (Lexington Books, 1972). He has contributed articles on political development, negotiations, and internal politics of South Vietnam to journals such as *Asian Survey, Orbis, Economic Development and Cultural Change, Yale Review*, and *Pacific Affairs.*

Paul M. Kattenburg has been professor of government and international studies at the University of South Carolina since 1973. From 1950-1972 he was a foreign service officer long concerned with Southeast Asian affairs. He is the author of "Vietnam and U.S. Diplomacy, 1940-70" (*Orbis*, Fall 1971), "Obstacles to Political Community: Southeast Asia in Comparative Perspective" (*Southeast Asia*, Spring 1973), and other articles and reviews on foreign policy and diplomacy.

Donald Kirk is Edward R. Murrow Fellow at the Council on Foreign Relations. He served as the Far East correspondent for the *Chicago Tribune* from 1971 to 1974 and as the Asia correspondent for the *Washington Star* from 1967 to 1970. He is the author of *Wider War: The Struggle for Cambodia, Thailand and Laos* (Praeger, 1971); *Tell It To The Dead: Memories of a War* (Nelson-Hall, 1975), and numerous articles that have appeared in such publications as *Asian Survey, New Leader, New York Times Magazine, Far East Economic Review*, and *Saturday Review/World*.

Milton Osborne is director of the British Institute in Southeast Asia. An Australian Foreign Service Officer in Cambodia from 1959-1961, he has taught in Australia, England, and the United States, most recently as a visiting professor at Yale University. He is the author of *The French Presence in Cochinchina and Cambodia: Rule and Response* (Cornell University Press, 1969); *Region of Revolt: Focus on Southeast Asia* (Penguin Books, 1971); *Politics and Power in Cambodia: The Sihanouk Years* (1973); "History of Cambodia" in the fifteenth edition of *Encyclopaedia Britannica* (1974); and articles that have appeared in journals such as *International Affairs, Journal of Asian Studies*, and *Australian Outlook*.

Peter A. Poole is chairman of Southeast Asian Studies at the Foreign Service Institute, adjunct professor of international service at American University, and chairman of the Laos-Cambodia Council of the Asia Society in New York. He served as a foreign service officer in Cambodia and Thailand during the 1960s. Dr. Poole is the author of *The Vietnamese in Thailand* (Cornell University Press, 1970), *The U.S. and Indochina from F.D.R. to Nixon* (Dryden Press, 1973), and *America in World Politics* (Praeger, 1975); and editor of *Indochina: Perspectives for Reconciliation* (Ohio University Center for International Studies, 1975). In addition, he has contributed articles to publications such as *Asian Survey, Pacific Affairs, Washington Monthly*, and *Yearbook of International Communist Affairs*.

Gareth Porter is codirector of the Indochina Resource Center in Washington, D.C. From 1972 to 1974 he was a research associate for the International Relations of East Asia Project at Cornell University. He is the author of *No Peace for Vietnam* (Indiana University Press, 1975) and has contributed to *The New Republic, The Progressive, Worldview, Current History*, and other periodicals.

Sheldon W. Simon is professor and chairman, the Department of Political Science, Arizona State University. He has also been a professor at the University of Kentucky and a visiting professor at the University of Hawaii, the University of British Columbia, and George Washington University. He is the author of *The Broken Triangle: Peking, Jakarta and the PKI* (Johns Hopkins, 1969), *War and Politics in Cambodia: A Communications Analysis* (Duke University Press, 1974), *Asian Neutralism and U.S. Policy* (American Enterprise Institute, 1975), and articles that have appeared in such journals as *Asian Survey, Pacific Affairs, Orbis, China Quarterly, Current Scene*, and *Journal of Conflict Resolution.*

Carlyle A. Thayer is a lecturer in the politics of China and Southeast Asia at the Bendigo Institute of Technology in Victoria, Australia. He is a candidate for the Ph.D. in the Department of International Relations, Research School of Pacific Studies, the Australian National University. For his dissertation, "The Origins of the National Front for the Liberation of South Viet-Nam, 1954-1960," he conducted field work in Hong Kong, Taiwan, Vietnam, France, England, Thailand, and the United States. Mr. Thayer has contributed to *Asian Survey, Australian Outlook, Dyason House Papers, Pacific Affairs*, and *Yearbook on International Communist Affairs.*

William S. Turley is assistant professor of political science at Southern Illinois University; he was a Ford Foundation Research Assistant in the Republic of Vietnam in 1972-1973. Dr. Turley has contributed articles on the DRV to journals such as *Asian Survey* and *Pacific Affairs.*